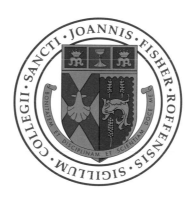

The Sociology
of the Economy

The Sociology of the Economy

FRANK DOBBIN

EDITOR

Russell Sage Foundation | New York

Library of Congress Cataloging-in-Publication Data

The sociology of the economy / Frank Dobbin, editor.
   p. cm.
  Includes bibliographical references and index.
  ISBN 0-87154-284-6
   1. Economic policy. 2. Economics—Sociological aspects. I. Dobbin, Frank.

  HD87.S64 2004
  306.3—dc22

2003068752

Text design by Suzanne Nichols

RUSSELL SAGE FOUNDATION
112 East 64th Street, New York, New York 10021
10 9 8 7 6 5 4 3 2 1

Contents

Contributors

FRANK DOBBIN is professor of sociology at Harvard University.

URS BRUEGGER is director of the Winterthur Institute of Health Management at Zurich University of Applied Sciences in Winterthur, Switzerland. He is a former economist and foreign exchange trader at a large Swiss bank.

KARIN KNORR CETINA is professor of sociology at the University of Konstanz, Germany, and member of the Institute for Global Society Studies at the University of Bielefeld.

DEBORAH S. DAVIS is professor of sociology at Yale University.

GERALD F. DAVIS is the Sparks/Whirlpool Corporation Research Professor, chair of organizational behavior and human resource management, and professor of sociology at the University of Michigan.

BAI GAO is professor of sociology at Duke University.

MAURO F. GUILLÉN is the Dr. Felix Zandman Professor of International Management at the Wharton School of the University of Pennsylvania, and visiting professor at Instituto de Empresa, Madrid.

HEATHER A. HAVEMAN is professor of management and, by courtesy, sociology at Columbia University.

KIERAN HEALY is assistant professor of sociology at the University of Arizona and postdoctoral fellow in the Research School of Social Sciences at the Australian National University.

LISA A. KEISTER is associate professor of sociology at Ohio State University.

PAUL D. MCLEAN is assistant professor of sociology at Rutgers, the State University of New Jersey.

MARK S. MIZRUCHI is professor of sociology and business administration at the University of Michigan.

JOHN F. PADGETT is research professor at the Santa Fe Institute, associate professor in political science at the University of Chicago, and senior fellow at the University of Bologna.

CHARLES PERROW is professor emeritus and senior research scientist of sociology at Yale University.

WILLIAM D. SCHNEPER is a doctoral student in the Management Department at the Wharton School of the University of Pennsylvania.

W. RICHARD SCOTT is professor emeritus of sociology at Stanford University with courtesy appointments in the Schools of Business, Education, and Medicine.

RICHARD SWEDBERG is professor of sociology at Cornell University.

Acknowledgments

This volume is the product of two conferences at Princeton University organized to take stock of the new economic sociology: "Contemporary Developments in the U.S. Economy" (April 2001) and "The U.S. Economy in Context" (February 2002). Included are half of the works presented at those two conferences: those that focus on product market characteristics and business strategies. I thank the Russell Sage Foundation for backing the conferences and for sponsoring the trips of graduate students from far and wide. For contributing funds, I thank Princeton's Department of Sociology, where I taught from 1988 to 2003, and Center for Migration and Development. Special thanks are due to Eric Wanner of Russell Sage, who shared our view that bringing together some of the most interesting scholars working in economic sociology was a worthy project, and to Thomas Espenshade, chair of sociology at Princeton and an economist by training, who thought that Princeton should be the place to do so. My thanks also to my colleagues at Princeton who helped to organize the two conferences: Paul DiMaggio, Alejandro Portes, Bruce Western, and Viviana Zelizer.

1

INTRODUCTION:
THE SOCIOLOGY OF THE ECONOMY

Frank Dobbin

IN RECENT years, sociologists have returned to study the field's first subject, economic behavior. Beginning in the 1840s, Karl Marx tried to understand the economic underpinnings of class relations and political activity. Forty years later, Émile Durkheim explored how work was divided up in modern societies and the implications for occupational behavior. By the end of the nineteenth century, Max Weber was concerned with understanding the origins of economic institutions and behavior patterns. Then, between about 1920 and 1980, sociologists turned away from the study of economic behavior per se. They studied economic institutions, such as firms and unions, but they tended not to study economic behavior in those institutions.

Since about 1980, sociologists have flocked back to the subject of economic behavior, bringing the tools they had developed to study other kinds of behavior. They had been asking why behavior varies so dramatically across societies but less so within them. Why are religious patterns, childbearing patterns, and voting patterns so regular within each society, yet so variable across different societies? Sociologists had traced behavior in these different realms to social conventions, and they came to believe that economic conventions are much like family or religious conventions. Conventions vary dramatically between Budapest and Seoul, but within Budapest, conventions tend to be quite pervasive and powerful.

Sociologists therefore began to argue that their theories explaining patterns of political, religious, and family behavior could explain economic behavior. Like families, polities, and religions, markets are social structures, with conventions and roles and conflicts (Fligstein 2001). The realization that modern, capitalist societies exhibit widely different patterns of economic behavior stimulated sociologists to treat economic conventions like other types of conventions, and this realization came about in part with the increasing awareness that East Asia provides a model of modernity different from the model that Europeans and North Americans were used to—or perhaps several different models. This new treatment of economic conventions was also fueled by the insight that despite their similarities, the economies of the United States, Germany, France, Sweden, and Britain are different in systematic and persistent ways. If such different kinds of economies can achieve high growth rates, sociologists reasoned, then economic behavior must be driven by more than narrow economic laws that determine what is efficient. Social processes must explain much of the variation in economic behavior.

This volume brings together the work of some of the most innovative and influential sociologists studying the economy. Each of the chapters tackles a pattern of economic behavior and tries to explain it using one or several of the conceptual tools honed by sociologists. Taken together, the chapters show not only the astonishing vitality of empirical research in the field of economic sociology but the remarkable explanatory power of sociological models.

The human species is a highly social one, and our behavior is shaped systematically by social context. By contrast, instinct explains the lion's share of behavior in other species. Even among other primates, such as gorillas, while there is good evidence that different "tribes" have different "cultures," most observable behavior is virtually identical across groups that have never come into contact. The same can hardly be said for humans. Across societies, the most basic human tasks are highly stylized—shaped by culture as much as by instinct, or by some interaction between instinct and culture. Food-gathering looks very different in different societies. Shelter-building looks very different. More arcane activities, such as stock trading and insurance peddling, look quite different as well. This variety raises the question: how exactly does social context shape economic behavior? This volume showcases the insights that are emerging in the new economic sociology.

Modern markets are social structures that consist of roles, conventions, and power struggles. The telecommunications market is thus analogous to the Lutheran Church, or to the Detroit school system. Sociologists have approached explaining the social structures and conventions found in markets much as they approach explaining structures and conventions in a church or a school system. Common sense tells us that that markets and economic conventions are shaped by economic laws. Sociologists find that concrete social processes matter too.

The authors in this volume use several classical sociological approaches to understand economic behavior. These different approaches do not represent competing theories of economic conventions and markets so much as different parts of the puzzle. If economic conventions vary significantly across societies and over time, where do they come from, and what leads them to change? The authors focus on four factors in particular that contribute to the shaping and evolution of economic conventions—political institutions, economic models, networks, and ideas—and attempt to answer these questions by combining the factors in different ways. Each chapter builds on fundamental sociological insights and demonstrates the utility of a sociological view of the economy. Although the chapters are divided into four parts based on the core mechanism at work, most explore several mechanisms at once.

How Political Institutions Shape Markets

Sociologists have long argued that political institutions shape markets. Common sense tells us that nations' political institutions converge on the policies that best support natural market mechanisms—that is, markets come first and political institutions evolve to support their natural form. Adam Smith (1776/1970) contributed to this view, insisting that universal economic laws force governments to adopt the same policies everywhere. Countries that adopt policies that are incompatible with economic laws will falter and change their ways. Ultimately, primordial markets shape politics, not vice versa. Smith believed that nations can "get it wrong"—that they can adopt growth policies and political institutions that impede economic growth. But he also believed that countries that "get it right" come to look the same.

Sociological studies, however, have suggested that political institutions create different sorts of markets in different countries. Karl Marx saw markets and economic conventions as being shaped by power, operating through political institutions. He also saw that modern societies can produce wealth in any number of different ways because economic laws are broad, permitting many kinds of markets and economic conventions to succeed. Political institutions can shape markets by making the state capable, or incapable, of pursuing particular policies; by favoring capitalists, or bureaucrats, in regulatory decision-making; and by creating models for corporate behavior.

Karl Marx and Max Weber cataloged the different varieties of feudalism and capitalism, recognizing that capitalism takes different forms based on different logics of accumulation. Studies of the most developed countries suggest that political institutions shape markets. Markets take myriad forms, and the insight that political institutions shape them is hardly unique to sociology. Political scientists have produced a series of comparative studies of capitalism (for reviews, see Hall and Taylor 1996; Thelen and Steinmo 1992; Campbell 1998). In the jargon of institutional economists, "property rights" regimes advantage different kinds of firms and different kinds of market arrangements (see, for example, North 1990; Greif 1993; Williamson 1975).

Students of economic history have made the same point. Alfred Chandler (1990) shows that political institutions forged national market structures, with Germany organized around strong cartels, Britain around insulated family-held firms, and the United States around diffuse stock ownership and oligopolies. Colleen Dunlavy (forthcoming) shows that political systems had produced different corporate governance systems in Britain, France, the United States, and the German states by the middle of the nineteenth century. Scholars from many camps have been interested in how political institutions shape markets. What distinguishes the sociological view is an emphasis on the relationship between political institutions, collective perceptions of the world—"frames," in Erving Goffman's (1974) term—and market behavior. What stabilizes nations' market arrangements, from the perspective of sociologists, is not merely the ongoing incentives that political institutions create but the ongoing ideas of causality that they represent. In my own research (Dobbin 1994), I have shown that political institutions produced very different ideas of economic efficiency in Britain, the United States, and France, centering on entrepreneurialism, market mechanisms, and industrial coordination, respectively. These ideas survived because they were written into industrial policy.

Chapters 2 through 4 of this volume explore how political institutions shape the economy. The commonsense view is that economies evolve according to their own rules and that they naturally become more efficient over time. The shorthand for this idea is that "history is efficient," meaning that markets and economic institutions evolve toward more efficient forms. Changes in an economic system are generally viewed as mutations that increase that system's efficiency. But analyses of the forces that shape markets and economic institutions *across countries* almost always identify political institutions as a principal cause of changes in economic systems, and they almost always find that changes do not necessarily improve efficiency.

Charles Perrow's chapter on the rise of oligopolistic enterprises in the United States and Bai Gao's chapter on the rise of business groups and cartels in Japan examine how *domestic political institutions* give nations distinct economic institutions and market forms. In the United States, a weak state that was politically porous enabled early capitalists to set the ground rules for business, and they set rules that favored huge firms. In Japan, an administratively strong state that was politically independent made it possible for state bureaucrats to effect their own vision of how the modern economy should be organized, which was through business associations.

Chapter 2 reprises the story from Perrow's book *Organizing America: Wealth, Power, and the Origins of Corporate Capitalism* (2002). Why did huge corporations dominate the American economy by the early twentieth century, a time when America's closest peers, England and Germany, still had relatively small firms? The United States saw the growth of huge firms even in industries where economies of scale could not be achieved. Power and political institutions, Perrow argues, were the ultimate causes.

In Perrow's story, a state structure that was designed to prevent government tyranny had the unintended consequence of permitting the fox to regulate the chicken coop. With no tradition of a crown exercising control over the elite—as most European states had—and with a strong constitutional mandate to maximize individual freedom, the American government was easily persuaded to go along with powerful proto-capitalists, who thus determined the laws by which they lived. Capitalists sought to shape government regulation to their taste in all countries, but not everywhere did they succeed. In 1819 in the United States, however, the Supreme Court changed the nature of incorporation, allowing the incorporation not only of "public" endeavors with public board members but of private endeavors with no public representation. Private corporations thus came to enjoy advantages designed for public-service corporations. Soon thereafter, Robert Lowell brought the "corporate company" model from Britain, where diffuse stockholding permitted corporations to amass the capital needed for huge enterprises.

Perrow argues that in textiles and elsewhere it was not economies of scale that led to consolidation but regulations that favored big corporations. The huge textile mills of Lowell, Massachusetts, were no more efficient than Philadelphia's smaller and more entrepreneurial mills, but they were favored by the law. Economies of scale may have motivated mergers in some industries, but in many others large firms had no advantages over small ones. Big corporations had legal advantages—especially limited liability—that small private firms lacked, and regulation did nothing to prevent huge companies from gobbling up their smaller competitors. The law thus helped to quash an equally practical model of efficiency: entrepreneurial capitalism.

Perrow argues that political institutions allowed the powerful to shape regulation to their own advantage so that it favored big corporations and did nothing to stem consolidation. Americans distrusted the huge firms that resulted, but they came to believe that "economies of scale," rather than political institutions and power, had ultimately produced them. This belief sustained large firms, which were seen as a natural consequence of an economic precept rather than an unintended consequence of America's peculiar political institutions.

In chapter 3, Bai Gao turns the sights of economic sociology on the associational economic order that arose in the interwar years and became Japan's claim to fame after World War II. The Japanese "business group" model contrasts sharply with the American model of huge firms operating under antitrust laws. How did political institutions facilitate the rise of Japan's interindustry business groups and intraindustry cartels? In the American case, Perrow traces the rise of the large oligopolistic firm to the administrative weakness and political porousness of the American state, which allowed capitalists with grand plans to steer public policy. Gao shows that the rise of intraindustry associations and interindustry business groups in Japan was also in part a consequence of political institutions—or the "constitutional order of the state." In Japan the state was organized to give much greater power to public bureaucrats. They chose how industry would be structured, and they chose an associational economy based on their perceptions of what had made Germany prosper.

Japan's state was modeled on Continental states that operated under administrative law, rather than common law, meaning that the executive rather than the judicial branch had the final authority to interpret and carry out the law. This structure made for strong state bureaucrats who were capable of carrying out their ideas about how the economy should be organized. In Japan state bureaucrats favored the system of business associations that Germany had embraced, and Japan's constitutional order closely resembled Germany's: the Japanese state's administrative competencies were similar to Germany's, and Japanese bureaucrats, like their German counterparts, had the wherewithal to implement their vision of how the modern economy should be set up.

Japan's associational order got its break during the Great Depression, and a comparison with the United States shows how important state institutions were at that time. Both Japan and the United States reacted to the Great Depression by trying to create greater cooperation among firms. The New Deal in the United States was designed to create cooperative cartels in a wide range of industries that would shield firms from destructive competition. The policy failed, however, because in the United States the state lacked the administrative capacity to carry it out (Skocpol and Finegold 1982). Japan also pursued an associational industrial policy, but in Japan the policy took hold and brought about a stable set of business associations. With nearly identical policy goals, two countries with very different sorts of political institutions ended up in very different places. In the civil law tradition, the Japanese state was neither administratively weak nor politically porous. Japan succeeded in creating an economy organized around business cooperation because its administrative corps had the power and resources to carry out its will, and also because the business community had come to expect that the state would assume this role. The associations that Japan put into place have shaped the economy ever since. What is fascinating in Gao's account is that, like their American counterparts, Japanese capitalists accepted the market order that emerged as natural and efficient, and their acceptance has been the key to its persistence.

In chapter 4, Richard Swedberg asks how *international political institutions* cause similarities in national political institutions. Like Perrow and Gao, Swedberg argues that national institutions determine the "property rights," or rules of economic exchange, that shape market behavior. This is true everywhere. What is interesting about the core property rights that govern most countries today is that they stem from a common set of international rules formed at a time when modern nation-states were just emerging. If *domestic* political institutions determine the differences in national markets, as Perrow and Gao argue, *international* political institutions determine many of the commonalities among markets across nations. This insight challenges Adam Smith's view that if nations have similar market traits it is because universal economic laws drive them to adopt identical institutions. Swedberg suggests that Western nation-states copied their economic regulations from the same place.

Swedberg argues that legal institutions are not well theorized by the law-and-economics paradigm that now dominates legal scholarship and that a more sociological understanding of how law shapes ongoing economic behavior is needed. Building on one of Weber's insights about the historical emergence of commercial institutions, he shows the utility of that insight today. The common commercial laws that emerged in Europe were based on the lex mercatoria—these were the rules of the "law merchants" who regulated commercial relations before a systematic order of commercial regulations had emerged among nascent states. Merchant markets established courts that heard cases and developed a sort of common law of market exchange that still serves as the foundation of commercial transactions. It included such principles as acquisition in good faith overriding original ownership, the economic corporation being a legal entity, and symbolic delivery through contract replacing the actual transfer of goods. It included such institutions as patents and trademarks, the bond, the modern mortgage, and the bill of lading. The commercial regulations that are common to modern countries, then, took parallel forms not because they arose, sui generis, as the most efficient forms of commercial regulation, but because they had a common historical source. The old lex mercatoria shaped political institutions and thereby shaped modern thinking about property, inheritance, the contract, and the corporation as a legal person.

Here Swedberg's argument resonates with Karin Knorr Cetina and Urs Bruegger's in chapter 7 about the informal rules of conduct that emerge out of international currency trading. Those rules appear to derive from participants' common understanding of an overarching system, that of economic theory. In this case, national rules and property rights emerged out of an overarching transnational system, the traditions of merchants. Swedberg notes that in the international economy a new lex mercatoria has emerged since the 1960s based on consensual principles of exchange. There are new law merchants who regulate international exchanges for a fee and enact principles that often come from economic theorists themselves.

Swedberg makes a sort of mimicry argument, akin to those elaborated in the coming section, in tracing the origins of the modern accoutrements of market exchange. These principles and institutions actually predated modern states, and when modern states emerged, they embraced the economic lingua franca of the day. This version of the story of how the modern set of market institutions emerged is entirely different from the two commonsense versions: that countries have similar economic institutions because they follow universal economic laws, or that they need common institutions to do business with one another. Swedberg's chapter shows the potential of historical sociology. At a time when regional governing regimes, such as the European Union, and international institutions, such as the World Bank, are putting pressure on countries to conform to a single regulatory model, Swedberg shows that international models have had important effects in the past. Neil Fligstein (2001) shows that economic globalization is not reshaping national markets and trade patterns as quickly as many expected it would, and this outcome suggests that the tension between the Perrow and Gao arguments on the importance of national institutions, on the one hand, and the Swedberg argument on the role of transnational political institutions, on the other, will continue to be where the action is.

How Economic Models Shape Markets

Another group of economic sociologists studies a supremely social form of behavior, mimicry. Early role theory in sociology suggested that we learn how to behave by copying those around us. Whether we copy our parents or our peers is a matter of some debate in developmental psychology, but we learn by copying in any event. The institutionalists John Meyer and Brian Rowan (1977) explored how organizations came to be isomorphic—that is, how, given the huge number of ways one *could* organize a school, all schools came to be organized in pretty much the same way. They found that organizations adopt rationalized practices ceremonially, reinforcing the myths of rationality that accompany those practices. If organizations look alike, it is not that they have identical needs and that each has discovered the one best way to fulfill those needs. They copy one another. When a group sets out to establish a bank or a hospital, it begins with a mental map of how a bank or hospital should be set up. The map itself comes from members' experiences with such organizations (Stinchcombe 1965; Baum 1996). Do the functions of a bank demand that banks be set up exactly as they are, with tellers and bank officers, counters and desks, loan departments and investment departments? Many of these structures arose historically for particular reasons having to do with power and politics and then persisted because new banks copy old ones. An important insight is that we read reason into existing economic conventions, reinforcing whatever economic models history has left us.

Economic models shape firms' behavior and market structure not only as new firms copy prevailing ways of doing business but also as existing firms follow fads that sweep across industry. Paul DiMaggio and Walter Powell (1983) term this process "mimetic isomorphism" and argue that although organizations try to identify efficient practices to copy, they seldom have hard evidence of whether the economic models they follow "work." The central idea is that we collectively make sense of organizational practices in rationalist terms—we see business practices and attribute efficacy to them. This process gives each of us a cultural tool kit full of canned solutions that we apply ritualistically when we encounter new situations. When we see new business models in leading firms, we instinctually imbue them with efficiency. It is not that we would not adopt the most efficient solution to any given problem if we knew a priori what that solution was, but that "bounded rationality" (March and Simon 1958) hinders us. We follow habits and fads because our ability to choose the optimal solution to any problem is limited by our cognitive incapacity to envision the full set of alternative solutions and by the practical problem of subjecting each alternative to a cost-benefit analysis.

Whereas common sense tells us that entrepreneurs, corporations, and central banks behave similarly in Argentina and Italy because there is one best way to behave in each role, sociologists find that mimicry is often at work. William Roy (1997) shows that states and nations copied the limited liability legal model of the firm in the nineteenth century, leading firms everywhere to take the same broad form. Studies have found that all sorts of economic models have spread around the world through imitation. Just as Roy follows the limited liability corporation, Bruce Carruthers and Terence Halliday (forthcoming) look at bankruptcy reform, Marion Fourcade-Gourinchas and Sarah Babb (2002) at neoliberal policies, Gili Drori, Yong Suk Jang, and John Meyer (2000) at government restructuring, and Gerald Davis and Christopher Marquis (2001) at corporate governance. Countries have copied all kinds of things.

The three chapters in part 2 explore different aspects of the diffusion of economic models, from setting up foreign branches to embracing the hostile takeover to developing rules of behavior that mirror wider global economic models of markets. In chapter 5, Mark Mizruchi and Gerald Davis show that American banks established foreign offices in droves in the 1960s and early 1970s, then stopped. What explains the rise and fall of the fad? Firms copied the business models of industry leaders, even in the absence of evidence that those strategies succeeded. In a classic article entitled "Follow the Leader" (1993), Heather Haveman has shown that California banks followed leading banks into new product areas with all of the forethought of lemmings. They followed the leaders without looking into whether the leaders had made money in the new product areas.

Mizruchi and Davis show that banking leaders, including Citibank, argued that global expansion could broaden the American market, and before there was any evidence that foreign offices paid off, their competitors jumped on the bandwagon. Did banks calculate the costs and benefits of setting up branches in Paris, or did they do so because their rivals had them? It looks like social emulation, rather than rational calculation, was at work among America's largest, most efficiency-oriented banks. The end of the fad came just as abruptly. After foreign market entries peaked in 1970, banks came to believe that participation in foreign markets was perilous, and they stopped branching out, long before the Third World debt crisis tarnished the idea of overseas loans. The fad came, then went, with surprising speed.

Some of the best evidence for Mizruchi and Davis's story about mimicry comes from their finding that network centrality—having a board of directors that is connected to other boards through cross-memberships—predicts the creation of foreign branches. It is through these networks of board members that firms learn what other firms are doing; in this case they learned that other banks and major bank customers were aggressively globalizing. Networks are as important to the story told here as they are to the stories told in part 3 on networks.

In chapter 6, William Schneper and Mauro Guillén explore the spread of hostile takeovers in thirty countries. Many studies have now shown that new economic conventions spread from country to country, but Schneper and Guillén's study is one of the first to look at the national factors that determine whether a country will jump on a new bandwagon. You might guess that the hostile takeover spread to all countries once it had been invented, around 1975 in the United States, because it solved problems of lax management by creating an efficient market for corporate control. Managers who were asleep at the wheel, or simply incompetent, were deposed during hostile takeovers and replaced by more efficient chiefs. Or so the story goes. But the hostile takeover did not take over everywhere. Schneper and Guillén show that hostile takeovers became common only in countries where existing institutional arrangements made the buying and selling of companies in a market "legitimate." For instance, in many developed, high-growth countries, stock trading is relatively rare because families or governments own major companies. In such places the idea of trading entire companies like baseball cards is not culturally acceptable and the hostile takeover never became common.

Schneper and Guillén provide compelling evidence that societal ideas about what is legitimate shape economic behavior, building directly on Guillén's influential book *Models of Management* (1994), which explores why three twentieth-century management paradigms spread unevenly across the United States, Britain, Germany, and Spain. In *Models,* Guillén finds that paradigms such as scientific management caught on only where they were culturally and politically acceptable. Not every country found the idea of the hostile takeover acceptable. In countries where the idea of the buying and selling of companies was not supported by tradition, the apparent efficiency of the practice was not enough to get it through the door. Building on a typology developed by W. Richard Scott (2001), Schneper and Guillén find that three sorts of factors were important. First, in countries where the state had given a *regulatory* nod to the buying and selling of companies—through legislation that put shareholder rights above those of labor and others—hostile takeovers were more likely to emerge. Second, in countries where there was *cognitive* acceptance of stock trading—that is, where the practice was highly institutionalized—hostile takeovers were more likely to emerge. Third, in countries where there was great *normative* legitimacy for private property, as evidenced by high levels of cultural individualism and weak labor movements, hostile takeovers were more likely to emerge.

Thus, in the decade ending in 1998, the United States saw 431 hostile takeover bids and Britain saw 220, but Japan had only one hostile takeover, Germany had 5, Sweden had 12, and France had 20. Whether a country was amenable to the idea of buying and selling companies, then, affected whether this particular fad made any headway there. It was not simply that growth-oriented countries embraced hostile takeovers—all of the countries Schneper and Guillén observe were oriented to growth. Like the chapters in part 1, this chapter shows that political institutions shape market behavior. In chapters 2 and 3, Perrow and Gao look at how political institutions distribute power among capitalists and bureaucrats, and they explain industrial regulations and market structure as consequences. In this case, political institutions (industrial policies, stock trading rules) have shaped ideas about how the market for corporations should operate, and they have thereby mediated the spread of a new global economic model—the hostile takeover.

In chapter 7, Karin Knorr Cetina and Urs Bruegger chart the emergence of global trading norms among a community of currency traders who interact electronically and at lightning speed. This market had reached an average *daily* turnover of $1.2 trillion by March 2001. How did this global market develop explicit conventions for conducting trading on computer screens—an etiquette of the trade? Knorr Cetina and Bruegger build on the symbolic inter-actionist, ethnomethodological, and phenomenological traditions in sociology. Their ethnographic analysis explores the informal rules governing the trade, which amount to the very rule structure of this market. Knorr Cetina and Bruegger find that despite the fact that the global currency market is virtual, disembodied, and geographically distributed, rules of etiquette emerge from interactions, just as they do in face-to-face communities.

The global currency market is a recent phenomenon, produced as nation-states have deliberately swept away trade and exchange barriers. It is globally dispersed, and buyers are also sellers. Building on Harrison White's (2002) insight that participants in a market tend to observe parallel participants for signals about how to behave (buyers watching buyers, sellers watching sellers), Knorr Cetina and Bruegger note that in this market the buyer-seller observes the emerging rules of trade from both sides of the transaction.

The rules of currency trading emerge out of a collective understanding of markets that reflects the modern lex mercatoria. Knorr Cetina and Bruegger identify a series of normative rules that have emerged to guide behavior in the global currency market. An offer to trade one currency for another must be neutral as to whether the trader is looking to buy or sell, and it must be accompanied by a buy price and a sell price so as not to bias the trade. Traders must stick by the offers they type and send, even when they make mistakes. Once a price is offered, it cannot be negotiated—there is no back-and-forth—and if a trader does not like the deal another trader offers, he can only wait for a better offer. These norms are guided by the neoclassical notion of the spot market and how it ought to operate. Traders break these rules at their peril, for they risk ostracism from the trading community. This apparently self-regulating market is in fact regulated by its own set of unwritten rules based on a shared economic model of the market.

As in face-to-face communities, the emergent rules of interaction mirror wider principles of the social system. Two groups of sociologists who have studied face-to-face interactions (symbolic interactionists and ethnomethodologists) have found principles of hierarchy and of democracy mirrored in dyadic interactions. Knorr Cetina and Bruegger build on this idea: "Strategies mirror and sustain the interactional principles of global spheres." What members of this international group of currency traders share is an understanding of the precepts of economic theory, and the informal rules of exchange they develop come to reflect and reinforce those precepts. This market thus comes to look like what economic theory suggests it should.

If Mizruchi and Davis in chapter 5 and Schneper and Guillén in chapter 6 look at how models of business behavior spread, across U.S. banks and across national stock markets, Knorr Cetina and Bruegger look at how a model of currency trading emerges and becomes institutionalized. In the case of the lex mercatoria, as Richard Swedberg describes it in chapter 4, the principles established by private merchant courts shaped the merchant regulations that individual countries established—that is, a transnational model shaped local market practices. Knorr Cetina and Bruegger show that global principles of market order have shaped how the virtual currency market is run as well.

How Networks Shape Markets

The French sociologist Émile Durkheim (1893/1933) argued that societies vary distinctly in the structure of their social connections. In premodern societies there are only one or two occupations—hunter-gatherer, witch-doctor— and thus people's identities and interaction patterns are shaped by the fact that they live a common life. In modern societies with complex divisions of labor, people's identities and interactions are shaped by their occupational groups. Occupational groups define how members should behave, and the groups themselves are interdependent and arrayed in a complex web of interactions. One identifies not with the people in the next hut or house, but with those with whom one shares a structural position. Members of occupational groups learn behavior from other members.

Firms, like individuals, are also embedded in ongoing social relationships, and these social relationships prevent them from acting as atomistic theories predict they will act. Firms depend on networks of other firms that occupy similar structural positions, as well as myriad networks of firms that occupy different structural positions. Placement in these networks shapes behavior in a variety of different ways, via mimicry and power plays, for instance.

In 1985 Mark Granovetter published an article in the *American Journal of Sociology* that developed Karl Polanyi's (1944) observation that economic behavior is socially embedded, in the sense that it is situated in a web of social relationships. Granovetter's article became the touchstone of the network paradigm in economic sociology. Granovetter argues that in matters such as pricing, the conventional atomistic view of human economic behavior is wrongheaded. Individuals are not free-floating atoms who will as readily interact with one alter as with another, seeking the best price in every situation, the social consequences be damned. Granovetter uses transaction cost economics (Williamson 1975) as a foil. Transaction cost economics suggests that parts suppliers price-gouge when they have the chance and that parts buyers can prevent gouging only by buying the firms that supply them. Where market conditions are ripe for price-gouging, firms will buy the companies that sell them parts. Granovetter counters that social networks punish price-gouging by closing off the gouger from future transactions. In his example, norms against malfeasance enforced by social networks shape prices just as surely as do individual norms of self-interest.

The two chapters in part 3 build on the general insight that economic transactions are embedded in social relationships and that the social inevitably affects the economic. People do not behave as isolated atoms in economic exchanges and they do not treat all others identically. For instance, prices have long been a central concern of neoclassical economists, but economic sociologists have only recently begun to look at how social ties influence pricing to find that network ties affect how much people pay for stock, computer components, and bank loans (Baker 1984; Carruthers 1996; Uzzi 1999; Zuckerman 1999; and Bothner 2002). Networks shape pricing, economic alliances, and corporate vitality in contexts as different as the banking and textile industries in Renaissance Italy and the California savings and loan industry. We have already seen the importance of social networks in chapter 5 by Mizruchi and Davis, which documented how corporate board networks diffused the idea that banks should set up foreign branches.

Chapter 8 explores the role of networks in the early Florentine economy. Paul McLean and John Padgett show that the silk industry developed the same business model as the wool industry through its ties with bankers, who served both industries in Renaissance Florence. Most studies of the relationship between social life and economic life have been concerned with distinguishing sharply between the two spheres, then showing the unexpected influence of social life on economic life. McLean and Padgett reiterate a point that Talcott

Parsons and Neil Smelser (1956) made in their early treatise on economic sociology, and that Durkheim made before them, namely, that economic life cannot be disentangled from social life. Economic life, even in the disembodied virtual transactions that Knorr Cetina and Bruegger observe in chapter 7, is inherently social. It is not just that social networks *affect* economic networks, but that economic networks are impossible to separate from social networks. Because of this connection—which was taken for granted before the rise of the Western view that the economy is a distinct sphere (Meyer 1988)—we must view the marriage, banking, class, and entrepreneurial connections in Renaissance Florence (to many minds the birthplace of capitalism) as a single integrated network.

Evidence that social networks shaped Florentine economic practices comes in several forms. In one set of analyses, business partnerships and marriage partnerships showed striking parallels, reflecting the move from a traditional and locally based system to a modern and cosmopolitan system. In the wool industry, partnerships among elites tended to be based on shared location, whereas elite bankers deliberately partnered with bankers from other locales. These differences are reflected in marriage patterns: a local pattern of marriages prevailed among wool-making families and a more cosmopolitan pattern of marriages among banking families.

Network connections also altered core economic behavior patterns, in part by serving as the conduits for the kinds of new economic models discussed in chapters 5 and 6. Bankers had extralocal networks from their long ties to the wool industry, and when they began to sponsor the growing silk industry as the wool industry declined, they brought those networks of raw materials providers, on the input side, and purchasers of finished products, on the output side, to the silk manufacturers they financed. A result was that silk manufacturing came to look modern in the way that wool manufacturing did, with its input and output networks of wide geographical scope. McLean and Padgett add yet another insight about how economic models spread to the insights offered by Mizruchi and Davis in chapter 5 and by Schneper and Guillén in chapter 6.

In the second chapter on networks, Heather Haveman and Lisa Keister explore how location in an industry network influences a firm's prospects. Neoclassical economics and industrial organizations theory, a game-theoretic approach developed by economists for understanding strategic market behavior (Tirole 1988), focus on competition among firms and how it affects their prices and vitality. Competition generally reduces prices, making it harder for firms to prosper. Sociologists from several camps—institutionalists, network theorists, and population ecologists—show that competitors actually have more complicated effects on one another. Two firms in the same industry may compete for clients in a zero-sum game. But a firm's apparent competitors may have positive effects on it as well.

Population ecologists discovered that in the early years of an industry an increase in the number of competitors actually makes existing firms more likely to prosper. As the number of competitors grows, a nascent industry gains a stable clientele and legitimacy among investors, and these developments help incumbent firms, contrary to the conventional wisdom that firms suffer when competitors enter the fray. Ecologists have found that in a wide range of industries the initial growth in the number of competitors is good for incumbents (Baum 1996).

Haveman and Keister build on these insights by exploring how connections among firms in a mature industry may have positive effects on those firms. In a sample of California savings and loan banks, they find that when firms compete directly, offering exactly the same services as others nearby, their profits, growth, and chances for survival suffer. By contrast, when savings and loans are located near other savings and loans that offer different sorts of services, "mutualism" improves their profits, growth, and chances for survival. All else being equal, it is better to have lots of other savings and loans around—as long as they specialize in different services.

How can competition from other firms in the same industry, but with different specialties, help a firm? Where there are concentrations of firms in a particular industry, clients may visit one firm and be referred to another firm that better suits their needs. It may be that as savings and loans come to specialize in more and more services, customers will look to them to solve a wider range of problems. By advertising new, specialized services, savings and loans create more interest in the industry. Haveman and Keister's findings provide striking evidence of a process that White (2002) and his colleagues have documented: firms seek to distinguish themselves from their nearby competitors so as to prevent head-to-head competition. Haveman and Keister show that when firms do this, by catering to customers with different needs and by drawing on different sets of environmental resources, they indeed do better.

Sociologists have argued that networks can serve as an alternative to bureaucracies, coordinating aspects of financing and production more flexibly and creatively than bureaucracies can (Powell 1990). The chapters in part 3 explore this aspect of networks by showing how they shape different sorts of economic behavior. In McLean and Padgett's analysis, overlapping social and economic networks brought new ideas about both marriage patterns and trade patterns to early Florence. Like the chapters in part 2, McLean and Padgett's chapter illuminates the role of new economic models, documenting the spread of a cosmopolitan model of trade through banking networks from wool to silk manufacturers. Haveman and Keister show that industry networks can have positive effects on firm performance and survival. When a new industry is emerging, each firm benefits from the establishment of other similar firms. But firms also reap advantages from being in a dense network of similar firms, as long as those firms do not offer exactly the same products.

How Economic Ideas Shape Markets

Max Weber (1905/1958), who is often described as the father of economic sociology, famously said that the spirit of capitalism was the offspring of the *ethic* of Protestantism. The religious ideas of the "calling" and of asceticism caused early Calvinists to act in ways that were good for capitalism: they devoted themselves to hard work and saving. A religious ethic thus influenced economic behavior. Students of modern ideas emphasize that there are many different notions of market rationality and that proponents of the different notions often slug it out in corporate offices or on regulatory boards. Thus, for instance, Fligstein (1990) shows that over time three different management groups have imposed successive ideas of corporate rationality, based in their own managerial traditions. As corporate reins have been taken by production managers, then marketing managers, then finance managers, they have brought a sequence of quite different notions of efficiency to the task. These different ideas produce corporate efficiency through different means, optimizing different functions of the firm. For students of ideas and markets, there is more than one way to skin most cats, and ideas about efficiency often determine which way is chosen.

Economic sociologists find that ideas shape economic conventions and are shaped by them. We derive ideas from economic practices, attributing efficacy to the practices we encounter. When we see competition among firms, we associate it with efficiency and then use the principle that competition breeds efficiency to design sectors such as health care and education. In the final part of the volume, three chapters tackle the relationship between ideas and economic practices. Does the abstract market described by neoclassical theory diffuse because economic forces favor it or because it is a powerful idea? Do sectors that embrace the model actually conform to its principles?

Sociologists have long emphasized the importance of ideas in shaping economic behavior. This was the principal theme of Weber's *The Protestant Ethic and the Spirit of Capitalism* (1905/1958), which shows how the Calvinist ethics of asceticism and a worldly calling stimulated capitalist behavior. Marx also believed that ideas shape economic behavior, arguing that the modern state is in the business of constructing ideologies of fairness and efficiency around institutions that favor the capitalist class.

In chapter 10, Richard Scott builds on his award-winning book *Institutional Change and Health Care Organizations* (Scott et al. 2000). In the health care sector, a market model of order won out over an early professional model of order and an interim bureaucratic model, which arose when the federal government got into the business of providing health care for the indigent and the elderly in the 1960s. How did the new market model of "managed care" arise?

Scott's analysis of the striking changes in the health care industry traces the eventual rise of managed competition as the state "deregulated" the industry and allowed "market mechanisms" to take over. Between the 1920s and the mid-1960s, the medical industry had been organized through professional control, with doctors making critical decisions. A shift in power and a change in public policy altered that model, as specialization divided the medical community and the federal government stepped in to cover a large number of people excluded by this system, imposing bureaucracy and a norm of equity. Equity in access to health care was the driving idea behind the new state model. A second shift in power and change in regulation then altered the state model as health maintenance organizations increased their market share and government sought to stem rising costs. Market efficiency was the new driving idea.

America's weak federal state facilitated these changes, just as it had facilitated the early rise of large corporations described by Perrow in chapter 2. After all, other countries had nationalized health care and dictated how providers would behave. In the United States the federal system permitted early professional groups to set their own terms, and doctors did this more successfully than any other group. The result was the early professional model of control, which set the United States apart from other developed nations. America's weak state also subsidized early health insurance with tax "expenditures" for employer-backed coverage and in so doing set the stage for the second phase: state takeover of insurance for excluded groups, the unemployed, and the retired.

Despite their rhetorical power, the ideas of equity in access and of market control of the industry were never very successful in practice. Under the state regime, many groups, notably the working poor, lacked health insurance. Under the managerial regime, the ideas of "deregulation" and "market mechanisms" are not actually matched by a decrease in regulation or, in most cases, by a rise in competition. Yet these ideas proved to be vital rhetorical tools in political struggles over how health care would be run. The ideas of professional domination, state-led equal access, and market coordination have proved to be powerful organizing principles, however, even if they have not been realized in practice.

In chapter 11, Deborah Davis explores resistance to the globalization of ideas about private ownership of real estate—specifically the resistance to a Western, capitalist real estate law that was instituted in China. Ideas about ownership and inheritance were dramatically different in pre-Communist China, when family rights of ownership and inheritance prevailed, and under communism, when collectivist ideas about real estate ownership prevailed. Familial conceptions of ownership remained surprisingly powerful even after half a century of Communist rule.

Davis's chapter demonstrates how differently new global ideas about property rights can be interpreted in particular settings. Her study brilliantly epitomizes the continuing relevance of Weber's caution to sociologists to try to understand the subjective meaning of practices to members of a society. Previous legal regimes had deeply embedded meanings to the Chinese, and when the government installed a new property law based on Western ideas, economic behavior and social relations were slow to change.

Davis finds that in focus groups conducted in 2000 and 2002—eight and ten years after China's collective housing policy had been replaced with private ownership and several years after a majority of city dwellers had become owners of their apartments—people evaluated competing claims to ownership not through the lens of the law but through the lens of either the traditional familial system or the system of state socialism. These systems had their own rational logics, and change in state policy did not destroy those logics.

Davis takes the same broad approach taken by Schneper and Guillén in their chapter on the spread of hostile takeovers. Schneper and Guillén use cross-national comparisons to show that the hostile takeover spreads only to countries where the cultural and legal systems legitimate the trading of companies. Davis shows that the new global ideal of a real estate market faces cultural resistance in a setting where previous systems of real estate law define the new model as illegitimate. In both cases, the success of new ideas about property based in Western economic theory is mediated by local traditions.

Davis studies the clash of three systems of economic ideas, using real estate as a lens through which to observe China as it moves toward Western market institutions and ideas. Kieran Healy's chapter explores the struggle to use market principles and ideas in another realm where they seem illicit. He tries to understand how the organ transplant industry has eluded the problem of the seeming commodification of human organs. Healy's analysis parallels that of Viviana Zelizer in *Morals and Markets: The Development of Life Insurance in the United States* (1983). Zelizer asks how life insurance, which provides a cash payout for the death of a loved one, could surmount cultural barriers to the idea of commodification—the idea that a value can be placed on life. Healy similarly asks how the proponents of rationalizing the allocation of human organs have managed to transcend resistance to the idea of trade in body parts.

Since the 1970s, a system of procuring and distributing organs has arisen in the United States that can only be described as a market, even if cash payments are in most cases avoided. The obstacle for early consumers—the groups that sought organs to transplant—was the resistance of families to appeals for the organs of their dead, or dying, loved ones. Simple rational arguments did not win the hearts and minds of the survivors. Family members did eventually respond, however, to a new idea, a new emotional discourse of donation: the act of donation would be a means of healing the family's loss and an ongoing gift of life from the deceased. The issue of how to introduce monetary compensation was particularly fraught, for payment for organs seemed to amount to trafficking in human lives. Proponents made payments culturally acceptable by disguising them. They proposed to discount insurance premiums for people who signed up for donation, creating a sort of futures market in organs. They won legislation in Pennsylvania to provide cash, but in the form of funeral expense assistance to be paid directly to the funeral home.

Healy's study illuminates a third dimension of the relationship between ideas and economic practices. Both Scott and Davis look at the effect of ideas on economic practices inside the market—in what became the health care "industry" and in the Chinese real estate market. By contrast, Healy follows in a long sociological tradition of trying to understand commodification in a realm that is culturally defined as outside of the market. Viviana Zelizer (1983) has done the same with the case of life insurance, which seems to place a value on human life, and Perry Anderson (1974) has done it for labor, which seemed under feudalism to be something inalienable and not something one could buy and sell. How quickly we came to accept the idea of placing a value on human life and on human time!

If economic theory and modern common sense suggest that there must be one "best way" to organize health care, real estate markets, or the market for human organs, the authors of these final chapters see that there are many effective ways to organize economic activity. Ideas help to select which among them will be identified as the one "best way." Is health care more effectively organized on the professional model, the state model, or the managerial model? It is virtually impossible to say, and each model has claimed to optimize a different sort of outcome—patient care, equality of access, and managerial efficiency, respectively. It may be that circumstances determine which of the several models of rationality will be most effective. Defining property inheritance rights by law rather than by tradition seems to foster opposition in China, and market incentives appear to be ineffective in the case of organ donation. The question of how economic activities *should* be organized may be more than a question of how one abstract model of the economy suggests they should be.

Conclusion

The great promise of economic sociology is that it can explain aspects of economic behavior and institutions that have been resistant to explanation. The chapters assembled in this volume represent the best empirical work being done in economic sociology today, and the payoff is a series of empirically verified insights about how economic behavior patterns come about—a sociology of the economy. The social mechanisms underlying economic behavior that these twelve studies document do not boil down to a single principle, such as the principle of self-interest in neoclassical economics. But neither do these chapters present a disorganized hodgepodge of ideas. They demonstrate four social processes at work:

1. The structure of political institutions determines who will shape economic institutions and conventions and what those institutions and conventions will look like.

2. Firms and nations follow the rational strategies of their role models, just as adolescents follow the behavior of their role models, and hence much economic behavior looks more like crowd behavior than like the result of pure rational calculation.

3. Social networks shape economic practices in a wide range of ways—by providing sanctions for malfeasance but also by providing cues that shape prices, by providing business strategies that industries can copy, and by shaping the competitive environment.

4. Ideas influence economic behavior and institutions, and ideas embedded in economic customs often shape new economic customs. For instance, the idea of market competition as efficient arbiter is well institutionalized in the industrial sector in the United States, and that idea has come to shape other sectors, such as health care. In the modern world there is a wide range of rational ideas—visions of how to rationalize things—and understanding their origins and influence promises to help us to understand why economic institutions and behaviors vary so significantly.

Economic sociology is built on the premise that narrow economic laws do not drive economic practices to become identical across societies. There may be many efficient ways to organize a transplant organ market, a market for corporate control, and the health care sector, as suggested by Healy; Schneper and Guillén; and Scott, respectively. Economic sociology has been reinvigorated since the 1980s in large part because nations that did not fit the model that Britain and later the United States seemed to epitomize grew at astonishing rates in the postwar period—chiefly the East Asian economies, but France, Germany, and Sweden as well. If there is more than one truly efficient solution to any economic problem, then the explanations of economic behavior that social scientists have been working with are too limiting. Most are based on the assumption that history is efficient, which suggests that economic practices evolve toward increasingly efficient forms. This kind of efficiency is certainly what nations oriented to growth strive for, and that striving has gone a long way toward increasing efficiency in the aggregate. But explanations of economic behavior have also been based on an assumption of optimality, which suggests that economic practices evolve toward a *single* efficient form. If economic practices are not evolving toward a single efficient form, it would appear that the ideal of the "perfect market" is not driving the evolution of economic practices and that we need to develop explanations that root economic behavior in society rather than in economic ideas that transcend society.

Taken together, these twelve chapters suggest that markets are social structures first and foremost. They are incompletely described by algorithms that predict prices and output. As social structures, they are composed of roles, conventions, and institutions, and they are characterized by ongoing disputes over what those roles, conventions, and institutions should look like. These disputes are typically framed as scientific and managerial disagreements over the most efficient means of organizing the world, and this characterization of the disputes—their seeming orientation to divining the true "best way" of organizing an economic sector—reinforces the notion that it is economic laws that drive change in the system. Our determined efforts to divine the character of those economic laws often blind us to the mundane social origins of many economic behavior patterns.

Put another way, even if universal economic laws select superior economic roles, conventions, and institutions for survival and doom inferior ones, it is important to understand where the great variety of roles, conventions, and institutions come from in the first place. And even if economic laws shape the long-run evolution of the economy, it is important to understand what shapes the short-run social perturbations that spawn new market forms and often extinguish them before economic laws have a chance to do their job of rewarding the best and destroying the worst.

The chapters assembled in this volume show that markets have the characteristics of other sorts of social structures, like religions or clans. Like religions and clans, markets can take any number of different forms. Some will not prosper, but history suggests that many different forms of markets can prosper—that different logics of efficiency exist. For economic sociologists, then, the most important questions concern how markets emerge, stabilize, and change. It is these processes that are explored by the chapters of this book. The chapters on political institutions sketch the effects of the political on the initial structuring of markets. The chapters on economic models show how economic conventions travel from one place to another, producing change in markets. The chapters on networks show how social relations modify market behavior, and the final chapters show how ideas can revolutionize markets or make them resistant to change.

If markets are social structures, on a par with other social structures, rather than price functions, we need to know more about their organization and why they change. The studies included in this volume demonstrate the ability of economic sociology to explain the emergence of various types of markets, their persistence, and change. How can we understand, for instance, the stability of the model of American corporate structure over the last one hundred years—the tendency for large firms to dominate even in sectors where there are no economies of scale? Economic theory alone does not explain the early rise of huge firms in the United States, and so Charles Perrow traces the initial political institutions that encouraged capitalists to shape the regulations that they had to live by. Here, as in Bai Gao's chapter on the rise of business associations in the Japanese economy, we see that political institutions shaped early policymaking and thereby affected industry structure. In both cases, new policy institutions and corporate practices became cognitively embedded and thus resistant to challenge.

How can we explain the fact that American banks set up foreign branches in droves around 1970 but had stopped by 1980? Conventional economic explanations fail here, and it is clear that two important sociological forces were in play: a tendency to mimic role models and a tendency to learn through social networks. Mizruchi and Davis's study thus provides strong evidence that what goes by the name of "rational calculation" is often based not on evidence but on mimicry of role models, and that face-to-face networks are often the conduits through which new putatively rational prescriptions diffuse.

How can we explain the fact that modern medical care moved from professional domination to managed care? The change fits the commonsense view that the world is being rationalized in the image of neoliberalism, but it in fact represents the shift from one ideological form of rationality, professional expertise, to an interim form, bureaucratic expertise, to a third and fragile form, "managed care." Underlying this story we find competing groups with different rationales who have played different roles at different times. These competing ideas of rationality seemed to give the health care industry coherence and meaning for participants, and each seemed like the ultimate and final ordering of the industry at the time. Ideas do matter, and ideas of rationality have a certain finality about them.

That economic sociology has produced such a wealth of empirical findings in the scant twenty years since its renaissance bodes well for its future. That so many of those findings can be traced directly to a handful of social processes that the first group of economic sociologists, Karl Marx, Max Weber, and Émile Durkheim, saw at work a century or more ago also bodes well, because it suggests that a finite number of social mechanisms typically shape economic behavior and that those mechanisms are relatively stable across contexts. The structure of political institutions and decisionmaking processes matters for the form taken by economic institutions and regulations. The human tendency to copy behavior and to copy institutions seems to operate in all social contexts, and it plays a large role in shaping economic behavior (a role that is often attributed to rational calculation). Social systems shape behavior of all sorts, both through networks that diffuse new ideas and through networks that constrain malfeasance. And ideas influence all kinds of social behavior, including economic behavior, despite the fact that the effects can be difficult to see in a world where the proponents of new economic conventions and institutions appeal to universal economic laws rather than human-made conceptions of rationality.

References

Anderson, Perry. 1974. *Lineages of the Absolutist State.* London: New Left Books.

Baker, Wayne. 1984. "The Social Structure of a National Securities Market." *American Journal of Sociology* 89(4): 775–811.

Baum, Joel A. C. 1996. "Organizational Ecology." In *Handbook of Organization Studies,* edited by Stewart R. Clegg, Cynthia Hardy, and Walter Nord. London: Sage Publications.

Bothner, Matthew S. 2002. "Structure, Scale, and Scope in the Global Computer Industry." Working paper. Chicago: University of Chicago, Graduate School of Business.

Campbell, John L. 1998. "Institutional Analysis and the Role of Ideas in Political Economy." *Theory and Society* 27(3): 377–409.

Carruthers, Bruce G. 1996. *City of Capital: Politics and Markets in the English Financial Revolution.* Princeton, N.J.: Princeton University Press.

Carruthers, Bruce G., and Terence C. Halliday. Forthcoming. "Institutionalizing Creative Destruction: Predictable and Transparent Bankruptcy Law in the Wake of the East Asian Financial Crisis." In *Neoliberalism and Institutional Reform in East Asia,* edited by Meredith Woo-Cumings. Ithaca, N.Y.: Cornell University Press.

Chandler, Alfred D., Jr. 1990. *Scale and Scope.* Cambridge, Mass.: Harvard University Press.

Davis, Gerald F., and Christopher Marquis. 2001. "The Globalization of Stock Markets and Convergence in Corporate Governance." Paper presented to the conference on the Economic Sociology of Capitalism. Cornell University, Ithaca, N.Y. (2001).

DiMaggio, Paul J., and Walter W. Powell. 1983. "The Iron Cage Revisited: Institutionalized Isomorphism and Collective Rationality in Organizational Fields." *American Sociological Review* 48(2, April): 147–60.

Dobbin, Frank. 1994. *Forging Industrial Policy: The United States, Britain, and France in the Railway Age.* Cambridge: Cambridge University Press.

Drori, Gili S., Yong Suk Jang, and John W. Meyer. 2000. "The Impact of Education and Science on Administrative Rationalization: Cross-National Analyses, 1985 to 1995." Unpublished paper. Stanford University, Department of Sociology, Stanford, Calif.

Dunlavy, Colleen. Forthcoming. *Shareholder Democracy: The Forgotten History.* Cambridge, Mass.: Harvard University Press.

Durkheim, Émile. 1893/1933. *The Division of Labor in Society.* Translated by George Simpson. New York: Free Press.

Fligstein, Neil. 1990. *The Transformation of Corporate Control.* Cambridge, Mass.: Harvard University Press.

———. 2001. *The Architecture of Markets: An Economic Sociology of Twenty-first-Century Capitalist Society.* Princeton, N.J.: Princeton University Press.

Fourcade-Gourinchas, Marion, and Sarah Babb. 2002. "The Rebirth of the Liberal Creed: Paths to Neoliberalism in Four Countries." *American Journal of Sociology* 8: 233–79.

Goffman, Erving 1974. *Frame Analysis.* Cambridge, Mass.: Harvard University Press.

Granovetter, Mark. 1985. "Economic Action and Social Structure: The Problem of Embeddedness." *American Journal of Sociology* 91(3, November): 481–510.

Greif, Avner. 1993. "Contract Enforceability and Economic Institutions in Early Trade: The Maghribi Traders' Coalition." *American Economic Review* 83: 525–48.

Guillén, Mauro F. 1994. *Models of Management: Work, Authority, and Organization in a Comparative Perspective.* Chicago: University of Chicago Press.

Hall, Peter A., and Rosemary C. R. Taylor. 1996. "Political Science and the Three New Institutionalisms." *Political Studies* 44(5): 936–58.

Haveman, Heather A. 1993. "Follow the Leader: Mimetic Isomorphism and Entry into New Markets." *Administrative Science Quarterly* 38(4): 593–627.

March, James, and Herbert Simon. 1958. *Organizations.* New York: John Wiley.

Meyer, John. 1988. "Society Without Culture." In *Rethinking the Nineteenth Century,* edited by Francisco Ramirez. New York: Greenwood.

Meyer, John W., and Brian Rowan. 1977. "Institutionalized Organizations: Formal Structure as Myth and Ceremony." *American Journal of Sociology* 83(2, September): 340–63.

North, Douglass. 1990. *Institutions, Institutional Change, and Economic Performance.* New York: Cambridge University Press.

Parsons, Talcott, and Neil Smelser. 1956. *Economy and Society: A Study in the Integration of Economic and Social Theory.* London: Routledge and Kegan Paul.

Perrow, Charles. 2002. *Organizing America: Wealth, Power, and the Origins of Corporate Capitalism.* Princeton, N.J.: Princeton University Press.

Polanyi, Karl. 1944. *The Great Transformation: The Political and Economic Origin of Our Time.* New York: Rinehart.

Powell, Walter W. 1990. "Neither Market nor Hierarchy: Network Forms of Organization." In *Research in Organizational Behavior,* vol. 12, *Leadership, Participation, and Group Behavior,* edited by Larry L. Cummings and Barry Staw. Greenwich, Conn.: JAI Press.

Roy, William G. 1997. *Socializing Capital: The Rise of the Large Industrial Corporation in America.* Princeton, N.J.: Princeton University Press.

Scott, W. Richard. 2001. *Institutions and Organizations.* 2nd ed. Thousand Oaks, Calif.: Sage Publications.

Scott, W. Richard, Martin Ruef, Peter J. Mendel, and Carol Caronna. 2000. *Institutional Change and Health Care Organizations: From Professional Dominance to Managed Care.* Chicago: University of Chicago Press.

Skocpol, Theda, and Kenneth Finegold. 1982. "State Capacity and Economic Intervention in the Early New Deal." *Political Science Quarterly* 97(2, Summer): 255–78.

Smith, Adam. 1776/1970. *The Wealth of Nations.* Baltimore: Penguin.

Stinchcombe, Arthur. 1965. "Social Structure and Organization." In *Handbook of Industrial Organization,* edited by James G. March. Chicago: Rand McNally.

Thelen, Kathleen, and Sven Steinmo. 1992. "Historical Institutionalism in Comparative Politics." In *Structuring Politics: Historical Institutionalism in Comparative Politics,* edited by Sven Steinmo, Kathleen Thelen, and Frank Longstreth. New York: Cambridge University Press.

Tirole, Jean. 1988. *The Theory of Industrial Organization.* Cambridge, Mass.: MIT Press.

Uzzi, Brian. 1999. "Embeddedness in the Making of Financial Capital: How Social Relations and Networks Benefit Firms Seeking Financing." *American Sociological Review* 64(4): 481–505.

Weber, Max. 1905/1958. *The Protestant Ethic and the Spirit of Capitalism.* New York: Scribner's.

White, Harrison. 2002. *Markets from Networks: Socioeconomic Models of Production.* Princeton, N.J.: Princeton University Press.

Williamson, Oliver E. 1975. *Markets and Hierarchies: Analysis and Antitrust Implications.* New York: Free Press.

Zelizer, Viviana A. 1983. *Morals and Markets: The Development of Life Insurance in the United States.* New Brunswick, N.J.: Transaction.

Zuckerman, Ezra. 1999. "The Categorical Imperative." *American Journal of Sociology* 104(5): 1398–1438.

Part I

HOW POLITICAL INSTITUTIONS SHAPE MARKETS

2

ORGANIZING AMERICA

Charles Perrow

A<small>T THE</small> table that historians and most social scientists have set for us to explain our national history sit three major figures: industrialization (including technological change), culture, and politics. In the volume upon which this article is based, *Organizing America: Wealth, Power, and the Origins of Corporate Capitalism* (Perrow 2002), I argue that scholars have largely ignored the eight-hundred-pound gorilla that came to dominate that table in the late nineteenth century and has continued to dominate it since. The gorilla is the large for-profit organization, barely regulated, vertically integrated, and bureaucratic. Its power and influence in shaping the direction of industrialization, of culture, and of politics have been neglected. We need to make an *organizational* interpretation of our history, and this chapter is an attempt to take a necessary first step in doing so. You may say, ah, Alfred Chandler (1977) and economic historians since his great work have done that. But theirs is a quite narrow efficiency interpretation of selected firms, just the winners; they show almost no concern with the losers, which represented alternative paths, or the broader social impact of the winners.[1]

I want to know how it came about that the United States developed an economic system based on large corporations, privately held, with minimal regulation by the state. Two hundred years ago there were none. Until the 1890s, there were only a few, in textiles, railroads, and the oil, steel, and locomotive industries. They hardly dominated society as yet, but they put the necessary legal and political structures in place. At the turn of the century they made their move, and in about five years mergers had produced most of the two hundred biggest corporations of the time. Most of these still rule their industries. What in our bucolic agrarian history made this sudden transformation possible?

Nothing comparable occurred in Europe. Until the 1950s, the corporate structure of the United States was unique (and also dominant in the industrialized world). One reason for this American "exceptionalism" is familiar: the industrial revolution found fertile ground in a resource-rich land with mass markets and democratic institutions and a culture of individual freedom and entrepreneurship. But this does not sufficiently emphasize the weakness of government and the ability of elites with organizational interests to change the legal system and institute bureaucratic employee controls. Rich resources, mass markets, and democratic institutions would not produce corporate capitalism on their own; nor would individual freedom and entrepreneurship. Indeed, many democratic institutions had struggled hard to prevent corporate capitalism from being the dominant form throughout the nineteenth century.

For large corporations to spring into existence at the end of the century the legal structure of the commonwealth had to be reworked. It had to favor the accumulation of private capital for large-scale production for national markets rather than the dispersion of capital into smaller enterprises with regional markets. The United States centralized private wealth and power a century sooner than Europe did. Our global success then forced our solution on Europe in the last half of the twentieth century. Distinctive organizational tools were required to transform agrarian republicanism. Organizations had to ensure that the labor force was dependent (unable to move freely among organizations or to survive outside of them), rule it with bureaucratic tools rather than force, and link organizational success to political access, often through corruption.

The weak state and the organizational arguments are interdependent. Assuming a minimal degree of democracy, a weak state allows private organizations to grow almost without limit and with few requirements to serve the public interest. Private organizations can shape the weak state to their liking.[2] This requires state action, in the form of changing property laws; thus, the courts did a lot for private organizations. The legislature of a strong state would be sufficiently independent of private economic organizations, and its executive branch would be strong enough to check their power. Together a strong state's legislative and executive branches could limit the growth of private organizations and require that they pay some attention to the public interest. This happened to a greater degree in Europe than in the United States.

Let me start with Europe, in the sixteenth to the eighteenth centuries. Agricultural production increased, leading to better diets, and with greatly improved disease control, Europe had a population increase. Stronger states appeared as the agricultural surplus and the first technological stirrings brought some prosperity, and these states were able to reduce the power of warlords and bandits, providing stability. With stable states, the new inventions of the industrial revolution could spread and develop. The population increase provided the manpower for the artisans, craftsmen, and small manufactories. Wealth increased, but it remained centralized in political-religious hands, resulting in even stronger states. These states restricted the size of private power sources, just as they beat down the nobility and sought to control the church.

Private economic organizations emerged anyway, because an industrial revolution was under way and there were democratic notions about exploiting it. But labor was still tied to the land, whereas industry was urban. The labor power had to be moved. In England the state allowed the nobility to reduce its historic obligations to the peasantry and remove them from the land—the enclosure movement—creating a small urban population wholly dependent on wage labor. Newly created profits from manufacturing began to be centralized in private hands, and private power that might challenge the state and the church appeared. In England the crown simply confiscated the estates of the newly rich upon their death—the mort main, or dead hand laws—and limited capital investment to the financial resources of business partners or a few stockholders. The primary means of raising capital had to be through joint ownership or joint stockholders. The sums were small, and the size of economic organizations was correspondingly limited throughout the nineteenth century and into the next one. There were some big organizations, such as the East India Company (but it had a royal charter with government representatives), and a few other big ones, such as the pottery giant Wedgwood, but there was not a free hand for private investment in big organizations. It was the United States that allowed that to happen.

The United States was blessed with a fear and hatred of two gigantic organizations the immigrants had experienced in Europe: the state church and the state itself. No national church was established, and the federal state was kept small, weak, and divided. With no significant state, there was no nobility. Without a nobility, there was no feudalism and none of those immobile peasants. With no strong state, there could be no strong church; it takes a state to impose one. Without a crown, church, and nobles to be jealous of the rise of private economic power, large organizations were able to flourish, though resistance to them was strong through much of the nineteenth century. Farmers and laborers and some politicians objected to the lack of regulation and the lack of public representation in the new corporations, and they also objected to their market control and ability to corrupt the legislature and the judiciary. But these objections had only a limited effect. The economy was growing fast, and there was a strong demand for the output of the new organizations. The culture presented contradictory scripts that enabled almost any arrangement to be defended.

There were a few legal impediments initially. Since organizations make use of all sorts of public services and benefits, the common law from England required that chartered companies serve a public interest and have public representatives on their boards. In 1819 the Supreme Court's *Dartmouth* decision struck out that provision, as successfully argued on Dartmouth's behalf by the lawyer Daniel Webster, who had been hired by New England merchant elites. That year also saw the dissolution of two other restraints on the private accumulation of power. One was limited liability: an entrepreneur who went bankrupt and could not pay his workers or his creditors did not have to pay them out of his own pocket; he could be very rich, but his personal wealth was separated from the assets of his business. Limited liability made it inconvenient for workers and creditors, who subsidized the failure of the business, and it encouraged mismanagement and lack of planning, but it also certainly encouraged risky business adventures.[3]

The second restraint on the private accumulation of wealth disappeared when the Supreme Court declared that the federal government acted for the people directly and that its laws would prevail over any laws of the individual states regarding the conduct of corporations. But the executive branch of the federal government hardly existed at that time, and the legislature was easily bribed, so this ruling led to the removal of local control over internal improvements, banking, and, significantly, the railroads when they appeared. The economy was to be largely unregulated.[4]

The third check on private power to be removed was the limited ability of partnerships and joint stock companies to raise enough capital to build really big organizations. In a quirk of history, when Robert Lowell went to England to steal the technology for building the new water-powered looms, he spent much of his additional time in Scotland, where he encountered a unique legal fiction: the corporate company. In a corporate company, any number of people could invest small amounts of money in one firm, and the officers were subject to few restrictions from the investors.[5] There were few such organizations; Scotland was not industrializing very quickly, and the heads of the state had little to fear from the small organizations that did incorporate. Lowell saw the advantage immediately and took it back, with the stolen machinery plans, to Boston, where he formed a series of true, interlocked corporations.

The emerging manufacturing elite was a motley bunch: there were gentlemen with landed wealth and wealthy merchants as well as farmers, small businessmen and craftsmen, and clever and ambitious immigrants. Indeed, the emerging elite could be almost anyone as long as they were white and not Irish. This is an important point because, in contrast to Europe, no particular culture shaped the American manufacturing elite. Lineage was scant, so wealth was more often gained than inherited, thus favoring the industrious. Moreover, with the varied background culture, more chances for the cross-cutting fertilization of ideas and practices arose, and there were few established traditions that might be blindly followed. The only check was a widespread fear among rural and labor interests that their freedom would be curtailed by large, private centers of wealth as these emerged. But the openness of organizational opportunities in the United States probably increased the legitimacy of the new forms.

Two additional forces were crucial, beyond a weak state that was not interested in limiting the private power of organizations and an elite that was neither hereditary nor ethnically and religiously homogeneous: these were capital and labor. Capital was initially scant and local. The Napoleonic Wars and our own War of 1812 shut off the import of the cheap manufactured goods needed for a rural, colonial nation. New England capital was diverted from shipping raw materials to manufacturing goods here. Had this not happened, the continent could have become like India—ruled by colonials who extracted the raw materials and shipped them abroad and shipped in the manufactured and consumer goods made in England. For a time this was Canada's fate, until the British empire began to break up and Canadians gained some economic independence.

In the United States, with independence and then with restrictions on importing European goods, the major center of wealth, the New England merchants, turned toward tariff-protected manufacturing and internal transport. With high tariffs, ample natural resources, and a steady labor supply from exhausted New England farms—and even more important, from immigration—European capital flowed in to invest in manufacturing and transport. European capital was especially important in satisfying the giant demands of the new railroad industry from the middle until the end of the century.

But there were important variations in capital formation among the states. In Massachusetts the state government allowed a free rein to banks, and the textile elites were able to put together the large sums needed to establish mass-production mills of unprecedented size. These were located in company towns that further centralized wealth and power. They used the corporate model, borrowed from Scotland, which allowed passive, remote investment from many stockholders. In contrast, in Pennsylvania the state closely regulated banks and favored investment in transportation. This limited the ability of elites to raise the capital for local enterprises, such as textiles, and their wealth went into railroads, mining and shipping, and, ironically, New England textiles. The conditions in Philadelphia were favorable for the first major industry in the first half of the century, textiles, but the lack of capital ensured a decentralized textile industry of small firms (Gumus-Dawes 2000). By the 1880s Philadelphia textile production was greater than New England's, with small firms and half the capitalization of the New England firms.

The towns along the mid-Atlantic and New England coasts soon filled with workers who were dependent on a wage for a living. This was new in the early nineteenth century. Many of these workers were immigrants, but many were also the younger sons of the farmers who could no longer subdivide the land into viable plots for all their sons. Others had become unable to work the exhausted New England soil or had found that easy migration to the West was no longer possible as the distances increased and the Indians blocked movement just east of the Great Lakes. As with England a few decades before, a wage-dependent population became available for manufacturing. Where there was no wage dependency—that is, where workers could choose farming, skilled trades, or a mix of these with some casual day labor—factories could not find workers (Shelton 1986).

As in England, a generation earlier, the first factories were manned by orphans, paupers, and criminals; no one else would accept "wage slavery" as it was called, so new was it. When the New England textile mills were built in the 1830s, they were in remote areas such as Lowell, Massachusetts, where water power was available and land was cheap. But there were no wage-dependent workers there. Mill owners had to recruit farmers' daughters, who worked for three or four years until they had a dowry and could marry. The mills had to treat these girls well: they were not wage-dependent, and they could always go back to the farm. This phase of the Lowell experience is rightfully treated as a model industrial community for the time, with literate, industrious young women living in dormitories and publishing a literary journal. But once the famished Irish came over and a railroad could bring them from the Boston port to the inland mill towns, a dependent workforce became available. Wages were cut, the New England daughters left, exploitation increased, and the handsome mill towns became slums. Profits soared with the cheap labor and slum rents; the companies were returning 25 percent per year on their investments. The firms of the Boston Associates, as they were called, completely dominated the market for low-cost, high-volume goods, in part thanks to the favorable tariffs they had pushed through Congress to keep out cheap foreign goods. Thus, their policy of labor exploitation and community disinvestment cannot be attributed to intense competition, since they had none. Beyond sheer greed, class power is the most likely explanation.[6]

This was one path of development available to the industrializing nation—centralized capital, high wage dependency, mass production of cheap goods, little technological development, and large externalities, or social costs, to be born by workers and communities. It did not become the dominant path until late in the century.

The other path is illustrated by the textile mills of Philadelphia. Though there were a few mass-production mills with unskilled and exploited immigrant labor (for a vivid account, see Shelton 1986), the lack of large amounts of capital for manufacturing, due to the state's restrictions on banks, kept textile mills small. Unable to compete with the Lowell mills in the low-end market, the Philadelphia mills developed high-end goods of a quality and innovative style that could not be copied by Lowell. These small firms spread the profits over many owners; exchanged personnel regularly, spreading the skills and innovations; did not build big integrated facilities but rented rooms with power, spreading the capital investment; and cooperated with each other as well as competed. In this environment, workers easily became owners and then workers again when another shop got the contracts. Wage dependency was reduced because there were many firms to choose from (there is no evidence that employees who left a firm were blacklisted, a standard practice in New England); higher skill levels also reduced wage dependency.

Status was not as fixed as in the Lowell mills. The small firms were profitable and prospered, and when owners achieved their modest financial goals, they often retired, further spreading the wealth and spending it locally. Labor policies were crude by our standards, but not for the time; there was child labor, but not as much as in the mass-production Lowell mills, because of the skills required. The Philadelphia mill owners invested in their communities by demanding paved streets and clean water and sewers and trade schools and by paying the required taxes. Philip Scranton (1983), in his brilliant account of these mills, discovered and theorized "small-firm networks" just one year before the immensely influential work on the small-firm networks of northern Italy and Europe by Michael Piore and Charles Sabel (1984).

A few communities in Philadelphia had large mills. These did not invest in infrastructure improvements, fired workers for voting for the wrong candidate, fought public schooling for children, and centralized the wealth in their community. They also eventually lost out to Lowell, whose mills were more massive and whose control of local communities was nearly absolute.

It is hard to generalize, but the small-firm network model appears to have been more representative of emerging industry from 1820 to about 1880 than the Lowell mass-production model. In Philadelphia there were no convenient accumulations of capital, as were provided by the Massachusetts state banking arrangement. In addition, mass-production techniques were surprisingly slow to develop for most of the industry and often resisted by owners (Hounshell 1984). Firms grew by adding more identical modules, or small shops, rather than by reorganizing work on a Fordist assembly-line model. Batch rather than mass production was the rule, and skills were reasonably high. Markets were small and local for most production, so economies of scale were not important. Of course, this all changed late in the century—and for other industries, such as petroleum, well before that.

Why did the United States have the surge of giant organizations at the end of the nineteenth century? Because of the railroads. First, they made mass markets possible, and for most economists and historians, including Alfred Chandler, this encouraged economies of scale, which in turn led to the development of national rather than regional railroad lines and national rather than regional industries. For most industries with late-nineteenth-century technologies, however, scale economies were small and achieved with only modest-sized firms of, say, five hundred employees. The cheap, dependable, all-weather transportation provided by the railroads would have been quite consistent with a decentralized, regionalized economy with modest-sized firms—the economy we had before the railroads arrived. Goods could be made in a variety of places and inexpensively distributed locally and regionally. Railroads also did not have to be national. One tristate railroad operated as a regional for several years, with efficient short-haul service and innovative maintenance and shipping practices that the national railroads copied, but it was bought out by a national line (Berk 1994, ch. 5).

The national lines (there were four major ones by the end of the century) could make the most money by promoting long-haul transport, charging low rates, because of the competition, but very high rates for short hauls where they had a monopoly. This pricing practice made a regional economy unviable. Railroads were capital-intensive and the biggest organizations in the world, with economic and political resources that allowed them to favor a national rather than a regional economy. Major centers for livestock processing, food processing, steel, petroleum, and durable goods manufacturing were established, with huge organizations dominating the national market. Since the national railroad system needed national production centers, the economy was centralized, and since it was in private hands, wealth and power were centralized as well.

It seems likely that the railroads were also responsible for the massive capital needed to establish massive industrial producers. Once the railroad system was built, with handsome and wasteful government subsidies, of course, its capital needs declined, while the railroads themselves were immensely rich. The investment banking houses, the banks, foreign capital, and wealthy railroad stockholders provided the funds for the massive merger movement at the end of the century, consolidating the industrial and retail sectors of the economy and reducing competition. In a few short years modest-sized firms were merged into the two hundred giant ones I referred to earlier, reducing competition, creating monopoly and oligopoly profits, and slowing innovation (Roy 1997). Many mergers failed, of course, but the surviving giant firms have dominated the economy ever since. The Philadelphia small-firm network model, though innovative and socially constructive, went into decline, and the Lowell mass-production model, with large, centralized, and bureaucratic firms and large social costs for workers and communities, was ascendant.

The key role of the railroads in organizing America was possible because they passed, quite quickly, into private hands with no significant regulation in the public interest. We were the only nation to allow the deregulated privatization of this immense public good. The railroads started out as quasi-governmental entities, with heavy local and state-level public investment and some public control. By the 1840s the public control was disappearing, and railroad owners began to build interstate, then national lines, with federal subventions.[7] The country needed and desperately wanted cheap transportation as it spilled westward, but in private hands the waste, inefficiency, and corruption that attended the growth of the system is legendary. Corruption in the railroads is treated as incidental by most historians and political scientists, whereas it should be seen as one important factor of production. Furthermore, by dwelling only on the corrupted—the judges and legislators—and ignoring the corrupters—the railroad organizations—they fail to see corruption as an exercise of power. Inventors in the United States were responsible for the major safety devices, such as automatic couplers and air brakes, but the U.S. railroads were the last to use them, so little concerned were they with the public good. The major scandal of the nineteenth century, the Crédit Mobilier scandal, and the fiercest strikes of the century were in the railroad industry. The railroads' labor policies set the antagonistic tone for all future capital-labor relations. And their bureaucratic control structure, so celebrated in organizational theory, became the model for both public and private organizations. Bureaucracy has proved to be the best unobtrusive control device that elites have ever achieved.

I have emphasized that a weak state allowed private organizations to grow and exploit wage dependency. But it was a path-dependent process, with some historical accidents; there was no inevitability to it until the end of the century, when the path was so firm that little could, or did, change it. Had the founding fathers not had such a taste of the costs of centralized power from England and Europe, they might have established something other than the federated political system that allowed private organizational wealth, when it appeared, such a free rein. The country was unformed when the industrial revolution came along. Had the U.S. population of, say, 1850 been achieved in 1650, a European structure of production with guilds and trades and tenant farmers could have been in place, and the tendency of unchecked industrialization to level social institutions could have been resisted. The actual United States of 1850, however, in contrast to Europe, had a small population, infirm traditions, weak local and regional centers, and a muddled class structure. This made private economic centralization easy. And it was not our culture, or the necessities of industrialization, or our political system that accomplished it, but organizations.

Had the Lowells and Cabots of Boston reinvested their wealth in an expanded merchant fleet instead of the power loom on remote rivers, we might have left mass-produced cheap textiles to the English to produce (and then to India—the Lowells had to get a special tariff to block Indian goods) and established instead a fine goods industry, with small organizations, on the low-powered streams that dot the New England coast. Had the Irish potato famine not occurred, wage dependency would not have overwhelmed the United States so quickly and easily, just when factories appeared. Had the panic of 1837 not occurred just as the railroads were getting under way, public investment could have been so paramount that effective governmental regulation of the railroads would have been demanded and perhaps achieved, despite a weak federal state.

But some things were "in the cards." A vastly resource-rich, virtually unpopulated land attracted settlers who needed vast quantities of cheap goods just when steam power permitted their production. This was a new market of unprecedented size, and because of the industrial revolution, it was more likely to be filled with mass-produced goods than with those of local artisans. Britain mass-produced goods for the rest of Europe, which was dominated by artisans and craftsmen, but it seems unlikely that with a market soon larger than Britain's markets that we would have left mass production to the British, though we could have had mass production on a regional rather than national scale, thus decentralizing wealth and power. Despite the conjunction of industrialization, mass markets, and untapped natural resources, the juggernaut of giant corporations at the turn of the century was far from inevitable, and it was far from efficient even in the narrow sense that economists employ, let alone in social terms.

Eventually the democratic ethos put something of a brake on the private accumulation of wealth and power. Labor unions did what they could, despite a hostile judiciary, and an increasingly broad electorate sent messages to the federal government about corporations and private wealth. Though sometimes misguided and full of bucolic idiocy, these messages often slowed centralization.[8] So it could have been far worse. Witness the imposition of Taylorism in Russia under Lenin—that was tried here, but success was limited, compared with Russia. Another reason economic elites could not walk away with the whole store was that big organizations generate structural interests that can run counter to those of their masters—organizations are tools, but large ones are quite recalcitrant tools.

Nevertheless, it could also have been far better. Look at what the United States had going for it: both the first and second industrial revolutions occurring in a nature-rich land that hardly had to be conquered; an ample labor supply; no fixed class structure or nobility; no religious wars to fight or religious traditions strong enough to uphold the subjection of women; early enfranchisement; and perhaps most often unnoted, only one war of consequence, our Civil War, in contrast to our competitors. Moreover, we were under the British umbrella on the high seas and used them to protect our expanding trade. A "far better" outcome would have meant less human carnage in the factories and mines, less unrestrained devouring of natural resources and less pollution, a far less steep rise in the degree of wealth and income inequality, smaller, more flexible, and competitive organizations, and stronger social welfare provisions by a strong federal government. (Something genuinely close to "wage slavery" were the orphan trains that were still running in the 1920s, handing out kids picked up on the streets of New York and Boston to midwestern farmers and factory owners.) And of course, we were behind England in abolishing slavery. A weak central government waffled and quivered about slavery under the pressure of a fabulously rich southern aristocracy and northern textile and shipping interests—organizations all.

To sum up, a weak state allowed the private accumulation of wealth and power through the medium of big organizations. Over the century economic elites developed modern bureaucracy, which was to be the means for the increasing centralization of wealth and power over the course of the nineteenth century (on the centralization of wealth, see Williamson and Lindhert 1980). The organization won the freedom to select its own officers, and thus it could keep public or governmental representatives off the board, even though it enjoyed public largess; it also won the right to choose its own successors, so that it could exist forever. Its owners and stockholders, who collected the profits, could not be sued for its debts or failures or accidents, and until the end of the century an employee or his or her family could not recover damages for any work-connected injury or death. The organization could control the social behavior of its employees. Initially such control was crudely, if legally, exerted, as when workers were fired for voting for the wrong candidate, not attending church, or not attending the right church; later the socialization of employees would rely on more subtle pressures. The strongest pressure the large organizations exercised was in building an economy that ensured wage dependency, initially with blacklisting, then with urban work that cut workers off from a rural or small-town environment that might have provided other means of survival. It was hard to get people to work in factories, but when they lived in large cities, they had little choice. It was declared legal for firms to pollute the environment, flood a farmer's land, and cause other negative externalities, and it was also legal for firms to discriminate on the basis of gender, race, and ethnicity in hiring. The firm was ruled to be a fictitious person, so it could buy up other firms, thereby increasing its market power, and use its resources to go into any business it wished, expanding its scope as well as scale.

These aspects of modern bureaucracy were all new, and often contested, since people feared centralized, uncontrolled power. But we take most of these powers for granted today. In 1820 about 20 percent of the population worked for wages and salaries; by 1900 it was 50 percent; today well over 90 percent of Americans work for wages and salaries, over half of them in big organizations, which often have the power to control small organizations. We have become a society of big organizations, and it was not inevitable.

Notes

1. I critique Alfred Chandler throughout my book *Organizing America* for ignoring the role of market power; for treating corruption as an incidental cost rather than a factor of production as important as land, labor, and capital; for ignoring the social costs of corporations; and in general for exercising his functionalist logic. But I mine his pathbreaking work for many insights and data. William Roy (1997) subjects the principal hypotheses in Chandler's *The Visible Hand* (1977) to empirical test and finds them wanting. Monographs on the railroads (Berk 1994; Licht 1983) also challenge Chandler's assertions in his work on the railroads (Chandler 1965; Chandler and Salsbury 1965), though mostly implicitly.

2. Bai Gao's contribution to this volume demonstrates the importance of the state in governing economic relations and aptly examines the three alternatives of state control, market forces, and associations as governing principles. Under the strong state in Japan, what he calls market forces had only limited impact. But the concept of "market forces" may mask the role of a more concrete actor, the corporation. The Japanese state kept the corporations at bay, just as did European states in the nineteenth century. His third alternative, associations, did play a role in the United States, which I do not deal with in my account. In the latter part of the nineteenth century, in order to discipline competition and stabilize markets, corporations explored cartels and other associational regimes, but the state blocked them at each turn, as Neil Fligstein (1990) shows. In Europe, strong states were able to use the cartels and associations to promote public interests; because the weak U.S. state could not control the cartels, it could only outlaw them.

3. The basic reference on how corporations got the laws they desired is Morton Horwitz's classic work *The Transformation of American Law* (1977). Charles Sellers (1991) elaborates on this in his valuable work, and an article by the editors of the *Harvard Law Review* (1989) further documents the changes.

4. Richard Swedberg's contribution to this volume necessarily discusses law in general terms that lend themselves to emphasizing the role of institutions, and how people orient themselves towards laws. While he ends his essay with the provocative suggestion that "interests help to lock in, to defend, and to legitimize" legal institutions, that is not a major concern of the sociology of law. The main concern of the sociologist, he says, is in the role of law as an "actual determinant of human behavior." My own effort here is to go behind the institutions and the actual laws that determine behavior and ask who writes the laws; how do they get written; what interests lie behind them? The laws, and the institutions, are not just "out there"; shaping behavior; they had to be constructed and enacted. Specific people with concrete interests fashioned them, and those interests were often organizational.

5. A dissertation by Zehra Gumus-Dawes (2000) makes this valuable point, for the first time, I believe.

6. The literature on the Lowell mills is vast. I have relied principally on Scranton (1983), Dalzell (1987), Dawley (1976), Dublin (1979), Gitelman (1967), Gumus-Dawes (2000), and Ware (1931). Robert Dalzell's account is much the rosiest, and I disagree with his interpretation.

7. To do this, significant legal innovations were necessary, such as allowing one firm to hold an interest in other firms, thus making mergers and giant firms possible. This controversial act was quietly achieved in Pennsylvania by bribing the legislature (Roy 1997, 295). Another innovation was New Jersey's liberal incorporation laws, which removed the last remaining hints of public responsibility.

8. For a few of the many instances of the opposition of labor and farmers throughout the century to the accumulation of private power, see Clawson (1980), Hall (1984), Keyssar (1986), and Wilentz (1984).

References

Berk, Gerald. 1994. *Alternative Tracks: The Constitution of American Industrial Order, 1865 to 1917.* Baltimore: Johns Hopkins University Press.

Chandler, Alfred D., ed. 1965. *The Railroads: The Nation's First Big Business.* New York: Harcourt Brace and World.

———. 1977. *The Visible Hand: The Managerial Revolution in American Business.* Cambridge, Mass.: Harvard University Press.

Chandler, Alfred D., and Stephen Salsbury. 1965. "The Railroads: Innovators in Modern Business Administration." In *The Railroad and the Space Program: An Exploration in Historical Analogy,* edited by Bruce Mazlish. Cambridge, Mass: Harvard University Press.

Clawson, Dan. 1980. *Bureaucracy and the Labor Process: The Transformation of U.S. Industry, 1860 to 1920.* New York: Monthly Review Press.

Dalzell, Robert F. 1987. *Enterprising Elite: The Boston Associates and the World They Made.* Cambridge, Mass.: Harvard University Press.

Dawley, Alan. 1976. *Class and Community: The Industrial Revolution in Lynn.* Cambridge, Mass: Harvard University Press.

Dublin, Thomas. 1979. *Women at Work: The Transformation of Work and Community in Lowell, Massachusetts, 1826 to 1860.* New York: Columbia University Press.

Fligstein, Neil. 1990. *The Transformation of Corporate Control.* Cambridge, Mass.: Harvard University Press.

Gitelman, Howard M. 1967. "The Waltham System and the Coming of the Irish." *Labor History* 8: 227–53.

Gumus-Dawes, Zehra. 2000. "Forsaken Paths: The Organization of the American Textile Industry in the Nineteenth Century." Ph.D. diss., Yale University.

Hall, Peter Dobkin. 1984. *The Organization of American Culture, 1700 to 1900: Private Institutions, Elites, and the Origins of American Nationality.* New York: New York University Press.

Harvard Law Review editors. 1989. "Incorporating the Republic: The Corporation in Antebellum Political Culture." *Harvard Law Review* 102(4–6): 1883–1903.

Horwitz, Morton J. 1977. *The Transformation of American Law: 1780 to 1860.* Cambridge, Mass.: Harvard University Press.

Hounshell, David A. 1984. *From the American System to Mass Production, 1800 to 1932: The Development of Manufacturing Technology in the United States.* Baltimore: Johns Hopkins University Press.

Keyssar, Alexander. 1986. *Out of Work: The First Century of Unemployment in Massachusetts.* New York: Cambridge University Press.

Licht, Walter. 1983. *Working for the Railroad: The Organization of Work in the Nineteenth Century.* Princeton, N.J.: Princeton University Press.

Perrow, Charles. 2002. *Organizing America: Wealth, Power, and the Origins of Corporate Capitalism.* Princeton, N.J.: Princeton University Press.

Piore, Michael, and Charles Sabel. 1984. *The Second Industrial Divide: Possibilities for Prosperity.* New York: Basic Books.

Roy, William G. 1997. *Socializing Capital: The Rise of the Large Industrial Corporation in America.* Princeton, N.J.: Princeton University Press.

Scranton, Philip. 1983. *Proprietary Capitalism: The Textile Manufacturers at Philadelphia, 1800 to 1885.* New York: Cambridge University Press.

Sellers, Charles. 1991. *The Market Revolution: Jacksonian America, 1815 to 1846.* New York: Oxford University Press.

Shelton, Cynthia J. 1986. *The Mills of Manayunk: Industrialization and Social Conflict in the Philadelphia Region, 1787 to 1837.* Baltimore: Johns Hopkins University Press.

Ware, Caroline F. 1931. *The Early New England Cotton Manufacture: A Study in Industrial Beginnings.* Boston: Houghton Mifflin.

Wilentz, Sean. 1984. *Chants Democratic: New York City and the Rise of the American Working Class, 1788 to 1850.* New York: Oxford University Press.

Williamson, Jeffrey G., and Peter H. Lindhert. 1980. *American Economic Inequality: A Macroeconomic History.* New York: Academic Press.

3

THE STATE AND THE ASSOCIATIONAL ORDER OF THE ECONOMY: THE INSTITUTIONALIZATION OF CARTELS AND TRADE ASSOCIATIONS IN JAPAN, 1931 TO 1945

Bai Gao

CARTELS experienced a rapid development in the Japanese economy during the Great Depression and World War II. Between the Sino-Japanese War of 1894–95 and World War I, a few voluntary cartels emerged, mostly among small-scale exporters; most were short-lived. The cartels in heavy industries that developed rapidly after the Russo-Japanese War of 1904–5 mainly controlled sales and seldom controlled production. Only after World War I did cartels begin to control production and sales simultaneously. Even then, however, they were still few in number (Haley 1991, 146; Takahashi 1933, 138–39). After World War I, while industrywide coordination was still weak, the zaibatsu became conglomerates. In contrast to cartels, which were usually confined to one industry and organized by similar types of organizations, all sorts of business organizations were members of conglomerates, which coordinated the businesses of their member companies in multiple industries (Kunihiro 1941, 7–9). In the early 1930s an associational order in the form of mandatory cartels began to emerge in the Japanese economy. During World War II they further developed into compulsory trade associations. As the war ended the associational order had become a major governance structure in the Japanese economy (Gao 2001a, 2001b).

The conversion to an associational order was an epical phenomenon among capitalist economies in the 1930s. Even the United States, which had a long antitrust tradition, supported cartels during its first New Deal program. What made the Japanese case distinctive? First, while both the United States and Japan tried to convert themselves to the associational order, the U.S. effort failed quickly after the Supreme Court ruled that the National Industrial Recovery Act of 1933 was unconstitutional in the case of *Schechter Poultry Corp.* v. *United States* in 1935. In contrast, Japan moved decisively toward mandatory cartels and compulsory trade associations. Second, although the Japanese state tried hard to follow the German model in an effort to create a comprehensive associational order, the effect in Japan was much weaker than in Germany. In reality, the compulsory trade associations were operated by the private sector. Third, despite these weaknesses, the continuities of the associational order in Japanese economic life in the postwar period were astonishing. How do we explain the rise of Japanese cartels in the 1930s, while taking into account its variations from other countries?

In this chapter, I examine how the state shaped the rise of the associational order in Japan during the Great Depression and World War II by highlighting three points. First, the rise of the associational order in the Japanese economy at this time was part of what Karl Polanyi (1944/1957) calls the Great Transformation. It was a trend that was common among major industrialized countries and directly sustained by the changing roles of the state in economic governance from protecting the liberties of private enterprises to maintaining political stability in economic crisis and allocating resources for war. Second, the constitutional order of the Japanese state shaped by the civil law tradition of the state had a great impact on the pattern of the associational order by enabling the executive branch of the state to use cartels as its policy tool. Third, the rise of the associational order and the changing roles of the Japanese state in economic governance were accompanied by a process of social reconstruction of property rights whose outcome was shaped in important ways by institutionalized beliefs about property rights. To demonstrate the characteristics of the Japanese experience, I make some brief comparisons between Japan and other countries. To illustrate the significance to contemporary Japan of what happened in this period, I also briefly discuss the postwar development of the associational order in the Japanese economy.

The Associational Order and the State

According to Mark Schneiberg and Rogers Hollingsworth (1991, 208–13), the associational order emerged to fix prices, limit output, and more generally facilitate and regulate conscious, coordinated efforts to control competition, stabilize profits, and shield members from the adverse consequences of untrammeled market competition. In essence, they were created for distributional purposes, that is, to protect and enhance firms' market positions, shift the burden of adjustment on to their transaction partners, and extract from these partners a form of rent. Price and production associations were primarily created to govern horizontal relations by firms that were looking for relief from intensive competition. Later on, trade associations further expanded their roles in economic governance by fortifying the associations' capacities, delegating rights and power to full-time professional staffs, and instituting a variety of bureaucratic controls.

For both the market order and the state order, the associational order is an alternative way of coordinating economic activities. In the market order, actors are independent, and the order is maintained through "dispersed competition" in the market. In the state order, actors are dependent, and the order is sustained by a hierarchical control and coordination. In contrast to both of these orders, in the associational order actors are strategically interdependent, and the order is maintained by "organizational concertation" of "private interest government" (Boddewyn 1985, 31; Streeck and Schmitter 1985, 9–10). In this type of social order, actors are defined by their common purpose of defending and promoting functionally defined interests. They negotiate for compromises as they recognize each other's status and entitlements. In the context of economic sociology, the associational order emerged to address the collective action issues as firms tried to organize cooperation among industry members and face enforcement problems. Trade associations are "a form of private government to the extent that peers rather than outsiders formally control or at least dominate the establishment and enforcement of self-imposed and voluntarily accepted behavior rules" (Boddewyn 1985, 36–37). As an alternative to the state, the market, and vertically integrated firms, associations can promote innovative and dynamically efficient production (Schneiberg 1999, 87).

Theoretically, the state plays a role in the associational order in a modern capitalist economy in two ways. First, the rise of the associational order in the form of cartels in the late nineteenth century directly raised the issue of public goods. Since cartels involved predation and monopoly power, they became subject to the state's scrutiny for legitimacy. In the United States the Sherman Antitrust Act was enacted in 1890. The attitudes of Continental European countries toward cartels were more favorable, but cartels had to be endorsed or at least tolerated by the state to play a role in economic governance. In contemporary capitalist economies, the state is under political pressure to watch cartels and trade associations. Depending on the circumstances, outsiders may no longer be willing to delegate public authority to sector organizations, and the state may withdraw its support to the industry. The associational order also faces an implicit threat: if the industry cannot police itself effectively, the state has to step in, pushing government regulations (Fligstein 1990; Schneiberg 1999).

Second, the state has often used the associational order as its policy tool. Since the state is limited in its capacity to control the negative impact of market forces, it has often been able to use the associational order as an alternative to direct government control (Streeck and Schmitter 1985, 16). The state not only can make independent and significant contributions to the negotiation of a more stable and institutionalized interest compromise but is also empowered to extract some "public-regarding" concessions from the bargaining associations (Schmitter 1985, 36). Relying on the associational order to govern the economy can help the state relieve to some extent the burden of the administration and the courts, cut costs, or reduce the complexity of its tasks (Boddewyn 1985, 33). By frequently encouraging and supporting the self-regulatory systems that complement the law, the state plays an important role in pushing industry to establish new norms and procedures (Boddewyn 1985; Tilton 1996; Upham 1997).

The existing literature mainly uses state capacity to explain the cross-national variations of associational order. Frans van Waarden (1991a, 1991b) holds that the differences in the development of trade associations during World War II in North America and Europe can be attributed to both the organizational capacity of the state and the prewar tradition of trade associations. In Canada and the United States, the history of statehood was relatively short, and the process of state-building continued into World War II. The state was restrained not only by the ideology of liberalism but also by powerful trusts and big corporations. In the meantime, these countries did not have interest associations in the pre-1930 period that could assume the role of economic governance or were strong enough to discipline their members. As a result, during the war mobilization the state relied not on trade associations but on businessmen-cum–civil servants who acted as interest intermediaries between the state and private companies (Coleman and Nossal 1991; Hooks 1991).

In contrast, in Germany and its occupied countries such as France, Belgium, and the Netherlands, the state created a comprehensive system of institutions to organize industry. In this pattern, associations became the tools of state control. They were established by the state and had compulsory membership, domain monopoly, complex and comprehensive sectoring, regional and functional differentiation, and hierarchical integration. The state controlled the appointment of the leaders of these associations and provided subsidies, statutory authorities, and public law sanctions. Early on in these countries, especially in France, the state distinguished itself clearly from civil society, and professional civil servants were created before industrialization took hold. In both Germany and France the state emerged in the mercantilist period and had dominant power in the economy. Germany had a long history of using cartels to self-regulate the industry, and France was also well known for its tradition of guilds and guild regulations, which were never abolished, not even after the French Revolution (Barnouw and Nekkers 1991; Luyten 1991; Rossiter 1991; Weber 1991).

Although state capacity is an important factor, it is also a factor that often demands further explanations. We are not satisfied with a simple dichotomy between weak states and strong states, and we want to know why some states have strong capacities while others do not.

In this chapter, I invoke three theoretical issues in order to enhance the explanatory power of the existing literature, not only for understanding the

Japanese case but also for further developing theories on associations, the state, the legal system, and economic governance in general.

The Great Transformation of Capitalism

The state has three objectives for its property rights policy: protecting the liberties of private enterprises, maintaining political stability, and allocating resources. *Legal protection of property rights* can create an incentive to use resources efficiently, and such efficiency leads, in turn, to economic growth (Posner 1986). By specifying the fundamental rules of competition and cooperation and enforcing them by its coercive power, the state can maximize the rents it receives. Of course, efficient property rights do not necessarily always lead to higher tax revenues for the state, because they may lead to higher income in the state but lower tax revenues (North 1981).

Maintaining political stability is another major objective in the state's property rights policy. When the wealth or income of societal groups is adversely affected by the present property rights structure, societal groups may support an alternative government, and the survival of the present government may be threatened, either through democratic election or social revolution. In many cases, the state has to agree to a property rights structure that is favorable to those groups, regardless of that structure's effects on efficiency (North 1981, 28).

Controlling resource allocation is a third major goal of the state in a property rights structure. Unlike the other two objectives, which are the ends themselves, controlling resource allocation is a means that can be used by the state to achieve multiple policy objectives. This type of control is often achieved through state procurement, subsidies, tariffs, state borrowing and provision of capital, and direct state investment in the production of education and training, research and development, and transportation and communications infrastructures. Nevertheless, the state can also use a property rights structure to prevent private companies from competing with the state in the use of certain resources (Lindberg and Campbell 1991, 361).

The changing role of the state in economic governance in the downturn of the last wave of globalization shaped the associational order in important ways (Gao 2001b). The last wave of globalization that started in the 1870s entered its downturn in 1914 as the gold standard collapsed and World War I broke out. The failure of the market forced the state to strengthen its intervention in the economy. This intervention in turn further stimulated the development of cartels, whose rise had already been evident since the 1870s. In the industrialization and revolutions, the state focused on protecting the liberties of private enterprises and releasing the market forces constrained by mercantilism and medieval guilds. It backed both civil and business laws to regulate and adjust the relationship between private individuals and juristic persons. In a sense, the state acted more like a "night watchman" and left the responsibility of maintaining stability to either the market or private ordering (Kunihiro 1941).

Between the 1870s and 1914, intense market competitions resulted in numerous bankruptcies. Responding to the negative impact of market forces, producers in the same industries began to reach minimum price agreements in order to ensure stability. The initial state reaction to the development of cartels emphasized the issue of public goods because the rise of monopoly power in various forms had presented a great challenge. From the late nineteenth century to the early twentieth century, the state in many industrialized countries had enacted either antitrust or cartel legislation. Although resource allocation had been a major concern of the state, since military power played an important role in the process of state-building in the early modern era, the scope of these endeavors was much more limited in comparison with what would happen in the twentieth century.

During the Great Depression and World War II, for the first time in modern history, I argue, the state in capitalist economies shifted the focus of its property rights policy from protecting private properties to maintaining political stability in economic hard times and allocating resources for national survival in war. This shift had important implications for the associational order. When the state focused on protecting the liberties of private enterprises, it tended to focus on the liberty of contracts, the promotion of market competition, and prevention of the associational order. If the associational order is set on a voluntary basis, trade associations are rarely able to intervene directly in firms' internal operations because trade associations neither consolidate ownership nor hire their members (Schneiberg and Hollingsworth 1991, 202). As the state shifted its focus to maintaining political stability and controlling resource allocation, in contrast, it began to concern itself with the effect of the associational order at the macro level. Consequently, cartels and trade associations often became a policy tool for the state. When the state made the associational order compulsory, agreements reached by participating companies could be legally enforced by the state. Since the objective of promoting efficiency often conflicted with the objectives of maintaining political stability and controlling resource allocation, a state endorsement of an associational order often led, in varying degrees, to a suppression of the liberty of private companies' contracts.

The Constitutional Order of the State

The constitutional order of the state played an important role in shaping the pattern of the associational order in the Japanese economy. The constitutional order of the state refers to both the state's structure and the people's liberties, as defined by a country's constitution (Siegan 1980, 11). The structure of the state includes the organization, composition, powers, and limitations of the state's executive, legislative, and jurisdictional branches. The structure of the state determines how property rights are defined and enforced. The liberties of the people define the relationship between the individual and the state and determine the extent to which property rights are granted and enforced by the state.

Legal tradition shapes the constitutional order of the state in a country to an important extent. Beyond a legal *system,* which refers to a set of rules about contracts, corporations, and crimes, a legal *tradition* is "a set of deeply rooted, historically conditioned attitudes about the nature of law, about the role of law in the society and the polity, about the proper organization and operation of a legal system, and about the way law is or should be made, applied, studied, perfected, and taught" (Merryman 1969/1985, 2). In other words, a legal tradition involves not only a country's legal system but also its political institutions. This is a major aspect of the Weberian perspective on the sociology of law. According to Weber, the rise of the formally rational legal system in Continental Europe was closely associated with the rise of the bureaucratic state (Trubek 1996, 224). In economic sociology, the impact of laws on the economy has received increasing attention (Fligstein 1990; Dobbin 1994; Roy 1997). In his chapter of this volume, Richard Swedberg calls for further studies of the impact on the economy of specific laws, such as property, inheritance, contract, and corporation laws. Adopting more of a macro-approach, I emphasize here the impact of a legal tradition, instead of specific laws, on the pattern of economic governance through the constitutional order of the state.

To demonstrate the impact of the constitutional order of the Japanese state on the rise of cartels in Japan, it is helpful to compare the civil law tradition that shaped the constitutional order of the Japanese state with the common law tradition to reveal the key differences between these two major legal traditions. The common law tradition is "an embodiment of fundamental liberties and human rights" (Hughes 1996, 12). This symbolic character of the common law is exemplified by various institutional arrangements. The rights of individuals in the common law countries are privately enforced. The method of regulating in the common law tradition relies mainly on private citizen-victims and their lawyers, and incentives to obey the law are created by the threat of having to compensate victims for the harm done them by a violation of the rules (Posner 1986, 343). Among different branches of the state, the common law tradition finds legal solutions by a technique that first considers judicial decisions, and the judges' decisions are supreme (David and Brierley 1964, 85; Dobbin 1994). Functioning within the confines of a structure of separating and limiting the powers of each branch of the state, judges can exercise a veto, or negative power, over legislation (Siegan 1980, 15).

In the United States the court plays an important role in safeguarding liberties consistent with the objectives of private property and private enterprise. The common law tradition in the United States protects private companies from being forced by the state to join an associational order without their consent.

The federal courts have used both the contract clause and the due process clause of the Constitution to secure economic liberties. The contract clause states that, "once a right had become 'vested' by either private bargaining or an arrangement with the state, the state could not take the right away or alter its fundamental character" (Hovenkamp 1991, 17). In the due process clause, the Constitution created rights against the sovereign. "Although these rights were characterized as a 'liberty of contract,' they were fundamentally different from the rights secured by the contract clause. They involved the liberty to contract—that is, to enter into prospective agreements—rather than the sanctity of contracts already in existence" (18).

The constitutional order directly shapes the pattern of economic governance, and the common law tradition does not provide a favorable environment for an associational order in the United States. The U.S. antitrust solution in the Sherman Antitrust Act was based on the common law's opposition to restraints of trade. Traditionally, the common law had treated restrictive contracts as "simply unenforceable," and it was always hostile toward the anticompetitive agreements among different firms (Stigler 1991, 38). In 1897 Justice Rufus Peckham rejected the rule of reason in the *Trans-Missouri* case, a suit brought against the railroad cartels. This decision greatly enhanced the role of the Sherman Antitrust Act as an anticartel device (Hovenkamp 1991, 248). From then on, the rule of per se illegality for cartel agreements (agreements whose purpose is not to produce efficiency but merely to eliminate competition) left a court no discretion to weigh other values that might legitimate the cartel (Bork 1991, 43). This significantly eliminated the probability of an associational order based on cartels being formed in the United States. However, addressing the antitrust issue through the common law tradition also left the door open for corporations to strengthen their market positions through merger and acquisitions (Fligstein 1990). Charles Perrow argues in his chapter in this volume that the rise of big corporations in the United States was primarily driven by the political power of these corporations. I contend that it was the institutionalized beliefs reflected in the common law's interpretation of the antitrust issue that legitimized these big corporations.

In contrast, there is a strong distinction in the civil law tradition between private law and public law. "The role of the state was not limited to the protection of private rights; on the contrary, the driving consideration was the effectuation of the public interest by state action" (Merryman 1969/1985, 92–93). As a result, "fundamental private law concepts have . . . been modified by the addition of social or public elements" (94–95). In the Continental civil law tradition, legal solutions are sought by a technique that first considers legislation (David and Brierley 1964, 85; Dobbin 1994). In other words, in the Continental legal tradition the law as a system of abstract rules is supreme and originates from statutes, which are enacted by legislative bodies and function as a general guide for behavior in society; the administrative bodies and the courts apply laws to specific situations. The constitutional order of the state in the Continental legal tradition gives more power and jurisdiction to the executive branch and less to the courts and the legal profession than is true in Anglo-Saxon legal systems of rule-making and rule enforcement. Unlike the common law system, in which private individuals or juristic persons seek remedy after they become victims of another party's behavior, the logic of the Continental legal tradition is to prevent injuries from occurring in the first place rather than to compensate victims of injuries (Posner 1986, 343). As a result, the state often passes more government regulations, relying on public laws to restrain the property rights of private enterprises, in an effort to reduce competition and prevent the negative impact of competition on the economy.

In the common law tradition, rules are built up over time by judges' decisions in individual cases, and laws are subject to judicial review. In contrast, in the civil law tradition "the formal legal code serve[s] as the ultimate arbiter of the law and judgments of policymakers are often immune to interference from the courts" (Dobbin 1994, 99). Moreover, in the constitutional order of the state in the civil law tradition, the executive branch often performs both the function of coordination and the function of adjudicating conflicts of interests among private individuals and juristic persons. Whereas the major concerns of the court system in the legal process are to enforce the rule of law, the executive branch of the state, which is more open to political pressures, has its own policy objectives in property rights policy. The priority of protecting the liberties of private enterprises often has to give way to other policy objectives, such as maintaining political stability and controlling resource allocation, especially when these goals conflict with each other.

Since the executive branch of the state has more power in rule-making and enforcement, and since it has additional policy objectives besides protecting the liberties of private enterprises (political stability and resource allocation), the state in the Continental pattern of constitutional order often regards cartels as "a convenient and low cost means of acquiring information about and influencing economic development" (Gerber 1998, 75). When the associational order becomes compulsory, the state relies on public law to enforce its operation. With the support of public law, the state can thus directly make appointments for the key posts of trade associations and ensure that trade associations' actions do not violate the state's policy objectives. Thus, the state is no longer simply a judge but also becomes a player itself. Accordingly, the definition of property rights goes beyond the domain of private law and enters the domain of public law. In the Continental constitutional order of the state, the scope of public law has traditionally been larger than it is under the constitutional order of the common law systems. Since World War I, the executive branch of the state has often obtained the authority of delegated legislation. These laws enable the state to rely more heavily on administrative instruments, such as penalties, imposed at bureaucrats' discretion, and economic police to enforce the law, reducing the role of the court system and the legal profession.

The Japanese state was modeled on the German constitutional order and adopted the Continental tradition of administrative law. Thus, the associational order in the Japanese economy had a favorable political environment.

The Social Construction of Property Rights

The constitutional order of the state did not shape the rise of the associational order of the Japanese economy in a static, path-dependent fashion. Rather, it did so in a dynamic process in which the institutionalized legal and economic beliefs profoundly affected the politics of the social construction of new property rights.

As William Roy points out (1997, 11):

> There are no inherent or natural "property rights." The conception of inalienable or natural property rights existing prior to society or history may have been an effective ideology for creating capitalism, but it has clouded the historical analysis of what specific rights, entitlement, and obligations govern economic relations. Rather, the content of property relations is historically constructed.

Institutionalized beliefs play an important role in the politics of the social construction of property rights because that process is often shaped by a legal environment dominated by deeply rooted symbols (Edelman 1990, 1992; Suchman and Edelman 1996). Within the same institution, moreover, there can be multiple or even competing institutional logics. Where to draw the line about the boundary of legitimacy for property rights is often subject to contention. The impact of institutionalized beliefs on the social construction of property rights is reflected not only in assertions of legitimacy for the old property rights structure by the incumbents of existing property rights but also in the innovative reinterpretation of the old institutional logic aimed at defining a new direction for the property rights structure.

Starting in the nineteenth century, when cartels raised the issue of public interest, the states in different capitalist economies demonstrated two distinctive patterns of preferences in their policies regarding the associational order. The United States showed a strong preference for promoting the liberties of private enterprises when it banned the loose combination represented by cartels. The U.S. preference for the protection of the liberties of private enterprises was articulated in a twofold manner in the Sherman

Antitrust Act of 1890. On the one hand, the common law was tough on any restraints of trade, and thus the Sherman Antitrust Act was rigid about cartels or other types of loose combinations. It asserted that cartels monopolized the markets and obtained huge profits at the cost of consumers and waged workers; the act identified cartels a major barrier to the promotion of efficiency. On the other hand, the act was rather ambiguous about the tight combinations resulting from corporate mergers. As a tool to prevent monopoly, the law of contracts in restraints of trade as the legal basis for antitrust law was weaker than a federal incorporation statute for firms seeking to do business in more than one state, which could have placed multistate firms' structural decisions immediately under federal control. The U.S. choice reflected a major concern of the Congress to preserve the liberties of private enterprises. A federal corporate law would not be able to prohibit monopoly while also making the distinctions necessary to permit firms to grow to a more efficient size. Such a law would be too heavy-handed, because it would forbid one corporation from owning another corporation's stocks, not only the anticompetitive ones (Hovenkamp 1991, 247). Canada, New Zealand, and Australia, which all shared the common law tradition, were also influenced by this school of thinking (Kunihiro 1941).

In contrast, Germany demonstrated a strong preference for both maintaining political stability and controlling resource allocation in its policy toward the associational order represented by cartels. In that country, rapid industrialization and the resulting social and economic disruptions had created great tensions and called for the state to manage the market competition (Gerber 1998). It was held that in a market economy recession would take place in the form of an economic cycle. This would waste an enormous amount of wealth. However, cartels could be used to adjust the balance between production and consumption (Kunihiro 1941). The bureaucracy of the German state often favored cartels because it regarded them as a convenient and low-cost means of acquiring information about and influencing the behaviors of private companies. At the same time, the German state also regarded cartels as important tools for supporting the state's goal of expanding Germany's international impact and building its military strength, because cartels predominated the heavy chemical industries (Gerber 1998, 75). In 1897 the highest court in Germany handed down a decision in the famous *Saxon Wood Pulp* case that formally legalized cartels and held the cartel agreements to be legally enforceable under German law. Despite the increasing number of cartels that were using their position to raise consumer prices, and several political attempts to enact anticartel legislation, cartels were basically left free in Germany until the late 1920s (Gerber 1998).

The preference of the Japanese state before the Great Depression was rather a mixture. On the one hand, it protected the liberties of zaibatsu companies, allowing these conglomerates to maintain their dominant market position under the name of advancing national interests. On the other hand, it encouraged medium-size and small companies to organize cartels and trade unions to reduce the number of bankruptcies in economic recessions.

A Brief History of the Japanese Economy

The Japanese economy by the early 1930s had gone through a decade-long stagnation. The Japanese banking industry was struck by a financial crisis in 1927 that resulted in the bankruptcies of thirty-one banks in two months. The government enacted the Bank Law in 1928 in an effort to consolidate the banking industry by eliminating small banks. As a result, Mitsubishi, Mitsui, Sumitomo, Yasuda, and Daiichi became the big five financial oligopolies. In 1929, to tighten finance and reduce national debt, the Japanese state lifted the ban on gold exports, which had been in effect since 1917. Removing the gold embargo, however, was not only strongly opposed by the stock market, as both stock and commodity prices declined rapidly, but also opened the Japanese economy to the international market at an inappropriate time. Only three months after Japan removed the ban on gold exports, the events of the day known as Black Tuesday struck the New York stock market, marking the beginning of the Great Depression. The depression that started in the United States was quickly transferred to Japan. This caused a further deterioration of the Japanese economic situation. Between 1929 and 1931, Japan's GNP declined 18 percent, exports 47 percent, household consumption 17 percent, and investment in plants and equipment 31 percent. Its stock market also crashed. If we set the January 1921 market average at 100, the average stock price in 1930 was only 44.6 (Arisawa 1976, 53–54).

The economic hard times also brought about an increase in labor disputes. In 1930, 195,805 Japanese workers were involved in 2,289 disputes, and 81,329 took part in 906 strikes. In rural areas the net production of agriculture, forestry, and fishing in 1931 was equal to only 57 percent of production in 1929 (Arisawa 1976, 56). Many families felt compelled to sell their daughters to work as prostitutes. In one hard-pressed village, one-fourth of the young girls were sold; the village office was even used as a marketplace for transactions in prostitution.

The Japanese Army provoked the Manchuria Incident on September 18, 1931, with the intention of surviving the economic crisis at home by expanding Japan's military power in mainland Asia. This choice had far-reaching consequences for the nation. It drove Japan into military confrontations not only with China but also with the Western powers that had vested interests in East Asia. Branded an aggressor, Japan was ostracized by the world. Because Japan strongly opposed any intervention by the League of Nations, it became more and more isolated from the international community. During the 1930s parliamentary power continued to decline, and in 1940 the government forced all the parties to disband and enter the political wing of the Imperial Rule Assistance Association. The purpose of the establishment of this association was to sponsor a nationwide popular movement, like the Nazi and Fascist parties.

The military conflicts had serious economic consequences for Japan. The Japanese government depended on an expansionary fiscal policy to enable the country to survive the economic crisis. Between 1931 and 1936, the size of the government budget increased nearly 200 percent. The weight of both the central and the local governments' budgets in the national income increased from 56 percent to 76 percent. During these five years military expenditures increased 2.4 times, from 1,477 billion yen in 1931 to 3,452 billion in 1937 (Rengō Jōhōsha 1938, 17), and their weight in the government budget increased from 30.8 percent to 45.8 percent (Arisawa 1976, 86). The rapid increase in military expenditures created huge government debts. These huge military expenditures inevitably weakened Japan's ability to make international payments. Japan's trade deficit in yen also jumped from 67 million yen in 1932 to 636 million yen in 1937 (203).

The Important Industry Control Law of 1931

The Important Industry Control Law enacted by the Japanese state in 1931 changed the nature of the private cartel from an organization that promoted the interests of its member companies to a policy instrument of the state. According to this law, when two-thirds of the companies in one industry joined a cartel, the state had the authority to order outsiders to obey the cartel's agreement. Prior to that time, a private company had the freedom to stay out of a cartel and did not have to honor any agreement reached by that cartel. Under the Important Industry Control Law of 1931, however, private companies were forced to obey the cartel agreement reached by the majority of companies in the industry. This law also stated that when the state believed that the cartel agreements violated the public interest, it had the power to change or dissolve them. By giving the state, rather than the court, this discretion, the law brought mandatory cartels under the control of the executive branch of the state.

The Important Industry Control Law of 1931 triggered a rapid development of mandatory cartels in Japan (see figure 3.1). Among the 110 cartels that existed in 1933, dates of establishment are available for 96. Among these 96 cartels, only 13 existed before 1920, 28 were established in the 1920s, and 55 were established between 1930 and 1933. Of the 110 cartels, 33 were in heavy industry, 30 in the chemical industry, and 11 in the textile industry (Takahashi 1933). These cartels organized the whole distribution process of the industry by enlisting companies in that industry (Shimizu 1940, 232–33). Mandatory cartels played an important role in restraining market forces

FIGURE 3.1   *Growth of Japanese Cartels, 1880 to 1933*

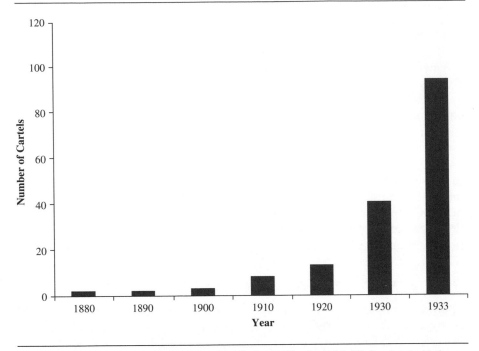

Source: Based on data in Takahashi (1933, 121–26); Gao (2001a, figure 3.1, 52). Reprinted with the permission of Cambridge University Press.

through a number of practices, including quotas on production and sales, minimum prices, and joint marketing and distribution. These practices significantly changed the way the economy operated. Although in every industry some private companies stayed outside the cartels, the markets became much more organized in comparison with the pre-1930 period as cartels intervened in several stages of the production cycle.

The enactment of the Important Industry Control Law indicates that during the Great Depression the Japanese state changed its priority from protecting the liberties of private enterprises to maintaining the economic order. Japanese legislators held at the time that the chaos of the Great Depression showed that private ordering could no longer effectively govern the economy because the desire for maximizing wealth was the direct cause of the Great Depression. Since the overbuilt Japanese production capacity during World War I could not be absorbed by the demand in the postwar period, private companies competed recklessly, often selling their products at prices lower than production costs. The country's international competitiveness suffered as a result (Tsusanshō 1964, 49–50). The aim of the Important Industry Control Law was to "battle the anarchy of Japanese industry and eliminate the root of economic instability." According to the minister of commerce and industry, Nakajima Kusamachi, the major concern of the state was to restrain surplus production and achieve a balance between production and consumption, and between supply and demand (cited in Takahashi 1933, 63).

Mandatory cartels represented a new stage of associational order; these cartels were very different from the traditional cartels based on private initiative. In this new stage of associational order, the property rights of private companies, including those of the zaibatsu conglomerates, were restrained. Private ordering by the zaibatsu in the past had transformed the atomized process of production into an integrated arrangement. It had enabled private companies to coordinate their pricing policy, marketing channels, and the amount of production, in order to avoid the zero-sum competition. However, coordination by the zaibatsu had still served to promote the interests of each business group rather than to maintain order for the entire economy. When the economy was confronted with a major crisis like the Great Depression, the state had to assume leadership to restore economic order. For this reason, the leading bureaucrat Yoshino Shinji argued, mandatory cartels were established to maintain economic order for the state rather than to pursue profits for private companies (Johnson 1982, 109).

While in many countries the rise and then wide expansion of the associational order reflected the failure of the self-regulated market, the Japanese response represented a distinctly different pattern. The competition policy adopted by the Japanese state before the Great Depression was distinctive from both the German model and the American model. On the one hand, the Japanese experience resembled that of Germany to some extent. Since the Meiji Restoration, the state had supported the development of the zaibatsu—which were big feudal merchant families with close ties to the state. The zaibatsu, represented by the Mitsui and Mitsubishi groups, were the major monopolies that dominated the market and restrained competition significantly. During this period the goal of the state was to enforce the property rights of the zaibatsu with the expectation that they would strengthen Japan's international competitiveness. On the other hand, the Japanese state had not rigidly followed the German model. Although the state had tried to encourage the formation of local chambers of commerce and industrial or commercial guilds for medium-size and small companies by giving them legal status and tax immunities from 1884 to 1902, there had been no mandatory cartels or compulsory trade associations.

The Important Industry Control Law of 1931 clearly reflected the constitutional order of the Japanese state, in which the executive branch of the state had great power in both rule-making and rule enforcement. According to John

Haley (1991), before the Meiji Restoration the Japanese legal system was influenced by the Chinese legal tradition, which did not require the principle of rights for enforcement. In this tradition, the word *law* meant punishment. Codes and statutes were administrative or penal. Legal rules were uniformly prescriptive. There were no rights, only duties. Although "civil" or private legal rules, as defined in substantive terms today, can be identified in traditional East Asian law, they were generally expressed as commands, a violation of which was subject to a prescribed penalty or incident that could be best described as an administrative enforcement by an essentially regulatory state (Haley 1991, 10–11). After the Meiji Restoration the Japanese legal system was strongly influenced by the Continental legal tradition, especially the German model. By the end of the nineteenth century, most of the important codes enacted in Japan bore the imprint of a strong German influence (Noda 1976, 196). By the end of World War I, the German influence on the Japanese legal system had reached its height. In the German model, as discussed earlier, the executive branch of the state held strong power. Once statutes were enacted, the bureaucrats had the authority to interpret them and apply them in actual situations. This is quite different from the common law system in which not only does the court have the authority to develop a ruling through its decision, but private individuals and juristic persons have the right to protect their own property rights in court.

As the Important Industry Control Law indicates, when the Japanese state decided to establish an associational order for the economy, it derived its means from its constitutional order by increasingly relying on punishment supervised by the state bureaucracy to ensure that its policy objectives were served. Among twelve articles of this law, for example, six concerned penalties. When private companies that did not join the cartels failed to obey the agreement reached by the cartels, or when cartel member companies disregarded the state's order of dissolution, they were fined. Penalties were also levied on cartels that did not register and on private companies that refused to allow examination by the government officials or provided fake information. Meanwhile, the constitutional order of the Japanese state at the time also prevented potential civilian challenges to the Important Industry Control Law. Opposition did exist in Japan, but it had no formal channel through which to challenge the state authority because there was no judicial review system on which it could rely. In contrast, in the United States the whole National Industrial Recovery Act of 1933 was brought down by a private company filing suit in the regular court system.

The National Mobilization Law of 1938

The Japanese state enacted the National Mobilization Law in 1938 after Japan declared a "semi-war situation" amid a full-scale invasion of China. Under this law, the state began to control the flow and distribution of capital, labor, and materials through a variety of laws and directly distributed these production factors through its annual national mobilization plans. Under the National Mobilization Law of 1938, the executive branch of the state gained unprecedented power in lawmaking. By then the Japanese state already had enacted a series of industry laws concerning artificial gasoline, iron and steel, machine tools, shipbuilding, aircraft, light metal, and organic chemistry. These laws made all businesses in these industries directly subject to state licensing. It also enacted more than eighty executive ordinances that were not subject to approval from the Diet.

Before 1937, the state had entrusted cartels with setting limits on minimum prices, since the dumping of products by private companies would result in massive bankruptcies. After the China War broke out, private companies quickly raised the prices of their products because strong military demands had created a wartime economic boom. In response to these circumstances, the state began to control the maximum price any cartel could set, and soon there was a shift to direct price control. These major adjustments in the economic governance structure inevitably led to the Japanese state imposing restraints on business freedom. Under the National Mobilization Law, private companies had to surrender to the state their rights in determining wages and employment. This measure was aimed at preventing a labor disturbance during the war mobilization. It led to the initial institutionalization of the contemporary practices of permanent employment, the seniority-based wage system, and company-based labor unions. Under this law, national security interests were given priority over private companies' profits. In the past, private companies had been able to lay off workers to reduce their production costs and increase their profits. Now that part of their property rights was restrained because it could lead to domestic political instability (Gao 1997).

The passage of the National Mobilization Law encountered strong resistance in the Diet. Many Diet members questioned the bill's legitimacy, pointing out that "since the Meiji constitution was enacted, the civilians' property rights protected by the constitution have never been taken away by a comprehensive delegation legislation" (Tsusanshō 1964, 182–83). Diet members added that they had never found any similar "legislation that reflected the will of the state to enforce its control by comprehensive penalty." Diet members labeled the bill "a kind of legislation for criminals." The response from the bureaucrats, however, was that the penalties were intended to stimulate the consciousness and self-control of private companies. To survive the unprecedented crisis, the state had to depend on tough punishment (Tsusanshō 1964, 52–58).

World War II made control over resource allocation in economic governance a major goal of states throughout the world (Gao 1994, 1997). States had always needed resources to build infrastructures, to maintain national security, and to redistribute economic welfare among citizens. Before the twentieth century, however, the scope of these activities had been relatively small. Two world wars, especially World War II, forced states to control resource allocation to an unprecedented level in all major industrialized countries. The German theory of total war, which emerged in World War I, gave strategic significance to economic governance. This theory maintained that modern war involved not only military forces but also the entire economy and that victory would be determined by the strength of economic institutions as well as the superiority of weapons. Accordingly, "the state is becoming increasingly important. It has to plan and organize the comprehensive employment of national resources even in peacetime" (Matsui 1938, 35). Since the pursuit of profits could jeopardize national mobilization, the state had to restrain the liberties of private citizens. When civilian goods production conflicted with the interests of national security interests, civilian goods production was strongly repressed by the state (Yomiuri Shinbunsha 1972).

Maintaining political stability was also an important reason for the state to control resource allocation in wartime. World War II marked an important new stage of state-building in the history of capitalism in many industrialized countries. Although the state-building process of modern capitalism in the eighteenth and nineteenth centuries had achieved enormous success in establishing democratic political institutions, underprivileged social groups still existed. In a total war the existence of these groups and the inequality they had suffered became the biggest political barriers in the war mobilization of human resources. By practicing compulsory equalization, many industrialized countries tried to make these social groups assume their political responsibility in war (Yamanouchi 1995). This explains not only why the state had to control resource allocation and why the warfare states became the welfare states, but also why the state had to restrain the property rights of private companies, whose interests conflicted with this goal.

The expansion of bureaucratic power by delegating legislation to the executive branch of the state came to characterize, in different degrees, all industrialized countries during World War II. Not only did a new type of economic governance emerge, with increasing restraints enacted by the state on the freedom of individuals in economic activities, but the legislative power of the state also shifted from the parliament to the administration. During this process, however, countries with a different constitutional state order still fell into two groups. In Japan, as well as in Germany and Italy, which adhered to the Continental legal tradition and were influenced by fascism, this trend took shape as a radical change of political institutions toward totalitarian regimes. The executive branch of the state obtained the power of legislation without any consultation with the legislative branch of the state. As Tanaka Jirō (1942, 796) pointed out:

In the past, laws emphasized legal stability and restrained the state intervention in the economy, aiming at nothing more than ensuring the intrinsic order of the economy. At present, laws reflect the will of the state on the economy, exemplify the detailed standards for the economy and establish an order for the economy. The transition of the mission of the legal system brought about changes in not only the content of laws, but also the form of laws. It is under this context the increase of delegated legislation, elastic definitions or comprehensive articles can be properly explained.

In contrast, in the common law countries such as the United States and Britain this shift appeared as a reform that maintained the previous general principles. Accordingly, the polity in these countries remained democratic, and the legislative branch maintained supervisory power even after the executive power was greatly expanded (Miyazawa 1940; Wagatsuma 1948, 7).

The National Mobilization Law reflected a strong German impact on the Japanese constitutional order of the state. In the German model of the state, there was a strict separation of powers. The competence of the judiciary to adjudicate direct appeals from administrative actions was denied, and a separate administrative court was created. In the Japanese adaptation, the judges of the administrative court could even hold other administrative posts concurrently. Administrative law is a systematic discipline in the Continental legal tradition that developed in the early French Third Republic. Japan adopted French administrative law through the intermediary of German legal teaching and created a body of administrative law doctrine, the principal pillars of which were a dichotomy between public and private law and the concept of the "administrative act." Contrary to a juristic act in private law, administrative acts were binding, unilateral government dispositions that imposed duties on private parties, granted licenses or approvals, and carried out other formal measures under legal authority that required no assent or special authority. As a practical consequence, they restricted the availability of legal relief from administrative conduct. Unless the allegedly illegal administrative act met the constitutive criteria of form and effect of an administrative act, its legality was not justifiable (Haley 1996). As Haley (1996, 636) states, "The public law conception of a hierarchy of power and status in which the state and its organs were superior countered the premise of equality in private law." In theory, the administrative authority was restricted by the limits and binding power of the law. In reality, however, state bureaucrats in prewar Japan held unlimited power in areas in which the state was sustained by administrative acts (Narita 1976, 359).

The National Mobilization Law of 1938 was a comprehensive delegation law that gave the executive office of the Japanese state unprecedented power in lawmaking and enforcement. Consequently, the state enacted many industry laws without any consultation with the private sector, and business interests were often disregarded. Once enacted, the laws were backed up by the coercive power of the state. The Ministry of Commerce and Industry alone issued more than eighty ordinances in two years to exercise its control over the economy (Nihon Keizai Renmeikai 1940, 305–8). Under the National Mobilization Law, the Japanese state also continued to rely heavily on the discretion of the executive branch of the state to use punishment to enforce its policy objectives. Among the fifty articles of this law, eighteen concerned penalties. Those people who violated state control over labor, trade, production, and use of resources were subject to a prison term of up to three years and a fine of up to five thousand yen.

To enforce its economic laws, the Japanese state also relied on economic police. Under the Administrative Enforcement Law of 1900, Japanese police were empowered to enforce administrative regulations and thus were able to arrest and hold in custody persons suspected of violating administrative orders and regulations, without the protection of the Code of Criminal Procedure (Haley 1996, 640). As many economic laws were enacted to restrain the freedom of private citizens and legal persons in economic activities after 1937, an economic security division was established in each prefecture's police department. According to statistics of the Economic Security Division at the Police Bureau of the Ministry of Home Affairs, by October 1939 more than 225,000 individuals had been charged with violating the state economic regulations. To promote the economic security divisions' effectiveness, the economic police established formal channels not only with state economic bureaucracies, by having regular coordination meetings with the Ministry of Commerce and Industry, the Ministry of Welfare, the Ministry of Finance, the Ministry of Justice, and the Economic Planning Board, but also with various business organizations. By the end of 1938, a council on economic police had been established in every prefecture; the councils became the center of coordination between the state and the private sector in enforcing government economic regulations. The operation of these councils was centered on and directed by the police department (Ogino 1988, 351–55).

The Important Industry Association Ordinance of 1941

By the eve of the Pacific War, the state had not yet intervened directly in the internal operation of cartels. Facing the challenge of waging a war with a major world power, however, the Japanese state replaced the mandatory cartels with compulsory trade associations by enacting the Important Industry Association Ordinance in 1941. Cartels were private organizations whose primary goal was to serve their own interests. The state may have controlled the cartels' pricing policy and decided the quota for the supply of capital, material, and labor, but as long as these measures remained exogenous constraints, private companies had the freedom to pursue their own goals, and the state was unable to ensure munitions production. The Japanese state intended to strengthen its control over the economy, not only because munitions production bore strategic significance for national survival in the coming war with the United States, but also because economic embargoes by the United States and its allies made resources more scarce.

The Japanese state tried to establish what was called an "economic new order," which consisted of making and implementing annual government plans for national mobilization and various laws that restrained the freedom of private companies. The economic new order contained several radical proposals to support the operation of control associations. First, managers would be given official status at both the company and trade association levels in order to free them from pressures from shareholders seeking to pursue profits. Second, "production corporations," which were fundamentally different from business associations, would be established and given the status of public organizations. Conglomerates could be dissolved and absorbed into these corporations. Third, the profits of private companies would be controlled (Tsusanshō 1964, 448).

Control associations were an important component of this new economic order because they dealt directly with the issue of how to make the government plans and supervise the implementation of those plans. Supported by the National Mobilization Law, the Important Industry Association Ordinance of 1941 took the form of an executive order, which did not need approval from the Diet. Control associations were established to remedy the weakness of the cartels. Whereas membership in cartels was voluntary, control associations were industrywide compulsory trade associations—every company in the industry was required to be a member. In contrast to cartels, which could make their own decisions within the constraints established by the state, control associations were more tightly controlled by the state. They played an important role in the war mobilization program. Control associations not only participated in government planning by collecting various data but also supervised the implementation of the annual national mobilization of resources in each industry. For example, the Japan Steel Association directly controlled steel distribution in the industry. Working closely with the state, the association had designated agents, designated wholesalers, and secondary wholesalers for each major specific product in the industry. These agents and wholesalers would make sure that raw materials and products were not distributed for any business purposes that conflicted with the policy objectives of the state. At the beginning of 1943, the state bureaucracy further empowered control associations to decide the quota of production, rations of production materials and equipment, and the distribution of products.

The German ideology of economic law had a great impact on the development of compulsory trade associations in Japan. In the 1930s the leading German ideology directly restrained private property rights. Economic law was a public law concept, and it first emerged in Germany during World War I. Sustained by the Delegated Legislation Law of 1914, the executive office of the German state gained absolute power in both administration and legislation, and the legislative function of the German Diet almost completely ceased. The German state subsequently issued numerous executive orders controlling the economy.

The World War I history of Germany was marked not only by delegated legislation but by "state intervention in private property rights and market economy," "the tremble of business contract," and a "new organizational pattern of business and industry under strong control by the state" (Kikuchi 1943, 3). Suffering from an unprecedented crisis created by war, revolution, and the collapse of the monetary system, the German state enacted numerous laws in the postwar period to maintain economic order. When the Nazis obtained power, the German concept of economic law was injected with a new element—totalitarianism. The Nazis held that economic organizations should be governed according to the same principle as the state. The economy should serve the political purpose of the nation. Economic activities should be viewed politically. To achieve these goals, all fields of the economy needed to cooperate with the state, obey its will, and move in the direction decided by the state. Economic law was perceived in Germany as an administrative law that would regulate all types of development of the Nazis' economic organizations (Kikuchi 1943, 101–5).

In the Japanese context, the German ideology of economic law enhanced the legitimacy of the efforts of the Japanese state to control the economy by issuing coercive executive orders, adjusting the relationships of private law and public law, and nationalizing the management of private properties (Minobi, cited in Shimizu 1940, 37; see also Shimizu 1940, 5). In the Japanese discussion, the German theory of economic law was perceived as an alternative to liberal legal theory. Liberal legal theory regarded law as an indispensable evil to ensure individuals' rights; the enforcement of individuals' duties was seen as only a secondary concern. Liberal legal theory held that the power of the law had to be minimized to maximize the freedom of individuals. In both civil law and business law, this individualistic ideology was reflected by three major principles: absolute property rights, limited liability, and freedom of contract. As private laws, both civil and business laws aimed to protect the independence of individuals and adjust the interpersonal relationship according to their own will.

Economic law, in contrast, was a major revision of civil and business laws. In place of the absoluteness of property rights, limited liability, and the freedom of contract, economic law emphasized "preventing the abuse of rights," "public order and morality," and the "safety of economic transaction." Economic law maintained that individual citizens were responsible for meeting the demand of the state even when doing so might violate private property rights. The state, moreover, might impose responsibilities on individuals even if they had done nothing wrong (Kikuchi 1943, 159–60). Rather than simply adjusting conflicting interests between two parties who had equal legal status, the state in economic law was a legal subject, and the relationship between the state and private individuals or juristic persons was subordinate. The ideology of economic law directly acknowledged the authority of the state in economic intervention and represented direct constraints by the state not only on the freedom of individuals and juristic persons in economic activities but also on the independence of private laws, even though economic law did not reject civil and business laws completely. In short, economic law reflected the "permeation of public law in the sphere that had formerly been dominated by private laws" (Shimizu 1940, 7). The advocates of this ideology in Japan contended that the theory of economic law was not a temporary measure during a crisis but a legal development that responded to the transformation of modern capitalism from a liberal stage to a monopoly stage (Minemura 1951, 4).

Although Japan was strongly influenced by Germany, the Japanese state failed to achieve the same degree of control over trade associations as did the German state. The daily operation of Japanese control associations was still in private hands. One important reason for this Japanese variation on the German model was the agency of actors. Since the Important Industry Association Ordinance significantly reduced the scope of the property rights of private companies, it encountered a much stronger resistance from the private sector than had been the case with the Important Industry Control Law of 1931 and the National Mobilization Law of 1938. The private sector charged that the state policy proposals under which managers were given official status and the profits of private companies were controlled were radically anticapitalistic, with a "communist orientation," and "violat[ed] the Constitution" (Yomiuri 1972). In December 1940, eight major business organizations together sent a statement to the government to oppose these initiatives. By mobilizing right-wing conservatives and drawing on the anticommunist orientation of fascism, they were even able to force the state to arrest several bureaucrats who had drafted the state policy proposal. As a result, although private companies had failed to protect their interests in the law as written, they succeeded in doing so in the law in action. The actual operation of control associations reflected a political compromise. It enabled the private sector to resist direct bureaucratic control of the internal affairs of private companies. It also enabled the state to restrain market forces from disturbing its policy objective. In this new governance structure, private companies worked closely with the state under the condition that they would maintain a certain degree of autonomy for running the daily operation of control associations.

Postwar Continuities

The rise of the associational order in the Japanese economy during the Great Depression and World War II was not simply an abnormal and temporary phenomenon under the strong influence of fascism. Cartels in Japan continued to evolve after the war in ways that further strengthen the argument I have laid out so far.

During the postwar occupation the United States forced Japan to enact its first antimonopoly law in 1947. The original version of the Japanese antimonopoly law was quite rigid and did not allow any kind of cartels to exist. However, since the constitutional order of the state changed little during the postwar democratic reforms, a pattern of economic governance driven by the market, as prescribed by the 1947 version of the antimonopoly law, did not have strong political support. As soon as the U.S. government changed its policy toward Japan from introducing democracy to turning Japan into an ally in the cold war, the Japanese state amended its antimonopoly law twice in 1949 and 1953 and also enacted about thirty cartel exemption laws.

The cartels exempted by these new laws included the cartels organized in industries, such as transportation and insurance, where competition might be harmful to the public interest; the cartels organized to encourage cooperation and organization among companies that operated on a small scale and tended to engage in excessive competition; the cartels organized to prevent excessive competition in the exports-related sector; the cartels organized during economic recession to adjust the balance between demand and supply; and the cartels organized to promote rationalization in the manufacturing industries, including automobile and electronic power (Kōsei Torihiki Iinkai 1977, 105–6).

In 1952 only 53 cartels were exempted by various pieces of legislation (see figure 3.2). That number grew to 79 in 1953, 162 in 1954, 348 in 1955,

FIGURE 3.2   *Cartels Exempted from the Enforcement of the Antimonopoly Law in Japan, 1952 to 1976*

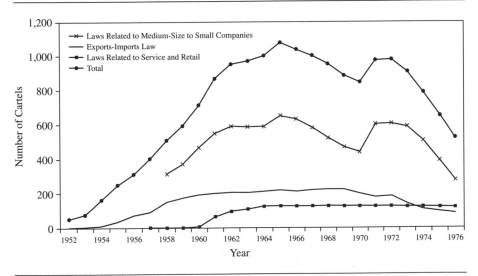

Source: Based on the data in Kōsei Torihiki Iinkai (1977, 767–69); Gao (2001a, figure 5.2, 133). Reprinted with the permission of Cambridge University Press.

312 in 1956, 401 in 1957, and 509 in 1958. By 1959 the number of cartels organized according to these exemption laws had reached 595. Among these, 370 were exempted by the Medium- and Small-Size Company Business Organization Law, and 172 were exempted by the Exports-Imports Transaction Law. Together, these two types of cartels constituted about 90 percent of the total (Kōsei Torihiki Iinkai 1977, 81). In the 1960s the cartel exemption laws emphasized the medium-size and small companies and the sunset industries. During the liberalization of trade in the 1960s, especially during the 1964 recession, the number of exempted cartels increased rapidly. In 1960 the total number was 714. It peaked at 1,079 in 1965 and stayed above 1,000 during 1966 and 1967. In 1970 Japan still had as many as 976 cartels exempted from enforcement of the antimonopoly law (Kōsei Torihiki Iinkai 1977, 769).

Why did the Japanese state allow cartels to exist in postwar Japan? The two reasons that had sustained the rise of cartels in the 1930s continued to be highly relevant. First, maintaining political stability and allocating resources were still higher priorities in the state policy than protecting the liberties of private enterprises (Gao 2001). If Japan had championed the American antitrust model, which prohibited cartels yet allowed mergers and acquisitions, many small companies in Japan would have disappeared as a result of the failure in the competition. However, medium-size and small companies provided more than two-thirds of Japanese employment opportunities in the manufacturing industries during the high-growth period. In many other industries the share of companies this size in total job creation was even higher: in 1975 that share was 99.9 percent in construction, 99.5 percent in manufacturing, 99.6 percent in wholesale and retail, 100 percent in real estate, and 99.5 percent in transportation and communication. Medium-size and small companies employed 92.9 percent of the total labor force in construction, 70.7 percent in manufacturing, 86.8 percent in wholesale and retail, 97.6 percent in real estate, 85.6 percent in transportation and communication, and 71.1 percent in service (Maotani 1978, 39). The Japanese state did not want to see massive bankruptcies and the resulting layoffs because major political instability would have ensued.

Second, the Japanese state continued to regard cartels as a useful policy tool. It even often acted as the organizer of joint actions among private companies in a number of forms during economic recessions, including "advised production reduction" (the state directly ordering private companies to restrain production), "freezing the stocks" (during a recession, directly advising private companies to freeze their stocks of certain goods that were in oversupply and then to "unfreeze" them when the market situation improved), and what was called "public sales." In public sales, manufacturers were responsible for reporting to the government an estimated amount of their monthly sales and the sales price negotiated with wholesalers. After the price was reported, it could not be changed. Manufacturers that violated the state-advised production amount and sales price would be punished (Kōsei Torihiki Iinkai 1977, 95–99).

Conclusions

What does the rise of mandatory cartels and compulsory trade associations in Japan tell us about the relationship between the associational order and the state in general?

First, this study demonstrates that the rise of the associational order in the Japanese economy was a result of the changing state property rights policy. It shows that when the globalization process reversed its course, the state in capitalist economies shifted the focus of its property rights policy from protecting the liberties of private enterprises to maintaining political stability and controlling resource allocation. When the state tried to reinstall economic order during the Great Depression, the old policy of achieving order by private means, using voluntary cartels and zaibatsu conglomerates, was no longer sufficient, and negotiated self-regulation through the use of mandatory cartels emerged. When the state was confronted with the tough task of mobilizing national resources for war, even mandatory cartels became inadequate. The modes of pure regulation and mandated self-regulation emerged in succession to sustain state control over the economy. The shifts among these three different modes of associational order in the Japanese economy within such a short period of time (and their postwar persistence in many capitalist economies) indicate that the Great Depression and World War II constituted a turning point in the long-term movement of capitalist economies after the previous wave of globalization headed toward a downturn, which in turn followed the collapse of the gold standard and the breakout of World War I in 1914.

Second, this study contributes to the social science literature on the state, on property rights, and on economic governance by highlighting the impact of the constitutional order of the state on the associational order of the economy. In recent years, law, as a variable in interpreting the outcome of economic governance, has received increasing attention in economic sociology (Dobbin 1994; Fligstein 1990; Roy 1997; Swedberg, this volume). Both Fligstein (1990) and Roy (1997) have demonstrated the impact of the law on the changes in American corporations. The independent variables of their analyses, however, are laws and public policies, not the constitutional order of the state. Dobbin (1994) compares the differences in the constitutional order of the state among the United States, Britain, and France but focuses on the cultural element of the issue. In his analysis of the U.S. case, for example, Dobbin emphasizes the active state and local government and the passive federal superstructure instead of the judge-supremacy of the common law and the law of contract in restraints of trade as the legal foundation of the antitrust law structure of the state. The literature associated with historical institutionalism in both political sociology (Weir and Skocpol 1985) and economic sociology (Campbell, Hollingsworth, and Lindberg 1991) focuses on whether the state has the capacity to implement a new policy. By highlighting the constitutional order of the state, in contrast, this study shows that whether the state can develop a certain capacity is constrained by the institutional logic of a specific constitutional order. Thus, the rise of the associational order in the Japanese economy is explained here by the institutional logic built into the Continental tradition of the state constitutional order, which gave more power to the executive branch of the state, which often relied on cartels and trade associations to achieve its policy objectives.

Third, the Japanese case also highlights the mechanism through which the institutionalized beliefs about the constitutional order of the state shape the outcome of a property rights redefinition and the resulting changes in economic governance. The study shows that institutional logic tends to be general and abstract and can be implemented in diverse ways in an actual situation. The diverse implementations of the institutional logic, however, can have quite different implications for the property rights structure, economic governance, and the interests of actors. For this reason, redefining property rights is a highly political process in which the state may try to expand the range of constraints on property rights, whereas private companies may strategically reinterpret the institutional logic in their own favor in order to protect their property rights. For example, in the early 1940s in the political struggle between the Japanese state and private companies over control associations, the private sector did not reject the state priorities of maintaining political stability and controlling resource allocation in its property rights redefinition. Instead, the private sector adopted a strategy of rejecting the specific government proposal that aimed to establish direct bureaucratic control over control associations, replacing it with a new proposal for privately managed control associations that would perform the same function of controlling the resource allocation in the war mobilization. Although these two proposals can be considered as having drastically different implications for property rights and the nature of the resulting control associations, they were both considered legitimate means for the state to use in controlling resource allocation.

This chapter is largely based on Gao (2001b).

References

Arisawa, Hiromi. 1976. *Showa Keizaishi* (The Economic History of the Showa Period). Tokyo: Iwanami Shoten.

Barnouw, David, and Jan Nekkers. 1991. "The Netherlands: State Corporatism Against the State." In *Organizing Business for War: Corporatist Economic Organization During the Second World War,* edited by Wyn Grant, Jan Nekkers, and Frans van Waarden. New York: Berg.

Boddewyn, Jean J. 1985. "Advertising Self-regulation: Organization Structures in Belgium, Canada, France, and the United Kingdom." In *Private Interest Government: Beyond Market and State,* edited by Wolfgang Streeck and Philippe C. Schmitter. Beverly Hills, Calif.: Sage Publications.

Bork, Robert H. 1991. "Legislative Intent and the Policy of the Sherman Act." In *The Political Economy of the Sherman Act,* edited by E. Thomas Sullivan. New York: Oxford University Press.

Campbell, John L., J. Rogers Hollingsworth, and Leon N. Lindberg. 1991. *Governance of the American Economy.* New York: Cambridge University Press.

Coleman, William D., and Kim Richard Nossal. 1991. "The State and War Production in Canada." In *Organizing Business for War: Corporatist Economic Organization During the Second World War,* edited by Wyn Grant, Jan Nekkers, and Frans van Waarden. New York: Berg.

David, Rene, and John E. Brierley. 1964. *Major Legal Systems in the World Today: An Introduction to the Comparative Study of Law.* London: Stevens.

Dobbin, Frank. 1994. *Forging Industrial Cultures.* Cambridge: Cambridge University Press.

Edelman, Lauren B. 1990. "Legal Environments and Organizational Governance: The Expansion of Due Process in the Workplace." *American Journal of Sociology* 95(6): 1401–40.

———. 1992. "Legal Antiquity and Symbolic Structure: Organizational Mediation of Civil Rights Law." *American Journal of Sociology* 97(6): 1531–76.

Fligstein, Neil. 1990. *The Transformation of Corporate Control.* Cambridge, Mass.: Harvard University Press.

Gao, Bai. 1994. "Arisawa Hiromi and His Theory for a Managed Economy." *Journal of Japanese Studies* 20(1): 115–53.

———. 1997. *Economic Ideology and Japanese Industrial Policy: Developmentalism from 1931 to 1965.* New York: Cambridge University Press.

———. 2001a. *Japan's Economic Dilemma: The Institutional Origins of Prosperity and Stagnation.* New York: Cambridge University Press.

———. 2001b. "The State and the Associational Order of the Japanese Economy: The Institutionalization of Cartels and Trade Associations in Japan, 1931 to 1945." *Sociological Forum* 16(3): 409–43.

Gerber, David J. 1998. *Law and Competition in Twentieth-Century Europe.* Oxford: Clarendon Press.

Haley, John O. 1991. *Authority Without Power: Law and the Japanese Paradox.* New York: Oxford University Press.

———. 1996. "Error, Irony, and Convergence: A Comparative Study of the Origins and Development of Competition Policy in Postwar Germany and Japan." Unpublished paper. University of Washington, Seattle.

Hooks, Gregory. 1991. "The United States of America: The Second World War and the Retreat from New Deal Era Corporatism." In *Organizing Business for War: Corporatist Economic Organization During the Second World War,* edited by Wyn Grant, Jan Nekkers, and Frans van Waarden. New York: Berg.

Hovenkamp, Herbert. 1991. *Enterprise and American Law 1836 to 1937.* Cambridge, Mass.: Harvard University Press.

Hughes, Graham. 1996. "Common Law Systems." In *Fundamentals of American Law,* edited by Alan B. Morrisson. New York: New York University School of Law.

Johnson, Chalmers. 1982. *MITI and the Japanese Miracle.* Stanford, Calif.: Stanford University Press.

Kikuchi, Haruo. 1943. *Keizaihō nyūmon* (Introduction to Economic Law). Tokyo: Tōyō Shoten.

Kōsei Torihiki Iinkai. 1977. *Dokusen kinshi seisaku sanjūnenshi* (The Thirty Years' History of Antimonopoly Policy). Tokyo: Kōsei Torihiki Iinkai.

Kunihiro, Kazuto. 1941. *Keizai dantai* (Economic Associations). Tokyo: Nihon Hyōronsha.

Lindberg, Leon, and John L. Campbell. 1991. "The State and the Organization of Economic Activity." In *Governance of the American Economy,* edited by John L. Campbell, J. Rogers Hollingsworth, and Leon N. Lindberg. Cambridge: Cambridge University Press.

Luyten, Dirk. 1991. "The Policy of the Lesser Evil: Corporatist Economic Organization in Belgium." In *Organizing Business for War: Corporatist Economic Organization During the Second World War,* edited by Wyn Grant, Jan Nekkers, and Frans van Waarden. New York: Berg.

Maotani, Tsutomu. 1978. "Wagakuni chūshō kigyō no chii to sono henka" (The Status and Its Change of Japanese Medium-Size and Small Companies). In *Chūshō kigyō run,* edited by Kiyonari Tadao, Maotani Tsutomu, Shōya Kuniyuki, and Akiya Shigeo. Tokyo: Yūhikaku.

Matsui, Haruo. 1938. *Nihon shigen seisaku* (Japan's Resource Policy). Tokyo: Chikura Shobō.

Merryman, John Henry. 1969/1985. *The Civil Law Tradition: An Introduction to the Legal Systems of Western Europe and Latin America.* Stanford: Stanford University Press.

Minemura, Teruo. 1951. *Keizaihō* (Economic Law). Tokyo: Sanwa Shobō.

Miyazawa, Kikoyoshi. 1940. "Gaikan narabi ni wagakuni" (Overview and Japan). *Kokkagaku kenkyū* 54(9): 1–16.

Narita, Yoriaki. 1976. "Administrative Guidance." In *The Japanese Legal System,* edited by Hideo Takana. Tokyo: University of Tokyo Press.

Nihon Keizai Renmeikai. 1940. *Genkōsangyō tōsei no kekkan jitsujo narabi ni sore ni taisuru gyojō betsu kaizen ikken* (The Present Problems in the Managed Economy and a Proposal for Improvement). Tokyo: Nihon Keizai Renmeikai.

Noda, Yoshiyuki. 1976. "Impact of Foreign Law and Legal Scholarship." In *The Japanese Legal System,* edited by Hideo Takana. Tokyo: University of Tokyo Press.

North, Douglass C. 1981. *Structure and Change in Economic History.* New York: W. W. Norton.

Ogino, Fujio. 1988. *Tokkō keisatsu taiseishi* (The Institutional History of Special Police). Tokyo: Sekita Shobō.

Polanyi, Karl. 1944/1957. *The Great Transformation: The Political and Economic Origins of Our Time.* Boston: Beacon Press.

Posner, Richard A. 1986. *Economic Analysis of Law.* 3rd ed. Boston: Little, Brown.

Rengō Jōhōsha. 1938. *Sensō keizai no zenshin* (The Progress of the War Economy). Tokyo: Rengo Jōhōsha.

Rossiter, Adrian. 1991. "Business and Corporatism in Vichy France." In *Organizing Business for War: Corporatist Economic Organization During the Second World War,* edited by Wyn Grant, Jan Nekkers, and Frans van Waarden. New York: Berg.

Roy, William G. 1997. *Socializing Capital: The Rise of the Large Industrial Corporation in America.* Princeton, N.J.: Princeton University Press.

Schmitter, Philippe C. 1985. "Neocorporatism and the State." In *The Political Economy of Corporatism,* edited by Wyn Grant. New York: St. Martin's Press.

Schneiberg, Mark. 1999. "Political and Institutional Conditions for Governance by Association: Private Order and Price Controls in American Fire Insurance." *Politics and Society* 27(1): 67–103.

Schneiberg, Mark, and Rogers Hollingsworth. 1991. "Can Transaction Cost Economics Explain Trade Associations?" In *Political Choice,* edited by Roland M. Czada and Adrienne Windhoff-Heritier. Boulder, Colo.: Westview Press.

Shimizu, Kaneo. 1940. *Nihon keizai tōseihō* (Japan's Economic Control Law). Tokyo. Genshōtō Shoten.

Siegan, Bernard H. 1980. *Economic Liberties and the Constitution.* Chicago: University of Chicago Press.

Stigler, George J. 1991. "The Origin of the Sherman Act." In *The Political Economy of the Sherman Act,* edited by E. Thomas Sullivan. New York: Oxford University Press.

Streeck, Wolfgang, and Philippe C. Schmitter. 1985. "Community, Market, State, and Associations? The Prospective Contribution of Interest Governance to Social Order." In *Private Interest Government,* edited by Wolfgang Streeck and Philippe C. Schmitter. Beverly Hills, Calif.: Sage Publications.

Suchman, Mark C., and Lauren B. Edelman. 1996. "Legal Rational Myths: The New Institutionalism and the Law and Society Tradition." *Law and Social Inquiry* 21(4): 903–42.

Takahashi, Kamekichi. 1933. *Nihon keizai tōseiron* (On the Japanese Managed Economy). Tokyo: Kaizōsha.

Tanaka, Jirō. 1942. "Keizai tōseihō no nerai to sono kiso kōzō" (The Goal of Economic Control Law and Its Basic Structure). *Kokkagaku kenkyō* 56(6): 103–26.

Tilton, Mark. 1996. *Restrained Trade: Cartels in Japan's Basic Materials Industries.* Ithaca, N.Y.: Cornell University Press.

Trubek, David M. 1996. "Max Weber on Law and the Rise of Capitalism." In *The Sociology of Law: Classical and Contemporary Perspectives,* edited by A. Javier Trevino. New York: St. Martin's Press.

Tsusanshō. 1964. *Shōkō seisakushi* (The History of the Commercial and Industrial Policies). Tokyo: Shōkō Seisakushi Kankōkai.

Upham, Frank K. 1997. "Retail Convergence: The Structural Impediments Initiative and the Regulation of the Japanese Retail Industry." In *National Diversity and Global Capitalism,* edited by Suzanne Berger and Ronald Dore. Ithaca, N.Y.: Cornell University Press.

Van Waarden, Frans. 1991a. "Introduction: Crisis, Corporatism, and Continuity." In *Organizing Business for War: Corporatist Economic Organization During the Second World War,* edited by Wyn Grant, Jan Nekkers, and Frans van Waarden. New York: Berg.

———. 1991b. "Wartime Economic Mobilization and State-Business Relations: A Comparison of Nine Countries." In *Organizing Business for War: Corporatist Economic Organization During the Second World War,* edited by Wyn Grant, Jan Nekkers, and Frans van Waarden. New York: Berg.

Wagatsuma, Sakae. 1948. *Keizai saiken to tōsei rippō* (Economic Reconstruction and Legislation for Control). Tokyo: Yōhikaku.

Weber, Hajo. 1991. "Political Design and Systems of Interest Intermediation: Germany Between the 1930s and the 1950s." In *Organizing Business for War: Corporatist Economic Organization During the Second World War,* edited by Wyn Grant, Jan Nekkers, and Frans van Waarden. New York: Berg.

Weir, Margaret, and Theda Skocpol. 1985. "State Structures and the Possibilities for 'Keynesian' Responses to the Great Depression in Sweden, Britain, and the United States." In *Bringing the State Back In,* edited by Peter B. Evans, Dietrich Rueschemeyer, and Theda Skocpol. Cambridge: Cambridge University Press.

Yamanouchi, Yasushi. 1995. "Hōhōteki joron: Sōryokusen to shisutemu tōgō" (On Methodology: The Total War and the Integration of the System). In *Sōryokusen to gendaika,* edited by Yamanouchi Yasushi. Tokyo: Kashiwa Shobō.

Yomiuri Shinbunsha. 1972. *Showashi no tennō* (The Emperor in Showa History). Vols. 17, 18, and 19. Tokyo: Yomiuri Shinbunsha.

4

ON LEGAL INSTITUTIONS AND THEIR ROLE IN THE ECONOMY

Richard Swedberg

O
NE OF the great achievements of twentieth-century sociology as a social science discipline is to have studied the role of institutions, in the economy and elsewhere.[1] Economists, as a result of the ill-fated Battle of the Methods toward the end of the nineteenth century, chose to disregard institutions and instead focus on the pure play of economic interests in the market. With the loss of interest in economic institutions, their attention to political institutions, including legal institutions, also suffered. Today, as we know, economists have put institutions on their agenda and have slowly come to understand that unless these are better understood, much of the way that the economy operates will remain a mystery. The economists, however, still have quite a way to go and need, among other things, to get much better acquainted with the sociological literature on institutions. Sociologists have had more than a century to work out their ideas on this topic and as a result have developed a number of important insights. One of these is that the same economic activity can be effectively organized in several different ways; another is that politics typically plays a key role in developing economic institutions (see, for example, Dobbin, this volume).

But even if sociologists are in many ways ahead of economists when it comes to studying institutions and how these operate in concrete reality, there still exist a number of unsolved problems as well as areas that need to be much better understood. One of these areas has to do with the role that legal institutions play in economic life—a topic to which sociologists, including sociologists of law, have not paid much attention. It is true that legal institutions are part of the political institutions of a country, and that today's sociologists have developed a good knowledge of political institutions and how these operate on an everyday basis. But even if legal and political institutions are strongly related to one another, they are by no means identical, and it would be a great mistake to equate the will of the legislator with the way that the legal system operates. While law in some ways is simply a tool for politicians, it can also be developed in the legal institutions themselves, as well as by economic actors such as firms. There are some parts of the law that can be changed more or less at will by the politicians—but other parts of a country's law go far back in time and follow a different rhythm of change.

I begin this chapter by speaking generally about the problem of how to conceptualize legal institutions and their role in economic life, drawing primarily on the work of Max Weber. I then discuss the lex mercatoria, since it was in the Middle Ages that the legal foundations of modern capitalism were laid. This discussion is followed by two sections on research by sociologists on the nature of these legal foundations, from the classics to today's sociologists. I end with a discussion on how to improve the sociological analysis of the role of legal institutions in capitalism.

Legal Institutions and the Economy: The Perspective of Max Weber

In studying institutions, sociologists have typically emphasized the element of rules or models: institutions tell you what type of behavior is permitted and what is not. Or alternatively, they tell you what rules to follow and what will happen if you do not follow them. Phrased in this manner, it is clear that this perspective can easily be expanded to law. If we take our lead from Max Weber's sociology, law is defined in the following manner: "An order will be called . . . *law* if it is externally guaranteed by the probability that physical or psychological coercion will be applied by a *staff* of people in order to bring about compliance or avenge violation" (Weber 1922/1978, 34; cf. 313ff.). An "order," as Weber uses this term, is a set of conventions or prescriptions for how to act.

Weber also pays attention to the enabling side of legal institutions, especially when it comes to the economy. Since this part of Weber's sociology of law is rarely mentioned, it may be useful to cite the relevant statement in full:

> To the person who finds himself actually in possession of the power to control an object or a person the legal guaranty gives a specific certainty of the durability of such power. To the person to whom something has been promised the legal guaranty gives a higher degree of certainty that the promise will be kept. These are indeed the most elementary relationships between law and economic life. But they are not the only possible ones. *Law can also function in such a manner that, in sociological terms, the prevailing norms controlling the operation of the coercive apparatus have such a structure as to induce, in their turn, the emergence of certain economic relations.* (Weber 1922/1978, 667; emphasis added)

Weber (1922/1978, 668, 730) explains that this type of "enabling" or "empowering law" law confers "privileges" of two distinct types: they "[provide] protection against certain types of interference by third parties, especially state officials," and they "grant to an individual autonomy to regulate his relations with others by his own transactions." As examples of this second type—legal institutions that further economic relationships—Weber cites the modern contract, agency, assignment, negotiable instruments, and the conception of the firm as an individual actor. We here have something of a Weberian research agenda for the economic sociology of law; several of these institutions will also be discussed later on in this chapter.[2]

Finally, Weber is very careful in his sociology, including his sociology of law, to point out that what an institution proscribes is not just translated into identical behavior by the actor, be it through socialization, respect for authority, or what not. What the actor does, on the other hand, is to *orient* his or her behavior to an institution; this is something quite different from mechanically following what the rules lay down. The actor may not know what the rules say; he or she may misunderstand them; or he or she may decide not to follow the law. To the empirical sociologist, what first and foremost matters about law is not so much what it says or how the court will interpret it, but how it influences the behavior of various actors. To the sociologist, in brief, what is most important about law is its role as an "actual determinant of human behavior" (Weber 1922/1978, 312).

Laying the Legal Foundation for Modern Capitalism: The Lex Mercatoria

The innovations in commercial law that were made in Europe during the period of the late eleventh and twelfth centuries still constitute the foundation for capitalism. What happened in commercial law during this brief period can, to some extent, be compared to the technological innovations that ushered in the industrial revolution or the change in economic mentality that according to Weber came about with Protestantism. Given the enormous importance of lex mercatoria—which created "all characteristic legal institutes of modern capitalism" (Weber 1922/1978, 1464)—it seems natural that it should occupy an important place in the economic sociology of law. After a presentation of the lex mercatoria—or the Law Merchant, as it is also known—I will address the question of why such great legal creativity came to characterize just this period.

During the eleventh and twelfth centuries the Western economy experienced a very rapid growth in agricultural productivity and trade. New cities were founded, and the number of merchants grew rapidly. Merchants crossed the sea as well as the countryside in search of profit, and they organized markets and fairs where these did not already exist. They also developed their own law, which soon came to coexist with canon law, urban law, manorial law, and so on. Buying and selling, transporting goods, and insuring them were all dealt with in novel legal terms in the collections of laws that now emerged from the merchants' communities. Together these made up a fairly coherent set of rules, the lex mercatoria, which was accepted all over Europe (on the lex mercatoria, see, for example, Weber 1889/2002; Goldschmidt 1891/1957; Berman 1983, 333–56).

The merchants had their own courts at the markets and fairs that they organized, and they appointed fellow merchants as judges. They were also often present as judges at guild courts and urban courts during the Middle Ages. The proceedings at the merchants' courts were typically conducted very quickly, and technical legal arguments were discouraged. Professional lawyers were not welcome, and equity inspired the verdicts. The merchants controlled what went on in the markets and fairs but had little power outside of these when it came to enforcing the decisions of their courts. Sometimes the local rulers assisted the merchants in jailing and tracking down those who had broken the lex mercatoria. Often, however, the merchants had to fend for themselves in punishing and pursuing law-breakers.

What is truly remarkable about the lex mercatoria is that it created a series of institutions that still constitute the legal foundation for capitalism. In doing so, it also helped to systematize and institutionalize a series of novel economic activities. A list of the most important achievements of the lex mercatoria includes (see Goldschmidt 1891/1957; Weber 1922/1978, 1464, 1923/1981, 341–42; Berman 1983, 333–56):

- Acquisition in good faith overriding original ownership
- Patents and trademarks
- The bond
- The modern mortgage
- The notion of the economic corporation as a legal entity
- Symbolic delivery through contract replacing the actual transfer of goods
- The bill of lading and other transportation documents

It is still somewhat unclear what accounts for the great legal creativity that in such a brief period of time could produce the lex mercatoria (on commercial legislation in non-Western legal systems, see, for example, Swedberg 1998, 90–98). In an aside, Weber (1922/1978, 688) suggests that the emergence of the Law Merchant was facilitated by the fact that medieval society allowed different legal bodies to exist side by side, and that each of these "corresponded to the needs of concrete interest groups." Harold Berman (1983, 334, 354), a historian of legal thought, has similarly argued that the merchants constituted a fairly coherent and autonomous group in medieval society and that they created a law that reflected this fact. They also lived in a period of great economic expansion—what has been called "the commercial revolution of the middle ages" (Lopez 1976)—and were quick to respond to the many opportunities that came in its wake.

A recent study of the lex mercatoria has drawn attention to the fact that the merchants' courts at the Champagne Fairs were effective in enforcing their verdicts even though they had no state or similar political institution to back them up (Milgrom, North, and Weingast 1990). What to some extent compensated for not having access to a coercive machinery was the fact that it was possible for the merchants' courts to destroy a merchant's reputation if he behaved in a dishonest way. This sounds plausible, even if a systematic study of actual cases would be more convincing than the game-theoretical exercises that have been marshaled as proof.[3] It also seems to be the case that even if the merchants did not have recourse to the coercive apparatus of some state, political rulers assisted them when called upon.

Key Legal Institutions

To investigate the legal institutions that make up the lex mercatoria and also to follow their development over the centuries until today constitute two important tasks for the economic sociology of law, just as it is necessary to discuss the emergence of more recent legal innovations that are central to modern capitalism. In this chapter, however, only a few of the legal institutions that are central to the modern capitalist economy are discussed. These include property, inheritance, the contract, and the notion of the corporation as a legal personality.

Property

The first of these legal institutions, property, is of fundamental importance to all economies and has, as a consequence, been heavily regulated in law and enforced on a continuous basis. Class as well as status is related to property. Marx paid less attention to the legal dimension of property than to its social meaning, and he basically subsumed it under his concept of "relations of production." Émile Durkheim lectured on the respect that people have for property in most societies and argued that the force behind this prohibition is ultimately derived from the moral force of society (Durkheim 1950/1983, 110–70). Durkheim's analysis of respect for property, it may be added, is highly evocative—but also speculative in nature.

Max Weber wrote voluminously on property, in his sociological as well as in his legal and historical writings (see, for example, Weber 1889/2002, 1923/1981). It is also Weber who has made the most sustained attempt to conceptualize property exclusively from a sociological perspective and to integrate the result into a broader framework of economic sociology (cf. Veblen 1898). Weber starts out from the idea that property, from a sociological viewpoint, represents a kind of social relationship—and more precisely, that it consists of a social relationship that allows for *appropriation* (Weber 1922/1978, 44; cf. Parsons 1947, 40ff.). For property to exist, the relationship has to be closed (other people have to be excluded from it), and this allows the actor to monopolize the use of X for himself. This X can be an object, a person, and so on. When an actor has a monopoly on the appropriation of something, he or she has what Weber terms a "right"; when this right also can be passed on through inheritance, there is "property." If the property in addition can be bought and sold, there is "free property."

We can find an enormous variation throughout history when it comes to property. We learn, for example, from Weber's (1891/1986) early work on Antiquity that property in land in Rome had to go through several stages before it could be freely bought and sold on the market. At first the land was owned by a community and could not be sold at all. At a later stage it could be sold by some individual, but only if the community gave its permission. And finally, land became perfectly alienable: it could be bought and sold at will.

Just as land and objects have been bought and sold throughout history, according to Weber, so have human beings. Weber's remarks on slaves as a form of property are well known, but not as well known is his observation that in many societies males have often had a legal power over wife and children that is similar to that which slave owners have over slaves:

> This *dominium* [over wife and children in, for example, Roman law] is absolute. . . . The power of the house father extends with ritualistic limitations to execution or sale of the wife, and to sale of the children or leasing them out to labor. (Weber 1923/1981, 48)

In *Economy and Society* (Weber 1922/1978, 130–50), Weber attempts to enumerate the most important sociological types of property that have existed throughout history in agriculture, industry, and so on. He also discusses what kind of property relations and forms of appropriation are most suitable for modern capitalism. When it comes to labor, his answer is identical to that of Marx: modern capitalism works best (for the owners, Weber specifies) if the workers do not own the means of production. When this is the case, the owner gets to choose which workers he or she wants to hire and is furthermore in a position to impose discipline on them. Weber also stresses that modern capitalism is more efficient (again, from the viewpoint of the owners) if the managers, as opposed to the owners, are allowed to run the corporations. While the original owner and creator of a business fortune may also have been a skillful manager, his heirs are much less likely to be so than a handpicked manager.

Modern sociology has not devoted much attention to the concept of property (see, for example, Gouldner 1970, 304–13). In recent economic sociology, however, a few attempts have been made to analyze property with the help of the concept of property rights. These studies have typically taken their inspiration from the law and economics literature, not from Weber.[4] It has been argued, for example, that sociologists tend to forget that the state can change existing property rights and introduce new ones and in this way influence the economy (Campbell and Lindberg 1990). In the United States this happened when AT&T's monopoly over the telecommunications sector was challenged in the late 1950s and replaced by a competitive market.

The notion of property rights has also been used to get a better grip on the transition to capitalism in eastern Europe and to theorize the "hybrid" type of property that emerged at one point—that is, property that is neither fully private nor public (see Stark 1996; for a critique of Stark's thesis, see Hanley, King, and Toth 2002). Drawing on the work of Harold Demsetz, some experts on China have also suggested that the social structure of rural industry in this country differs depending on the structure of the property rights, which are of four kinds: the right to ownership, the right to manage, the right to the income that is generated, and the right to enforce the existing order (Oi and Walder 1999; cf. Walder 1992). The great variety of social arrangements under which rural industry in China currently operates lends itself very well to a flexible notion of property of this type.

A topic that has not been much explored in the sociology of property is that of intellectual property rights, which cover such items as patents, copyright, trade secrets, and trademarks. The Statute of Monopolies from 1523 in England is often cited as the first patent law, but the American Constitution of 1787 also includes a famous passage on patents and copyright. According to the Constitution, the U.S. Congress has the power "to promote the progress of science and useful arts, by securing for limited times to authors and inventors the exclusive right to their respective writings and discoveries." The attempt to secure the rights of the "authors and inventors," however, was soon replaced by the use of the law of intellectual property to secure the rights of corporations (Friedman 1985, 255–56, 435–38). This had already taken place in the nineteenth century when the first patent pools were organized; corporations, in other words, could buy and sell patents from each other. The value of intellectual property to big corporations increased enormously during the twentieth century with the emergence of the music industry, the drug industry, the computer industry, and so on.

An interesting aspect of this type of law has been noted by Robert Merton (1935; 1973, 286–312; personal communication, November 14–15, 2001), namely, that the effort to encourage "the inventive interest" of the individual scientist was soon taken over by the internal reward system of scientists. The scientist publishes his or her results and essentially gets awarded with the esteem of colleagues. As science has become much more profitable, however, the applicability of this type of award system has shrunk considerably

(Zuckerman 1988). This leads to the question of whether the current legal system still properly safeguards the interest of the inventor and encourages his or her activities.

Inheritance

Inheritance is closely related to the concept of property, as Weber's definition of property illustrates. As such, inheritance is also part of the more general social mechanism of appropriation, or the closing out of people from the opportunity to use a certain utility. Although contemporary sociologists have paid little attention to inheritance, this is not the case with the classics (see, however, McNamee and Miller 1989; cf. Beckert, forthcoming). In *Democracy in America* (Tocqueville 1835–40/1945, 1:48–54, 380–81; 2:368–70), for example, Alexis de Tocqueville devotes several pages to inheritance, which he regards as a legal institution of great political importance. According to Tocqueville, primogeniture is associated with the aristocratic type of society, and the equal right to inheritance with the democratic type. What especially impresses Tocqueville is that once a certain type of inheritance law is in place, it slowly but inexorably reshapes society:

> When the legislator has once regulated the law of inheritance, he may rest from his labor. The machine once put in motion will go on for ages, and advance, as if self-guided, towards a point indicated beforehand. When framed in a particular manner, this law unites, draws together, and vests property and power in a few hands; it causes an aristocracy, so to speak, to spring out of the ground. If formed on opposite principles, its action is still more rapid; it divides, distributes, and disperses both property and power. (Tocqueville 1835–40/1945, 1:50)

Tocqueville (1835–40/1945, 1:50-1) also draws a distinction between the "direct" and the "indirect" impact of inheritance. By the former, he means the impact of inheritance on some material object—say, a landed property being divided into a certain number of parts. By indirect impact, he refers to the fact that when landed property is divided, the feeling for the family property and the desire to keep it together tends to dissolve.

Durkheim and Weber both judge inheritance to be of great importance to economic life. According to Durkheim (1950/1983, 213), inheritance in modern society represents the survival of an archaic and collective form of property that leads directly to inequality. "It is obvious," he argues in one of his lectures, "that inheritance, by creating inequalities amongst men from birth that are unrelated to merit or service, invalidates the whole contractual system at its very roots." In Durkheim's opinion, inheritance is incompatible with the spirit of individualism in modern society and should be abolished; he also predicts its disappearance (216–17; cf. Schwartz 1996).

Like Durkheim, Weber (1922/1978, 669) regards the concept of inheritance as belonging to the legal past, since it deals with the actor in her capacity as a member of a family rather than in terms of what she herself has accomplished. Weber ascribed the increasing freedom of testation in modern society to, among other things, the need in families to adjust inheritance to the injustices of life. People "aim, in addition to munificence regarded as an obligation of decency, at the balancing of interests among family members in view of special economic needs" (670). Finally, Weber (1923/1981, 108) challenged the easy identification of primogeniture with aristocracy by pointing out that equal division of land was the rule in France before as well as after the creation of the famous Napoleonic Code.

The Contract

When it comes to *the contract,* the most frequently cited work in sociology is without a doubt *The Division of Labor in Society* by Durkheim. In a rebuttal to Herbert Spencer, who wants modern society to operate exclusively on the basis of individual contracts, Durkheim (1893/1933, 211) points out that a contract can work efficiently only if there also exists a social structure to support it. "Everything in the contract is not contractual. . . . Wherever a contract exists, it is submitted to regulation which is the work of society and not that of individuals." When he lectures on the contract, Durkheim also discusses its evolution throughout history. What especially fascinates him, as well as several of his students, is the fact that once a contract has been entered into, it is respected by the actors as well as by society. That a contract in this way can acquire a truly "binding force" is the result, he suggests, of "a revolutionary innovation in law" and it can be explained only with the help of sociology (Durkheim 1950/1983, 178, 203; cf. Cotterrell 1999, 119–33).

To Weber (1922/1978, 666–752), the law of contracts represents an "enabling law" par excellence, since a contract allows the actors to engage in new types of behavior that they agree upon. Contracts were used very early in history, but not in the economy; at that early stage they also typically involved the whole person ("status contracts," in Weber's terminology). The modern type of contract, in contrast, is primarily used in the economic sphere and has a narrow scope ("purposive contracts"). For rational capitalism to operate efficiently, it is absolutely essential that the transfer of property be stable and operate smoothly; only the modern purposive contract can ensure such transfers.

Weber never got around to writing on the contract and its role in modern capitalism. He does, however, occasionally touch on the structure of the modern employment contract; what he has to say on this point is reminiscent of Marx, namely, that the asymmetry of power between the worker and the employer makes the freedom of contract largely illusory (Weber 1922/1978,

729–30; cf. Marx 1867/1906, 195–96). Enabling laws, in other words, tend to promote formal freedom as opposed to real freedom:

> This type of rules [enabling rules] does no more than create the framework for valid agreements which, under conditions of formal freedom, are officially available to all. Actually, however, they are accessible only to the owners of property and thus in effect support their very autonomy and power positions. (Weber 1922/1978, 730)

At one point in *Economy and Society,* Weber (1922/1978, 328) notes that businessmen rarely go to court to settle their disputes over a contract. This insight is also central to an important article by the legal scholar Stewart Macaulay (1963), which deserves a special mention. Macaulay argues that a common reason why businessmen hesitate to use the court system is that they feel that this is not the way to deal with business associates. He quotes a businessman in his article:

> If something comes up, you get the other man on the telephone and deal with the problem. You don't read legalistic contract clauses at each other if you ever want to do business again. One doesn't run to lawyers if he wants to stay in business because one must behave decently. (Macaulay 1963, 61)

Subsequent research has tended to confirm Macaulay's argument that businessmen avoid litigation (see also Macaulay 1977). Macaulay himself has suggested that managers mainly avoid going to court because it is more expensive than settling a dispute through other means. In an interesting twist on this, he points out that money is also the reason why insurance companies do go to court in cases that involve huge claims in automobile accidents. "In such cases, the amount involved is so substantial that no official in the company wants to assume responsibility for writing the check; it seems safer to do this under the compulsion of a court order" (Macaulay 1977, 514).

Modern economic sociologists, as opposed to the classical sociologists, have on the whole tended to ignore the contract. The reason for this neglect may well be related to the more general fact that modern sociologists have not done much work on the contract in the first place. There are some exceptions, however, including a traditional concern with the labor contract (see, for example, Streeck 1992, 41–75). Oliver Williamson's argument (Williamson 1975) that the contract is linked to the market, just as authority relations characterize the firm, has also led to some debate among sociologists, including the suggestion that things are considerably more complex in reality (see, for example, Stinchcombe 1985). A special mention should also be made of Carol Heimer's (1985) study of insurance contracts, in which she investigates how risk is managed in this type of contracts. By trying to control for those parts of risk that have their origin in the fact that actors' behavior is interrelated ("reactive risk," in Heimer's terminology), the probabilities for loss are stabilized.

The Corporation as a Legal Personality

It is clear that the legal evolution of the modern corporation is of great interest to an economic sociology of law and that the notion of the firm as a *legal personality* holds a special place in this. Most important, it is by virtue of this particular notion that the firm has been able to acquire full legal independence from individual persons. To cite Weber: "The most rational actualization of the idea of legal personality of organizations consists in the complete separation of the legal spheres of the members from the separately constituted legal sphere of the organization" (Weber 1922/1978, 707). The notion of legal personality represents, in other words, a legal mechanism that allows individuals to act in novel ways. It is also an integral part of the modern Western firm.

Only two sociologists have paid more than cursory attention to the notion of legal personality—Max Weber and James Coleman. According to Weber (1922/1978, 705–29), this notion falls under the heading of "associational contracts" and can consequently be characterized as an enabling law. Weber unfortunately traces only the early history of the notion of legal personality, which was used for political and religious organizations rather than for economic ones during the Middle Ages. He does mention, however, that the complementary notion that a firm can own property of its own, which is distinct from the personal property of individuals, had already started to emerge during the early fourteenth century in Florence (Weber 1923/1981, 228). The notion of legal personality was eliminated from French law during the Revolution but was soon reintroduced in order to facilitate market transactions. No such interruption occurred in England, where the notion of legal personality was first used in the thirteenth century when charters were issued to towns. Still, it was not until the nineteenth century that the notions of limited liability and the joint-stock corporation became common (for how these notions developed in the United States, see, Horwitz 1992, 65–108; for how they developed in England, see Harris 2000).

While Weber primarily discusses the notion of legal personality in his sociology of law, James Coleman (1974, 1982, 1993) assigns it a place in his general sociology. According to Coleman, to study the notion of legal personality constitutes a way of tracking the evolution of a revolutionary innovation in human history, namely, the discovery that people can create groups for their own special purposes. People have always lived in groups, but it was at a relatively late stage in history that they consciously began to create new ones. The conceptual breakthrough, according to Coleman, came in the thirteenth century when an Italian jurist named Sinibaldo de' Fieschi (later known as Pope Innocent IV) introduced the notion that a "persona ficta" or a "fictitious person" should have the same legal standing as an individual, even though it lacked a physical body (Coleman 1993, 2). This also meant that organizations could have their own interests, a notion that has led to the creation of an "asymmetric society" (2ff.; cf. Coleman 1990, 145–74).

Current Research

Although no effort has been made in contemporary sociology to develop a general and systematic analysis of the role that law plays in ongoing economic life—what has here been called an economic sociology of law—there do exist a number of studies that naturally would fall into such a field (see, however, Swedberg 2003b; Edelman and Stryker, forthcoming; Stryker, forthcoming). In some studies, for example, economic sociologists have included a discussion of law in their analyses. One example of this is Neil Fligstein's (1990) analysis of the way that antitrust legislation influenced the various strategies and structures of American firms during the twentieth century. There are also a number of studies in organizational sociology and in the sociology of law that have produced valuable insights into the relationship of legal and economic forces (see, for example, the study of law firms in Silicon Valley in Suchman 1985, 2000). The law and economics movement has also served as an object of critique in the area of gender and inequality of pay (Nelson and Bridges 1999).

It is also possible to pick out a few research themes on some aspect of the role that law plays in the economy. There is, for example, the attempt in a few studies to focus on the firm as a distinct legal actor in its own right. Several attempts have also been made to study the role of bankruptcy and what happens when a firm or some of its employees break the law. A few words need to be said about each of these.

The most innovative research may well be the work on *the firm as a legal actor*. This type of research has grown out of new institutional analysis in organizational sociology and uses as its point of departure the idea that law is part of every firm's surroundings (Edelman 1990; Edelman and Suchman 1997). Through a series of studies of the Civil Rights Act of 1964 and related legislation, it has been shown why certain firms rather than others have responded positively to this type of law and implemented a series of legal measures, such as formal grievance procedures for non-union members and special offices for equal employment opportunity and affirmative action (for individual studies, see Sutton et al. 1994; Dobbin and Sutton 1998; Kelly and Dobbin 1999; for a summary, see Sutton 2001, 185–220). It has also been noted, however, that many of the measures that make up this "legalization of the workplace" mainly serve to legitimize the firm in the eyes of its surrounding community, and that management carefully ensures that these new legal measures do not interfere with important interests in the firm. In Lauren

Edelman's (1992, 1567) formulation: "Organizations' structural responses to law mediate the impact of law on society by helping to construct the meaning of compliance in a way that accommodates managerial interests."

Some interesting sociological studies have been carried out on *corporate crime*—when firms break the law as well as when employees engage in criminal activities. Policing the stock exchange is an important and difficult task, given the enormous values that are at stake and the temptations it poses for the individual (Shapiro 1984; cf. Zey 1993; Abolafia 1996). While insider crimes and embezzlement are fairly straightforward phenomena from a conceptual viewpoint, this is much less the case with whistle-blowing and organizational crimes. Enormous pressure is put on any single employee who dares to publicly challenge a firm for some wrongdoing (Miceli and Near 1991). One example of organizational crime—criminal behavior that benefits the firm but not necessarily the individual—is price-fixing, which is common in all industrial countries and involves enormous amounts. In a recent study of price-fixing, it has been shown that the social structure of secret cartels lends itself very well to networks analysis (Baker and Faulkner 1993). Price-fixing of standard products (switchgear and transformers) typically leads to decentralized networks, this study shows, since little direction is needed from above; the opposite is true for more complex products (turbines). The more links there are to an actor in a price-fixing network, the larger the risk that he or she will be found out.

One form of economic legislation that has been studied quite a bit by sociologists is *bankruptcy*. Research on personal bankruptcies has been conducted in the United States for more than a decade, and one of the findings is that during the 1977 to 1999 period bankruptcies increased more than 400 percent and often involved middle-class people (Sullivan, Warren, and Westbrook 1989, 2000). Also growing in number, however, are studies of corporate bankruptcies. The most important of these, *Rescuing Business* by Bruce Carruthers and Terence Halliday (1998), is a comparative study of the 1978 U.S. Bankruptcy Code and the English Insolvency Act of 1986 (see also Carruthers and Halliday 2000). According to the authors, research on law and society has failed to understand that legal professionals play a role not only in interpreting the law but also in shaping how it is changed and reformed. They also argue that when a firm fails in the United States, the law favors attempts at reorganization rather than liquidation (as in England).

Conclusion

Although it is clear that a beginning has been made to developing an economic sociology of law, it is equally clear that most of the work remains to be done. Much better knowledge, for example, is needed about the basic legal institutions of capitalism that have been touched on in this article (such as property, the contract, inheritance, and so on). The innovative idea of the corporation as a creator of law needs to be better fleshed out, and research could also focus on other issues in economic life besides employment discrimination. The general dilemma of how legislation tries to catch up with the rapid pace of innovations in modern capitalism—say, in the financial sector—has not been given the attention it deserves. Moreover, the legal dimension of the process of globalization needs to be much better understood. Although some studies have been made of international arbitration (Dezalay and Garth 1996), there is, for example, the issue of legal implants in the economic sphere—how models of antitrust legislation, bankruptcy law, and commercial legislation more generally are spread from the powerful countries to countries that are trying to catch up economically. And as always in economic sociology, much more attention should be paid to the gender issue.

Finally, there is also a need to better understand the concept of legal institutions and the relationship of this type of institution to political institutions. The role that coercion plays in the definition of law has been much discussed, for example, and coercion also plays a central role in Weber's definition of law as a set of conventions enforced by a staff. We generally adhere to conventions themselves, however, on a voluntary basis, and this dimension of law has been considerably less theorized in sociology. When it comes to law and the economy, for example, it would be interesting to know more about what may be termed the legitimation of economic inequality— that is, why and to what extent people are willing to put up with huge economic inequalities—and how this issue is related to the norms of economic justice.

It also seems to me that the role played by *interests* in the structure of institutions—both political and legal—has been greatly underemphasized in contemporary sociology. The central role played by interests in the basic structure of society is well understood by the classics (such as Tocqueville, Marx, and Weber), and some inspiration can be had from this source. There is in fact already a tradition in legal thought of looking at the role of interests (Jhering 1872/1915; Pound 1920; Schoch 1948). Drawing on these various sources, I would suggest that interests help to lock in, to defend, and to legitimize various types of institutions, including legal institutions (Swedberg 2003). Using the concept of interest, in all brevity, may be useful in breathing new life into a study of legal institutions that looks at the role these play in the economy and how they are related to political institutions.

Notes

1. Some of the material in this chapter can also be found in Swedberg (2003a).
2. It can also be added that the legal historian Willard Hurst would later develop ideas that are parallel to those of Weber about the way that the law enables economic actions and helps modern capitalism along (see also North and Thomas

1973). According to Hurst, American law played this role especially during the nineteenth century when it helped "the release of [economic] energy," to cite Hurst's famous phrase (see, for example, Hurst 1956, 1964; for an introduction to Hurst, see Novak 2000). Hurst himself has characterized his work as "legal economic history" and "law and the economy" (see especially Hurst 1981, 43–53).

3. The work of Avner Greif, on the other hand, is characterized by a judicious mixture of game-theoretical arguments and historical data; see Greif (1989, 1993, forthcoming).

4. The early law and economics literature is radically economic and nonsociological in nature; see, for example, Posner (1998), Coase (1960), and Mercuro and Medema (1997). Recent work, however, is closer to sociology and in some areas ahead of sociology; for the former, see Ellickson (1991), and for the latter, see La Porta et al. (1998).

References

Abolafia, Mitchel Y. 1996. *Making Markets: Opportunism and Restraint on Wall Street.* Cambridge, Mass.: Harvard University Press.

Baker, Wayne, and Robert Faulkner. 1993. "The Social Organization of Conspiracy: Illegal Networks in the Heavy Electrical Equipment Industry." *American Sociological Review* 58(6): 837–60.

Beckert, Jens. Forthcoming. *Negotiated Modernity: Inheritance in France, Germany, and the United States Since 1800.* Berlin: Campus Press.

Berman, Harold J. 1983. *Law and Revolution: The Formation of the Western Legal Tradition.* Cambridge, Mass.: Harvard University Press.

Campbell, John, and Leon Lindberg. 1990. "Property Rights and the Organization of Economic Activity by the State." *American Sociological Review* 55(5): 634–47.

Carruthers, Bruce, and Terence Halliday. 1998. *Rescuing Business: The Making of Corporate Bankruptcy Law in England and the United States.* Oxford: Clarendon Press.

———. 2000. "Professionals in Systemic Reform of Bankruptcy Law: The 1978 U.S. Bankruptcy Code and the English Insolvency Act of 1986." *American Bankruptcy Law Journal* 74(Winter): 35–75.

Coase, Ronald H. 1960. "The Problem of Social Cost." *Journal of Law and Economics* 3(October): 1–44.

Coleman, James. 1974. *Power and the Structure of Society.* New York: W. W. Norton.

———. 1982. *The Asymmetric Society.* Syracuse, N.Y.: Syracuse University Press.

———. 1990. *Foundations of Social Theory.* Cambridge, Mass.: Harvard University Press.

———. 1993. "The Rational Reconstruction of Society." *American Sociological Review* 58(1): 1–15.

Cotterrell, Roger B. 1999. *Émile Durkheim: Law in a Moral Domain.* Stanford, Calif.: Stanford University Press.

Demsetz, Harold. 1982. *Economic, Legal, and Political Dimensions of Competition.* Amsterdam: North-Holland.

Dezalay, Yves, and Bryant Garth. 1996. *Dealing in Virtue: International Commercial Arbitration and the Construction of a Transnational Legal Order.* Chicago: University of Chicago Press.

Dobbin, Frank, and John Sutton. 1998. "The Strength of a Weak State: The Rights Revolution and the Rise of Human Resources Management Division." *American Journal of Sociology* 104(2): 441–76.

Durkheim, Émile. 1893/1933. *The Division of Labor in Society,* translated by George Simpson. Glencoe, Ill.: Free Press.

———. 1950/1983. *Professional Ethics and Civic Morals.* Westport, Conn.: Greenwood Press.

Edelman, Lauren. 1990. "Legal Environments and Organizational Governance: The Expansion of Due Process in the American Workplace." *American Journal of Sociology* 95(6): 1401–40.

———. 1992. "Legal Ambiguity and Symbolic Structures: Organizational Mediation of Civil Rights." *American Journal of Sociology* 97(6): 1531–76.

Edelman, Lauren, and Robin Stryker. Forthcoming. "Law and the Economy." In *The Handbook of Economic Sociology,* 2nd ed., edited by Neil Smelser and Richard Swedberg. New York and Princeton, N.J.: Russell Sage Foundation and Princeton University Press.

Edelman, Lauren, and Mark Suchman. 1997. "The Legal Environments of Organizations." *Annual Review of Sociology* 23: 479–515.

Ellickson, Robert. 1991. *Order Without Law: How Neighbors Settle Disputes.* Cambridge, Mass.: Harvard University Press.

Fligstein, Neil. 1990. *The Transformation of Corporate Control.* Cambridge, Mass.: Harvard University Press.

Friedman, Lawrence. 1985. *A History of American Law.* 2nd ed. New York: Simon & Schuster.

Goldschmidt, Levin. 1891/1957. *Universalgeschichte des Handelsrechts.* Stuttgart: Verlag von Ferdinand Enke.

Gouldner, Alvin. 1970. *The Coming Crisis of Western Sociology.* New York: Avon.

Greif, Avner. 1989. "Reputation and Coalitions in Medieval Trade: Evidence on the Maghribi Traders." *Journal of Economic History* 49(4): 857–82.

———. 1993. "Contract Enforceability and Economic Institutions in Early Trade: The Maghribi Traders' Coalition." *American Economic Review* 83: 525–48.

———. Forthcoming. *Institutions: Theory and History.* Cambridge: Cambridge University Press.

Hanley, Eric, Lawrence King, and Janos Istvan Toth. 2002. "Path Dependence or Structural Autonomy? The State, International Agencies, and Property Transformation in Post-Communist Hungary." *American Journal of Sociology* 108: 129–67.

Harris, Ron. 2000. *Industrializing English Law: Entrepreneurship and Business Organization, 1720 to 1844.* Cambridge: Cambridge University Press.

Heimer, Carol. 1985. *Reactive Risk and Rational Action: Managing Moral Hazard in Insurance Contracts.* Berkeley: University of California Press.

Horwitz, Morton. 1992. "Santa Clara Revisited: The Development of Corporate Theory." In *The Transformation of American Law, 1870–1960: The Crisis of Legal Orthodoxy.* New York: Oxford University Press.

Hurst, James Willard. 1956. *Land and the Condition of Freedom in the Nineteenth Century*. Madison: University of Wisconsin Press.

———. 1964. *Law and Economic Growth: The Legal History of the Lumber Industry in Wisconsin 1836 to 1915*. Cambridge, Mass.: The Belknap Press of Harvard University Press.

———. 1981. "J. Willard Hurst: An Interview Conducted by Laura L. Small." Madison: University of Wisconsin, University Archives Oral History Project.

Jhering, Rudolf von. 1872/1915. *The Struggle for Law*. 2nd ed. Chicago: Callaghan.

Kelly, Erin, and Frank Dobbin. 1999. "Civil Rights Law at Work: Sex Discrimination and the Rise of Maternity Leave Policies." *American Journal of Sociology* 105(2): 455–92.

La Porta, Rafael, Florencio Lopez-de-Silanes, Andrei Shleifer, and Robert W. Vishny. 1998. "Law and Finance." *Journal of Political Economy* 106(6): 1113–55.

Lopez, Robert. 1976. *The Commercial Revolution of the Middle Ages, 950 to 1350*. Cambridge: Cambridge University Press.

Macaulay, Stewart. 1963. "Noncontractual Relations in Business: A Preliminary Study" *American Sociological Review* 28(1, February): 55–67.

———. 1977. "Elegant Models, Empirical Pictures, and the Complexities of Contract." *Law and Society Review* 11: 507–28.

Marx, Karl. 1867/1906. *Capital: A Critique of Political Economy*. New York: Modern Library.

McNamee, Stephen, and Robert Miller. 1989. "Estate Inheritance: A Sociological Lacunae." *Sociological Inquiry* 59(Winter): 7–29.

Mercuro, Nicholas, and Steven Medema. 1997. *Economics and the Law: From Posner to Postmodernism*. Princeton, N.J.: Princeton University Press.

Merton, Robert K. 1935. "Fluctuations in the Rate of Industrial Invention." *Quarterly Journal of Economics* 49(3, May): 454–74.

———. 1973. *The Sociology of Science*. Chicago: University of Chicago Press.

Miceli, Marcia, and James Near. 1991. "Whistle-blowing as an Organizational Process." *Research in the Sociology of Organization* 9: 139–200.

Milgrom, Paul, Douglass North, and Barry Weingast. 1990. "The Role of Institutions in the Revival of Trade: The Law Merchant, Private Judges, and the Champagne Fairs." *Economics and Politics* 2(1): 23.

Nelson, Robert, and William Bridges. 1999. *Legalizing Gender Inequality: Courts, Markets, and Unequal Pay for Women in America*. Cambridge: Cambridge University Press.

North, Douglass, and Robert Thomas. 1973. *The Rise of the Western World*. Cambridge: Cambridge University Press.

Novak, William. 2000. "Law, Capitalism, and the Liberal State: The Historical Sociology of James Willard Hurst." *Law and History Review* 18(1): 97–145.

Oi, Jean, and Andrew Walder, eds. 1999. *Property Rights and Economic Reform in China*. Stanford, Calif.: Stanford University Press.

Parsons, Talcott. 1947. "Weber's 'Economic Sociology.' " In Max Weber, *The Theory of Social and Economic Organization,* edited by Talcott Parsons. New York: Oxford University Press.

Posner, Richard. 1998. *Economic Analysis of Law*. 5th ed. Boston: Little, Brown.

Pound, Roscoe. 1920. "A Theory of Social Interests." *Papers and Proceedings of the American Sociological Society* 15: 17–45.

Schoch, Magdalena, ed. 1948. *The Jurisprudence of Interests.* Cambridge, Mass.: Harvard University Press.

Schwartz, T. P. 1996. "Durkheim's Prediction About the Declining Importance of the Family and Inheritance: Evidence from the Wills of Providence, 1775 to 1985." *Sociological Quarterly* 37(3, Summer): 503–19.

Shapiro, Susan. 1984. *Wayward Capitalists: Target of the Security and Exchange Commission.* New Haven: Yale University Press.

Stark, David. 1996. "Recombinant Property in East European Capitalism." *American Journal of Sociology* 101(4): 993–1027.

Stinchcombe, Arthur. 1985. "Contracts as Hierarchical Documents." In *Organization Theory and Project Management,* edited by Arthur Stinchcombe and Carol Heimer. Oslo: Norwegian University Press.

Streeck, Wolfgang. 1992. *Social Institutions and Economic Performance: Studies of Industrial Relations in Advanced Capitalist Societies.* Newbury Park, Calif.: Sage Publications.

Stryker, Robin. Forthcoming. "Mind the Gap: Law, Institutional Analysis, and Socioeconomics." *Socioeconomic Review.*

Suchman, Mark. 1985. "On Advice of Counsel: Law Firms and Venture Capital Funds as Information Intermediaries in the Structuration of Silicon Valley." Ph.D. diss., Stanford University.

———. 2000. "Dealmakers and Counselors: Law Firms as Intermediaries in the Development of Silicon Valley." In *Understanding Silicon Valley: The Anatomy of an Entrepreneurial Region,* edited by Martin Kenney. Stanford, Calif.: Stanford University Press.

Sullivan, Teresa, Elizabeth Warren, and Jay Lawrence Westbrook. 1989. *As We Forgive Our Debtors: Bankruptcy and Consumer Credit in America.* New York: Oxford University Press.

———. 2000. *The Fragile Middle Class: Americans in Debt.* New Haven, Conn.: Yale University Press.

Sutton, John. 2001. *Law/Society: Origins, Interactions, and Change.* Thousand Oaks, Calif.: Pine Forge Press.

Sutton, John, Frank Dobbin, John Meyer, and Richard Scott. 1994. "The Legalization of the Workplace." *American Journal of Sociology* 99(4): 944–71.

Swedberg, Richard. 1998. *Max Weber and the Idea of Economic Sociology.* Princeton, N.J.: Princeton University Press.

———. 2003a. "The Case for an Economic Sociology of Law." *Theory and Society* 32(1): 1–37.

———. 2003b. *Fundamental Principles of Economic Sociology.* Princeton, N.J.: Princeton University Press.

Tocqueville, Alexis de. 1835–40/1945. *Democracy in America,* translated by Henry Reeve. 2 vols. New York: Vintage Books.

Veblen, Thorstein. 1898. "The Beginnings of Ownership." *American Journal of Sociology* 4(3, November): 352–65.

Walder, Andrew. 1992. "Property Rights and Stratification in Socialist Redistributive Economies." *American Sociological Review* 57(4): 524–39.

Weber, Max. 1889/2002. *The History of Commercial Partnerships in the Middle Ages.* New York: Rowman & Littlefield.

———. 1891/1986. *Die römische Agrargeschichte in ihrer Bedeutung für das Staatsrechtund Privatrecht. Max Weber Gesamtausgabe I/2.* Tübingen: J. C. B. Mohr.

———. 1922/1978. *Economy and Society: An Outline of Interpretive Sociology.* 2 vols. Berkeley: University of California Press.

———. 1923/1981. *General Economic History.* New Brunswick, N.J.: Transaction Books.

Williamson, Oliver. 1975. *Markets and Hierarchies: Analysis and Antitrust Implications.* New York: The Free Press.

Zey, Mary. 1993. *Banking on Fraud: Drexel, Junk Bonds, and Buyouts.* New York: Aldine de Gruyter.

Zuckerman, Harriet. 1988. "Introduction: Intellectual Property and Diverse Rights of Ownership in Science." *Science, Technology, and Human Values* 13(Winter and Spring): 7–16.

Part II

HOW ECONOMIC MODELS SHAPE MARKETS

5

THE GLOBALIZATION OF AMERICAN BANKING, 1962 TO 1981

Mark S. Mizruchi and Gerald F. Davis

THE ONGOING debates over globalization highlight the inextricable link between political economy, finance, and the management of corporations. From the ongoing protests at meetings of the World Trade Organization (WTO) to governmental interventions in cross-border hostile takeovers in Europe, politics and the governance and management of corporations are intertwined. At the center of this nexus are capital flows and the ways in which they are channeled. The 1990s witnessed an enormous expansion of financial flows around the globe, from trade in currencies to cross-border investments in domestic corporations. Enabled by information technology, upwards of $1.5 trillion flows across borders daily, far outstripping the nominal value of trade flows. The much-heralded triumph of markets is in many ways the triumph of *financial* markets as a means of allocating capital. The consequences for local economies can be substantial, from the management of the currency supply to traditional understandings of the purpose of the corporation.

In this chapter, we seek to unpack a particular aspect of financial globalization—the expansion (and contraction) of American commercial banks through locating (and closing) branches abroad. There are many ways for American businesses to operate outside U.S. borders, but bank branching is a particularly significant form of global expansion. First, banks are unlike other businesses in what they make and sell and in the breadth of consequences of their actions. In principle, banks can make capital from wealthy countries available for businesses in low-income countries with limited indigenous savings, thus jump-starting economic development (McMichael 1996). They can also serve as templates for the practices of well-regulated financial institutions, transferring economically useful know-how as well as capital (World Bank 1997). Second, branches represent a substantial commitment by the bank to the host nation. Where industrial companies might set up local subsidiaries that are separated from the parent company by a legal firewall, branches have neither a separate legal personality nor their own assets and liabilities. Rather, the branch is legally part of its American parent, and its officers are officers of the parent bank (Robinson 1972).

Examining banks' choices to go international also allows us to assess the fruitfulness of studying globalization at a disaggregated level. Cross-border financial flows implicate political choices as well as organizational decisions. Historically, American banks faced strict limits on the geography of branching and on the range of industries they could enter at home (Roe 1994), and regulations both constrained and enabled banks' foreign operations. But banks did not respond to regulatory changes in identical ways: they varied enormously in where and to what extent they chose to open foreign branches.

> The social-organizational approach depends upon political economy to explain the frameworks in which economic action proceeds, the rules and legal systems that constitute such objects as firms and markets, and the pressure to which the accumulation process subjects owners and managers. At the same time, political-economic analysis requires models of the forms of social organization that mediate the effects of macroscopic processes, and cause variation in their consequences at the level of industries and national economies. (Zukin and DiMaggio 1990, 3)

In this chapter, we focus on the latter process. We argue that globalization is usefully seen as an organizational phenomenon, enacted (or resisted) by organizations and their decisionmakers. It is thus susceptible to organizational analysis.

By taking an organizational approach, we draw on two prominent perspectives within the new economic sociology: social network analysis and neo-institutional theory. We use network theory to argue that the banks' positions within interfirm social structures influenced their decisions to open overseas branches. We use neo-institutional theory to argue that as the process evolved, the opening of overseas branches came to be defined as an appropriate strategy within the community of large U.S. banks. We suggest that this new definition of expected behavior played a role in the diffusion of foreign branches: bank officials observed their peers engaging in the practice and subsequently followed suit.

In focusing on the role of networks and socially accepted behaviors, we touch on themes raised by several of the other chapters in this volume. William Schneper and Mauro Guillén, for example, show that the practice of hostile takeovers diffused from the United States to other countries after its inception in the 1970s, but that it became widespread only in nations in which the state had defined such practices as legitimate, through the institution of regulations that emphasized the rights of shareholders as opposed to workers or the larger public. Karin Knorr Cetina and Urs Bruegger document the development of norms among international currency traders. They show that these norms developed in part as traders observed and mimicked the behavior of those they defined as peers. Heather Haveman and Lisa Keister, in their study of California banks, find that banks performed best when they were able to distinguish themselves (in terms of the services they provided) from their direct competitors. This raises an issue that informs the larger study of which our chapter is a part: To what extent does interfirm influence lead firms to mimic their peers rather than try to distinguish themselves from them? In this chapter, we focus on direct mimicry by examining banks that followed their peers into foreign branching. In subsequent work, we plan to focus on banks' specific locational decisions by examining the extent to which banks open branches in countries distinct from those of their peers as a means of identifying a unique niche.

We begin by describing the theoretical background on banking and globalization, both at the macro level of Lenin and Braudel and at the micro level of social network analysis and neo-institutional theory. We then give a précis of the history of U.S. banks abroad during the twentieth century, focusing on the expansion period of the late 1960s and 1970s. We describe some of the policy changes that altered the context for global banking, as well as the Third World debt crisis that began in 1982 and radically altered the desirability of overseas expansion by banks. We analyze data on all foreign branch openings by the fifty largest U.S. commercial banks from roughly 1960 until 1999, linking the timing, intensity, and locational choices of the banks to their network ties to large U.S. corporations that were themselves globalizing. We find that the heyday of American bank globalization peaked in the late 1970s and that—with a very small number of exceptions—U.S. commercial banking has returned to being a resolutely domestic business, in sharp contrast to both investment banking and the broader sweep of American industry. The proportion of U.S. banks that do *any* commercial lending outside the United States is minuscule; one bank—Citibank—now holds over 40 percent of all corporate loans outside the country. We conclude with a discussion of the appropriate forms of analysis of financial globalization.

The Place of Banks in the Project of Globalization

The power and influence of "international bankers" has fascinated theorists from V. I. Lenin to Pat Robertson. In *Imperialism: The Highest Stage of Capitalism,* Lenin (1916/1939, 40–41) described the trajectory of haute finance within the major capitalist economies, in which banks became increasingly concentrated and ultimately formed a "bank trust" with significant power over the national economy. In the United States, he argued, two banks (those of Rockefeller and Morgan) predominated. Moreover, the business of banks under monopoly capitalism became increasingly international, and nations came to focus less on the export of goods than on the export of capital; thus did Britain transform itself from an industrial state to a "rentier state." For Lenin, this system of capitalist imperialism was unsustainable—finance capitalism was "moribund capitalism" bent on expansionist aggression (126). Karl Polanyi (1944/1957, 13–16) argued instead that representatives of haute finance were responsible for maintaining the peace, at least among the Great Powers, while Fernand Braudel (1984, 246) echoed Lenin's assessment, finding that significant expansion of foreign lending was a "sign of autumn" for global hegemons.

In their ambitious effort to assess regularities in hegemonic transitions in the world system, Giovanni Arrighi and Beverly Silver (1999) assert that the transitions from Dutch to British hegemony and the transition from British to American hegemony share underlying patterns that allow us to understand the (evidently forthcoming) end of American hegemony. Their conclusion is stark:

> The global financial expansion of the last 20 years or so is neither a new stage of world capitalism nor the harbinger of a "coming hegemony of global markets." Rather, it is the clearest sign that we are in the midst of a hegemonic crisis. As such, the expansion can be expected to be a temporary phenomenon that will end more or less catastrophically, depending on how the crisis is handled by the declining hegemon. (Arrighi and Silver 1999, 259)

Financial expansion, by this account, increases the power of "finance capital" with respect to states, generates interstate competition, and brings about "massive, systemwide redistributions of income and wealth from all kinds of communities to the agencies that control mobile capital" (259). But what exactly are these "agencies that control mobile capital"?

Discussions of financial power in the global economy often obscure the identities of the relevant operators. Peter Gowan (1999, 26), for instance, refers to "Wall Street" as synonymous with American private banking (including, for example, "the big, internationally-oriented U.S. money-centre banks"). But money-center banks and other commercial banks in the United States have historically been quite idiosyncratic, both in their local orientation and in their constrained ability to serve corporate clients. (They could make loans but not underwrite securities.) Nationally chartered banks could not open foreign branches until 1913 (although state-chartered banks could), and banks were restricted to within-state domestic branching until quite recently. A strong current of populist mistrust toward concentrated economic power left the United States with a far more fragmented banking industry than any other industrialized nation (Roe 1994). As a result, with the exception of a handful of money-center banks, large U.S. banks were relatively small by world standards through the first half of the twentieth century and overwhelmingly oriented toward local and regional businesses. This was reflected in their boards of directors, which were typically composed of prominent local businessmen (Mills 1956; Davis and Mizruchi 1999). "Wall Street" seems an inapt label for the geographically dispersed, highly localized business that was American commercial banking at midcentury. Yet by 1980 there were 150 American banks with foreign branches, spread across most of the globe. Virtually every major bank had branches in London and elsewhere. Something changed to draw Main Street to Bond Street.

We argue that a fruitful way to make sense of the contemporary process of financial globalization is to understand what large banks did when they expanded overseas, and why. To the extent that there are identifiable "agencies" controlling cross-national capital mobility, large commercial banks are among the most important. One indication of this is the composition of cross-border capital flows, particularly to low-income countries. Commercial bank lending was the overwhelming source of private capital flows to developing countries by the early 1980s (World Bank 1997, 14), and from 1970 to 1980 bank loans increased their share of Third World debt from 13 percent to 60 percent (McMichael 1996, 117). Banks during this period increasingly replaced states and multilateral aid agencies as sources of capital for both states and businesses in developing countries (for a historical perspective, see Manzocchi 1999). Thus, "by becoming truly international actors, banks have entered as full participants into the realm of foreign policy" (Cohen 1986, 56).

We seek to unpack the mechanisms by which domestic commercial banks came to be "truly international actors" during the 1960s and 1970s. Organizational decisions—the strategies followed by banks—are the micro components of financial globalization. The strategies followed by banks are in turn under the guidance of their top managers and boards of directors—typically local members of the corporate elite. Thus, we try to make sense of these decisions as a way to link the local economy to financial globalization (Sassen 1994).

American Commercial Banks Abroad

By the standards that apply to a global power, American commercial banks in 1960 were remarkably provincial. Only eight U.S. banks had *any* overseas branches, and most of these branches were owned by one bank, First National City Bank (the predecessor to Citibank; see Brimmer 1973). The modest international presence of American banks at this time was comparable to the situation in 1920 and had changed relatively little since the period just after the Second World War. In contrast to Great Britain, whose banks were allowed substantial leeway in international operations for many decades, U.S. national banks were allowed to establish branches outside the United States only with the Federal Reserve Act of 1913 (Brimmer and Dahl 1975, 342–43). Moreover, the fact that only eight of the several thousand U.S. banks in 1960 had any foreign operations contrasts sharply with other industries in the United

States. In the mid-1960s, American manufacturers were well on their way to being multinational enterprises: IBM had operations in 81 nations, Singer was in 64, and Mobil, Exxon, and Texaco were each in dozens. Among the 389 large manufacturers that shared a director with a major bank in 1966, the median firm operated in three nations outside the United States, and over 70 percent had at least some international operations (*Directory of American Firms Operating in Foreign Countries* 1966).

American banks can do business outside the United States in a number of forms. A U.S. bank can rely on a local bank in a foreign country to act as its agent, that is, as a correspondent bank. It can open a representative office to handle the local affairs of the U.S. bank's clients, but it cannot perform "banking" (taking deposits, making loans). It can take an equity stake in a local bank. It can acquire or establish a subsidiary in the local country—the pattern most frequently followed by industrial firms. Or it can open a branch, which is legally part of the parent bank and books its business on the parent's balance sheet (for a discussion of these alternatives, see Robinson 1972). A branch is the most consequential local presence a bank can have in another country, since it has essentially the same status as a domestic branch. That is, it can take deposits that may be used elsewhere in the bank, and it can make loans relying on the parent company's capital. Both of these functions can provide a motive for overseas expansion by U.S. banks. A branch (in contrast to a subsidiary) can be used to gather Eurodollars (U.S. currency held in banks outside the United States, typically generated through foreign trade) to be recycled through lending to domestic businesses in the United States. Branches can also make loans, whether to American corporations doing business overseas, local businesses, or sovereign states.

Although few U.S. banks had international operations in 1960, during the subsequent twenty years the foreign assets of U.S. banks increased one-hundredfold, and the number of banks operating branches outside the United States increased from 8 to 150 (Hallow 1993). By this time, Citicorp operated branches in 93 countries, BankAmerica had branches in roughly 50 nations, and American banking was a truly global industry. National Bank of Detroit was in Germany, Japan, and London. Harris Bank of Chicago was in Brazil, France, Mexico, and Singapore. North Carolina National Bank was in Australia and the Cayman Islands. In short, during the 1960s and 1970s banking began to catch up with the rest of American industry. But why then, and not before? And what accounts for the wide variation in the patterns of expansion of U.S. banks?

In outline form, U.S. banks went international owing to a combination of institutional and regulatory changes and because of the increasing internationalization of their domestic corporate customers. Perhaps the most significant regulatory change was the Voluntary Foreign Credit Restraint (VFCR) policy enacted by the Johnson administration in early 1965. For several years the United States had run a substantial balance-of-payments deficit, exporting more capital than it earned. Johnson sought to remedy this by restricting the flow of foreign direct investment by U.S.-based multinationals and limiting foreign lending by commercial banks. VFCR guidelines, issued by the Federal Reserve Board in March 1965, sought to restrict the growth of foreign lending to 5 percent per year (Brimmer and Dahl 1975; Dombrowski 1996, 46). Crucially, foreign branches of U.S. banks were exempt from these restrictions. Thus, branches outside the United States served two essential functions: London branches (and later branches in the Bahamas and Cayman Islands) could gather deposits to be lent in the United States, while other international branches could be used to make loans outside the purview of the VFCR. The VFCR "encouraged the establishment of an institutional structure abroad that would enable American banks to undertake a major and permanent commitment to overseas markets" (Hallow 1993, 84).

Once in place, the international branch network proved useful as a mechanism to recycle the "petrodollars" generated as a result of the steep rise in oil prices following the 1973 energy crisis. As integral parts of the parent bank, foreign branches could in principle take in dollar-denominated deposits in Bahrain and lend them in Brazil (although other forms of intermediation were also possible). Bank lending came increasingly to replace official sources of development aid during the 1970s (Manzocchi 1999, 56), and the largest banks found foreign business to be their primary source of profit growth. By 1976, 49 percent of the profits of the twelve major multinational banks came from international operations; for Chase Manhattan the figure was 78 percent (Hallow 1993, 95).

The two decades after 1980 saw, if not a complete reversal, then at least a substantial attenuation of the trend toward bank branch globalization. In December 1981 the Federal Reserve authorized the creation of international banking facilities, which were essentially "virtual branches" of U.S. banks able to book foreign deposits and loans as if they were transacted with an offshore branch. This allowed banks to participate in the Eurodollar market without having to establish "real" branches in London or shell branches in the Bahamas or Cayman Islands. Of more long-lasting significance was the Mexican debt crisis of 1982, which began when Mexico suspended its external debt service and nearly every debtor nation in Latin America and Africa ended up effectively in default. The consequences of this crisis are still widely felt in low-income countries in the form of IMF structural adjustment programs and other interventions, but the most immediate consequence for the banks was an immediate contraction in their overseas lending and a lingering malaise on their balance sheets. Figure 5.1 shows the cumulative number of nations in which the fifty largest U.S. banks operated for each year between 1963 and 1998. As the figure indicates, the year 1978 was the high-water mark for American banks' international activities.

FIGURE 5.1   *Foreign Branches of the Largest Fifty U.S. Banks, 1963 to 1998*

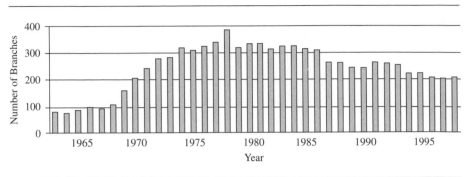

Year

Source: Authors' compilation.

Commercial banks faced their own form of structural adjustment at home during the 1980s and 1990s as market-based forms of funding increasingly took over their core business of corporate lending. As we have documented elsewhere (Davis and Mizruchi 1999), large banks substantially retreated from domestic corporate lending during this time, turning increasingly to fee-based businesses and other nontraditional activities. Some (notably JPMorgan and Bankers Trust) effectively abandoned commercial banking and morphed into investment banks. Those that maintained significant foreign lending were battered the hardest: Congressman John Dingell of Michigan, chair of the House Committee on Energy and Commerce, stated in 1991 that Citicorp (the most "international" of American banks) was "technically insolvent" and "struggling to survive" (*Business Week Online* 1995). Banks with the highest exposure to foreign loans were those with the most unfavorable stock market valuations. At the same time, the number of nations with stock exchanges doubled, and portfolio investment (primarily purchases of stocks and bonds by institutional investors) and foreign direct investment (investment by foreign businesses) increasingly replaced bank lending as the predominant forms of capital flows from wealthy nations to low-income nations (World Bank 1997; Weber and Davis 2002). Banks availed themselves of other new opportunities after 1989 as former Communist nations formed markets for U.S. banks. But the basic business model of commercial banks—taking in deposits and lending them out at higher rates of interest—had been largely superseded both at home and abroad, in wealthy nations as well as low-income countries. As Norwest CEO Dick Kovacevich put it, "The banking industry is dead, and we ought to just bury it" (Pare 1995).

The net result of these trends is that U.S. banking has returned from a substantial international presence to an overwhelmingly domestic business, while at the same time "financial markets have been transformed . . . from relatively insulated and regulated national markets toward a more globally integrated market" (World Bank 1997, 14; Knorr Cetina and Bruegger, this volume). There were 129 U.S.-owned banks with 737 foreign branches in 1975. By 2001 only 30 of the more than 2,500 U.S.-owned bank holding companies operated any branches outside the United States, while 38 had international banking facilities. Of the 824 foreign branches, more than half (413) were owned by Citibank, while the foreign presence of Chase Manhattan (successor to Manufacturers Hanover, Chemical Bank, JPMorgan, and the original Chase) and Bank of America (the successor to NationsBank and the original BankAmerica) were substantially attenuated compared with 1975. For American banks, international business lending is almost entirely the province of three organizations, and international business lending is a relatively modest part of global capital flows. Again, this contrasts sharply with the trends in other industries: for the median Fortune 500 manufacturer, the proportion of revenues accounted for by international business steadily increased, from under 15 percent to about 25 percent between 1986 and 1999. It is possible that the "signs of autumn" for U.S. hegemony have actually heralded an Indian summer (Arrighi and Silver 1999).

Why Overseas Expansion?

In this chapter, we limit our attention to the expansion phase of U.S. overseas banking and leave a detailed account of its contraction to another paper. Sociologists and organizational theorists have done little theorizing on the reasons for overseas banking. Most writing on the topic has been done by economists, although sociologists of development have studied overseas economic expansion in general. In addition to the fact that the topic received little publicity until recently, one reason that sociologists have not addressed overseas banking may be that the reasons provided by economists have been plausible, straightforward, and largely intuitive—exactly the kind of explanations that sociologists would tend to find uninteresting and unworthy of study. Of the several accounts that have been proposed (Baker and Bradford 1974; Darby 1986; Dombrowski 1996; Hallow 1993; Peter Merrill Associates 1981), most focus on the reactions of banks to U.S. government regulations that placed restrictions on their activities, the incentives provided by foreign countries, or banks' general attempts to increase profitability by diversifying risk. Michael Darby (1986, 405) asserts, for example, that "the onset of American banks' foreign thrust can be attributed to avoidance of U.S. regulations." He goes on to cite "deposit interest ceilings, reserve requirements, and various capital controls." James Baker and Gerald Bradford (1974, 3) note the persistent U.S. balance-of-payments deficit during the 1960s and the economic opportunities resulting from the emergence of the European Economic Community (EEC).

Hallow (1993) notes the importance of regulations, such as the Interest Equalization Tax of 1963, which taxed the foreign stocks and debt obligations of American firms and individuals (Americans circumvented this by depositing their earnings overseas, which increased the demand for American banking in these locales), and the VFCR program, which was instituted on a voluntary basis in 1965 and made mandatory in 1970. (This program placed a limit on the amount that U.S. banks could lend overseas but exempted their overseas branches.) These arguments are difficult to test empirically. For one thing, even when these authors specify the particular regulations they believe triggered overseas activity, it is difficult to predict when their effects will occur. Did the banks respond immediately or within two, three, or four (or more) years? Second, even if these factors account for aggregate level increases in the number of U.S. banks operating abroad, they do not allow us to specify which particular banks opened overseas branches.

Another (related) argument suggested by Hallow (1993, 75) is that the imposition of tight monetary policy in the late 1960s, which restricted the amount of capital available to lend, led U.S. banks to rely increasingly on the Eurodollar market. In particular, Hallow notes, large U.S. banks circumvented the tight monetary policy by importing funds from their foreign branches. Although at first only the banks that already had overseas operations could take advantage of this, once other banks recognized the advantages of foreign branches, Hallow argues, they rapidly established their own. If this is the case, then we should witness increases in foreign branching in response to tight monetary policy, although again, the precise timing of the effect is difficult to predict.

The argument that U.S. banks went overseas in response to declining profits at home also contains problems. Virtually any action that firms take can be assumed to be an attempt to improve profitability. Highly profitable banks might be just as likely as less profitable ones to adopt a new strategy, on the ground that it would lead to even higher profits. It may therefore be difficult to predict an association between profitability and entry into foreign activity. Still, the hypothesis that banks moved overseas to compensate for declining profit opportunities at home is testable. If the argument is tenable, we would expect overseas branching to increase in response to low profitability and to be especially likely to occur during contraction periods in the economy.

A fourth argument, suggested by both Baker and Bradford (1974) and Hallow (1993), is both tenable and empirically testable, however. In this view, the proliferation of foreign banking was a response to the increased overseas activities of American banks' primary customers, large nonfinancial corporations. Banks were seen as moving overseas to accommodate the overseas moves of their corporate customers. American banks were uniquely suited to do this, in this view, because they had already established informal operating procedures based on continued personal contacts and the trust they entailed.

This ability to make use of personal contacts gave U.S. banks an advantage compared with banks in the host countries.

If this argument is correct, then banks that conducted business with corporations with high levels of overseas activity should be those most likely to open overseas branches. Systematic data on bank-customer relations in the 1960s are unavailable, so it is not possible to directly test this argument. An indirect test is possible, however. One indicator of a link between nonfinancial corporations and banks is the extent to which the firms share directors, in particular whether officers of one of the firms are represented on the board of the other. During the 1960s leading commercial banks were filled with CEOs of major nonfinancial corporations. Beth Mintz and Michael Schwartz (1985) suggest that this was a means by which banks gleaned information about conditions in various industries. If this account is accurate, one consequence would be that banks whose boards included officers of firms with high foreign involvement would be more likely to become involved themselves.

This suggests an organization-level mechanism for financial globalization, particularly for banks outside the major money centers. As we have seen, manufacturers were internationally active well before most banks, and American banks have historically been locally oriented, by regulation and custom, with boards comprising the notables of local industry. Thus, ties through boards of directors are plausible sources of influence for the international locational decisions of commercial banks and a way to link global and local economic decisions. We might expect that as Emerson Electric, Monsanto, and Ralston Purina expanded operations overseas, First National Bank in St. Louis—whose board contained executives from each of these three local businesses—would follow suit, and that St. Louis bankers might find themselves stationed at branches in Brazil, India, or Switzerland. Once in place, the branch network served as a circuit of capital as new contingencies arose, for example, following the oil crisis of 1973 (on linking cities and globalization see Sassen 1994).

It is possible that banks' decisions to move overseas were driven by other forces as well. Neo-institutional theorists have emphasized the socially constructed nature of much economic activity (Dobbin 1994; Fligstein 1990). Ideas about what constitute appropriate firm strategies often take on an independent existence, becoming defined as "appropriate" forms of behavior even when evidence of their effectiveness is nonexistent or ambiguous. These ideas often diffuse through social networks among firms. In a study of the adoption of the takeover defense plans known as "poison pills," Gerald Davis (1991) finds that in addition to direct ties to prior adopters, firms that were centrally located in the interlock network were more likely to adopt these plans. Studies by Joseph Galaskiewicz and Ronald Burt (1991) and Mark Mizruchi (1992) show that being centrally located led firms to engage in behaviors that were dominant within the network. One possible reason for these findings is that centrally located actors are in a position to dictate prescribed forms of behavior. As new developments occur, central actors may be the first to adopt new behaviors—or if not the first, then most likely to have their behavior mimicked. This means that other organizations that are close to the center have a greater opportunity to be exposed to these prescribed behaviors, a process akin to what Michael Useem (1984) has termed "business scan."

The preceding suggests that being centrally located in interfirm social networks may have an independent effect on the adoption of a behavior that emanates from central organizations. Put another way, banks may learn where they should be doing business not so much from listening to their customers and advisers as from observing each other (White 1981). During the 1960s the most central firms in the U.S. corporate network were the leading New York commercial banks, in particular the six major money market banks, all of which were among the early participants in overseas banking. Roy Smith (1989, 35) contends that Walter Wriston at Citibank almost single-handedly brought about the globalization of U.S. banking through his example of aggressive overseas expansion: "Few individuals have influenced a whole industry as much as Wriston in getting all the others to follow him . . . in trying to escape the fate of being permanently just another dull company from a highly regulated business." Foreign banking, in other words, was a behavior that was endorsed by centrally located organizations. We therefore hypothesize that the closer a bank was to the center of the corporate network (that is, the higher its centrality), the more likely it was to open an overseas branch.

Data and Measures

The banks in our dataset were drawn from the Mathematical Analysis of Corporate Networks (MACNET) project at the State University of New York at Stony Brook under the direction of Michael Schwartz (see Mintz and Schwartz 1985, app. 1). This dataset includes information on ties among the boards of directors of over one thousand large American corporations during 1962, 1964, and 1966 and includes sixty-five commercial banks that were ranked among the fifty largest by *Fortune* magazine at least once between 1962 and 1973. After eliminating subsidiaries, we were left with a panel of fifty-four independent banks. We supplemented the director data with data drawn from various sources, primarily *Moody's Financial Manual* (annually from 1962 through 1999) for financial data and information on foreign bank branches, *Who Owns What in World Banking* (various years), and the *Directory of American Firms Operating in Foreign Countries* (various years) for information on overseas activity among the nonfinancial corporations whose officers sat on the boards of the banks. The financial data for our analyses came from Standard and Poor's COMPUSTAT files.

Our focus in this chapter is on the establishment and proliferation of overseas branches. We will focus on the specific location of these branches in a subsequent paper. We examine two dependent variables in the analyses that follow: the time to a bank's establishment of its first overseas branch, and the number of new branches that the bank established in a given year. Our analysis is informed by two factors noted earlier. First, only nine U.S. banks had foreign branches in 1962. Second, virtually all of the proliferation of overseas branching by U.S. banks had ended by 1980. We therefore focus on the forty-five banks in our dataset that were at risk of entering into foreign branching beginning in 1962. Missing data reduced the total number of banks to forty-one, thirty-three of which were at risk of opening their first foreign branches. We followed these thirty-three banks from 1963 through 1981 (that is, just prior to the Mexican debt crisis and the enabling of international banking facilities). The fact that we are omitting from our analysis the nine major banks that were previously involved in overseas activity creates the potential for sample selection bias. In an earlier analysis (Mizruchi and Davis 2000), we found, through an examination of a sample selection model, that the omission of these nine banks had no effect on the prediction of entry into foreign banking among the remaining forty-five banks. We therefore focus only on the latter here, although we do discuss the role of the original nine banks in our conclusion.

Our dependent variables were drawn from data on the overseas branches of U.S. banks available in yearly editions of *Moody's* and *Who Owns What in World Banking*. A team of six research assistants coded, by year and location, all non-U.S. branches of the fifty-four banks, beginning in 1962 and ending in 1999. We can group our hypotheses into two broad categories, based on those suggested by the economic literature and those consistent with organizational and sociological arguments. The former includes tests of the effects of regulation, profitability, and macroeconomic conditions. The latter involves those based on the foreign activities of the banks' interlock partners and the banks' network centrality. The effect of the foreign activities of the banks' interlock partners actually follows from both the economic and organizational literature, which suggest that the banks moved overseas to preserve their relations with their corporate customers.

One way to test the regulation arguments would be to examine a series of year dummy variables. There are two problems with this approach. First, as noted earlier, even though we can pinpoint our two key regulations in 1963 and 1965, it is difficult to predict the point at which their effects, if existent, were likely to emerge. Second, the use of year dummies makes it difficult to examine simultaneously the macroeconomic variables because they are year-specific. This means that it is necessary to examine the regulation hypotheses separately. Because the firm-level variables tend to be either highly stable over time (size and age, the latter of which varies consistently each year), measured at a single point in time (the director data), or uncorrelated with time, the most feasible way to test the regulation hypotheses is to examine a simple frequency count of the number of banks that opened their first foreign branch in each year.

To examine whether tight monetary policy led to an expansion of overseas banking, we examine two variables: the cost of AAA bonds and whether the Federal Reserve Bank was following a "tight" monetary policy. The effect of the condition of the economy is a dummy variable, coded one for years when the U.S. economy was in an expansion period and zero for years when it was in a contraction period. Monetary policy is a dummy variable, coded one when the Federal Reserve was following a "loose" policy and zero when it was following a tight policy. These data were derived from the National Bureau of Economic Research (NBER) and the *Federal Reserve Board Bulletin,* respectively. We used return on assets as our indicator of firm profitability. These data were derived from the COMPUSTAT files.

As we have already noted, we can test the hypothesis involving the foreign activities of the banks' customers only indirectly, by examining the foreign activities of their interlock partners. To address this, we coded a variable for the number of officers of companies conducting business overseas who sat on the board of the particular bank. We expect this variable to be positively associated with a bank's decision to open overseas branches. To test the centrality hypothesis, we examined the number of firms among nonbank members of the Fortune 800 (the sample of firms in the MACNET dataset) with which the bank shared directors. Although this is not the only possible measure of centrality, it has been found to be highly correlated with the commonly used eigenvector centrality measure developed by Phillip Bonacich (1987; see also Mizruchi and Bunting 1981). Although our analyses stretch from 1963 through 1980, we currently have full director data for only 1962, 1964, and 1966, and we use the 1966 data in our analyses. This is not ideal, but we believe that it is adequate for our purposes, for three reasons. First, Peter Mariolis and Maria Jones (1982) have shown that the interlock data from the MACNET dataset tend to be highly stable over time. Our own analysis indicates that the data from 1962 and 1966 yield virtually identical results. Second, although beyond a ten-year period there is likely to be some instability in centrality, major U.S. commercial banks remained highly central in interlock networks into the early 1980s (see table 5.1). Their centrality declined markedly in later years (Davis and Mizruchi 1999), but those years are beyond the scope of the current analysis. Most important, the vast majority of the banks in our sample had opened foreign branches well before 1980—twenty-seven of the thirty-three had done so by 1972, and thirty-one of the thirty-three by 1976. Despite these compensating factors, this measure is likely to yield a certain amount of error. Whatever error exists in our centrality measure is likely to render our results more conservative than they would be if we had

TABLE 5.1   *Ten Most Central Firms in the Interlock Network,*
1962, 1982, and 1999

1962	1982	1999
JPMorgan (56)	AT&T (43)	Chase Manhattan (34)
Chemical Bank (51)	JPMorgan (48)	Sara Lee (34)
Chase Manhattan (50)	Chase Manhattan (43)	American Express (32)
First National City Bank (47)	Citicorp (43)	Bell Atlantic (34)
Manufacturers Hanover (43)	IBM (38)	Ameritech (26)
Southern Pacific RR (38)	General Foods (31)	Xerox (29)
Ford Motor Co (34)	Chemical NY (38)	Lucent Techs (22)
AT&T (31)	Bankers Trust (39)	Cummins Engine (28)
Chrysler (28)	Manufacturers Hanover (36)	Ryder System (22)
Bankers Trust (41)	Mobil (28)	Procter & Gamble (26)

Source: Authors' compilation.
Notes: Rankings are based on Bonacich's (1972) eigenvector measure of point centrality, in which a node is more central if the nodes it is connected to are also central. Numbers in parentheses are counts of interlock ties.

interlock data for all of the years. We are therefore confident that any interlock effects we observe are unlikely to be overestimated.

In addition to our substantive predictors, we examined two control variables: the size of the bank (in assets, which we examined both in their raw value and in logarithms), and the age of the bank (in years). Because larger firms tend to be more heavily interlocked, it is possible that any observed effect of centrality could be a spurious consequence of size. The bank's age could have either a positive or a negative effect on its decision to move overseas. On the one hand, we would expect older banks to be more likely to have as customers the major firms with overseas operations. In that case, age would be positively associated with foreign branching. On the other hand, it is possible that younger banks would be more open to innovation and thus more likely to engage in new activities. In this case, age would be negatively associated with foreign branching. We suspect that the latter is unlikely, since the nine banks that were operating outside the United States before 1960 were among the oldest, most well-established U.S. institutions. Regardless of which view is correct (or if either is correct), we include the bank's age as a control.[1]

Estimation Procedure

Our dependent variables are the establishment of the bank's first overseas branch and the number of new branches the bank established in a given year. The first is binary; the second is a count. Because our data are temporal, we can treat the establishment of the first branch as an event and examine the process through the use of event-history analysis. At time zero, 1963, there were thirty-three banks in our dataset "at risk" of establishing a foreign branch. Once the bank established the branch, we dropped it from the analysis. We used a discrete-time event-history model, in which our units of analysis were bank-years (Allison 1984). There were a total of 233 bank-years in the event-history models we describe here.

The dependent variable in our second set of analyses, the number of new branches in a given year, is a count variable. This type of variable is most appropriately handled with a Poisson regression model. Poisson models require the assumption that the variance is smaller than the mean. When this is not the case—a situation referred to as "overdispersion"—then the negative binomial model is preferable. Because that was the case with our data, we estimated negative binomial models for the analyses involving the number of new branches in a given year. The standard negative binomial model includes a term, ln α, that represents the level of overdispersion. This value is assumed to equal zero in a Poisson model. Because our data are longitudinal, we have reason to suspect that ln α may vary systematically over time. We therefore used a generalized negative binomial model, in which we estimate ln α as a function of time. Unlike the conventional negative binomial model, which estimates a single coefficient for ln α, the generalized model that we estimate produces two ln α coefficients: a constant and one for the year effect.

As in the analysis of entry into foreign branching, our units of analysis for these models are also bank-years. Because all of the banks, including those that were involved in foreign banking prior to 1963, have the possibility of opening new branches in any given year, however, the observations remain present for all years in the sample. For these models there were forty-six banks that were at risk of opening at least one branch in a given year. These analyses included 775 observations. Because the number of new branches that a bank opens may be affected by the number of branches the bank already has, we controlled for the existing number of branches. Given the pooled nature of our data—the fact that the same banks appear in multiple observations in both sets of analyses—it was necessary to control for the within-bank variation across these multiple observations. One possible way to do this was through the use of firm-level dummy variables. An alternative approach was to adjust the standard errors using Halbert White's robust standard error transformation (Huber 1967; White 1978), combined with the algorithm for clustered observations developed by Rogers (1993; for a description of this model, see Mizruchi and Stearns 2001, Appendix A). We used robust standard errors with clustering in all of the models we present here.

Results I: Entry into Foreign Markets

Table 5.2 presents the means, standard deviations, and correlations among the variables. Table 5.3 presents a frequency distribution of the number of banks opening their first foreign branch for each year between 1963 and 1979 (at

TABLE 5.2 Entry into Foreign Markets by U.S. Banks: Means, Standard Deviations, and Correlations Among Variables

	Mean	Standard Deviation	2	3	4	5	6	7	8	9	10	11	12
1. Open first branch (1 = yes)	.117	.322	949	225	231	063	096	-186	286	-289	033	071	na
2. New branches opened	.473	1.653	—	120	232	-035	118	001	036	-033	184	217	248
3. Size (in assets)	9136.27	14717.2		—	790	-226	150	-170	-151	-038	434	504	840
4. Log size	8.456	1.077			—	-288	178	-231	-145	-108	541	652	702
5. Profitability (ROA)	.643	.246				—	-097	058	098	067	-077	-120	-206
6. Age of bank	93.836	43.032					—	-061	-027	-030	267	341	280
7. Federal monetary policy (1 = loose)	.523	.500						—	-116	485	002	002	-076
8. Cost of AAA bonds	5.308	.706							—	-499	-001	004	-101
9. Business cycle (1 = expansion)	.680	.467								—	001	001	-024
10. Officers of multinationals	4.430	3.481									—	825	410
11. Centrality (interlocks)	22.520	14.572										—	465
12. Branches established	5.304	10.806											—

Source: Authors' compilation.
Notes: Decimal points are omitted from the correlation coefficients to conserve space. Pairwise, N = 281 for variable 1, 898–923 for variables 2–12.

TABLE 5.3   *Number of Banks Opening First Foreign Branch,*
            1963 to 1979

Year	At Risk	Entering	Cumulative
1963	33	0	0
1964	33	1	1
1965	32	2	3
1966	30	1	4
1967	29	0	4
1968	29	2	6
1969	27	5	11
1970	22	11	22
1971	11	2	24
1972	9	3	27
1973	6	0	27
1974	6	0	27
1975	6	3	30
1976	3	1	31
1977	2	0	31
1978	2	1	32
1979	1	1	33

Source: Authors' compilation.

which point all thirty-three banks in our analysis had opened branches).
Table 5.4 presents the results of a discrete-time event-history analysis of the
banks' opening of their first foreign offices. Because the data are pooled, the correlations in table 5.2 have limited statistical meaning. They do provide some
interesting summary information, however. Consistent with the regulation
hypotheses, for example, banks tended to open overseas branches when the Federal Reserve was engaging in a tight monetary policy (and the cost of capital was
high). Concurrently, the banks tended to open overseas branches during contraction periods in the economy. The simple correlations for the interlock variable were also positive, as expected, although relatively small. And larger banks,
as expected, were more likely than smaller banks to open foreign branches.

Table 5.3 indicates that banks' entry into overseas banking occurred relatively constantly across time, with two exceptions, 1969 and 1970. Those two
years saw sixteen of the thirty-three banks in our analysis open their first overseas branches. It is difficult to know what this says about the regulation
hypotheses. The two policies suggested in the literature to have significantly
affected U.S. banks' decisions to move overseas, the Interest Equalization Tax
and the Voluntary Foreign Credit Restraint program, were instituted in 1963
and 1965, respectively. Even if we assume a time lag, it is difficult to argue
that it took six or seven years for the Interest Equalization Tax to trigger movement overseas. The effect of the VFCR program is more complicated, because although the program was voluntary when it was instituted in 1965, it

TABLE 5.4   *Determinants of Banks' Establishment of a First Foreign Branch (Discrete-Time Event-History Models with Clustering)*

Independent Variables	(1)	(2)	(3)	(4)
Constant	−10.800***	−7.251**	−4.401***	−4.906***
	(−4.243)	(−2.690)	(−4.459)	(−4.841)
Size	.0005***	—	.0004***	.0005***
	(4.570)	—	(3.998)	(6.473)
Profitability	0.303	−0.251	0.714	1.243
	(0.301)	(−0.292)	(0.696)	(1.016)
Age	0.023***	0.014**	0.021***	0.019***
	(3.213)	(2.984)	(3.280)	(3.299)
Monetary policy (1 = loose)	0.207	0.616	0.051	−0.929*
	(0.210)	(0.560)	(0.071)	(−2.212)
Cost of AAA bonds	0.996**	0.732	—	—
	(2.386)	(1.625)	—	—
Business cycle (1 = expansion)	−0.757	−1.410	−1.515*	—
	(−0.810)	(−1.388)	(−1.939)	—
Officers of multinationals	−0.106	−0.081	−0.067	−0.039
	(−1.036)	(−0.827)	(−0.647)	(−0.384)
Centrality (interlocks)	0.027	0.060*	0.017	−0.005
	(0.734)	(1.971)	(0.498)	(−0.144)
χ^2	75.39***	31.84***	56.44***	57.25***
df	8	7	7	6
Log likelihood	−77.423	−82.646	−80.095	−83.336

Source: Authors' compilation.
Notes: *p < .05; **p < .01; ***p < .001; probabilities for substantive variables are one-tailed; those for control variables are two-tailed. N = 233 in all models. Logit coefficients are presented, with Z-statistics, based on robust variance estimates with clustering, in parentheses.

became mandatory in 1970. Anticipation of this change may have led to the extensive movement observed in 1969 and 1970. At the same time, the Federal Reserve Bank's tight monetary policies and the concomitant high cost of capital described earlier may have been equally responsible. The real cost of AAA bonds was higher in 1969 and 1970 than in any other year in our time series. The correlation between year dummy variables and the cost of AAA bonds was .52 for the 1970 dummy and .35 for the 1969 dummy. The Fed was also following a tight monetary policy in those two years, although it also followed a tight monetary policy in 1966 and only one bank opened its first foreign office that year. On the other hand, 1969 and 1970 represented the first time in our dataset that the Fed followed a tight monetary policy for two consecutive years. The hypothesis for the effect of the VFCR program therefore receives some support from our data. The Interest Equalization Tax of 1963 appears to have had little if any effect.

Turning to the event-history models in table 5.4, we have included tests of our hypotheses with various combinations of variables. As is evident from table 5.2, the three macroeconomic variables (federal monetary policy, the cost of AAA bonds, and whether the economy was experiencing an expansion or contraction) and the two interlock variables (the number of companies with foreign operations represented on the bank's board and the bank's number of interlocks) were highly correlated, creating the possibility of multicollinearity. We therefore present equations in table 5.4 with different combinations of these variables in order to more carefully identify their effects. Although both bank size and the number of interlocks were right-skewed, their correlations with each other and with the bank's opening of a foreign branch were very similar. We therefore present models based on the raw values of assets and interlocks.

Equation 1 includes all of our predictors: the size, age, and profitability of the bank, the number of officers of companies doing business overseas represented on the bank's board, the bank's number of interlocks with other Fortune 800 firms, and the three macroeconomic indicators. Interestingly, the only substantive variable that significantly predicts the opening of the bank's first foreign office is the cost of capital, which, as predicted, is positively associated. The controls for the size and age of the bank are also significant positive predictors. Neither the other macroeconomic variables (stage of the business cycle and federal monetary policy) nor the two director variables (the number of firms with overseas operations represented on the bank's board and the bank's centrality in the interlock network) were significantly associated with the bank's opening of an overseas branch. This latter finding is interesting in light of an earlier analysis (Mizruchi and Davis 2000) in which we found that centrality in the interlock network predicted a bank's likelihood of opening a London office between 1962 and 1970, even when we controlled for the bank's size and profitability. The earlier analysis did not include the macroeconomic factors, so it is possible that the inclusion of these effects is what caused the centrality effect to disappear. To examine this, we recomputed equation 1 omitting these variables. The findings (not shown here but available on request) revealed no changes. The controls for size and age remained strongly positive and significant, and the effect of profitability approached statistical significance (although in a positive direction, contrary to what the earlier arguments would suggest). The effects of the board of director variables remained nonsignificant, however. A further analysis examining the effects of the two board variables separately (the two have a correlation of .82) revealed no differences. Why the network centrality measure does not significantly predict entry into foreign banking can be seen when we remove size from the equation. As shown in equation 2, removing the size variable causes the centrality effect to become significantly positive. Our analysis suggests, then, that there is a positive statistical association between network centrality and entry into foreign branching that disappears when we control for the size of the bank. Unlike our earlier analysis of the establishment of a London office, the effect of centrality is not independent of size.

To further examine the effects of the macroeconomic variables, we computed models in which we omitted one or more of the three variables. Equation 3 shows that when we remove the cost of AAA bonds, the effect of stage of the business cycle becomes significant in the predicted direction. Banks were more likely to open overseas operations during contraction phases of the business cycle. The monetary policy variable continues not to be significant in this equation. When we remove both the cost of AAA bonds and stage of the business cycle from the model, however (equation 4), monetary policy emerges as a significant predictor. Banks were more likely to open their first overseas branch during periods of tight federal monetary policy. The general effects of these three variables provide support for the hypothesis that U.S. banks moved overseas in response to restrictive federal monetary policies and recession stages of the business cycle.

Results II: Predicting the Number of New Nations Entered

In addition to predicting the initial establishment of a foreign branch, we also used our variables to predict the number of new branches that a bank would open in a given year. Unlike the previous analysis, in which entry into foreign branching is an end point that removes the bank from the analysis, all banks remain at risk of opening new branches during every stage, regardless of whether they had previously opened one or more branches. The new branches variable thus includes the first branches that were the subject of the models in table 5.4 but includes additional new branches as well. Because the number of new branches that a bank opens in a given year may be affected by the number it has already opened, we controlled for the number of existing branches that the bank had in the previous year. The number of observations in these analyses is 775, nearly four times as high as in the analysis of entry into foreign branching.

As noted earlier, our dependent variable here is a count variable. Because the variance of this variable exceeds its mean and because it is possible that this overdispersion was not constant over time, we computed generalized negative binomial regression models. They are presented in table 5.5, where equation 1 presents the full model, with all of the predictors and controls. The findings contain both similarities with and differences from those in equation 1 of table 5.4. As in the earlier analysis, the cost of AAA bonds is positively associated with foreign branching. The other variables that were nonsignificant in table 5.4 are nonsignificant here as well, although the effect of stage of the

TABLE 5.5 *Determinants of Number of Banks' New Foreign Branches (Generalized Negative Binomial Models with Clustering)*

Independent Variables	(1)	(2)	(3)	(4)
Constant	−3.361***	−15.000***	−1.424**	−1.530*
	(−3.415)	(−7.053)	(−2.417)	(−2.528)
Size (ln size in equation 2)	.0000	1.110***	.0000	−.0000
	(0.309)	(6.160)	(0.011)	(−0.304)
Profitability	−0.507	0.599	−0.387	−0.446
	(−0.937)	(1.554)	(−0.689)	(−0.790)
Age	0.003	0.007**	0.003	0.002
	(0.906)	(3.035)	(0.776)	(0.699)
Monetary policy (1 = loose)	−0.037	0.196	0.020	−0.354*
	(−0.172)	(1.014)	(0.093)	(−2.160)
Cost of AAA bonds	0.334**	0.064***	—	—
	(2.491)	(4.586)	—	—
Business cycle (1 = expansion)	−0.366	−0.174	−0.662**	—
	(−1.515)	(−0.750)	(−3.169)	—
Officers of multinationals	−0.047	−0.030	−0.050	−0.048
	(−1.181)	(−0.996)	(−1.143)	(−1.041)
Centrality (interlocks)	0.287*	−0.005	0.031**	0.031**
	(2.215)	(−0.492)	(2.427)	(2.472)
Cumulative total branches	0.043**	−0.002	0.047**	0.047**
	(2.911)	(−0.223)	(2.912)	(2.790)
Ln alpha (year)	0.080*	0.062	0.076*	0.064
	(2.424)	(1.386)	(2.109)	(1.574)
Ln alpha (constant)	−156.737*	−122.550	−148.136*	−125.241
	(−2.409)	(−1.379)	(−2.095)	(−1.561)
χ^2	76.24***	205.45***	77.88***	71.13***
df	9	9	8	7
Log likelihood	−608.589	−585.042	−611.249	−615.966

Source: Authors' compilation.
Notes: *p < .05; **p < .01; ***p < .001; probabilities for substantive variables are one-tailed; those for control variables are two-tailed. N = 775 in all models. Poisson coefficients are presented, with Z-statistics, based on robust variance estimates with clustering, in parentheses.

business cycle has a probability level of below .10 (.065). The most striking difference in this model is that the effect of network centrality is significantly positive, while that of size is not. Further examination (not shown here) indicates that the effect of size is significantly positive when we remove the control for the prior number of branches. Once we control for this variable, then, size does not significantly increase the model's explanatory power.

Examination of the correlations, especially considering the presence of the cumulative number of branches that the bank had established, indicates the potential for serious multicollinearity. This is especially the case with the role of bank size. We saw earlier that size, measured as the bank's assets, is highly skewed. The simple correlation between size and establishment of the bank's first foreign branch is virtually identical regardless of whether we use the log of size, and the correlations of both raw and logged size with the other exogenous variables are generally similar, although they tend to be larger when size is logged. The simple correlation between size and the number of new branches is considerably stronger when we log size, however, than when we do not. The log of size is also correlated .65 with centrality, compared with only .50 between raw size and centrality. As equation 2 of 5.5 illustrates, taking the log of size significantly affects our findings. The effect of log of size is strongly positive, and inclusion of this variable nullifies the effect of centrality, regardless of whether we take the log of interlocks or the raw number. (The equation with the log of interlocks is available on request.) The effects of age and the cost of AAA bonds also increase when we take the log of size, although the effect of stage of the business cycle appears to decline.

Before we conclude that the control for size has nullified an otherwise positive effect of centrality, however, we need to consider an important aspect of our measurement. We were able to measure bank size, in terms of assets, on a yearly basis for each bank. The asset values are also unadjusted for inflation, so that they tend to increase, sometimes sharply, with time. Our centrality measure, on the other hand, is based on the bank's number of interlocks in a single year, in this case 1966. This value remains constant throughout the period of the study, which continues through 1980. Our measure of network centrality is therefore significantly less valid than our measure of size. Its lack of variation and (despite the stability of interlocks) its possibly decreasing connection with our endogenous variables over time suggest that our observed effects of centrality may be underestimated. For this reason, we believe that the results in equation 1 may be no less valid than those in equation 2.

Whether we use raw size or its log affects the strength of some of the other coefficients as well. Equation 3 of table 5.5 shows, similar to equation 3 of table 5.4, that when we remove the cost of AAA bonds, the effect of stage of the business cycle becomes strongly significant; banks are likely to open more branches during contraction periods than during economic expansions. This effect holds, and the Z-statistic actually becomes stronger (increasing in strength from −3.169 to −4.155) when we include the log of size in the equation (not shown here). When we include the log of size, the effect of federal monetary policy, which is virtually zero in equation 3, has a positive Z-statistic (1.609) that, were we not using a one-tailed test with a negative alternative hypothesis, would be nearly significant in the opposite-from-predicted direction. The effect of federal monetary policy is significantly negative, as predicted, in equation 4, when we use the raw number of assets as our indicator of size. When we use the log of size, however (not shown here), the effect of monetary policy remains negative, but it is no longer close to statistically significant ($Z = -0.790$).

Our analysis of the number of foreign branches opened thus yields findings similar to those of the analysis of the opening of the first foreign branch, with the exception of the relation between size and network centrality. In the former analysis, size had a strong effect, and centrality had no significance when size was controlled. In the latter analysis, however, centrality did have a significant positive effect on the number of new foreign branches when we controlled for the bank's raw volume of assets. The effect of centrality disappeared when we controlled for the log of assets, but as we noted, our measure of bank size is accurate to the year, while our measure of interlocking is based on a single year (1966) that may have limited relevance to the later years of our data. Multicollinearity among the exogenous variables and controls may also have contributed to the nonsignificant effects when we used the log of size.

Discussion

Our results indicate that American banks expanded outside the United States for a combination of macroeconomic, public policy, and organizational reasons. Tight money at home and a policy to limit lending directly from domestic offices provided the initial impetus for banks to open foreign branches. London branches provided access to Eurodollars to be lent through American branches; by 1970, twenty-two of our thirty-three previously domestic banks had opened their first foreign office. We find only some suggestive evidence for any network effects here. In contrast, opening other branches did reflect social influences. We consider two possibilities. Banks might have followed their customers, opening branches close to the operations of their major customers (as proxied by the locational choices of their board members' companies). Or banks might have looked to each other for guidance on appropriate actions for a multinational bank. Our results are most consistent with the second possibility. (In subsequent work, we will examine in greater detail the linkages between the locational choices of banks and the industrial firms they were tied to over time.)

Even as foreign activity proliferated among U.S. banks, the bulk of the activity remained concentrated in a small number of institutions—primarily the six major New York money market banks plus a few leading banks in Boston, Chicago, and California. These were the same institutions that had been involved in foreign banking prior to the 1960s. By the late 1990s, only five banks remained that had 25 percent or more of their revenues from overseas activities: Bank of Boston, Bankers Trust, Chase-Chemical, Citicorp (now Citigroup), and JPMorgan.[2]

In a recent paper (Davis and Mizruchi 1999), we find that the role of large commercial banks in the U.S. economy declined between the early 1980s and the mid-1990s. The proliferation of alternative sources of financing reduced major U.S. firms' dependence on commercial banks. Corresponding to this shift, the presence of commercial banks in the center of the interlock network, a phenomenon that had held steady since the turn of the twentieth century, declined as well. In that paper, we suggest that one possible reason for this decline was the banks' increasing attention to overseas activity. As the profitability of domestic lending declined, the banks were presumed to be searching elsewhere for profitable activities, such as service-related functions with U.S. firms and increased lending overseas. Our findings from this paper show that the foreign banking portion of this account was at best overstated. The major U.S. banks had gone multinational long before the 1980s. If anything, in the 1980s and 1990s they became less focused on foreign activity.

Still, there was variation in the original entry into foreign banking, and to this day there remains considerable variation in the amount of foreign banking. Which banks were most likely to enter foreign banking in the 1960s, and which ones are most heavily involved at present? Clearly size is a primary factor. The largest banks were more likely to be early entrants and are more likely to continue to have significant foreign operations. But size alone does not explain these behaviors. Even when we control for size, banks' ties to other members of the corporate network play a significant role in predicting overseas activity. Banks that were integrated into the larger corporate network, where general ideas about prescribed strategies are likely to prevail, were more likely to join the growing trend toward internationalization.

How did these effects operate? If we consider a social network as an arena in which ideas are generated and disseminated, then the prevailing ideas and behaviors are likely, if not initially then eventually, to be adopted by the actors most integrated into the network. Thus, the closer an actor is to the center, the greater the probability that it has been exposed to the prevailing ideas and behaviors. To the extent that the internationalization of banking in the 1960s was a prevalent trend, we would expect that banks that were central in the network would be most likely to adopt this behavior. This is precisely what we find. The socially central banks also tend to be the largest, and depending on the measure we use, consideration of the bank's size may dampen the effect of centrality. Given the high correlation between centrality and size and the imperfections in measuring the former, size may also be a proxy for status within the banking community. Even taking into account the limited network data in our current analysis, centrality appears to be a significant positive predictor of a bank's involvement in overseas activity.

Coda: What Happened Next

We cannot comment at length on the subsequent two decades, but we can give a brief outline. In addition to the branch data described in previous sections, we have assembled data on board ties among the several hundred largest U.S. corporations from 1982 through 1999 (which includes a panel of the largest banks), as well as annual data on the foreign operations of the major corporations tied to banks through shared directors (reported in annual 10K reports). We have also put together annual data on the volume of domestic and foreign corporate lending by every commercial bank holding company in the United States from 1986 through 1999 (from quarterly Federal Reserve call reports). Descriptively, the data point to four trends:

1. Manufacturers gained an increasing proportion of their revenues from overseas, with the average firm's foreign sales increasing from under 15 percent to 25 percent of its total (see figure 5.2).

2. The number of banks doing business with foreign customers dropped by one-third, owing in part to a consolidation in the banking industry.

FIGURE 5.2   *Growing Volume of Sales Made Outside the United States by Two Hundred Large U.S. Manufacturers, 1985 to 1998*

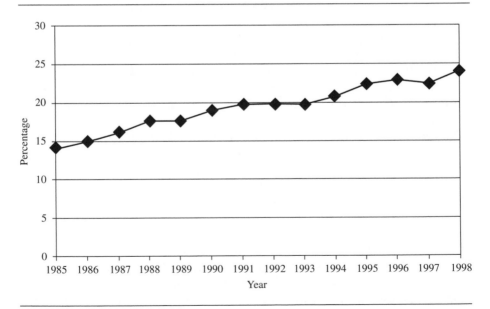

Source: Authors' compilation.

3. The volume of loans to non-U.S. businesses held by U.S. banks declined steadily from 1986 to 1992 but recovered by 1997 and remained at roughly the same level through the rest of the decade.

4. Foreign loans were increasingly held by a very small number of banks. Citibank's share of foreign corporate loans increased from 22 percent to 42 percent of the total held by U.S. banks between 1986 and 1999, and the four largest lenders collectively held roughly 78 percent of all commercial and industrial loans to addresses outside the United States.

In short, while the average American manufacturer grew increasingly multinational, bank holding companies split into two camps: a tiny handful of large multinationals, dominated by Citibank (now Citigroup), and roughly 2,500 domestically oriented banks (see figure 5.3).

Our initial analytical results indicate that the processes of globalization and "de-globalization" were not symmetric. Banks did not pull out of foreign operations at the speed with which they entered them. Instead, the decline in overseas activity was more gradual and operated partly through attrition as a number of leading banks were absorbed by other banks, including non-U.S. ones. The processes that accounted for overseas banking activity, however, have been, if anything, even more prominent in recent years. In an analysis of the proportion of banks' commercial and industrial lending that took place outside the United States (Mizruchi and Davis 2000), we found that network centrality and interlocks with U.S. nonfinancial corporations that did business

FIGURE 5.3 *Growing Concentration of Commercial and Industrial Loans Made Outside the United States by U.S. Banks, 1986 to 1998*

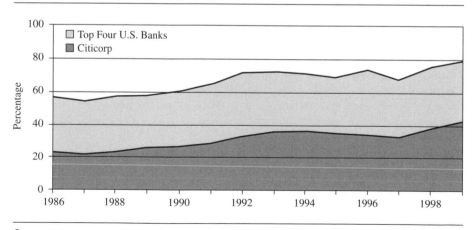

Source: Authors' compilation.

overseas were consistently strong predictors of involvement in foreign lending, with effects considerably stronger than those we observed in the 1963 to 1980 period. The factors that we predicted would influence involvement in foreign banking appear to have solidified in recent years, as numerous banks have reduced their overseas activities. For the few U.S. banks that remain as global institutions, proximity to the center of the corporate network is a primary predictor of their level of foreign activity. This suggests a puzzle: If centrality is associated with adopting "normatively appropriate" practices, why then are *only* the most central firms heavily involved in international banking?

Conclusion

We have tried to unpack the mechanisms behind the international expansion phase of American commercial banks during the 1960s and 1970s. Over the course of a few years large banks went from overwhelmingly domestic institutions to major players in the international economy, and the industry's foreign assets increased one hundred times over. Nearly every major bank that did not already have branches abroad opened them, and the largest banks greatly expanded their foreign operations, to the point that half the profits of the dozen largest multinational banks came from outside the United States. We find that this came about through a combination of opportunities and constraints at the level of political economy and network processes at the organizational level. Once a branch network was in place, new opportunities became available, such as new sources of deposits in oil-exporting nations and new outlets for lending in low-income countries.

The watershed in this process was the Third World debt crisis of 1982, and in the subsequent years U.S. banking as an industry substantially retrenched. By 2001, through a combination of mergers and exits, the number of U.S.-owned banks operating foreign branches dropped from 150 to 30. Branches on-site are not the only way to do foreign business, of course, but the number of bank holding companies booking *any* corporate loans to businesses outside the United States dropped by about one-third from 1986 to 1999, and only 38 banks maintained international banking facilities. One bank in particular, Citigroup, dominates U.S. overseas banking. As noted earlier, between 1986 and 1999 Citigroup's share of foreign corporate loans among U.S. banks increased from 22 percent of all foreign loans to 42 percent. Of the 824 foreign branches of U.S.-owned banks in March 2001, Citigroup operated 413 of them, and the three largest parents (now Citigroup, Fleetboston, and JPMorgan Chase) owned 87 percent of the total. International banking, at least for U.S. commercial banks, is in effect synonymous with these three organizations.

International financial expansions are taken by some as signs of impending "hegemonic crises" in global capitalism (see, for example, Arrighi and

Silver 1999), and international banks have at various times played a critical part in this process. We have argued that the activities of banks are susceptible to organizational analysis, and we have traced the history of American banks abroad by linking their strategies to developments at the level of political economy and organizational networks. In particular, we find evidence that in addition to economic and regulatory forces, the proliferation of foreign branching by U.S. banks was driven by a process of social definition: banks that were centrally located in interfirm social networks were those most likely to open overseas branches. Consistent with both social network and neo-institutional theory, this suggests that this particular business strategy may have diffused in part because it was defined by leading actors in the banking community as a socially appropriate activity. Our findings indicate a great U-turn, however, with American banks going from an overwhelmingly domestic business to a substantially international one—and back again. This finding of contraction clearly calls for further study.

As Schneper and Guillén (this volume) show, innovations do not always diffuse in a linear manner. They may catch on under some conditions but fail to go anywhere under other conditions. Although all of our banks eventually opened foreign branches, most reduced their operations over time. To what extent was this contraction related to the lack of a fit between the banks' missions and their actions? To what extent was the contraction based on location decisions that prevented the banks from occupying a unique niche in the international distribution of U.S. banking, as Haveman and Keister's (this volume) findings might suggest?[3]

At the same time, we should not lose sight of what is perhaps our most notable finding: the remarkable stability of the dominant foreign-oriented U.S. banks. The five U.S. banks with the greatest international business in 1960, accounting for almost all activities by the industry, were Citibank, Chase Manhattan, Bank of America, Bank of Boston, and JPMorgan. These were exactly the same banks—in the same rank order—that dominated foreign corporate lending in 1999. The average American bank is far less international than the average American manufacturer; with the exception of a half-dozen firms, American banking is almost exclusively domestic. The relevant tools for studying American international banking are perhaps those of the biographer rather than the demographer's.

In arguing against the notion that the current phase of globalization is simply a replay of prior historical occurrences, or that nothing much has changed at base in the world economy, Anthony Giddens (2000, 27) points to financial globalization as perhaps the central distinguishing feature. "Geared as it is to electronic money—money that exists only as digits in computers— the current world economy has no parallels in earlier times." One way in which the current era is distinctive is that identifiable actors, such as banks, are far less important to global financial flows than they were as recently as

1980. Since then, market-based flows have emerged as far more central (World Bank 1997). In that sense, the current era of financial globalization looks very much like the "coming hegemony of global markets" (Arrighi and Silver 1999, 259), which is itself a distinctively American form.

We thank Paul DiMaggio, Frank Dobbin, Gunter Dufey, and three anonymous reviewers for their helpful comments on an earlier draft of this chapter. We also thank Donald Palmer for providing the director interlock data. We are grateful to the Undergraduate Research Opportunity Program at the University of Michigan for providing funds for the data collection, and our team of Michigan undergraduates—Ignacio Benedetti, Terrence Griffin, Amber Thomas, Lihan Wang, Melissa Wong, and Cora Yeung—for their assistance with the data collection. Our thanks also to Princeton University for supporting the conference at which the paper was presented and the Russell Sage Foundation for support in the final stages of writing and preparation.

Notes

1. A reviewer suggested to us that the rate of inflation might have also played a role in banks' decisions to open foreign branches, since high rates of inflation during the 1970s lowered real rates of return domestically. To examine this possibility, we inserted a variable for the rate of inflation for each year in our data. The effect of this variable was significantly positive in two of the four equations involving the opening of the first branch, but its inclusion had no effect on the strength of the remaining coefficients. The variable had no significant effect in any of the equations involving the number of foreign branches, although it was strongly negative (in the opposite from the expected direction, which in a one-tailed test rendered the effect nonsignificant) in one equation. Because inflation was highly correlated with the three macroeconomic variables—monetary policy, the cost of AAA bonds, and the stage of the business cycle—this null effect appears to have been due to multicollinearity: when we removed the macroeconomic variables from the model, the effect of inflation on the formation of new branches became significantly positive. In none of the equations did inclusion of the inflation variable alter the substantive conclusions for the remaining variables in the model.

2. Chase and Morgan subsequently merged.

3. A third possible explanation for the banks' reduction in foreign branching has been suggested to us by Gunter Dufey, a professor at the University of Michigan Business School and a former banker. Dufey notes that when they opened their foreign branches, U.S. banks made special efforts to train personnel from the host country. This training was so successful, he argues, that many of the indigenous bankers left the U.S. banks and went to work for local institutions, taking their American customers with them. We thank Professor Dufey for this point.

References

Allison, Paul D. 1984. *Event-History Analysis: Regression for Longitudinal Event Data*. Beverly Hills, Calif.: Sage Publications.

Arrighi, Giovanni, and Beverly J. Silver. 1999. "Hegemonic Transitions: Past and Present." *Political Power and Social Theory* 13: 239–75.

Baker, James C., and M. Gerald Bradford. 1974. *American Banks Abroad: Edge Act Companies and Multinational Banking*. New York: Praeger.

Bonacich, Phillip. 1987. "Centrality and Power: A Family of Measures." *American Journal of Sociology* 92: 1170–82.

Braudel, Fernand. 1984. *Civilization and Capitalism, Fifteenth to Eighteenth Century*, vol. 3, *The Perspective of the World*. New York: Harper & Row.

Brimmer, Andrew F. 1973. "American International Banking: Trends and Prospects." Paper presented to the fifty-first annual meeting of the Bankers' Association for Foreign Trade. Boca Raton, Fla. (1973).

Brimmer, Andrew F., and Frederick R. Dahl. 1975. "Growth of American International Banking: Implications for Public Policy." *Journal of Finance* 30(2): 341–63.

Business Week Online. 1995. Chapter excerpt from *Walter Wriston, Citibank, and the Rise and Fall of American Financial Supremacy,* by Philip L. Zweig. Available at: www.businessweek.com/chapter/zweigch.htm. Downloaded on September 25, 2003.

Cohen, Benjamin J. 1986. *In Whose Interest? International Banking and American Foreign Policy*. New Haven: Yale University Press.

Darby, Michael R. 1986. "The Internationalization of American Banking and Finance: Structure, Risk, and World Interest Rates." *Journal of International Money and Finance* 5: 403–28.

Davis, Gerald F. 1991. "Agents Without Principles? The Spread of the Poison Pill Through the Intercorporate Network." *Administrative Science Quarterly* 36(4): 583–613.

Davis, Gerald F., and Mark S. Mizruchi. 1999. "The Money Center Cannot Hold: Commercial Banks in the U.S. System of Corporate Governance." *Administrative Science Quarterly* 44(2): 215–39.

Dobbin, Frank. 1994. *Forging Industrial Policy*. New York: Cambridge University Press.

Dombrowski, Peter. 1996. *Policy Responses to the Globalization of American Banking*. Pittsburgh: University of Pittsburgh Press.

Fligstein, Neil. 1990. *The Transformation of Corporate Control*. Cambridge, Mass.: Harvard University Press.

Galaskiewicz, Joseph and Ronald S. Burt. 1991. "Interorganization Contagion in Corporate Philanthropy." *Administrative Science Quarterly* 36(1): 88–105.

Giddens, Anthony. 2000. *Runaway World: How Globalization Is Reshaping Our Lives*. New York: Routledge.

Gowan, Peter. 1999. *The Global Gamble: Washington's Faustian Bid for World Dominance*. London: Verso.

Hallow, M. J. S. 1993. *Over There: American Banks Abroad*. New York: Garland.

Huber, Peter J. 1967. "The Behavior of Maximum Likelihood Estimates Under Nonstandard Conditions." *Proceedings of the Fifth Berkeley Symposium on Mathematical Statistics and Probability* 1: 221–33.

Lenin, Vladimir I. 1916/1939. *Imperialism: The Highest Stage of Capitalism*. New York: International Publishers.

Manzocchi, Stefano. 1999. "Capital Flows to Developing Economies Throughout the Twentieth Century." In *Financial Globalization and Democracy in Emerging Markets,* edited by Leslie Elliott Armijo. New York: St. Martin's Press.

Mariolis, Peter, and Maria H. Jones. 1982. "Centrality in Corporate Interlock Networks: Reliability and Stability." *Administrative Science Quarterly* 27: 571–84.

McMichael, Philip. 1996. *Development and Social Change: A Global Perspective.* Thousand Oaks, Calif.: Pine Forge Press.

Mills, C. Wright. 1956. *The Power Elite.* New York: Oxford University Press.

Mintz, Beth, and Michael Schwartz. 1985. *The Power Structure of American Business.* Chicago: University of Chicago Press.

Mizruchi, Mark S. 1992. *The Structure of Corporate Political Action.* Cambridge, Mass.: Harvard University Press.

———. 1996. "What Do Interlocks Do? An Analysis, Critique, and Assessment of Research on Interlocking Directorates." *Annual Review of Sociology* 22: 271–98.

Mizruchi, Mark S., and David Bunting. 1981. "Influence in Corporate Networks: An Examination of Four Measures." *Administrative Science Quarterly* 26: 475–89.

Mizruchi, Mark S., and Gerald F. Davis. 2000. "The Globalization of American Finance: Sources of Foreign Activity Among Large U.S. Commercial Banks." Paper presented to the annual meeting of the Academy of Management. Toronto (August).

Mizruchi, Mark S., and Linda Brewster Stearns. 2001. "Getting Deals Done: The Use of Social Networks in Bank Decisionmaking." *American Sociological Review* 66(5): 647–71.

Pare, Terence P. 1995. "Clueless Bankers." *Fortune* 132(2): 150.

Peter Merrill Associates. 1981. *The Future Development of U.S. Banking Organizations Abroad.* Washington, D.C.: American Bankers Association.

Polanyi, Karl. 1944/1957. *The Great Transformation: The Political and Economic Origins of Our Time.* Boston: Beacon Press.

Robinson, Stuart W., Jr. 1972. *Multinational Banking.* Leiden: A. W. Sijthoff.

Roe, Mark J. 1994. *Strong Managers, Weak Owners: The Political Roots of American Corporate Finance.* Princeton, N.J.: Princeton University Press.

Rogers, William H. 1993. "Regression Standard Errors in Clustered Samples." *Stata Technical Bulletin* 13: 19–23.

Sassen, Saskia. 1994. *Cities in a World Economy.* Thousand Oaks, Calif.: Pine Forge Press.

Smith, Roy C. 1989. *The Global Bankers.* New York: Dutton.

Useem, Michael. 1984. *The Inner Circle.* New York: Oxford University Press.

Weber, Klaus, and Gerald F. Davis. 2002. "The Global Spread of Stock Exchanges, 1980 to 1998." Unpublished paper. University of Michigan Business School, Ann Arbor.

White, Halbert. 1978. "A Heteroskedasticity Consistent Covariance Matrix and a Direct Test for Heteroskedasticity." *Econometrica* 46: 817–38.

White, Harrison C. 1981. "Where Do Markets Come From?" *American Journal of Sociology* 87(3): 517–47.

World Bank. 1997. *Private Capital Flows to Developing Countries: The Road to Financial Integration.* Oxford: Oxford University Press.

Zukin, Sharon, and Paul DiMaggio. 1990. "Introduction." In *Structures of Capital: The Social Organization of the Economy,* edited by Sharon Zukin and Paul DiMaggio. New York: Cambridge University Press.

6

CORPORATE GOVERNANCE, LEGITIMACY, AND MODELS OF THE FIRM

William D. Schneper and Mauro F. Guillén

O NE OF the central tenets of both neo-institutional theory and economic sociology is that economic practices occur with greater frequency if they are legitimate. In this chapter, we provide a comparative study that examines the legitimacy of the hostile takeover, a prominent yet highly contested market activity that is often regarded as serving an important corporate governance function. Drawing heavily on neo-institutional theory, we predict that regulative, cognitive, and normative institutional variables affect the legitimacy of hostile takeovers and hence their likelihood. Using data on thirty-nine countries between 1988 and 1998, we find that hostile takeovers occur more frequently the greater the regulative legitimacy of shareholder rights as enshrined in corporate legislation, the greater the cognitive legitimacy afforded by institutionalized stock trading, and the greater the normative legitimacy due to low levels of labor militancy, restrictions on bank ownership, and high cultural individualism. These findings support our claim that these structural and institutional characteristics help constitute each nation's prevailing conception of the firm. This socially constructed model defines the role of the business organization and continues to differ dramatically across countries.

The modern corporation is a contested entity. There is little agreement as to who should be involved in its governance, how the risks and rewards associated with its activities ought to be allocated, and which methods of transferring ownership and control are considered to be acceptable. One point of view holds that the firm is merely a bundle of assets, or resources, whose true value is determined by the cash flows that it provides to its shareholders. Accordingly, transfers in corporate control are deemed to be not only justifiable but economically advantageous provided that such actions remove underperforming or self-serving managers and increase shareholder wealth. From an opposing perspective, the firm is an integral component of the social fabric and is characterized by the intersecting interests of various stakeholders, including not only shareholders and managers but also employees, suppliers, creditors, and the surrounding community (Davis and Stout 1992; Fligstein 1990; Guillén 2000). Following this view, the benefits to shareholders that might arise from changes in ownership and management need to be weighed against the costs that could be imposed on the other constituents.

The study of hostile takeover provides a means to illuminate this debate since the practice's claim to legitimacy depends on the presumed role of the corporation in society. Hailed by some as an effective way to discipline managers and ensure that shareholders maximize their wealth, hostile takeovers are denounced by others as one of the worst manifestations of "predatory" capitalism (Hirsch 1986; Jarrell, Brickley, and Netter 1988; Kelly 2001). Given the intensity of this long-standing controversy, it is not surprising to note that the level of hostile takeover activity differs massively across countries. Between 1988 and 1998, for example, 431 hostile takeover attempts were announced in the United States and 220 in Britain. By contrast, only twenty were announced in France, twelve in Sweden, five in Germany, three in Malaysia, two in Thailand, and just one each in Chile and Japan. We seek to understand these types of differences by exploring how various institutional actors interpret hostile takeovers and react to their potential practice.

A hostile takeover can be defined as corporate acquisition that is actively opposed by the target firm's management or board of directors. Within the realm of corporate governance scholarship, however, the practice has taken on a supplemental meaning. Under the premise that there is a market for corporate control, the stock exchange can be viewed as an arena in which alternative management teams compete for the right to organize corporate resources (Davis and Stout 1992; Jensen and Ruback 1983; Manne 1965). Since corporate share price signifies the most objective and meaningful measure of a company's worth and of its managers' performance, poor stock market performance provides both an incentive and a justification for a more competent management team to take control in an effort to maximize shareholder value. Similarly, the threat of a hostile takeover, it is argued, disciplines incumbent managers and prevents them from straying too far from the best interests of shareholders.

Not surprisingly, the placement of shareholder interests ahead of those of other stakeholders in the firm—managers, workers, suppliers, creditors, and the community—is a most disputed idea. Organizational and economic sociologists have noted that, even in the United States the frequency of hostile takeovers has varied over time. Paul Hirsch (1986, 801) shows that hostile takeovers in the United States have followed the characteristic pattern of a deviant innovation. Initially treated as dubious, owing to the "ominous implications for workers and managers of the target corporations," hostile takeovers gained increasing social acceptance during the 1980s. As a result, the hostile takeover came to be considered a normal and routine governance mechanism within the American business community (Davis and Stout 1992; Fligstein 1996, 663). In other countries, by contrast, the hostile takeover and its socially disruptive effects continue to be framed pejoratively, albeit to different degrees (Bühner et al. 1998; Guillén 2000). Previous research has neither proposed a theory about the factors that may drive the institutionalization of this practice nor used a cross-national sample to test it.

Our theoretical approach is indebted to two streams in the sociological literature. First, we adopt a neo-institutional perspective by proposing that the frequency of hostile takeovers depends on the extent to which the practice is considered legitimate. Mark Suchman (1995, 574) defines social legitimacy as "a generalized perception or assumption that the actions of an entity are desirable, proper, or appropriate within some socially constructed system of norms, values, beliefs, and definitions." We treat the concept of legitimacy as an inherently multidimensional one. Neo-institutional theory recognizes three "pillars" of institutions that serve as the "bases" of legitimacy—the regulative, the normative, and the cognitive (Scott 1995, 34–47). The regulative pillar sanctions the types of behavior that are consistent with established rules and laws. The cognitive pillar helps actors create symbolic representations of the world that inform behavior and infuse it with meaning. The normative pillar tells actors what behavior is culturally appropriate, preferred, and consistent with accepted values and norms, especially those espoused by powerful or influential actors.

The second theoretical stream relevant to the study of hostile takeovers is the economic sociology of markets. Although much work in this area has focused on production markets rather than capital markets, the theory provides important insights into which actors and practices will achieve acceptability and status (Dobbin and Dowd 2000; Podolny 1993; Podolny and Phillips 1996). Markets cannot be taken for granted, do not exist everywhere, and cannot be assumed to develop naturally (Fligstein 2001; Stark and Bruszt 1998). Economic sociology seeks to understand the conditions under which stable and effective markets emerge and develop. In its explanation of the evolution and architecture of markets, economic sociology proves largely compatible with neo-institutional theory. Markets are social and political constructions that "involve both cognitive understandings and concrete social relations" and "reflect the unique political-cultural construction of their firms and nations" (Fligstein 2001, 32, 97; see also White 1981a, 1981b). They are the "outcome of an institutionalization project" that confers legitimacy on market participants and on the interaction between buyers and sellers (Fligstein 1996, 664; Zuckerman 1999). Specifically, we follow Fligstein (2001) and Dobbin and Dowd (2000) in underscoring both cultural and power-related factors in understanding the legitimacy of actors and practices.

Hostile Takeovers and National Corporate Governance Models

Previous research comparing national corporate governance practices and the occurrence of hostile takeovers has most commonly yielded descriptive and qualitative results. Eric Gedajlovic and Daniel Shapiro (1998) apply the taxonomy of James Walsh and J. K. Seward (1990) to show that many countries appear to conform to one of two archetypal models of corporate governance. Germany and France, for instance, adhere to a so-called internal constraints model, in which processes, relationships, and structures inside the firm impose the most salient limits on managerial behavior. Companies in these countries are often judged as having boards of directors that can serve as effective mechanisms to discipline managers. Under this system, directorial boards also often exhibit broad stakeholder representation, including such groups as labor and prominent equity shareholders (Alonso and Iturriaga 1997; Charkham 1994; Prowse 1995). Ownership concentration is viewed as another internal control mechanism, since large block holdings of shares make it relatively easier for equity investors to protect their interests (La Porta, Lopez-de-Silanes, and Shleifer 1999). Investors with comparatively high ownership levels generally hold greater sway over managerial behavior owing to their voting power, their increased economic incentive to invest in firm monitoring and "shareholder activism," and management's awareness of their importance in maintaining share price (Pedersen and Thomsen 1997; Prowse 1995; Useem 1996). The comparative literature often suggests that when such internal mechanisms prove effective, hostile takeovers are economically unnecessary and comparatively rare.

The United States and the United Kingdom are often identified as exemplars of the second ideal-typical model of corporate governance, which is based on external constraints, dispersed ownership, and liquid equity markets. Management's ultimate contractual responsibility is described as being the maximization of shareholder value or wealth (Guillén 2000; OECD 1998). As Michael Seely (1991, 35–36) proclaims, "Public companies are not in the business to reward creditors, inspire devotion of their employees, win the favor of the communities in which they operate, or have the best products. These are all means to an end—making shareholders richer." This view represents a triumph of what Neil Fligstein (1990, 1996) terms the financial conception of control, since it advocates measures of shareholder wealth as the most appropriate means of evaluating managerial and company performance (see also Davis and Stout 1992). In countries where the external constraints paradigm prevails, the hostile takeover tends to play a more important role as a mechanism for disciplining executive management (Roe 1993; Davis and Stout 1992). Other so-called external mechanisms include such financial incentives as stock options, which seek to direct managers toward maximizing stock market performance. In such countries, internal constraints most typically are characterized as weak and slow, with boards of directors that lack independence from management, individual stakeholders that do not engage in direct monitoring, and a minimal presence, if any, of large shareholders and workers on directorial and advisory boards (Becht 1999; Jensen 1989; Roe 1993).

Despite the progress made by prior research in highlighting international variations in corporate governance, little empirical work has been aimed at testing for specific causal factors. In this chapter, we seek to explain differences in the frequency of hostile takeovers from a theoretical perspective that emphasizes the conditions that enhance or undermine the legitimacy of the practice. Our empirical analysis is unique in that it offers the first explanation of cross-national differences in hostile takeover activity using a large and diverse sample of countries over time.

An Institutional Perspective on Hostile Takeovers

As with all business or economic practices, hostile takeovers do not occur in an institutional vacuum. Economic behavior is embedded in social, political, and cultural structures (Granovetter 1985; Scott 1995). Local institutions shape the ways in which various stakeholders of the firm view each other's roles and behavior (Pedersen and Thomsen 1997; Prowse 1995; Roe 1993). Economists argue that institutions are "the rules of the game in a society . . . the constraints that shape human interaction" (North 1990, 3). Sociologists, for their part, further propose that institutions enable, inform, and legitimate action as well as constrain the way in which knowledge and action are constructed (Scott 1995, 51). Institutions constitute actors as well as provide stability and meaning to action, and as such they are expected to provide definitions of what behavior is legitimate, acceptable, appropriate, or reasonable under various circumstances (Biggart and Guillén 1999; Dobbin and Dowd 2000; Guillén and Suárez 1993; Scott 1995).

From an institutional perspective, corporate governance is a social as well as a technical issue. Managers, owners, creditors, workers, and other stakeholders participate in an elaborate organizational field that shapes a country's distinctive corporate governance system. The goals of these various groups, however, are often conflicting and ill defined. Questions regarding the utility of various corporate governance practices also contribute to the ambiguity of the environment in which these institutional decisionmakers must operate.

Owing to this high level of uncertainty and sociopolitical complexity, it follows that organizational actors choose among various corporate governance mechanisms with an eye on more factors than just optimal performance and economic efficiency. We propose that organizational actors introduce, adopt, and perpetuate corporate governance strategies as a means of achieving social legitimacy (DiMaggio and Powell 1983; Meyer and Rowan 1977). Organizational actors strive for legitimacy in an effort to secure their credibility and survival. This quest for legitimacy suggests that the use of hostile takeovers depends on the degree to which they are deemed to be a congruent and accepted part of a country's overall institutional landscape.

National contexts differ widely in terms of how much legitimacy they may confer on hostile takeovers as a means to transfer the ownership of corporate assets, discipline management, achieve an efficient allocation of resources, or make certain stakeholders richer at the expense of others. Following Scott (1995, 34–47), the regulative pillar of legitimacy is fundamental to an understanding of hostile takeovers because states differ in how they define property rights (Campbell and Lindberg 1990; Fligstein 1996, 661; Sutton and Dobbin 1996), with direct consequences for the possible ways in which to transfer ownership and control of corporations, including through a hostile takeover. The second pillar of legitimacy, the cognitive, is also relevant because markets in general and takeover attempts in particular are facilitated by stable and regularized interactions among actors (Fligstein 1996, 658; White 1981b). The third pillar, the normative, highlights the degree to which hostile takeovers are consistent with the values and norms of powerful actors that are either involved in corporate governance or potentially affected by it (Dobbin and Dowd 2000; Fligstein 1996, 662).

In this chapter, we identify six institutional variables that may provide hostile takeovers with regulative, cognitive, or normative legitimacy. We begin by examining the effects of corporate legal traditions as the main institution providing hostile takeovers with regulative legitimacy. We then consider the degree of environmental uncertainty and formalized stock trading, two institutional factors that may help actors engage in hostile takeovers because they provide a cognitive template making such actions possible and meaningful to them and to other stakeholders. Finally, we explore how three key stakeholder groups—labor, banks, and the community—may affect the normative appropriateness of hostile takeovers depending on each group's power and influence.

Regulative Legitimacy: Corporate Law

Corporate law exerts a regulatory effect on corporate governance because it sets the general parameters of permissible behaviors and control mechanisms. Researchers in the field of corporate finance have argued and documented that the extent to which the rights of investors and creditors are protected in a country generates distinct patterns of ownership, governance, and financing of business firms (La Porta et al. 1998). Most crucially, corporate law defines the property rights of owners and the possible ways of transmitting shares in a corporation's stock. Hostile takeovers offer shareholders the opportunity to relinquish ownership and transfer managerial control to the highest bidder. As the Organization for Economic Cooperation and Development contends (OECD 1999, 18), the ability to convey and transfer ownership of shares is perhaps the most fundamental shareholder right. The OECD further argues that "anti-takeover devices should not be used to shield management from accountability." Hence, hostile takeovers are expected to be more frequent to the extent that the corporate legal system privileges the interests and perspectives of shareholders, as opposed to those of managers or other stakeholders.

Corporate legislation differs substantially across countries. Drawing on comparative legal scholarship (Glendon, Gordon, and Osakwe 1994; Reynolds and Flores 1989), Rafael La Porta and his colleagues (1998, 1999) classify countries into five main corporate legal traditions: English common law, French, German, Scandinavian, and formerly socialist. The English common law tradition is shaped by the decisions of judges ruling on specific issues. By contrast, French and German law emerged from Roman civil law, which "uses statutes and comprehensive codes as a primary means of ordering legal material" (La Porta et al. 1998, 1118). The French Commercial Code was issued by Napoleon in 1807, while the German Commercial Code was adopted in 1897 under Bismarck's influence. Scandinavian legal systems are based in part on civil law.

English, French, and German corporate law diffused widely throughout the world following patterns of imperial, military, economic, or cultural influence. Thus, former British colonies—including the United States, Canada, Australia, Ireland, and Singapore—adopted English common law. French law spread to the francophone colonies in the Near East, North and sub-Saharan Africa, Indochina, Oceania, and the Caribbean, and also to the Netherlands, Portugal, Spain, Italy, and their respective colonies. The German legal tradition shaped corporate laws in Austria, Switzerland, Greece, Hungary, Yugoslavia, Japan, Korea, Taiwan, and China, among other countries. Lastly, the former socialist countries need to be treated as a separate category because their legal systems, while in many cases influenced by either French or German law, have been in flux since 1989 and have largely failed to provide a sound basis for effective corporate governance (Spicer, McDermott and Kogut 2000).

A comparative analysis of corporate legal traditions reveals that the best protection of shareholder rights is awarded by English common law, followed by Scandinavian and German law. French law provides the worst protection. Shareholders are better protected when certain standards are ensured by corporate law, including: one share equals one vote; proxy by mail; nonblocking of shares before the shareholders' meeting; cumulative voting or proportional representation; oppressed minority protection; a preemptive right to new issues; and a relatively low percentage of shareholders required to call an extraordinary meeting (see La Porta et al. 1998). In Belgium (French legal tradition), none of these seven provisions are part of the law, as compared with five of them in Canadian and U.S. law (English tradition). Tests of means across legal traditions confirm that the English tradition awards the best shareholder protection (mean of 4.0 provisions), followed by the Scandinavian (3.0), German (2.33), and French (2.33) traditions (La Porta et al. 1998, 1999).

The variety of ways in which countries define and regulate shareholder rights provides an opportunity for making a theoretical prediction as to the legitimacy of the hostile takeover. We expect fewer impediments to hostile takeovers in countries that privilege shareholder rights relative to those of managers and other stakeholders. We thus predict that *the legitimacy of hostile takeovers will be greater in countries with an English corporate legal tradition based on common law than in other countries* (hypothesis 1).

Cognitive Legitimacy: Uncertainty and Routine Interactions

While the regulative pillar of institutional legitimacy underlines conformity with established rules, the cognitive pillar emphasizes "the extent to which choice is informed and constrained by the ways in which knowledge [of reality] is constructed" (Scott 1995, 51). Cognitive frames help actors understand reality and arrive at courses of action that make sense to them. Meanings arise in the course of interaction between actors and are maintained or adapted over time as they are employed to make sense of reality. We focus our analysis on two factors that affect cognitive legitimacy: uncertainty, and routine interactions among the actors in the market. We argue that the actors involved in the launching of a hostile bid or those affected by it either directly or indirectly find it easier to assess the attractiveness of a takeover target and its consequences in the absence of uncertainty. Likewise, a history of institutionalized, routine interaction among the participating actors facilitates sense-making and mutual adjustment. The basic argument is that economic practices and markets can emerge and develop only when stable and regular transactions are part of the experience of participants and other affected parties (Fligstein 1996, 658).

Uncertainty   Uncertainty about the future state of the world makes it more difficult for actors to understand the consequences of their actions in the market and for others to perceive them as appropriate. If markets are social constructions, and actors need to make sense out of them (Biggart and Guillén 1999; Fligstein 1996; Podolny 1993; Zuckerman 1999), then uncertainty is likely to undermine the legitimacy of economic practices or markets. For hostile takeovers to emerge as a legitimate practice, the consequences of such forced corporate restructurings need to be understood by the participants (current shareholders, hostile bidders, managers) and other potentially affected parties (the firm's other stakeholders, the overall community). We distinguish between political and economic uncertainty, which both differ substantially from country to country, as well as over time.

Political certainty depends on the predictability of the "rules of the game." When the government's commitment to a set of rules for doing business (regulation, taxation, property rights, trade policy) can easily change, uncertainty becomes greater (Henisz 2000a). Economic uncertainty refers to the extent to which the evolution of key macroeconomic variables such as growth, interest, or inflation rates can be accurately known or predicted. Political and economic uncertainty are inimical to hostile takeovers because neither the participants nor the other potentially affected parties can be reassured as to the accuracy of their predictions of future consequences. For example, the prices that acquirers pay for their targets are based on the assumption that the regulations, taxes, and property rights at the time of the acquisition are not likely to change in an unpredictable or unforeseen way. Similarly, higher uncertainty makes it harder for creditors and workers to assess and respond cooperatively to an acquirer's promises of improvements arising from restructuring.

From a cognitive point of view, reduced political or economic uncertainty helps participants and other potentially affected parties make sense of the situation. Thus, we predict that *the greater the political and economic uncertainty in a country, the lesser the legitimacy of hostile takeovers* (hypothesis 2).

Routine Interactions   A corporate acquisition tends to be a remarkably elaborate process requiring the coordinated efforts of numerous actors operating both inside and outside of the two firms, all with segmented responsibilities (Jemison and Sitkin 1986). The process becomes even more complex when the target firm resists the takeover. If a hostile takeover is to take place, managers, financial officers, investment bankers, outside auditors, and government regulators need to develop a common language and understanding. We argue that these shared understandings are formulated, routinized, and reinforced over time through institutionalized stock trading. The stock market provides the setting where many of the various organizational agents involved in a hostile takeover interact and exchange information using a standardized language.

Such a shared framework, however, takes much time and effort to develop. Therefore, the hostile corporate acquisition process will be regarded as a more complex and formidable task in countries with little cumulative experience in institutionalized stock trading. While stock markets in some countries were established by merchants several hundred years ago, routine stock trading in some other nations has existed for only a few years. Through ongoing stock trading, actors such as local firms, investment bankers, investors, brokers, and regulatory bodies have an opportunity to stabilize and regularize the ties and behaviors that constitute the marketplace (Podolny 1993; Zuckerman 1999). Given that the legitimacy of hostile takeovers depends on the complex interaction of several actors, acquirers will find it easier to organize and execute a hostile takeover attempt to the extent that stock trading has become a routine and taken-for-granted activity. We further predict that the incremental effect of cumulative trading experience is nonlinear, in the sense that it is stronger at lower than at higher levels of experience. Thus, each additional unit of stock-trading experience is expected to enhance the legitimacy of hostile takeovers at a decreasing rate. We therefore predict that *cumulative experience in stock trading increases the legitimacy of hostile takeovers, but at a decreasing rate* (hypothesis 3).

Normative Legitimacy and Power: Labor, Banks, and the Community

From a normative point of view, a practice is legitimate to the extent that it is perceived as consistent with the values and norms espoused by the various actors involved in it. Values define the preferred or desirable goals, while norms state the appropriate means to achieve those goals. Values and norms are prescriptive, evaluative, and binding (Scott 1995, 37–40). In many social settings, however, values and norms are not shared by all actors. In these situations it becomes imperative to analyze whose values and norms have become most influential, frequently as the result of power structures and dynamics (Perrow 1986; Pfeffer and Salancik 1978).

The modern corporation is one such setting because not all stakeholders share the same values and norms and there is no agreement as to whose should take precedence (Bühner et al. 1998; Guillén 2000; Pedersen and Thomsen 1997; Roe 1993). While some actors argue that hostile takeovers are a means to attain goals such as efficiency and profitability, others find them at odds with values such as stability and solidarity. Hostile takeovers are a particularly disruptive means of corporate reorganization because asset disposals, layoffs, and other traumatic events tend to occur in their wake (Hirsch 1986). Sociologists characterize corporations as beset by perennial conflicts over whose values and norms should be upheld (Fligstein 1990, 2001; Guillén 1994). Other theoretical perspectives agree on this point. Agency theory and the property rights literature suggest that the firm is a "nexus of contracts" between groups of stakeholders and that the architects of the corporate governance system must not only reconcile each group's divergent interests but also allocate resources in a manner that is deemed acceptable by all parties (Jensen and Meckling 1976; Fama 1980; Jensen 2000).

Jeffrey Pfeffer and Gerald Salancik (1978) argue that current management and potential acquirers remain most cognizant of the values and norms of the powerful constituents who supply the organization with the resources that are deemed most critical. Labor and credit are perhaps the most significant examples, especially because their supply is frequently controlled by organized actors such as unions and banks. We also consider the impact of the community's values and norms as another relevant stakeholder.

Organized Labor   The ability of organized labor to influence organizational arrangements, strategic decisionmaking, and performance outcomes at the national, industry, and firm levels of analysis is one of the earliest and best documented findings of cross-national comparative research on organizations (Bendix 1956/2001; Cole 1985; Guillén 1994). The bulk of this research suggests that the values and norms espoused by organized labor generally oppose the usually disruptive effects of corporate reorganizations. Consistent with this prior research, we argue that organized labor views most hostile takeover activity unfavorably because of its potentially disruptive consequences. Labor emphasizes job security and solidarity over efficiency and profitability. The hostile takeover, as a method of corporate reorganization, may help achieve efficiency and profitability, but frequently at the cost of reducing job security. This argument is accepted not only by sociologists (for example, Hirsch 1986) but also by economists. According to Andrei Shleifer and Lawrence Summers (1988), for instance, a hostile takeover affords the incoming management team a special opportunity to violate the implicit long-term contract between the target firm's incumbent management and its workers. This breach of contract often takes the form of layoffs and an increase in the demands imposed on the remaining workers.

The actions that workers can take to combat the threat of hostile takeovers are likely to vary depending on the institutional role and militancy of the organized labor movement. National labor organizations differ substantially in those two respects (Guillén 2000; Roe 1993). In some countries labor unions have aligned themselves closely with one or more of the leading political parties, while in others labor's voice has been effectively silenced. In Germany as well as in several other central and northern European countries, for instance, powerful labor unions have been able to gain legal and regulatory mandates that ensure worker representation on corporate boards of directors. This affords labor an improved ability to block unwelcome takeover attempts or to moderate their negative consequences. In other countries—especially in southern Europe, Latin America, and East Asia—labor unions do not enjoy those institutional roles but have a demonstrated ability to engage in organized protest, including strikes and other types of collective action. Our argument is that the militancy of organized labor will be associated with fewer hostile takeovers because it imposes additional costs on acquirers. Although unions can implicitly exercise power if they enjoy institutional representation in the company's governance structures (for example, on the board of directors), it is the threat of disruptive action on the part of organized labor that reduces the attractiveness of a hostile takeover from the point of view of the actor launching it. Thus, we propose that *the greater the militancy of organized labor in a country, the lesser the legitimacy of hostile takeovers* (hypothesis 4).

Banks Commercial banks constitute a second important firm stakeholder, but the functions they perform differ substantially across countries (Glaeser and Shleifer 2000; Prowse 1995). In the United States, for instance, banks largely serve as lenders and face severe restrictions in their ability to own shares in nonfinancial corporations and to engage in such stock market activities as underwriting, brokering, and dealing. This limited role for American commercial banks appears to have become solidified in part as a result of growing populist sentiments during the Great Depression. In other countries banks fulfill a more central role in the economy, not only by providing loans but also by acting as prominent stock market intermediaries and equity holders. In many countries banks also exercise a monitoring function on behalf of customers who own small amounts of equity in firms. This is accomplished through the mechanism of proxy representation and vote at the annual shareholders' meeting. Thus, it is not uncommon in certain countries for a bank to exercise more than half of a company's voting rights even though the bank may own only 10 to 15 percent of its stock.

Banks that directly control large blocks of stock in nonfinancial companies, act as stock market intermediaries, or represent a large proportion of the stockholders through the proxy mechanism could be seen as benefiting from a hostile takeover in the same way that other shareholders would. In reality, however, the literature points out that banks generally prefer stable systems of corporate control over the potentially destabilizing effects of hostile takeovers. Deutsche Bank director Ellen Schneider-Lenné (1993, 22) offers an example of this perspective by denouncing the "excesses of takeover battles such as those witnessed in America and Britain," the "resultant high indebtedness of companies involved," and "the practices of corporate raiders who, after taking over a company, strip its assets to make a quick profit."

There are three main reasons why banks are likely to oppose a takeover attempt over a company in which they hold equity or exercise representation and voting rights. First, banks with large shareholdings and voting privileges are firm insiders and operate from a position of strength that typically enables them to dispatch directors to the board and appoint the CEO. Thus, they have little need to mount a hostile bid in order to exercise influence and control (Davis and Stout 1992).

Second, in many countries banks become large owners of nonfinancial companies to ensure an exclusive access to lucrative commercial transactions. Salient examples are electrical utilities and telecommunications operators, which need a "house bank" to handle their banking needs, including financing infrastructure projects and managing their extensive commercial payments and receipts operations. Thus, even though the shareholding bank obtains income in the form of dividends, these revenues tend to pale by comparison with those obtained from the commercial relationship between the bank and the firm in which it owns stock. An unsolicited outside bid for the company would disrupt this profitable commercial relationship from the point of view of the bank (Bühner et al. 1998; Guillén 2000; Roe 1993).

Third, the highly visible and central position that banks with shareholdings in other companies hold in some economies suggests that they are often placed under intense scrutiny by other stakeholder groups. Consequently, banks might often find that the reputation costs associated with negative public opinion easily outweigh any tangible financial gains from a hostile takeover (Baums 1993). Rolf Bühner and his colleagues (1998) found this to be precisely the case when Deutsche Bank tried to finance steel manufacturer Krupp's hostile takeover of its competitor Thyssen. After announcing its intentions, Deutsche Bank faced a public relations crisis when steelworkers began picketing the bank's Frankfurt headquarters and the unions threatened to withdraw their financial deposits. In response to the media outcry, Deutsche Bank withdrew its financial support of the takeover, which took place only after the two companies agreed to a friendly merger one year later. For these three reasons, we expect that *the greater the restrictions on banks to act as shareholders of nonfinancial firms or as stock market intermediaries in a country, the greater the legitimacy of hostile takeovers* (hypothesis 5).

The Community   Like organized labor and the banks, the community is an important stakeholder in the firm whose values may or may not be consistent with those of a corporate raider or of the shareholders. From the viewpoint of the acquirer, the most reasonable justification for a hostile takeover is the opportunity to create or capture more wealth, either through synergy or through a favorable redistribution of economic gains and losses. In this context, synergy signifies increases in the efficiency and productive output that accrue to the merged company owing to complementary resources or capabilities that could not have been achieved by the two firms acting separately. Redistributions refer to the appropriation of a portion of another party's economic welfare. Although the labor force and the current managers of the target firm provide the most frequently cited victims of a hostile takeover, sociologists and economists have also noted that welfare losses can accrue to the general public (Hirsch 1986; Shleifer and Summers 1988). Such losses become readily apparent, for instance, when a takeover leads to the closure of a small-town factory or to the rapid consumption of a previously preserved natural resource (Harris 1996).

While synergistic gains might be welcomed as an economic boon to society, redistributions raise obvious ethical dilemmas and result in power contests. The extent to which a given society alternatively highlights the potential benefits of synergies or dwells on the negative aspects of redistribution depends, at least partially, on its overall cultural values. Geert Hofstede (1980, 213–19) distinguishes among several cultural value dimensions that in his study vary systematically across countries. In particular, he conceptualizes and measures individualism as the degree to which the values of the members of a society focus on satisfying the interests of the individual over those of the group, community, or collectivity. Individualism is consistent with the goals and values of efficiency and profitability, while collectivism is consistent with security and social justice. Thus, individualism affects people's perceptions in such a way that they behave normatively according to the values of their culture. Hostile takeovers are perceived as consistent with individualist norms but inconsistent with collectivist values (Hirsch 1986; Shleifer and Summers 1988).

The relationship between individualist values and hostile takeovers can be conceptually articulated at the level of both the national culture and the organization. In individualistic countries we predict that society will consider the acquirer's efforts to create value for itself and its shareholders to be legitimate and acceptable since it regards such efforts as promoting greater wealth in the long run. This individualistic framing is consistent with Fligstein's (1990) description of the financial conception of corporate control, which regards the maintenance and enhancement of shareholder wealth as focal concerns. In more collectivist or communitarian cultures, by contrast, it seems unlikely that the financial conception of control would prevail. The central problem of corporate governance would naturally entail a more harmonious and equitable reconciliation of the interests and needs of the various stakeholder groups. In collectivist cultures the motives of the hostile acquirer will tend to be judged to a greater degree in light of the possible ill effects on society. Therefore, collectivist or communitarian values impose more significant normative barriers on hostile takeovers, while individualist values foster them. At the level of the organization, collectivist values "call for greater emotional dependence of members on their organizations" (Hofstede 1980, 217). Thus, employees who espouse collectivist values are less likely to accept the often traumatic reorganizations and adjustments that hostile takeovers entail. Accordingly, we predict that *the greater the degree of individualism in a country, the greater the legitimacy of hostile takeovers* (hypothesis 6).

The Empirical Study

We collected data on sixty-one countries for the eleven years between 1988 and 1998. Information on takeover activity was taken from the Securities Data Company's *SDC Platinum* database (SDC 1999). This source starts its international coverage in 1985, but the quality of the data is not appropriate for our purposes until 1988. Our findings did not change when the records from these early years were included.

The database includes both public and private transactions. SDC classifies a takeover as "hostile" when the target firm's board of directors officially rejects an offer but the acquirer persists with the takeover. In a comparison of four operational definitions of hostile takeovers based on a sample of 2,346 takeover contests that occurred between 1975 and 1996, William Schwert (2000) finds SDC's definition to be the most highly and positively correlated with the one used by the Wall Street Journal/Dow Jones News Retrieval Service (WSJ/DNJR). *SDC Platinum*'s categorization can be regarded as a relatively conservative definition of hostile takeovers in that it produces higher counts of hostile takeovers than WSJ/DJNR but significantly lower counts than classifications based on non-negotiated bids or an evaluation of pre-bid events. For the purposes of this study, SDC holds the obvious advantage of being the data source with the best worldwide coverage. SDC draws on over two hundred English- and foreign-language news sources, SEC filings and their international counterparts, trade publications, wires and proprietary sources of investment banks, law firms, and other advisers. Although such important issues as variations in reporting standards and data availability should always raise concerns regarding the validity of cross-national tests, SDC is often regarded as the best resource for drawing inferences on global takeover activity (Guillén 2000; Prowse 1995).

We used the count of announced hostile takeover bids as an indicator of the legitimacy of this practice in different countries. Taking into account only consummated hostile takeovers would have amounted to sampling on the dependent variable and would therefore have introduced serious biases into the analysis. We followed several steps to construct our dependent variable. We first downloaded SDC's complete listing of corporate takeover bid announcements for the years under investigation. Next, we classified these records by year, by the attitude of the corporate transaction (either hostile or nonhostile), and by the home country of the target firm. We successfully classified a total of 249,028 of SDC's records and had to omit fewer than 1 percent of the total number of entries because of missing information regarding one or more of these three categorizations. This classification process yielded aggregate count data for hostile and nonhostile takeover announcements in each country and year.

We used a variety of sources to calculate indicators for our independent variables. We used the classification of national legal traditions used by La Porta and his colleagues (1999). We adopted Witold Henisz's (2000a, 2000b) methodology to quantify political uncertainty as a time-varying attribute of each country. His indicator of "political constraints" captures "a government's ability to credibly commit not to interfere with private property rights" (see also North 1990). Henisz's political constraints index incorporates information on the number of independent branches of government with veto power (executive, higher legislature, lower legislature, judiciary, subnational government) and the distribution of preferences across and within those branches. He gathered data on 157 countries for each year between 1960 and 1998 characterizing the political system in terms of the number of branches of government, the partisan alignments across each of them, and the party composition of legislatures. The political constraints index theoretically ranges between zero (no constraints) and unity (totally constrained), and increases with the number of de jure veto points in the political system, the degree to which veto points are controlled by different parties, and the extent to which the preferences of decisionmakers are aligned with party preferences within the legislature or the judiciary. To create a variable in which higher values represent greater political uncertainty, we reversed Henisz's original measure. We used Luis Servén's (1998) methodology for measuring unexpected macroeconomic changes and calculated the natural logarithmic of the conditional variance of nominal GDP growth in a given year fitted by using a generalized conditional heteroskedasticity (GARCH) specification.[1] The correlation between the measures of political and economic uncertainty is +0.37. We entered them separately in all of our analyses.

To determine when a country first instituted formalized stock trading, we initially referred to the *MSCI Handbook of World Stock, Derivative and Commodity Exchanges* (MSCI 1999), which contains brief histories of most major national equity exchanges. We considered the inception date (or year of incorporation) of the country's largest stock exchange as the starting point of formalized equity share trading. In cases where the currently leading stock exchange had a clear historical predecessor, we used the starting date associated with the earlier stock market. We found many instances in which the histories detailed in the *MSCI Handbook* were ambiguous in regard to the timing of the stock market inception (often by just a few years). In these cases, we also referred to that stock exchange's website. After conducting this additional search, ten countries were still considered to have ambiguous starting points for formalized stock trading. Each of the two authors made independent judgments of the appropriate inception year for these countries using all of the collected data. Inter-rater reliability was 80 percent. In the two remaining cases for which the authors came to different conclusions, they reviewed the information together and reached a mutually acceptable decision. To calculate the number of years of formalized stock trading, the stock market's inception date was subtracted from the observation year in the sample, thus obtaining a time-varying measure. To capture the nonlinear effect predicted in hypothesis 3, we included linear and quadratic terms.

The International Labor Organization's *Yearbook of Labor Statistics* (1994–1999) provided a proxy for the militancy of each country's organized labor movement: the number of workdays lost due to strikes for each year.

Since yearly strike data tend to be volatile, we calculated three-year moving averages.[2] Our measure of the banks' ability to own stock or act as brokers was calculated by examining in each country their ability to own and control nonfinancial firms and to "engage in underwriting, brokering, dealing and all aspects of the mutual fund industry" along two four-point scales created by James Barth, Gerald Caprio, and Ross Levine (2000, 14). Scores of one (unrestricted) or two (permitted but limited) suggest a more central role for banks in the national economy, while scores of three (restricted) and four (prohibited) reflect banking systems that have a narrower influence. We combined these two banking measures to create a composite scale that could theoretically range between two and eight. Since higher scores indicate greater restrictions on banking, we predict a positive relationship between this measure and hostile takeover activity. We were able to construct a time-varying measure, since Barth and his colleagues detail the various changes to national systems since 1980.

We measured the degree of individualism in a country with Hofstede's (1991) score. Since cultural inclinations are considered to be a relatively stable attribute (Hofstede 1980, 1991), all yearly records relating to the same country were coded with identical individualism scores.

We also compiled information on six groups of additional control variables, which were included in all models. Prior research has suggested that hostile takeovers occur in waves and are sensitive to changes in the business cycle. Therefore, we included yearly GDP growth rates. Since it could be argued that the level of hostile takeover activity largely represents a function of the overall takeover activity, we also controlled for the number of non-hostile corporate takeovers. This control also provides an indication of the extent to which a given country allows for market-mediated transfers of corporate control. To account for the total level of economic activity, we included annual GDP figures (measured in billions of U.S. dollars) in our models. The size of local stock markets in relation to the size of the overall economy differs dramatically across countries. Therefore, we also accounted for stock market capitalization (in billions of U.S. dollars) as a potentially relevant determinant of hostile takeover activity. To estimate differences in industrial composition, we calculated the percentage of all takeover targets for each country and year that SDC categorized as primarily operating in agriculture and mining, industrial and manufacturing, and the services sectors. Finally, we included a set of year dummy variables.

The dependent variable for our analysis (number of hostile takeover bid announcements) has certain important characteristics: it is non-negative; it is integer-valued, denoting counts of hostile takeovers; it exhibits overdispersion; and it is longitudinal, including observations per country and per year. When the outcome variable is non-negative and integer-valued, Poisson regression is more appropriate than ordinary least squares. To adjust for overdispersion, we used the negative binomial model, a generalization of the Poisson model where the assumption of equal mean and variance is relaxed (Cameron and Trivedi 1998; Hausman, Hall, and Griliches 1984). When longitudinally clustered data violate the underlying assumption of independence between observations, it is possible to adjust the parameter estimates and their standard errors by using the generalized estimating equations (GEE) approach (Liang and Zeger 1986; Zeger, Liang, and Albert 1988). The GEE algorithm accounts for correlation between records within the same cluster, thus providing efficient estimates of coefficients and improved standard error estimates (see Allison 2000; Diggle, Liang, and Zeger 1994). The GEE approach enjoys some advantage over random-effects models in that it is less computationally intensive and is therefore less subject to instability and specification problems. This feature of GEE is especially attractive for our analysis given the high prevalence of records with a value of zero for the dependent variable. We ran negative binomial analysis using GEE estimation and assuming an exchangeable correlation structure, which assumes an equal correlation structure between all records within the same country cluster.[3]

Although we were sometimes unable to find all of the data necessary for each of the eleven annual records for each country, there was no reason to suspect that yearly information was made unavailable owing to the (potentially unfavorable) nature of the data. Therefore, we continued our analysis with the use of an unbalanced panel. Table 6.1 presents the sample descriptive statistics, correlations, and composition. The samples used in the analyses contain a mix of developed and emerging economies.

Results

Table 6.2 shows the empirical results. Given the large amount of missing data on two of the independent variables (banking restrictions and the individualism score), we report our main results based on two different samples of countries. Model A is the baseline model with the control variables only. In model B we add our regulative, cognitive, and normative variables: the English legal tradition dummy, uncertainty, stock market age, and labor militancy. Models A and B are both based on our larger sample (483 cases, 61 countries, 11 years). Model C has the same specification as B, but we use a smaller sample (330 cases, 39 countries, 10 years), after deleting observations with missing data for our two remaining normative variables, namely, banking restrictions and individualism, which we add to the equation in model D. All models show significant levels of goodness-of-fit (p < 0.001). Comparisons of the Wald chi-squares indicate that model B represents a statistically significant improvement over model A, and that model D offers an improvement over model C (p < 0.001 for each test).

The results in models B through D provide strong support for hypothesis 1 on the regulative effect of legal institutions. Countries with English-origin

TABLE 6.1 Sample Descriptive Statistics, Correlations, and Composition

	Mean	SD	1	2	3	4	5	6	7	8	9	10	11	12
1. Number of hostile takeovers	1.97	7.88	—											
2. English legal tradition = 1	.37	.48	.28*	—										
3. Political uncertainty	.63	.21	-.05	.06	—									
4. Economic uncertainty	-5.74	2.80	-.17*	-.16*	.37*	—								
5. Stock market age	94.88	76.50	.29*	-.19*	-.22*	-.25*	—							
6. Stock market age squared	14,842.27	24,152.35	.22*	-.15*	-.20*	-.24*	.91*	—						
7. Working days lost to strikes (thousands)	1,917.49	11,327.16	.04	.13*	.05	.02	.01	-.01	—					
8. Banking restrictions[a]	3.98	1.49	.09	-.07	.09	.27*	-.28*	-.30*	.02	—				
9. Individualism score (log)[a]	3.82	.59	.31*	.06	-.47*	-.54*	.52*	.41*	.08	.27*	—			
10. GDP (billions of U.S. dollars)	503.94	1,239.79	.60*	.05	-.13*	-.22*	.35*	.25*	.03	.28*	.28*	—		
11. GDP growth rate (percentage)	3.39	3.69	-.03	.16*	.11	.02	-.09	-.09	-.02	.15*	-.48*	-.07	—	
12. Stock market cap (billions of U.S. dollars)	322.14	1,152.93	.58*	.14*	.10	-.21*	.28*	.21*	.02	.26*	.24*	.89*	-.02	—
13. Number of nonhostile takeovers	456.83	1,499.21	.75*	.23*	-.07	-.21*	.35*	.27*	.04	.14	.32*	.78*	-.05	.88*

Source: Authors' compilation.
Notes: N = 483 country-years, 61 countries.
Country composition:
The thirty countries included in the smallest sample are: Australia, Austria, Belgium, Brazil, Canada, Chile, Denmark, Finland, France, Germany, Greece, India, Italy, Japan, Malaysia, Mexico, the Netherlands, New Zealand, Norway, Philippines, Portugal, Singapore, South Africa. Spain, Sweden, Switzerland, Thailand, Turkey, the United Kingdom, and the United States.
The thirty-nine countries in the next larger sample are these thirty countries plus: Argentina, Colombia, Ecuador, El Salvador, Indonesia, Israel, Luxembourg, Pakistan, and Peru.
The sixty-one countries in the largest sample are these thirty-nine countries plus: Bangladesh, Botswana, Costa Rica, Cyprus, the Czech Republic, Egypt, Ghana, Hungary, Iceland, Jamaica, Kenya. Mauritius, Morocco, Namibia, Nigeria, Panama, Poland, Romania, Russia, Sri Lanka, Trinidad and Tobago, and Tunisia.
a. For this variable, sample size equals 330 country-years (39 countries).
* p < .01

TABLE 6.2   *Negative Binomial Regressions of the Number of Hostile Takeovers*

	Expected Effect	Model A	Model B	Model C	Model D
English legal tradition	H1: +	—	2.14*** (4.77)	2.23*** (5.57)	1.70*** (4.29)
Political uncertainty	H2: −	—	−2.01*** (−3.53)	−2.07** (−3.00)	−.58 (−.66)
Economic uncertainty	H2: −	—	−.06 (−0.86)	−.02 (−.22)	.11† (1.72)
Stock market age	H3: +	—	.04*** (5.20)	.05*** (5.28)	.03** (3.01)
Stock market age squared[a]	H3: −	—	−.09*** (−4.72)	−.10*** (−4.91)	−.06** (−3.20)
Working days lost to strikes[a]	H4: −	—	−.08* (−2.44)	−.09* (−2.26)	−.09† (−1.80)
Banking restrictions	H5: +	—	—	—	.18* (2.49)
Individualism score	H6: +	—	—	—	2.66*** (3.94)
GDP[a]	—	−.40 (−1.27)	−.04 (−.34)	.01 (.11)	−.01 (−.05)
GDP growth rate	—	−.03 (−1.51)	.02 (.44)	.05 (.87)	.13 (1.61)
Stock market capitalization[a]	—	−2.05*** (−6.71)	−.64*** (−4.01)	−.68*** (−4.56)	−.67** (−3.47)
Number of nonhostile takeovers[a]	—	2.33*** (5.49)	.67** (3.13)	.60** (3.33)	.58** (2.75)
Annual dummies	—	Included	Included	Included	Included
Industrial composition	—	Included	Included	Included	Included
Intercept	—	−2.04	−9.97	−15.13	−40.41
N (number of observations)	—	483	483	330	330
Number of countries	—	61	61	39	39
Wald chi-square	—	687.7***	1,334.75***	1,087.65***	1,714.16***

Source: Authors' compilation.
Notes: Using generalized estimating equations (GEE) approach for panel data.
z scores are shown in parentheses beneath regression coefficients.
a. coefficient multiplied by 1,000.
*** p < .001; ** p < .01; * p < .05; † p < .10 (two-tailed tests)

corporate laws have a greater number of hostile takeovers. We find mixed results regarding hypothesis 2 on the cognitive effect of uncertainty. Economic uncertainty never reaches significance (except marginally in model D, albeit in the wrong direction). Political uncertainty is highly significant in models B and C but loses significance in model D once we control for banking restrictions and individualism. Since political uncertainty is significant and the point estimate is very similar with either the larger sample of model B or the smaller one of model C, but loses significance in model D owing to the addition of new variables, we must conclude that there is no support for hypothesis 2 once the regression model is fully specified. This loss in significance might be attributable to the high correlation of political and economic uncertainty with individualism. Another contributing factor may be the reduced variation of political and economic uncertainty found in the countries that compose the smaller sample sizes, which excludes most of the less developed countries often associated with higher levels of these forms of uncertainty (see table 6.1).

We find significant results regarding the cognitive effect of stock market age that are robust to changes in the size of the sample and the number of variables included in the equation (see models B, C, and D). The consistently positive coefficient for the linear term of stock market age combined with a negative coefficient for the quadratic term suggests that increasing stock market age contributes to greater hostile takeover activity, but at a decreasing rate, thus supporting hypothesis 3. The effect of stock market age peaks at a level of 241 years in model B, 236 in model C, and 232 in model D. Only four countries have exchanges older than the peak points. In results not shown here, we used the cumulative number of nonhostile takeovers as the proxy for routine stock trading and obtained similar results.

Turning to normative effects, we find significant and robust support for hypothesis 4 on the effect of labor militancy on hostile takeover activity, for hypothesis 5 on the effect of banking restrictions, and for hypothesis 6 on the effect of individualism. These three hypotheses receive robust support from our analysis regardless of the sample size and the specification. The values and norms espoused by militant labor movements, banks with few operating restrictions regarding stockholding or stock brokerage, and non-individualist communities are found to reduce the number of hostile takeovers in our sample.

Given the large numbers of hostile takeovers in the United States and the United Kingdom, we repeated the analysis after removing these two countries from the samples in table 6.2. These tests yielded results consistent with those reported, except that labor militancy lost significance in model D.

To test whether our statistical models also predict nonhostile takeover activity, we repeated our analyses with nonhostile takeovers as the dependent variable (results not shown here). In general, these models produced relatively poor and unstable results. In the specification analogous to model B, English legal tradition and political uncertainty lost statistical significance, while labor militancy reversed sign. It is important to note that we specifically formulated our hypotheses with hostile takeovers and their role in corporate governance in mind, and this is the main reason why our models cannot explain nonhostile takeovers nearly as well.

Discussion and Conclusion

The literature on cross-national differences in corporate governance practices has produced valuable descriptive analyses. However, this research has often obscured the profound variation that continues to persist among national systems. Furthermore, prior work has largely failed to explore the causes underlying these differences. Our aim in this chapter has been to provide an explanation as to why cross-national variations exist in the case of hostile takeovers. We started the chapter by conceptually linking those differences to the specific institutional characteristics of countries that provide this organizational practice with legitimacy from regulative, cognitive, and normative points of view. The regulative pillar includes the basic rules and laws that make hostile takeovers possible. The cognitive pillar provides the frames that help actors cope with the uncertainty surrounding the practice. The normative pillar indicates to actors whether the practice is consistent with the norms and values espoused by various other actors in the environment of the practice. We proposed to use corporate legal traditions as the proxy for the regulative institutional pillar, economic and political uncertainty and stock market age as the indicators of the cognitive pillar, and stakeholder effects (labor militancy, banking restrictions, individualism) as the measure of the normative pillar. Our empirical results based on samples of sixty-one and thirty-nine countries over an eleven-year period allow us to claim that each of the three institutional pillars helps explain the differences across countries in the prevalence of this important corporate governance practice. We formulated six predictions and found consistent and robust support for all but one of them, even with changing samples and model specifications.

While U.S. corporate governance research typically focuses on the respective interests of shareholders and managers, this chapter illustrates the impact of other stakeholder groups on corporate control practices. Consistent with previous comparative research, we find significant cross-country variation in the relative level of influence of various stakeholder groups (Blair and Roe 1999, 163–93; La Porta et al. 1998, 1999). Research on the German system of codetermination, for instance, has chronicled how labor has secured a role in various internal control mechanisms, including workers' councils at the shop-floor level and supervisory boards at the company level (Streeck 1992; Rogers and Streeck 1995; Pistor 1999). The influential role that banks play in the Japanese keiretsu system has been equally well documented (Anderson 1984; Streeck 1992; Gerlach and Lincoln 2000). Through our discussion and analysis of hostile takeovers, we have attempted to show how stakeholders act as the arbitrators of social legitimacy and how their influence over firm control extends well beyond any traditionally recognized corporate governance position.

While there is no agreement as to whether hostile takeovers are "good" or "bad," our analysis provides a deeper understanding of the drivers of this important phenomenon. The regulative, cognitive, and normative variables used in the empirical analysis characterize countries in fundamental and momentous ways. Companies look so different because they themselves vary substantially in terms of legal provisions, stock-trading history, and stakeholder power and influence. Our point is that discussing the vices and virtues of hostile takeovers is only one way of looking at the problem; examining their legitimacy in various countries is another, perhaps complementary way of looking at them that yields further insights. In its emphasis on legitimacy, this chapter shares an important theoretical thread with Gerald Davis and Henrich Greve (1997), who outline how regulative, cognitive, and normative factors have influenced U.S. patterns of diffusion for "poison pills" and "golden parachutes," two other corporate governance mechanisms related to the market for corporate control. Of course, the study of how the processes underlying social legitimacy enable and constrain economic action has not been lost to researchers working outside the field of corporate governance. Within this volume, Kieran Healy provides a detailed account of how transplant advocates have worked to transform organ donation into a legitimate market activity.

This chapter also speaks to the differing ways in which the public corporation is conceived across countries. Like the chapters by Charles Perrow and Bai Gao, we point to the important role that institutions play in shaping the beliefs surrounding the firm. While Perrow finds that the political and legal institutions of the United States have contributed to an industry model favoring massive hierarchical corporations, Gao shows how the Japanese institutional environment led to a view that smaller firms tied together by complex interindustry arrangements provides the economically superior alternative. Our results indicate that hostile takeovers are more prevalent when the institutional conditions in a country are more consistent with the view of the firm as a bundle of financial assets than with the view of the firm as a social entity. Thus, this empirical study of hostile takeovers can be used to assess the conception of the firm that tends to predominate in different societies. Although much research in the sociology of organizations has emphasized the fact that the corporation is embedded in a wider social context, on which it depends for critical resources (see, for example, Perrow 1986; Pfeffer and Salancik 1978), almost no cross-national evidence has been produced to show that there is a systematic pattern of institutional variables that accounts for the differences.

It is worth noting that this association between the differing conceptions of the firm and the legitimacy of hostile takeovers has not been lost to practicing managers. In his polemic on the pros and cons of hostile takeovers, the corporate attorney and antitakeover advocate Edmund J. Kelly (2001, 1, 28) envisions a conversation between two persons. The advocate for takeovers argues that business corporations are merely paper entities and that their managers "ought to have one allegiance above all others—maximizing shareholder wealth." In contrast, the opponent characterizes the firm as "an elegant and exciting new medium for social as well as economic progress" whose primary objective is "preservation and growth for the benefit of society, including . . . but not exclusively the shareholders." From the perspective of this chapter, the efforts of Kelly and other like-minded activists to lobby for greater antitakeover legislation, challenge assumptions regarding the merits of takeovers, and appeal to powerful stakeholder groups can be regarded as attempts to deinstitutionalize the practice. Recent decreases in hostile takeover activity in the United States might suggest that they have realized some success. We approach this inference with much caution, however, since the frequency of hostile takeovers is subject to cyclical fluctuations.

Our findings are consistent with many of the key principles shared by both economic sociology and neo-institutional theory. Organizational practices do not diffuse broadly and rapidly solely because they are proven to be superior in some universal economic sense. Similarly, evidence of inefficiency and utility loss will not always be held as sufficient grounds for curtailing a well-established course of action. A sociological perspective on markets and the economy holds that so-called rational behavior is intersubjectively determined (Smelser and Swedberg 1994; Dobbin and Dowd 2000). As Mark Mizruchi and Gerald Davis do in their chapter on the globalization strategies of U.S. banks, we argue that the adoption and spread of an economic activity hinges on the preferences and perceptions of a society's most influential actors. In contrast with Mizruchi and Davis, however, this chapter focuses on a practice in which mimicry and diffusion have often failed to occur. Countries differ in how power is distributed among the stakeholder groups. Therefore, a practice that promises to disrupt the allocation of social welfare as dramatically as the hostile takeover has failed to gain acceptance in many countries.

Our empirical results also shed some light on the debate over the convergence in corporate governance practices across countries (Guillén 2000). The fact that differences across countries can be traced back empirically to the institutional and structural characteristics of countries means that we cannot assume that corporate governance practices, no matter how desirable or efficient, will diffuse widely. Widespread diffusion can be expected only if the relevant institutional features converge across countries. Previous research has pointed out that legal institutions, for instance, are unlikely to change in the foreseeable future (La Porta et al. 1998; Roe 1993). Our empirical evidence suggests that hostile takeovers are consistent with certain regulative, cognitive, and normative institutional circumstances but not others. Thus, we expect differences across countries in the level of hostile takeover activity to persist into the future.

Finally, our analysis speaks to the comparative study of institutions. Our theoretical and empirical analysis confirms the usefulness of examining the sources of institutional legitimacy of organizational structures, behaviors, and practices. Institutions provide the foundations for organizational life, the taken-for-granted regulative, cognitive, and normative pillars that enable and shape action. Our analysis shows that national institutions can be conceptualized and measured in a way that captures institutional variations across a large number of countries, which then can be used to explain differences in an outcome variable of interest. This approach lends itself to examining dependent variables defined at many levels of analysis, including the organization, the industry, and the country.

Our theoretical and empirical analysis is limited in several respects. First, we have focused on explanations at the country level of analysis. While we tried to control for industry effects using available data, firm-level variables surely have an impact on the frequency of hostile takeovers that we neglected here. Second, we obviously did not control for all possible alternative corporate governance mechanisms. Future research may develop ways of measuring other alternatives for which no readily available empirical indicators currently exist.

We envision several ways of refining and expanding the analysis of corporate governance practices reported in this chapter. First, other corporate governance mechanisms could be studied cross-nationally using a similar institutional framework of analysis, including board-of-director composition and employee stock options. Second, rather than aggregating the dependent variable at the country level of analysis, researchers could also test for firm-level explanations. Finally, case studies of firms across many national settings could be useful in generating more nuanced hypotheses and in understanding the basic underlying causal processes. These research avenues will provide fertile ground for formulating and testing sociological propositions about corporate governance practices and about the role of the corporation in society that strike a balance between large-scale, cross-national differences and microlevel processes.

We thank Frank Dobbin, Marion Fourcade-Gourinchas, Witold Henisz, Charles Perrow, and participants in the Princeton Economic Sociology Conference and the Academy of Management annual meetings for helpful suggestions. This research has been supported by a series of generous grants from the Center for Leadership and Management Change at the Wharton School.

Notes

1. Servén (1998) estimates the following GARCH(1,1) model originally suggested by Tim Bollerslev (1986):

$$y_{it} = \alpha_1 t + \beta_1 y_{i,\,t-1} + \varepsilon_t; \, t = 1, \ldots, T;$$

$$\sigma_t^2 = \gamma_{i,0} + \gamma_{i,1} \varepsilon_{i,t-1}^2 + \delta_i \sigma_{i,t-1}^2$$

with σ_t^2 denoting the variance of ε_t conditional on the information up to year t, which is estimated separately for each country.

2. Another indicator of organized labor's role in a country would be the proportion of workers who are unionized. Unfortunately, this variable is available only for a very small set of countries (the richest in the world), and for only a few years. Using it would reduce our sample by two-thirds.

3. We do not report results using country fixed effects because so doing would preclude us from testing the first and last hypotheses using legal traditions and individualism scores as the empirical indicators, respectively. The reason for this is that these two variables are not time-varying in nature, as explained in the data section.

References

Allison, Paul D. 2000. *Logistic Regression Using the SAS System*. Cary, N.C.: SAS Institute.

Alonso, Pablo de Andres, and Felix J. Lopez Iturriaga. 1997. "Financial System Models, Corporate Governance, and Capital Investment in OECD Countries: Some Stylized Facts." *EIB Papers* 2(2): 68–95.

Anderson, Charles A. 1984. "Corporate Directors in Japan." *Harvard Business Review* (May–June): 30–38.

Barth, James R., Gerald Caprio Jr., and Ross Levine. 2000. "Banking Systems Around the Globe: Do Regulations and Ownership Affect Performance and Stability?" Working paper. Washington, D.C.: World Bank.

Baums, Theodor. 1993. "Takeovers Versus Institutions in Corporate Governance in Germany." In *Contemporary Issues in Corporate Governance*, edited by D. D. Prentice and P. R. J. Holland. Oxford: Clarendon Press.

Becht, Marco. 1999. "European Corporate Governance: Trading Off Liquidity Against Control." *European Economic Review* 43: 1071–83.

Bendix, Reinhard. 1956/2001. *Work and Authority in Industry*. New Brunswick, N.J.: Transaction.

Biggart, Nicole Woolsey, and Mauro F. Guillén. 1999. "Developing Difference: Social Organization and the Rise of the Auto Industries of South Korea, Taiwan, Spain, and Argentina." *American Sociological Review* 64(5, October): 722–47.

Blair, Margaret M., and Mark J. Roe, eds. 1999. *Employees and Corporate Governance*. Washington, D.C.: Brookings Institution Press.

Bollerslev, Tim. 1986. "Generalized Autoregressive Conditional Heteroskedasticity." *Journal of Econometrics* 31: 307–27.

Bühner, Rolf, Abdul Rashee, Joseph Rosenstein, and Toru Yoshikawa. 1998. "Research on Corporate Governance: A Comparison of Germany, Japan, and the United States." *Advances in International Comparative Management* 12: 121–55.

Cameron, A. Colin, and Pravin K. Trivedi. 1998. *Regression Analysis of Count Data.* Cambridge: Cambridge University Press.

Campbell, John, and Leon Lindberg. 1990. "Property Rights and the Organization of Economic Activity by the State." *American Sociological Review* 55(5, October): 3–14.

Charkham, Jonathon P. 1994. *Keeping Good Company: A Study of Corporate Governance in Five Countries.* New York: Oxford University Press.

Cole, Robert E. 1985. "The Macropolitics of Organizational Change: A Comparative Analysis of the Spread of Small-Group Activities." *Administrative Science Quarterly* 30: 560–85.

Davis, Gerald F., and Henrich R. Greve. 1997. "Corporate Elite Networks and Governance Changes in the 1980s." *American Journal of Sociology* 103(1): 1–37.

Davis, Gerald F., and Suzanne K. Stout. 1992. "Organization Theory and the Market for Corporate Control: A Dynamic Analysis of the Characteristics of Large Takeover Targets, 1980 to 1990." *Administrative Science Quarterly* 37: 605–33.

Diggle, Peter, Kung-Yee Liang, and Scott L. Zeger. 1994. *The Analysis of Longitudinal Data.* New York: Oxford University Press.

DiMaggio, Paul J., and Walter W. Powell. 1983. "The Iron Cage Revisited: Institutional Isomorphism and Collective Rationality in Organizational Fields." *American Sociological Review* 48(2): 147–60.

Dobbin, Frank, and Timothy J. Dowd. 2000. "The Market That Antitrust Built: Public Policy, Private Coercion, and Railroad Acquisitions." *American Sociological Review* 65(5): 631–57.

Fama, Eugene F. 1980. "Agency Problems and the Theory of the Firm." *Journal of Political Economy* 88(2, April): 288–307.

Fligstein, Neil. 1990. *The Transformation of Corporate Control.* Cambridge, Mass.: Harvard University Press.

———. 1996. "Markets as Politics: A Political-Cultural Approach to Market Institutions." *American Sociological Review* 61(4, August): 656–73.

———. 2001. *The Architecture of Markets.* Princeton, N.J.: Princeton University Press.

Gedajlovic, Eric R., and Daniel M. Shapiro. 1998. "Management and Ownership Effects: Evidence from Five Countries." *Strategic Management Journal* 19: 533–53.

Gerlach, Michael L., and James R. Lincoln. 2000. "Economic Organization and Innovation in Japan: Networks, Spin-offs, and the Creation of Enterprise." In *Knowledge Creation: A New Source of Value,* edited by Georg Von Krogh, Ikujiro Nonaka, and Toshihiro Nishiguchi. London: Macmillan.

Glaeser, Edward L., and Andrei Shleifer. 2000. "Legal Origins." Working paper. Cambridge, Mass.: Harvard University, Department of Economics.

Glendon, Mary Ann, Michael W. Gordon, and Christopher Osakwe. 1994. *Comparative Legal Traditions.* St. Paul, Minn.: West.

Granovetter, Mark. 1985. "Economic Action and Social Structure: The Problem of Embeddedness." *American Journal of Sociology* 91(3, November): 481–510.

Guillén, Mauro F. 1994. *Models of Management.* Chicago: University of Chicago Press.

———. 2000. "Corporate Governance and Globalization: Is There Convergence Across Countries?" *Advances in International Comparative Management* 13: 175–204.

Guillén, Mauro F., and Sandra L. Suárez. 1993. "The Institutional Context of Multinational Activity." In *Organizational Theory and the Multinational Corporation,* edited by Sumantra Ghoshal and Eleanor Westney. New York: St. Martin's Press.

Harris, David. 1996. *The Last Stand: The War Between Wall Street and Main Street over California's Ancient Redwoods.* New York: Times Books.

Hausman, Jerry A., Bronwyn H. Hall, and Zvi Griliches. 1984. "Econometric Models for Count Data with an Application to the Patents-R&D Relationship." *Econometrica* 52(4): 909–38.

Henisz, Witold J. 2000a. "The Institutional Environment for Economic Growth." *Economics and Politics* 12(1): 1–31.

———. 2000b. The Political Constraint Index Database. http://www-management. wharton.upenn.edu/henisz/POLCON/ContactInfo.htm.

Hirsch, Paul M. 1986. "From Ambushes to Golden Parachutes: Corporate Takeovers as an Instance of Cultural Framing and Institutional Integration." *American Journal of Sociology* 91(4, January): 800–37.

Hofstede, Geert. 1980. *Culture's Consequences: International Differences in Work-Related Values.* Newbury Park, Calif.: Sage Publications.

———. 1991. *Cultures and Organizations.* New York: McGraw-Hill.

International Labor Organization (ILO). 1994–1999. *Yearbook of Labor Statistics.* Geneva: ILO.

Jarrell, Gregg A., James A. Brickley, and Jeffrey M. Netter. 1988. "The Market for Corporate Control: The Empirical Evidence Since 1980." *Journal of Economic Perspectives* 2(1): 49–68.

Jemison, David B., and Sim B. Sitkin. 1986. "Corporate Acquisitions: A Process Prospective." *Academy of Management Review* 11(1): 145–63.

Jensen, Michael C. 1989. "Eclipse of the Public Corporation." *Harvard Business Review* 67(5): 67–74.

———. 2000. *A Theory of the Firm: Governance, Residual Claims, and Organizational Forms.* Cambridge, Mass.: Harvard University Press.

Jensen, Michael C., and William H. Meckling. 1976. "Theory of the Firm: Managerial Behavior, Agency Costs, and Ownership Structure." *Journal of Financial Economics* 3: 305–60.

Jensen, Michael C., and Richard S. Ruback. 1983. "The Market for Corporate Control: The Scientific Evidence." *Journal of Financial Economics* 11(1–4): 5–50.

Kelly, Edmund J. 2001. *The Takeover Dialogues: A Discussion of Hostile Takeovers.* San Jose, Calif.: Authors Choice Press.

La Porta, Rafael, Florencio Lopez-de-Silanes, and Andrei Shleifer. 1999. "Corporate Ownership Around the World." *Journal of Finance* 54(2, April): 471–517.

La Porta, Rafael, Florencio Lopez-de-Silanes, Andrei Shleifer, and Robert W. Vishny. 1998. "Law and Finance." *Journal of Political Economy* 106(6): 1113–55.

———. 1999. "The Quality of Government." *Journal of Law, Economics, and Organization* 15: 222–79.

Liang, Kung-Yee, and Scott L. Zeger. 1986. "Longitudinal Data Analysis Using Generalized Linear Models." *Biometrika* 73(1): 13–22.

Manne, Henry G. 1965. "Mergers and the Markets for Corporate Control." *Journal of Political Economy* 73: 110–20.

Meyer, John W., and Brian Rowan. 1977. "Institutionalized Organizations: Formal Structure as Myth and Ceremony." *American Journal of Sociology* 83: 340–63.

Morgan Stanley Capital International (MSCI). 1999. *The MSCI Handbook of World Stock, Derivative and Commodity Exchanges.* London: Mondo Visione.

North, Douglass C. 1990. *Institutions, Institutional Change, and Economic Performance.* New York: W. W. Norton.

Organization for Economic Cooperation and Development. 1998. *Corporate Governance: Improving Competitiveness and Access to Capital in Global Markets.* Paris: OECD.

———. 1999. *OECD Principles of Corporate Governance.* Paris: OECD.

Pedersen, Torben, and Steen Thomsen. 1997. "European Patterns of Corporate Ownership: A Twelve-Country Study." *Journal of International Business Studies* 28(4): 759–78.

Perrow, Charles. 1986. *Complex Organizations.* New York: Random House.

Pfeffer, Jeffrey, and Gerald R. Salancik. 1978. *The External Control of Organizations: A Resource Dependence Perspective.* New York: Harper & Row.

Pistor, Katharina. 1999. "Codetermination: A Sociopolitical Model with Governance Externalities." In *Employees and Corporate Governance,* edited by Margaret M. Blair and Mark J. Roe. Washington, D.C.: Brookings Institution Press.

Podolny, Joel M. 1993. "A Status-Based Model of Market Competition." *American Journal of Sociology* 98(4): 829–72.

Podolny, Joel, and Damon J. Phillips. 1996. "The Dynamics of Organization Status." *Industrial and Corporate Change* 5: 453–72.

Prowse, Stephen D. 1995. "Corporate Governance in an International Perspective." *Financial Markets, Institutions and Instruments* 4: 1–63.

Reynolds, Thomas H., and Arturo A. Flores. 1989. *Foreign Law.* Littleton, Colo.: Rothman.

Roe, Mark J. 1993. "Some Differences in Corporate Structure in Germany, Japan, and the United States." *Yale Law Journal* 102: 1927–93.

Rogers, Joel, and Wolfgang Streeck, eds. 1995. *Works Councils: Consultation, Representation, and Cooperation in Industrial Relations.* Chicago: University of Chicago Press.

Schneider-Lenné, Ellen R. 1993. "Corporate Control in Germany." *Oxford Review of Economic Policy* 8(3): 11–23.

Schwert, G. William. 2000. "Hostility in Takeovers." *Journal of Finance* 55(6): 2599–2640.

Scott, W. Richard. 1995. *Institutions and Organizations.* Thousand Oaks, Calif.: Sage Publications.

Securities Data Company. 1999. SDC Platinum Product Guide. http://www.tfsd.com/pdfs/sdcplatinum_pg.pdf.

Seely, Michael. 1991. "A Vision of Value-Based Governance." *Directors and Boards* 15: 35–36.

Servén, Luis. 1998. "Macroeconomic Uncertainty and Private Investment in LDCs: An Empirical Investigation." Working paper. Washington, D.C.: World Bank.

Shleifer, Andrei, and Lawrence H. Summers. 1988. "Breach of Trust in Hostile Takeovers." In *Corporate Takeovers: Causes and Consequences,* edited by Alan J. Auerbach. Chicago: University of Chicago Press.

Smelser, Neil J., and Richard Swedberg. 1994. "The Sociological Perspective on the Economy." In *The Handbook of Economic Sociology,* edited by Neil J. Smelser and Richard Swedberg. Princeton, N.J.: Princeton University Press.

Spicer, Andrew, Gerald A. McDermott, and Bruce Kogut. 2000. "Entrepreneurship and Privatization in Central Europe: The Tenuous Balance Between Destruction and Creation." *Academy of Management Review* 25(3): 630–50.

Stark, David, and László Bruszt. 1998. *Postsocialist Pathways: Transforming Politics and Property in East Central Europe.* New York: Cambridge University Press.

Streeck, Wolfgang 1992. *Social Institutions and Economic Performance: Studies of Industrial Relations in Advanced Capitalist Economies.* London: Sage Publications.

Suchman, Mark C. 1995. "Managing Legitimacy: Strategic and Institutional Approaches." *Academy of Management Review* 20: 571–610.

Sutton, John R., and Frank Dobbin. 1996. "The Two Faces of Governance: Responses to Legal Uncertainty in U.S. Firms, 1955 to 1985." *American Sociological Review* 61(5): 794–811.

Useem, Michael. 1996. *Investor Capitalism: How Money Managers Are Changing the Face of Corporate America.* New York: Basic Books.

Walsh, James P., and James K. Seward. 1990. "On the Efficiency of Internal and External Corporate Control Mechanisms." *Academy of Management Review* 15(3): 421–58.

White, Harrison C. 1981a. "Production Markets as Induced Role Structures." In *Sociological Methodology,* edited by Samuel Leinhardt. San Francisco: Jossey-Bass.

———. 1981b. "Where Do Markets Come From?" *American Journal of Sociology* 87(3, November): 517–47.

Zeger, Scott L., Kung-Yee Liang, and Paul S. Albert. 1988. "Models for Longitudinal Data: A Generalized Estimating Equation Approach." *Biometrics* 44(4): 1049–60.

Zuckerman, Ezra W. 1999. "The Categorical Imperative: Securities Analysts and the Illegitimacy Discount." *American Journal of Sociology* 104(5): 1398–1438.

7

GLOBAL MICROSTRUCTURES: THE INTERACTION PRACTICES OF FINANCIAL MARKETS

Karin Knorr Cetina and Urs Bruegger

IN THIS chapter, we begin to develop an analysis of "global microstructures." We use the term to mean patterns of relatedness and coordination that are global in scope but microsocial in character and that assemble and link together global domains. We argue that features of the interaction order, loosely defined, have become constitutive of and implanted in processes that have global breadth; it is microsocial structures and relationships that instantiate some of the most globally extended domains we can think of—for example, global financial markets.

In the last few decades we have witnessed a rise to structural equivalence of what Erving Goffman (1983, 9) calls the interaction order and macrosocial phenomena. The rise to equivalence came with an understanding of forms of life in the interaction order as relatively autonomous, and not prior to, fundamental to, or constitutive of, the shape of macroscopic phenomena (Collins 1981, 88ff.; Knorr Cetina 1981). It also came with an understanding of the microworld as situational—that is, as tied to the physical setting and the social occasion, which were thought to be governed by principles and dynamics not simply continuous with or deducible from macrosocial variables (Goffman 1972, 63). Both assumptions—that of the relative autonomy of micro-orders and that of their confinement to the physical setting—are questioned in this chapter. We turn to the study of financial markets as they are played out on the trading floors of large investment banks to submit that these global contexts run on a largely interactional machinery disembedded from the local and extended to a worldwide setting.[1] On a more general level, the expansion of societies to global societies need not imply further expansions of social complexity along the lines of highly differentiated organizational and institutional arrangements. Rather, the installation of global social forms that are not nationally bound would seem to be feasible with the help of individuals and social microstructures and perhaps becomes feasible only in relation to such structures.[2]

The argument just made holds for areas of "global practice" in which participants are tied together in transnational domains of transaction. The global sphere upon which our discussion is centered differs from ordinary domains of transaction through its institutional character; we will be looking at interbank trading in foreign exchange markets, a particular category of financial markets. The "cambist" (trader) form of these markets—and the wide-ranging issues they raise as institutions that are increasingly defining post-industrial societies—deserve attention not only from the perspective of globalization but also from the new sociology of economics, whose major concerns so far have been institutions and relations of production, consumption, and social distribution (DiMaggio 1994, 28; Smelser and Swedberg 1994, 3; Portes 1995, 3; for exceptional early analyses of the stock market, see Smith 1981; Baker 1984; Abolafia 1984). Two central propositions of the new sociology of economics are that economic action "is a form of social action" and that it is "embedded" in social relations (Swedberg and Granovetter 1992, 6; Swedberg 1997, 62). In bringing out the microsocial patterns of global foreign exchange activities, we offer a view of the standard "shape" of the respective social action. We also show how the institutionality of the domain, which is of interest to institutional theory in economic sociology (for example, DiMaggio and Powell 1991; Dobbin 1994), manifests itself in these patterns, exemplifying what one might call an interactional institution. Finally, we address the specific form of embeddedness (Granovetter 1985) in knowledge that characterizes this action.

Global microstructures encompass a variety of phenomena that we discuss in subsequent sections, but we should first mention two conditions on which such micro-orders rest. The first is that the transactions that make up the global domain can be accomplished symbolically through, for example, linguistic utterances, which must be used in a "performative" (action-performing; see Austin 1962) way. In the domain considered, the performative vehicle of global transactions—and the hub of global relatedness—is the "conversation": a sequence of utterances that do not just convey information but accomplish or perform economic actions. The second condition is the presence of electronic information technologies, the "arteries" of global connectedness through which the symbols flow.[3] The idea of global microstructures captures the sociological side of these technologies: global microstructures instantiate technology systems as sequentially and culturally specific accomplished social action.

We begin by discussing some general characteristics of cambist markets and saying more about the empirical domain from which our data are derived. The next section turns to the microsocial literature and specifically to the body-to-body starting point from which much of the discussion develops; we show that these ideas need to be extended to a concept of face-to-screen interaction and a split in orientation in the interaction order to accommodate global spheres. The next section presents and explains global trading conversations and their underlying interactional dynamics. We take this one step further in the following section by showing that the observed "appresentation" of local knowledge in the global sphere through exchanges and displays of information may sustain a notion of global situatedness or embeddedness. Finally, we discuss the possibility of a global we-relationship as a form of integration that has its basis in shared temporal orientations and in the synchronicity of time frames. It is also possible to show that organizational strategies mirror and sustain the interactional principles of global spheres, but this is something we can only hint at within the space available here.

One important purpose of this chapter is to bring together elements of several microsociological literatures—interactionism, ethnomethodology, phenomenology—with elements from the new economic sociology, specifically, its interest in institutions (that is, the institutional dimension of global conversations), in embeddedness, and in the symbolic and expressive dimension of economic objects and activities (see also Zelizer 1988, 1994; Smith 1993; Carruthers and Babb 1996).

The Cambist Orientation, Knowledge-Embeddedness, and Globality of Financial Markets

The sociology of economics defines economic behavior in terms of the institutions and relations of production, consumption, and social distribution (DiMaggio 1994, 28; Smelser and Swedberg 1994, 3; Portes 1995, 3). Financial markets, however, are primarily concerned with neither the production of goods nor their distribution to clients, but with trade—the trading of currencies and financial instruments not designed for consumption. Though it might be relevant for some concerns to study financial markets in terms of industrial organization and workforce variables, or in terms of the specific consumer culture of investment bankers, the distinctiveness of these markets lies elsewhere: in the differentiation and recent massive proliferation of trading cultures involving the trading of money, entitlements (Zelizer 1998), risks, and debts. To capture the distinctiveness of these markets, we call them "cambist," by which we mean that they are centered on the social role of the trader and on behavioral and other repertoires that feature trading as an economic activity in its own right, not one geared to merely assuring the supply of goods for consumption or production.[4] On a more general level, the distinctiveness of cambist markets that we emphasize is rooted in a particular historical development:

the emergence of an international system of credit and securitization that is separate and desynchronized from the global system of production and distinct from the role of money as a means of circulation (Strange 1988; Lash and Urry 1994, 285ff.).

A general understanding of financial markets as trading cultures required further research that also considers the early and important work of Charles Smith (1981, 1990, 1993), Wayne Baker (1981, 1984, 1990), and Mitchel Abolafia (1981, 1996a, 1996b). But we can start with some characteristics that distinguish these markets from production markets (see, for example, White 1981b) and bring out the concerns of this chapter. First, cambist markets of the kind studied revolve around *exchange* activities performed through and encapsulated in *communication;* hence, we must pay some attention to the *platforms of symbolic exchange* that instantiate transnational markets. Second, attention must be paid to the role of individual traders as providing the *social links that sustain the market* when it would otherwise lose its processual continuity. At the core of institutionalized currency trading is the individual trader who is also a "market maker"—someone who trades to gain from price differences while also offering trades to other market participants, thereby providing liquidity for the market and sustaining it, if necessary by trading against his or her own position (see also Baker 1984, 779; Abolafia 1996a, 2ff.). In other words, as a social form these markets depend on keepers who survive and restart markets—who fulfill bridging and liquefying functions when activity streams start to "gel," gaps arise, and the fluidity and continuity of the whole is threatened. Sociologically speaking, a form of market "liquidity" is also provided by the intense levels of communication that we begin to characterize in this chapter.

Third, in cambist markets we must look at organizational subunits and the local settings out of which market participants operate—arrangements such as trading floors, dealing rooms, trading pits, and exchanges. Trading floors tend to belong formally to large corporations (such as investment banks), but they are at the same time separated from the other corporate activities in terms of their location, restricted access, distinct forms of governance, traders' pay structure and self-understanding, and so on. In other words, trading units are institutional hybrids located at the boundary between organizations and markets that combine principles of both. Exchanges are similar hybrids; they tend to be membership rather than employee organizations, offering facilities to independent contracting members. More generally speaking, cambist markets require a differentiated view of the firm that recognizes the organizational distinctiveness and separateness of trading units as penetrated by markets, and of the role of traders as "continuators" engaged not only in performing markets but in keeping them afloat as sequential structures. In addition, the markets studied call for an analysis of the ongoing globally distributed conversation in which market activities appear to be embedded. This situation differs from that of production markets, which have been inspiringly analyzed as networks of interorganizational relations (see, for example, White 1981a, 1981b, 1993; Burt 1983, 1992; Uzzi 1997). In these, agency has been located with the firm as a whole. and the social role of the trader appears to be absent or absorbed into that of distributors in supply chains. We attempt in this chapter to put forward and illustrate a *micro- or practice approach to markets* that focuses on enacted market features and supplements the structural approach to markets that has dominated recent work (for overviews, see Swedberg 1994, 267ff.; Baker, Faulkner, and Fisher 1998). Empirically, we focus on the activities of traders in foreign exchange markets as observed on the trading floor of a global investment bank (GB1)[5] in Zurich, where it is legally based, and two other banks. The data on which our discussion is based derive from observation of and participation in spot and option trading in interbank activities.[6] The foreign exchange market has been the largest and fastest-growing financial market in the world, featuring $1.2 trillion worth of transactions every day in 2001 (Bank for International Settlements 2002). In June 1998, *FX Week* reported that GB1 had continuously been ranked as one of the top five or seven most profitable banks worldwide by reported foreign exchange trading revenues over recent years.

In cambist behavior, the strategic variable would appear to be the decision to buy, sell, or do nothing (to "hold" a position). Such decisions result in a trader's shifting his or her position in the market—for example, to being "long" or "short" on a currency he or she trades. One positions and repositions oneself in relation to market movements, economic indicators, and signs of future development—all of which are intently observed and professionally researched and assessed. This points to a second characteristic of these markets that we address in this chapter: their deep involvement with *knowledge*—the content of most of the communications mentioned. In an early and influential article, Harrison White (1981b, 518) argues that markets are self-reproducing structures in which the key variable is that participants "watch each other within a market." White has in mind production markets, and his point about producers monitoring the competition is directed against an understanding of markets as being defined by buyers or a firm's speculation about buyers. In cambist markets, traders also watch one another. This includes watching buyers and indeed finding out whether someone is a potential buyer or seller; market participants cannot be sorted into one or the other camp on a long-term basis as producers and consumers can. To trade with financial instruments one must be ready to switch sides instantaneously—usually spurred on by some new information that suggests profit can be made or loss averted by a buying or selling move. This further distinguishes cambist markets from production markets, but it also points to the relevance of knowledge in driving market action. Foreign exchange markets include several levels of knowledge production: knowledge is created by professional analysts and specialists who work on trading floors and in separate research departments; research firms provide it; and traders and salespeople pursue it through their own qualitative observations, personal models, and technical analyses. Financial markets are perhaps the most pronounced example of a knowledge-based economy—an area in which information is a productive force (Drucker 1993) in the sense of driving market action. They also exemplify a situation where the market reality itself is knowledge-generated (as discussed later in the chapter).

A third characteristic of cambist markets to which we want to draw attention up front is that they are, or tend to become, *global* markets. The foreign exchange markets studied have a *specific global form* that we can characterize by first drawing a distinction between a globally inclusive and exclusive system. A globally inclusive financial marketplace would be one where individual investors in any country are able to trade shares freely across national boundaries. Such a system requires the computer penetration of investor locations (such as households), language capabilities or unification, Web architectures, payment and clearing arrangements between stock exchanges, regulatory approvals, and national security systems that support individual financial planning.

Such systems are being created in some regions (Europe, for example), but they are far from being in place on a worldwide basis. On the other hand, in the area of institutional trading considered in this chapter, a global market of a different kind has been evident for some time. This form of globality is not based on the penetration of countries or on individual behavior. Instead, it rests on the establishment of bridgehead centers of institutional trading in the financial hubs of the three major time zones: New York, London, Tokyo, and perhaps Zurich, Frankfurt, or Singapore (for a description of this global urban system, see Sassen 1991). The centers cover the world by covering the clock (time zone), and they provide trading opportunities for banks and institutional investors on the three major continents of predominant interest to financial service industries (North America, Southeast Asia, and Europe) during their respective working times.

For example, the interbank activities studied at GB1 have been concentrated in four centers worldwide: New York, London, Zurich, and Tokyo.[7] Institutional investors in these regions are linked up with GB1 (and other banks) through "open" or immediate access phone lines. The bank's relevant centers and facilities are also connected through elaborate "intranets"—computer linkages within the bank that extend across the globe. The intranets include electronic information and brokerage services provided exclusively for institutional customers by firms such as Reuters, Bloomberg, and Telerate. Foreign exchange deals through these channels start at something on the order of several hundred thousand dollars per transaction and may reach a hundred million dollars or more. The deals are made by investors, speculators, financial managers, central bankers, and others who want to avert, and hedge against, adverse currency moves, who want to profit from expected currency moves, or who need currencies to help them enter or exit transnational investments. In sum, a system of this sort is global and exclusive at the same time; it is a supranational platform for transactions involving relationships between "elite" units (highly specialized organizational divisions mutually accrediting one another), enacted by individual traders (including proprietary traders who bet the bank's own money on the direction of currencies), salespersons, and their customers. Globality and temporality are intricately connected in this system, a topic we discuss in the final section.

From the Face-to-Face to the Face-to-Screen Situation

We now want to take a closer look at these features as they come together in global currency trading, starting from the key assumption that global financial markets run on patterns of coordination that rely on—but also break away from—the vehicles and structures of ordinary interaction. To do this, we draw on various dimensions of an arena that captures microsociological concerns like no other, that of the face-to-face situation.[8] This also allows us to begin with the local settings out of which market participants operate, and which we cannot consider further in this chapter (but see Heath et al. 1995). The notion of face-to-face epitomizes the idea that the territory of microanalysis is that (rather large) fraction of social life that we spend in the immediate presence of others. The term also has been crucial for social scientists' understanding of social relatedness, stripped to the basics. For Georg Simmel, George Herbert Mead, Alfred Schutz, and others, the face-to-face domain accounts for what are perhaps the most primordial forms of sociality (see, for example, Schutz 1964, 27ff.; Natanson 1962, 13; Simmel 1981; Mead 1934). For Goffman, the notion of face-to-face is identical with that of the interaction order, and both concepts refer less to a pattern than to a domain of activity that Goffman takes as the natural theater for the expressive displays and strategic games of all human interaction.[9] The face-to-face domain's interactional dimensions that are also of interest for global spheres include specific communicative functions (oral conversations), expressive repertoires, and moral codes, some of which have to do with the fact that participants are exposed to "the naked glance" (and potential violence) of others, binding effects that derive from joint experiences and time frames, and the reciprocal orientation of participants toward one another. The assumption of global microstructures implies that fewer of these patterns than perhaps thought are bound to the physical presence of participants, and that those that are not carry over and become extended into global spheres—though they are also "worked over" in the process. The transition to the global sphere involves, interactionally speaking, a break in participants' reciprocal orientation, which we discuss later as a switch from the face-to-face to the face-to-screen situation. In the next section, we turn to the micro-structuration of global spheres in terms of these communication structures.

"When in each other's presence," Goffman (1983, 3) says, "individuals are admirably placed to share a joint focus of attention, perceive that they do, and perceive this perceiving." The principles that have been, at a minimum, associated with the face-to-face domain are the co-bodily presence of partic-ipants and the cognitive-subjective state of the reciprocal orientation of those present toward one another and toward the situation. Consider now a trading floor such as that of GB1 in Zurich on which we conducted the present study. About two hundred traders engaged in stock, bond, and currency trading work on the floor. Dealers sit at "desks" consisting of a row of several (six to twelve) single desks; they have a range of technology at their disposal, most of which displays market data or serves to conduct trading and other conversations. Dealing takes place electronically over the Reuters dealer, sometimes involv-ing a "voice broker" (the voice of a broker coming out of an intercom system continuously shouting prices and demanding deals) and the phone. Before looking in more detail at these deals, we turn to the question of the refiguring of the face-to-face domain in such a setting.

The first point to note is that a dealing room is a collective setting fea-turing co-bodily present participants. Traders, salespeople, and a few others such as analysts and managers share a common space in the flesh; they are not remotely or virtually but physically present on the trading floor. Though the presence of a multitude of "voice" and "electronic" agents (brokers) is cer-tainly striking, so is that of young males and some females in their early twen-ties and thirties, in dark suits and ties, their jackets off. Thus, the first criterion for a face-to-face setting and Goffman's definition of an interaction order as emerging when persons are in each other's physical response presence is clearly fulfilled. Moreover, co-bodily presence may be not only given but deliberately enhanced: traders appear to be seated closer together than is needed for the routine cooperations between traders and salespeople—or between the former when they need to help each other out—to take place (see Heath et al. 1995). They are placed in a situation where they can "observe" one another and "feel" the mood of the market(s) from the responses of the single individuals dealing in them.

A closer look at the setting reveals, however, that the vividly descriptive notion of the face-to-face is in some respects strikingly inadequate. Traders do not face one another but face their screens, an arrangement that transforms the face-to-face situation literally into a back-to-back situation instead. The face-to-face notion is tied to the idea of the visual and physical orientation of participants toward one another. It is also tied to the idea of intersecting lines of visual regard or at least of intersecting facial orientations sustaining the possibility of a certain amount of synchronization of experience and of intersubjectivity. Can the back-to-back situation similarly deliver the empirical foundation of intersubjectivity? We return to this question in the final section. The point we want to make here is that the particular back-to-back arrangement found in trading rooms implements a *split in orientation* in the interaction order, forcing, on the one hand, an orientation toward the screen that links the physically present person with a global sphere and, on the other hand, a secondary orientation to the local setting and the physically present others participating in it. Perhaps we can distinguish here between the *vivid presence* of the trading room, with its possibilities of immediate rapport, and the *engrossing presence* of the screen and the global sphere, which does not quite break off this rapport but becomes superimposed on it, turning it into a vivid background experience. The double orientation requires, and is made possible by, a certain division of labor between the senses. The screen, and through the screen the global sphere of transactions, is what holds the line of visual regard—apart from certain points where the screen action is interrupted by brief glances at others in the room. At the same time, traders tune in to the trading floor (the local sphere) through the auditory channel, overhearing others' "response cries" (Goffman 1981, 78ff.), shouted questions, and oral conversations. In other words, the local goings-on become a sensorily specific segment of the actors' multiple awareness and orientation. The simultaneity sometimes collapses into a sequential back and forth, when traders lean back from their screens to survey the scene in the room and talk to other traders. There is a certain amount of turn-taking between the global and the local, in addition to the simultaneity of foregrounding and backgrounding. Multitasking is pervasive: traders engage simultaneously in several attention tasks— watching scrolling information on screen windows, perhaps conducting a phone conversation, remaining oriented toward immediate reaction to trade requests coming in over the Reuters dealer, overhearing others in the room, or addressing them with a question.

It should be noted that the split in orientation is institutionally supported and sustained by a number of arrangements. One example is the bonus system of pay, in which traders receive a basic salary and a yearly bonus, often several times as large, whose size depends on the money they make for the bank. Those traders who have investments of their own may also manage them while doing their work for the bank. The basic salary epitomizes the trader's employee status—his dependence on the bank for his livelihood, resources, and institutional identity. His bonus and private investments, on the other hand, mark the trader as an independent entrepreneur whose financial well-being depends on his success in the market. As Abolafia (1998, 72) has shown, traders also feel themselves to be such entrepreneurs. Split pay arrangements are, of course, also used in other sectors of the economy to enhance motivation and competition. But in the present case, we need to draw attention to the membership categorization accompanying the split pay. The domain "out there" to which traders belong, as market participants and as market makers, is one they want to be connected to and to keep track of. Traders who leave their job and are no longer connected may feel that they have been stripped of part of their selves, and some of them buy little hand-held Reuters screens to reconnect themselves, however scantily.

Global Conversations

We return later to the screen-world to which traders are drawn; here we first want to discuss the patterns that lie at the heart of global transaction and relatedness—the patterns that the term "global microstructures" is designed to capture. The performative vehicle of global transactions is, in native terminology, "conversations." The currency flows that circulate the globe are initiated, energized, and partitioned when traders and others willing to make deals open "conversations" with one another. The conversational interactions of traders and salespeople (the other category of players on the trading floor) and their counterparts elsewhere are performed by typing messages (and receiving typed messages) on the dealing screen; the messages are automatically printed out and serve as records of the deal. Consider the following example of a typical trading conversation, rendered as is (except with names deleted and line numbering added; see note 5 on the printouts we obtained):

1. FROM GB2L GB2NY GLOB SPOT LDN * 0923GMT 251196 */3377
2. Our Terminal: GB1Z Our user: [name of spot dealer]
3. CHF 10 PLS
4. # InSD>6267
5. 67
6. # 10 MIO AGREED
7. # VAL 27NOV96
8. # MY CHF TO DIRECT
9. # THANKS AND BYE
10. # #INTERRUPT#
11. #
12. # #END LOCAL#

The example illustrates the shortest (ten to twenty seconds or less) and most common trading sequence. The interaction begins with an *identification* (the first two lines), which appears on the screen and tells the trader where the caller is located: at another large and globally active bank's (GB2) spot desk in

London ("GB2L . . . SPOT LDN"), where currencies (rather than options on currencies and similar long-term instruments) are traded directly, on the spot. Also indicated are the date and time and an identification number, as well as the terminal in Zurich and the name of the Zurich trader. The core of the trading exchange begins in line 3 with a question, or *initiation,* in which the London dealer asks for the price of 10 million U.S. dollars against Swiss francs by typing the sequence "CHF 10 PLS [please]." The Zurich trader whose initials are given (InSD) *responds* by typing a price range, "62" and "67," meaning that he is willing to buy U.S. dollars at a rate of 1.4062 Swiss francs per dollar and to sell them at a rate of 1.4067. The *initiation-response* sequence is followed by a *selection:* the London dealer indicates that he wants to buy dollars by typing the last two digits of the Zurich trader's selling price ("67"). The conversation concludes with a preprogrammed closing sequence confirming the size of the deal, the date of the deal's settlement ("VAL27NOV96"), the account to which the Swiss francs should be paid ("MY CHF TO DIRECT," meaning GB1 Zurich), and thanks and a greeting. If we include the identification part in the initiation, the sequential structure of global trading conversations corresponds to the pattern initiation-response-selection, followed by a closing sequence.

Several further characteristics of this short, fast sequence need to be pointed out. The first is the *global* character of the conversation, made apparent in the language used, the identification sequence, and the exchange rate given in line 4. All trading conversations are conducted in English, even when both traders are Swiss bankers who, in the face-to-face situation of a trading room, converse with each other professionally in the local idiom, Swiss German. Switching from the face-to-face to the face-to-screen situation entails switching to English, which is used in all trading rooms around the world. Second, the identification sequence indicates three global centers of trading: New York ("GB2NY"), London ("L" and "LDN"), and Zurich ("GB1Z"). Banks are never indicated by just their name but also by their global location. The abbreviation "GB2NY GLOB SPOT LDN" adds a further detail: the caller works in London but the global headquarters of the calling global investment bank's spot trading is in New York. A further indication of globality, still in the identification sequence, is the announcement of the Greenwich Mean Time ("GMT") in line 1. Greenwich Mean Time serves as a reference time for the respective markets (for its interesting historical origin, see Zerubavel 1982, 12ff.). Since these markets have no central location, time is fixed to a place to ensure global identification of the correct transaction date. Finally, a more hidden reference to the global world lies in the exchange rates of line 4. The "6267" typed by the Zurich trader means that the exchange rate for interbank dollar-Swiss trading on this day at this particular point in time lies where the two traders make the deal. In other words, the rate and the deal, if it is made, constrain and to some degree select the terms of the next trade of dollars against Swiss francs in the market. Participants in the field learn about this rate either directly (from the listing of the deal on the GB1-intranet) or, outside the GB1 network, indirectly from the electronic broker indicating the price at which the last deal was made; they then construe the next price, or trade, taking their lead from the one they learned. The price retains its validity and its market-defining power only until the next deal changes the rate.

A second feature of the conversation is its *institutional* character, manifest in conversational presuppositions and specificities, which include the institutionally limited access to such conversations, the presupposed intranet and phone connections, and the institutional identifications within conversations. But there is more. As Paul Drew and John Heritage (1992, 22ff., 43) have argued, institutional talk typically involves more constraints than ordinary conversations—on the goal orientations informing the talk, on allowable contributions, on the inferential frameworks particular to specific contexts, and on the overall structural organization of the talk. In the present case, some structural limitations of trading conversations result from the fact that they are conducted within a specialized and computerized turn-taking system that allows no overlaps: only one party can type a message at a time, and the sender "formally" passes the turn on to the other participant at the end of a message by pressing a key. The system provides "interrupt" keys, though, that force a change of turn and are used to gain time. Institutionalized reductions and specializations are also apparent in the more substantive aspects of conversational patterning—for example, in the way information is requested, delivered, and received. Such constraints were found in the past to be strongest in courtroom settings when participants orient their conduct by reference to legally enforceable constraints.

In the present case, convention and expedience rather than legal constraints appear to guide conversational form: the desire is to perform deals *swiftly,* without cost in terms of time and money for oneself and others; *transparently,* oriented to the fact that deals are recorded and open to inspection by supervisors and others; and *without conflict,* free of tangled and complex interpretative issues. Expedience translates into minimalism: deals are basically performed in three turns (lines 3 through 5), each specifying bare essentials: the volume and kind of currency ("CHF 10"), the price ("6267"), and the buy or sell request ("67"). There is typically no greeting at the beginning, though standards of politeness are maintained through the use of the "please" abbreviation and the "thank you" and greetings at the end. And there is variability. For example, the caller may equally well respond by typing his or her intent verbally rather than by indicating the rate (for example, "I BUY" or "BUY" or "MINE"), and the abbreviation for Swiss francs on some of our transcripts is "SFR" and even "SWISSI." There appears to be no variability, though, in standard sequences with respect to a trader's price indication ("6267"), which is unhedged, non-negotiable, and normally unaccompanied by other words.

The caller's buy or sell response, a central component of the trading conversation, is offered in equally unambiguous terms, cleared of other content.

The minimalism of trading conversations may count as one of their "identifying details" (Garfinkel, Lynch, and Livingston 1981), one that displays not only their institutionality but also—and this is the third feature we want to mention—participants' orientation to the *economic* aspects of the interaction. The speed with which conversations are performed, which points to global competition and price volatility, illustrates this orientation.[10] The economic character also emerges in a number of conversational implicatures and understandings that are interesting in that they mainly attempt to preclude traders from uninhibited profit-seeking.[11] For example, initiating questions must be uttered in a neutral way without disclosing the caller's intention to buy or sell; to receive a fair price response, callers contacting traders (unlike clients discussing options with a salesperson) are expected to have formed such an intention. The responding trader, in his turn, is constrained to respond by indicating a price for both (buy and sell) options. Another important and sanctionable understanding is that traders commit themselves to the price they indicate. They are bound to honor it even if they have made a mistake—as long as the caller's response comes within the "understood" time frame of approximately two seconds, and the trader hasn't snatched the conversation back by an "interrupt" to invalidate the price. A third understanding of interest with regard to economic theory and auctions, bazaars, outdoor markets, and other markets, where the opposite obtains (Smith 1990; 1993; Geertz 1978; DeLaPradelle 1995; Clark and Pinch 1995; see also Callon 1998, 264–66), is that the price is non-negotiable within a trading interaction; all a counterparty can do is forgo the trade and hope for a better price to be offered at a later time or somewhere else. Conversationally, this means that there are no turns allowed that challenge a price range—other than a turn that ends the conversation prematurely, without a deal. Frequent premature endings, however, reflect back on the trading parties and their "relationship," to which we return later in the chapter.

These institutionalized expectations are extended by an informal code of honor.[12] Traders are informally assessed according to this code, which also constrains trading behavior. The code challenges traders to respond to trading questions nearly instantly, to provide a narrow spread between the buying and selling prices, and to "make a price" (trade) even when they stand to lose from the deal—what Baker (1984, 780) has called their "affirmative obligation." The constraints are imposed on precisely those parameters that traders might be inclined to manipulate to their advantage through behavior that lies somewhere between simple self-interest-seeking and "opportunism"—self-interest-seeking with guile, as the transaction-cost approach has it (Williamson 1981, 553). Traders can increase the spread between the bid and sell prices to diminish their risk, and they can delay their response, hoping perhaps that a caller will lose interest. They can also simply limit their participation when the market goes against them. It is acceptable to tinker with the price—for example, to offer a higher price for a currency they expect to go up than the price the market is currently offering—in order to induce others to sell to them and allow them to "go long" on an article that will be in demand. Traders may also drive the price in a particular direction when they can "read" the counterparty's intention. However, consistently shaping the response in some of these ways may have relationship costs; a trader may lose prestige and his or her good reputation and may no longer be contacted. On the other hand, conforming to the code may also be problematic under some circumstances. For example, when a caller wants to distribute a trade across several banks and contacts them simultaneously, a trader who responds fast may lose out. The counterparty may wait until all prices are in before disclosing the deal, not wanting a fast trader to learn about it early and make similar moves, which might destroy the market for the caller.

What this sort of reasoning reveals is that participants' orientation to the economic character of the transaction at the same time involves them in an *interactional and emotional dynamic* that is sealed into trading conversations and discloses itself only when conversations collapse into more informal talk (as illustrated later in the chapter). This is the fourth feature we want to put forward, one that brings us to the undertow of tensions and conflicts associated with the opposing needs of buyer and seller and the conflicting demands of profit-seeking and restraint. Consider how this interactional dynamic may play itself out in a trading conversation. In the first movement, the initiation sequence, a caller's identity appears on the screen, followed by the indication of the size of a potential deal. If the caller is of the type from a large hedge fund or an important investment bank, these lines may be received as a "danger" signal that alerts the trader to the market price movements that could be ignited by the caller's actions. The lines may also be received as setting up two potentially conflicting goals: the challenge of interpreting the caller's undisclosed intention and anticipating the market repositionings that a realization of these intentions may bring about, and the challenge of serving the caller well while at the same time calculating a price range that protects the trader's position and also serves him well. Traders meet the challenge by typing their commitment to a price range. The second movement begins with and centers on this commitment; it leaves the trader exposed to adverse market movements while he or she is waiting for the caller's response (for example, ones that might leave him or her "long" on a currency whose market price goes down) and to the risk of having committed time and resources to a conversation that might not end in a deal. In the following example, a conversation that erupts into a side-sequence exhibits some of the dynamic of the second movement.

1.   FROM GBI [name of bank]MILAN *1135GMT 251196 */3447

2.   Our terminal: GB1Z Our user: [name of spot dealer]

3. SPOT CHF 5
4. # InSD> 6364
5. FROM IS>
6. # #INTERRUPT#
7. #
8. #INTERRUPT#
9.
10. # #INTERRUPT#
11. # HALLOOOOOO THIS IS SPOT AND NOT FWDS OK?/
12. YES MATE SRY CUST.
13. #
14. #INTERRUPT#
15. MY RISK PSE
16. #
17. NWOSPE
18. # 6263
19. SELL
20 to 27.   [Confirmation and closing sequence]

In this conversation, the trader, who is "king of the floor" in terms of his earnings for the bank, reputation among traders, and importance of the currency traded, offers a narrow price range (line 4). He is then kept waiting by the caller, who does not respond and tries to snatch the turn back from the trader (line 8), who also holds on to the turn or interrupts (lines 6 and 10). This back-and-forth ends when the Zurich trader interjects angrily: "HALLOOOOOO THIS IS SPOT AND NOT FWDS OK?/" This reprimand reminds the caller that in spot trading a response must come forth immediately, in contrast to situations where long-term instruments are traded. The caller, accepting this, apologizes by pointing out that he himself was kept waiting by a customer who had not reached a decision (line 12 reads in full: "Yes, mate, sorry customer"). He interrupts the flow once more and then offers "my risk please"—meaning, he considers the Zurich trader no longer committed to the price. He accordingly repeats the price question when ready: "Now please" (this is misspelled in line 17), receives a new price offer with an equally narrow spread ("6263"), and selects the deal ("SELL").

The conversational turbulence and repair show how the conventions of global conduct are interactionally upheld. Note again that unlike other exchange situations, interactional means play no role here in bringing about and negotiating situational outcomes—for example, price or buying commitments.

Rather, they are used to manage and sustain a global order through a variety of means of the sort indicated, which include overtly stating that one is "noting" someone's misbehavior or stating the break-off of the business relationship. It is this *structural* rather than *situational* deployment of interactional means to sustain a social form that we want to bring out as another facet of global microstructures. It occurs in a domain where legal sanctions are hardly available and would be considered inefficient by participants.

A further microstructural element also springing into view with the interactional dynamic of trading takes us back to the notion of the face-to-screen situation. Consider the fact that the profits and losses made by spot traders are marked to them individually at the end of every day; they are also marked to them as their contribution to the "desk"—the group of traders dealing in the same instrument at a particular location. Traders keep track of their profit-and-loss balance with practically every trade; their "worth" is explicit not only to themselves but also to supervisors at every moment in time. In this situation traders put themselves on the line with every move they make. Losses in particular arouse "fear" and perhaps "greed" and are expressed in a vocabulary that resounds with the emotions of felt violence and attack. As a trader on the Zurich floor put it, the terms refer "basically [to] sex and violence and a lot of them seem to have to do with anal penetration." The list we accumulated included: "I got shafted," "I got bent over," "I got blown up," "I got raped," "I got stuffed/The guy stuffed me," "I got fucked," "I got hammered," and "I got killed."

One interesting facet of this vocabulary is that it displays the assaults implicit in global trading conversations as analogous to bodily assaults. Goffman (1983, 4) takes it to be evident that we can "participate in social situations only if we bring our bodies and their accoutrements along with us," and he saw this equipment as vulnerable to physical assault, sexual molestation, and so on, by virtue of the instrumentalities that others bring along with their bodies. Traders think of their market presence in terms of "exposures" and "vulnerabilities," talking, for example, about upside and downside exposures to markets by virtue of being long or short on a currency from whose price direction they stand to lose money. On record-keeping forms, initiating parties are called "aggressors," while traders quoting prices are the "non-aggressors." Beyond indicating economic danger, the vocabulary of aggression and assault displays traders' emotional engagement with the market and other market participants. Participants appear to be viscerally plugged into the screen reality of the global sphere, and they indicate this when they refer to market actions in terms of the penetration of their bodily preserves. One way to make sense of this felt physical connectedness is to return once more to the concrete setup of a trading desk. Through their face and body front, traders reorient a significant fraction of their sensory equipment and bodily reaction capabilities to the "lifeform" (native term) of the market—to its glaring and eye-catching presence on screens, its continual vocal demands (phone, voice broker), and its rousing and sometimes frenetic effects on other traders. Though traders are not able to slip through the screen and walk into this lifeform, they stand, we might say, within its intimate space—close enough to feel every "tick" of its movements and to tremble and shake whenever it trembles and shakes. Perhaps we might think of a trader's reactions to the market in terms of Mead's (1934, 144ff.) picture of a conversation of gestures: of reflex-like actions that mirror market movements and respond to them and are possible only in a situation of sensory attunement and attachment to a co-present other. For those engaged with it, the market, we want to argue, is a co-present other; in this sense the face-to-screen situation retains characteristics of a physical response setting continuous with the face-to-face situation (see Goffman 1983, 2).

The Relational and Knowledge Embeddedness of Global Spheres

We have now introduced the performative structures of global transactions, which are in fact conversation patterns, and we have illustrated the global references, the institutional and economic features, and the interactional dynamics that converge in global talk. From the viewpoint of these dimensions, global "talk-in-interaction" (Schegloff 1987) is intricately constructed, even when it is merely "standard"; it is talk in which the discrepancy between the seemingly innocuous surface and the background assumptions and processes is relatively large. We have also attempted to convey a sense of the structural role of interactional devices in sustaining a global order and of the continued relevance of the visceral features of the face-to-face situation. We now want to turn from the conversation/interaction structures that span up global markets to the relationships that inhere in them, arguing that these relationships are significantly based in exchanges of information. We also work with the notion of "embeddedness" as proposed by Mark Granovetter (1985), but add one level: knowledge.[13] The idea of the social embeddedness of economic action as discussed in the new sociology of economics has been tremendously suggestive, shifting, as Richard Swedberg (1997, 62) points out, the critique of economics from its emphasis on the unrealistic conception of rationality to the failure of economists to incorporate social structure into their analysis. But embeddedness has been understood in different ways. Alejandro Portes (1995, 6) summarizes the discussion by distinguishing between market exchange as interdependent with (embedded in) a whole set of cultural, political, and social background variables described by Barber (1995), DiMaggio (1994, 24), Fligstein (1996), Abolafia (1996a), Lash and Urry (1994), and others, on the one hand,[14] and "relational embeddedness," the phenomenon that exchange tends to flow through interpersonal and interorganizational ties based in rules of trust, exclusivity, and loyalty which structure markets and influence exchange outcomes, on the other (for example, Geertz 1978; White 1981b, 543; Baker 1981; Uzzi 1997; Fligstein and Mara-Drita 1996, 14f.; Baker, Faulkner, and Fisher 1998, 148ff.). The present conception sits well with the last one in stressing embeddedness in its tangible and concrete form of ties; an important component of the idea of knowledge embeddedness is that global financial market activities are embedded in ongoing relationships between market participants that turn around the exchange of information. However, knowledge embeddedness cannot be limited to this relational component. In a sense, the global financial market to which traders are oriented is itself a knowledge construct: knowledge-based figures, descriptions, and accounts provide for the reality of global markets as an experiential reality on screen, where this reality appears as an ongoing process of price information and of continuously updated and interpreted details from geographically dispersed corners of the world and their cultural, political, and social events and trends. The information that flows through relationships contributes to this construct. But there are also other important channels, such as intranet bulletin boards on which traders in worldwide trading centers enter "what they see," banks' own research that assembles, interprets, and distributes global market information to the floor and to clients, and specialized firms such as Reuters, Bloomberg, and Telerate whose services render markets (in the sense of price action and contextual information) present on screen. In sum, knowledge embeddedness is relational, but it is also constructive and constitutive of global financial markets.

Within the space of this chapter, we can only briefly illustrate the relational component of these markets and its role as a channel for (market-constitutive) information. Consider the following trade between a dealer from a large and important American global investment bank and Zurich's dollar–Swiss franc trader:

1. FROM GB3 [name of bank]INTL LONDON * 1301GMT 251196*/3514

2. Our terminal: GB2Z Our user: [name of spot dealer]

3. # TEST BACK LOWER RATES NOW . . .

4. #

5. #INTERRUPT#

6. CAN I GIVE YOU 15 MIO USDCHF PLS

7. # SURE 83

8. GTEATEE TREE GREAT. TKS

9. # WELCOME . . .

10. # BUYING DM SFR HERE. . . .

11. # AROUND 150 MI. . . .

12. # BUT LOOKS DAMN TOPPSIH HERE. . . . THINKING [GB4] . . . ON THE TOP

13. # . . .

We begin with the specifics of this conversation as compared with the earlier trading conversations. First, the Zurich trader in line 3 does not initiate a trade in the sense shown before but makes reference to the ongoing character of the conversation (to the open line of communication these participants have) by offering a piece of information that is in fact a warning: he says the dollar is moving lower. Upon receiving this information, the London dealer takes the turn back (line 5) and then asks whether he can sell the Zurich trader $15 million against Swiss francs. The "sure" with which the Zurich trader begins his response may give him a fraction of a second to think about the price, which he then offers. He receives a misspelled "great" and "thanks" and closes the deal with a "welcome." Note that the central conventions of global trading are passed over and to some degree ostentatiously broken in the deal: the caller discloses his intention instead of keeping it silent, obtains just a one-way price, thanks the Zurich trader in the slot where the standard pattern exhibits a deal selection, and is greeted by a "welcome" that ignores the prescribed confirmation sequence. What this means is that the two parties affirm, through the specific formulations used, that they have a long-standing relationship based on trust that needs no precautions and formalities. They also begin the conversation with an information exchange and continue this exchange after the deal is completed. The Zurich trader offers that the Zurich dealing room is buying a rather large sum of German marks against Swiss francs (around 150 million), adding that he thinks the rate will not go higher from here ("BUT LOOKS DAMN TOPPSIH HERE") and that he believes a particular bank is selling German marks against Swiss francs.

The relational component in this deal is not an isolated event. Traders say they tend to know their interaction partners and see themselves engaged in ongoing (business) relationships. Personal knowledge about the other—derived from visits, phone calls, and the like—defines many business relationships and at the same time personal ties. The two components run together, and they also become mixed with informational content. This informational content resides not only in the observations offered by the Zurich trader in lines 3 and 10 through 12. It also resides in the deal itself, which contributes to his picture of the market by telling him how a significant market participant moves his positions and places his bets. This conversation illustrates a global tie in which an orientation toward maintaining the relationship takes priority over profit-making. By linking themselves in deals with important market actors, traders are able to track the market "as it is made"; they gain bits and pieces of information before others and are able to assess future trading opportunities and constraints from the positions their counterparties have taken. In this case, the Zurich trader returns the favor by offering a good price—and local knowledge from the trading room in Zurich and his position in the screen world.

To repeat, everything is mixed into this relationship: a long-term relational commitment involving trust and perhaps friendship, business exchanges, and knowledge obtained on both sides. But there are also other information-relationships that traders have with former colleagues and others with whom they do not trade. For example, the proprietary trader in foreign exchange who had worked in Singapore for years before he came to Zurich called four to six people every morning when he arrived, often before 7:00 A.M., to question his Asian colleagues about the Asian markets the night before. He also kept screen and phone conversations open with several distant colleagues during the appropriate times of the day, exchanging observations ("what we see"), interpretation, and comments about market events. The following gives an example:

1. TO GB5 [name of bank]HK * 0458GMT 210597 */6309
2. Our terminal: GB1Z Our user: [name of spot dealer]
3. # PEI
4. HIHIIH LATRRY
5. # InSD> HIHI YOUNG GIRL
6. # BUSY DAY ON THE YEN PERHAPS TODAY
7. # THESE MOVES I FIND JUST UNBELIEVABLE
8. # ESP IN THE CONTEXT OF THE CENTRAL BANKS WANTING TO
9. # CONTAIN VOLATILITY WHEN IN REALITY THEY ENHANCE IT . . .
10. # GUESS SHOULD BE THANKFUL AS THEY ARE PROLONGING THE
11. # EMPLOYMENT PROSPECTS OF MANY IN OUR FIELD
12. HAHAHA TRUE
13. WE ARE SEEING JAPANESE LIFE AND TRUST BUYING USD TODAY
14. ON RUMORS THAT MOF SAID THEY SHOULD BUY USD
15. AND ALSO BUNDLES OF COMMENTS ABOUT MOF NO LONGER
16. CONCERN OF YEN WEAKNESS/WE ALSO SEE TECHNICAL GUYS AS
17. BUYERS BUT 114.50 IS P/T LEVEL FOR THOSE WHO WENT LONG
18. YDAY AND ALSO EARLY THIS MORNING

19. RIDICULOUS RUMOUR THAT SWISS IS GOING TO HIKE RATE!
20. DEMCHF DOWN A LOT TODAY AND PROBABLY RUMOUR OF THIS
21. #
22. #INTERRUPT#
23. BECAUSE OF PRICE ACTION.
24. THIS IS VERY VOLATILE
25. [etc.]

In this conversation the trader in Zurich contacts a former colleague whom he knows from his "time in Singapore." He appears to create a friendly atmosphere by commenting ironically on central banks being responsible for the high dollar-yen volatility observed. (Central banks normally want to contain volatility.) His Hong Kong contact Pei then offers local information about the Asian market (lines 13 through 18, 20)—about Japanese life insurance companies and trusts buying dollars on rumors relating to the Japanese Ministry of Finance (MOF), which dictates the policy of the Central Bank of Japan, about the MOF's alleged unconcern about the yen weakness, about the German mark (DM) against Swiss franc rate coming down during Asian market hours, and about buys prompted by technical analyses. She also comments negatively on a rumor about the Swiss National Bank's intention to raise interest rates (line 19), which appeared "ridiculous" against her background knowledge that the bank was concerned at the time about the Swiss franc's strength. The conversation continues (not illustrated) for another twenty lines with the Zurich trader offering his interpretation of the dollar–Swiss franc low in Asia against the meaning of rate falls in the European and American market.

Besides illustrating an information relationship, this sort of global conversation also illustrates what we want to call, borrowing a term of Edmund Husserl's (1960, 49–54) and Alfred Schutz and Thomas Luckmann's (1973, 11), the strategy of *appresentation:* the transport of local details from particular time zones and geographic regions where they are observed to the global arena on screen—to the world of "everyone" logged on and having access to the respective channels. The choice of the term "appresentation" is meant to suggest that the global market on screen is not simply a representation of markets that exists independently elsewhere by participants such as Pei or the two Zurich traders we quoted and by professional knowledge providers—the "screen world" *is* the global market *into which* local details are transposed. The global market continually assembles and updates itself from such knowledge fragments. The scrolling screen windows in front of traders are central in holding the relevant information and in providing the means for transactions to take place; they are supplemented and surrounded by other components attendant to the screen, such as phone/voice channels, information "on paper" (such as written analyses provided by in-house research groups or financial papers), and media units (for example, financial news and analyses offered by TV channels, such as CNN, that traders can watch at their desks and at home).

The Possibility of a Global We-Relation

We now turn to another meaning of the notion of embeddedness, one that it has in debates between communitarianism and liberalism and more generally in political philosophy: embeddedness as rootedness in and integration with a community to which one belongs (Etzioni 1993; Sandel 1982; Walzer 1990). We discuss this by drawing on Schutz's idea of a "We-relation," the term with which he attempts to circumscribe intersubjectivity as arising in the face-to-face situation (see, for example, Schutz 1964, 25). The question to ask is whether the idea of a We-relationship can be extended to global domains whose participants are not in one another's physical response presence and may in fact never even have met one another. The proposal adds a further conceptual level to the argument that (some) global social fields are organized in terms of principles and structures that have been extended from, or closely resemble, structures of the face-to-face domain. What we have claimed in the last section is that global fields depend on the mapping of regional and local events onto the global arena of a screen world and that the multiple and overlapping mappings in fact constitute this screen world. Here we submit that the common orientation to knowledge on screens—combined with temporal mechanisms—may constitute a basis for a form of intersubjectivity and integration of global spheres.

Schutz associates his theory of intersubjectivity closely with the bodily presence of participants in the same situation. He speaks of the "interlocking of the glances" and the "thousand-faceted mirroring of each other" that he sees as a unique feature of face-to-face situations (Schutz 1967, 169). Going beyond overt communication, to the degree of underemphasizing it, Schutz, like Simmel, points out the role of nonverbal signs in making accessible another person's meaning, intentions, and "consciousness" in embodied interaction:

> In the face-to-face situation, the conscious life of my fellow man becomes accessible to me by a maximum of vivid indications. Since he is confronting me in person, the range of symptoms by which I apprehend his consciousness includes much more than what he is communicating to me purposefully. I observe his movements, gestures and facial expressions, I hear the intonation and the rhythm of his utterances. Each phase of my consciousness is coordinated with a phase of my partner's. (Schutz 1964, 29)

In trying to unpack intersubjectivity further, Schutz arrives at another idea that becomes central to his conception, that of temporal coordination. As one of his followers puts it, "The reciprocal interlocking of time dimension is for Schutz the core phenomenon of intersubjectivity" (Zaner 1964, 75). As much as the "spatial immediacy" of embodied encounters, Schutz notes the "temporal immediacy" that obtains in this situation. He contends that this temporal immediacy allows one to recognize and follow another person's experience (say, of a bird in flight) as contemporaneous with one's own experience. Schutz (1964, 24–26) tries his hand at a number of formulations of the temporal coordination of "phases of consciousness"; he speaks of the "synchronization of two interior streams of duration" and of the fact that during this synchronization, "we are growing older together."

The point for us is that in emphasizing temporal coordination, Schutz moves away from any attempt to base social relatedness on the idea of shared (in the sense of identical) experience or on any real understanding of other minds. Instead, he leaves things with the subject recognizing the other as a fellow human being here and now, evidently paying attention to the same event. What turns this experience into a "We-relation," as he calls it, is the contemporaneousness of the event, one's experiencing it, and the indications of the other's attentiveness to it: "Since we are growing older together during the flight of the bird, and since I have evidence, in my own observations, that you were paying attention to the same event, I may say that *we* saw a bird in flight" (Schutz 1964, 25).

Much depends on temporal synchronization in this argument, which is what we want to work with in addressing global spheres, but we should also note two problems. The first is that if Schutz leaves the question of understanding other minds behind in basing his We-relationship in a community of time, he does not also leave spatial immediacy behind. For Schutz, sharing the same segment of time implies the "genuine simultaneity" of participants' streams of consciousness only if they share a common space—the space that affords them the possibility of partaking in the "step-by-step constitution" of experience of an unfolding event. Schutz evidently sees no distinction between spatial immediacy and the possibility of "paying attention to the same event." But this distinction is a crucial one when events mediated by electronic transmissions (television, for example) can be witnessed in real time worldwide without one's sharing a common space. The trading context is specific yet again in that central market events have no physical location outside the screen world. In a sense, the common space of global financial markets is the space on screen. We might claim that spatial immediacy still obtains in global contexts within particular time zones, but the space involved is a layered hybrid that consists of a central and shared electronic center and a dispersed human periphery of trading floors. This sort of spatial immediacy, however, no longer is what it is for Schutz—a situation of bodily co-presence. A second problem with Schutz's ideas about temporality is that he bases his analyses on processes of short duration, like listening to a musical performance or watching a bird flying (Schutz 1964, 159–78). Markets of the kind discussed, however, are ongoing collective processes of indefinite duration. Many different temporal structures come into play in organizing these processes, and some are consciously adopted to manage market events. Nonetheless, we can take Schutz's argument about social binding arising from the reciprocal interlocking of time dimensions as a basis for the claim that the idea of a global We-relationship is entirely plausible and that it provides for a form of sociality and integration of global groups.

To illustrate this now in regard to financial markets, we can start with the question what the *same events* might be that could plausibly be construed as *globally* observed in the same binding fashion in which events are observed in the face-to-face situation. These events are delivered, we argue, by the knowledge-created phenomena on screen and the content of the supplemental channels to which traders are oriented. In other words, the bird that traders watch together around the clock is "the market," as it is assembled in identical (price actions, market analyses, news descriptions, and so on, furnished by global information providers), overlapping (information exchanged through personal relationships), and coordinated fashion in the many windows and channels to which participants are attached. In these windows and channels the "same" market has a vivid presence; it speaks out to participants and demands from them continuous attention—and action.

This action component is implicated in a second requirement associated with the We-relation, that of *reciprocity:* it must somehow be noticeable that others are watching the same events and that they are attuned to one another's presence. For Schutz, observing the other observe is crucial for any interlocking of subjectivities to come about; his emphasis is on nonverbal expressions as signals of the other's attention and attunement to the situation. On the global plane, this attention and attunement to the market—comprising price action, economic context, *and* a set of market participants—is presupposed and hardly needs to be expressed. We assume that no professional trader or salesperson can survive financially if he or she pays no attention to the market, and floor managers watch over participants' attention signals. Nonetheless, there are a variety of indicators of others' active interest in the market that traders observe, most notably the deal requests they make, the messages they send, and the price movements they trigger. Through these signals, absent market participants have what Charles Goodwin (1995, 260) has called a "mediated" presence on screen. Market activities can be considered as signals not only of economic opinion but also of social connectedness—of participants' reciprocal awareness of others' presence and constitutive involvement in an unfolding market situation.

The reciprocity just indicated marks the current context as also involving what Schutz (1964, 55) calls the "interlocking of motives characteristic of interaction in the We-relation"—the possibility of one's "in-order-to" motive becoming the other's "because" motive. A trader selling a currency in order to take a profit may trigger trading responses in others because of what he or she did. Here reciprocity points to the fact that global financial markets are fields of interaction: at any point in time all traders watch the same events and one another, but some also interact (trade), and in interacting they may add new levels of reciprocity and reflexivity (see Soros 1994). But we should turn now to the third feature on which Schutz bases the We-relation, that of temporal coordination (see also Zerubiavel 1981). First, traders, salespeople, and others on trading floors located within a particular time zone share a *community of time*. They watch the market as it comes into view in the morning and builds up during the day virtually continuously in synchronicity and immediacy during their working (and waking) hours.[15] All three aspects are important here: synchronicity refers to the phenomenon that traders and salespeople observe the same market events simultaneously over the same time period; continuity means they observe the market virtually without interruption, having lunch at their desks and asking others to watch when they step out; and temporal immediacy refers to the immediate real-time availability of market transactions and information to participants within the appropriate institutional trading networks. Local news is also transmitted on screen "live" when the events are scheduled at a particular time (for example, announcements of economic indicators), or they are transmitted with as little delay as possible. Traders, investors, and others attempt to gain advance knowledge of special developments, but these pursuits presuppose rather than undercut the community of time that obtains with respect to the market.

Second, time coordination also involves a temporal division of labor across time zones, to the effect that the community of time extends around the clock. As an example, take the trading instrument of an "option" to buy or sell a currency at a particular point in the future at an agreed price. In contrast to the instantaneously completed on-the-"spot" sales and purchases of currencies discussed so far, options expire weeks or months after the deal is made; hence, unlike a spot trader's accounts, an option trader's accounts cannot be closed every night. One way to organize such long-term transactions globally is to pass on a desk's option accounts every evening to the same bank's option traders in the next time zone, who manage the accounts and add deals during their working hours. The "option book" that circles the globe indicates global financial cooperation: one extends the surveillance of the "bird in flight," the market, through the eyes of others when it threatens to disappear from view during the night. As a result, the coordination of consciousness that Schutz discusses becomes more inclusive, encompassing groups that are not simultaneously present but that take turns sequentially and overlappingly in observing and acting on the market. Traders coordinate trading intentions and philosophies with both the next and the previous desks in time in evening and morning phone calls and mails, and the book remains on their mind (and available on their screens) while it is out of their hands. In other words, the circling book can be seen as an attempt to weave together the consciousness of those attending to it in different time zones, with the effect of creating an around-the-clock synchronization of observation and experience.

A third aspect of time coordination beyond this attempted global contemporaneity brings into view market "*calendars*" and *schedules:* dates and hours set for important economic announcements and for the release of periodically calculated economic indicators and data. These calendars and schedules structure and pace participants' awareness and anticipation. They create an atmosphere of collective anticipation and preparation for specific events that pace and interrupt the regular flow of market activities. Temporal structures of this sort recurrently focus a global field of watchers on possible changes of direction of the "bird in flight." They bind the field to specific time frames around which global attention is heightened and in relation to which expectations build up. The ordinary temporal flow of synchronous and sequential time-zone observation is thus punctuated regularly by potentially trend-changing occurrences. The scheduled character of these events not only synchronizes experience on a collective and global level but adds to it a measure of emotional arousal.[16] Durkheim considers such arousals to be central to bringing about a feeling of "solidarity": he assumes that the We-experience arises when a group becomes excited. We should note that the Durkheimian "force field" (Wiley 1994, 106, 122) of social solidarity is energized by feeling or sentiment, but it also entails the unity of something shared. With Durkheim, this something shared is either moral or semantic—that is, a unity of meaning. In the present case, the unity of meaning has much to do with knowledge—with the punctuation of existing trends by new information.

To conclude, we should note that we use the notion of a We-relation as a linker concept to connect microsociological concepts with questions of global embeddedness and integration; in so doing, we have asked whether our ideas about core phenomena of sociality (construed as intersubjectivity) have any relevance to global fields. Schutz's ideas are important to us because he provides a starting point for an analysis of global forms of binding based on temporal coordination rather than exclusively on the spatial immediacy and co-bodily presence from which most microsociological analyses take their lead. On a different level, we have argued that the diminishing relevance of the physical setting in defining global domains cannot be taken to imply that microsocial processes in general are also becoming increasingly irrelevant. In fact, the opposite is just as plausible: we might speculate that global domains of practice evolve instead in conjunction with microsocial principles, since other means of organizing become ineffectual on a global plane.

With the phenomena we have illustrated—hybrid settings situated at the boundary between organizations and global fields, conversation structures as the performative vehicles of global transaction and relatedness, the structural use of interaction devices, the reciprocal interlocking of time dimensions that sustain global forms of binding, and knowledge embeddedness—we have attempted to provide an overview of relevant principles and dimensions. With regard to these dimensions and others, more research that investigates the changing features of an interactional machinery as it begins to shape what Martin Albrow (1996) calls our "global age" is needed. The present study also complements earlier work on financial markets in the new sociology of economics by discussing these markets from a practice perspective rather than from that of (interorganizational) networks or fields and by bringing into view the global character of these markets. The continued development of the study of global financial markets would enhance our understanding of a defining characteristic of contemporary society—its most mythologized and perhaps most powerful economic substructure, as intertwined with its forms of sociality and social structures.

Our greatest debts lie with the managers, traders, salespersons, and analysts at GB1 and two other banks whose help proved invaluable in making this study possible and who so generously shared with us the information we collected. We acknowledge gratefully the helpful comments, suggestions, and ideas provided by Klaus Amann, Paul DiMaggio, Frank Dobbin, Stefan Hirschauer, Michèle Lamont, John Lie, Andrew Pickering, Alexandru Preda, Harrison White, Viviana Zelizer, Eviatar Zerubavel, and many others at the occasion of the presentation of earlier drafts at seminars and at the 1998 meeting of the American Sociological Association in San Francisco, where Charles Smith provided especially detailed and constructive comments. Karin Knorr Cetina prepared this chapter while she was visiting at the Department of Sociology, Princeton University, supported by a grant by the Deutsche Forschungsgemeinschaft.

Notes

1. Anthony Giddens (1990, 21ff.) uses the notion of "disembedding" to refer to the "lifting out of social relations from local contexts." In this chapter, we are concerned with how interaction principles traditionally associated with local contexts shape global domains.

2. Globalization may, of course, also lead to increasing complexities—for example, when transnational components or levels replicate national or local ones but with greater extension. (A possible example is the political-administrative institutions of the European Community (EC); these complement the national institutions that they also attempt to penetrate and change.) But this situation needs to be distinguished from the one we analyze in which the global system operates

decoupled from national or local ones according to its own principles, as if in a single differentiated layer.

3. Most accounts of information and communication media treat them as technologies. These accounts have been important in pointing out the direct and indirect effects of information and communication technologies (ICTs) on employment and skills (deskilling), on the rise of particular industries and occupations, on network-based reorganizations of firms, and on the potential implications of ICTs for politics and government (for an overview of current work, see Dutton 1996).

4. Financial markets might be seen as focused on exchange, but the notion of an exchange market has often been reserved for pre-industrial economies and their marketplace interactions, gift exchanges, potlatch ceremonies, auctions, and domestic transfers (see, for example, Davis 1992; Swedberg 1994, 268).

5. Throughout this chapter, we refer to global investment banks and other globally operating banks as GBs, in accordance with banking confidentiality requirements. The banks are numbered, and GB1 designates the Swiss bank we studied; we do indicate the trading location. Names of individual traders, salespersons, or managers have been eliminated. Where trader initials occur in transcripts, we abbreviated the initials and indicated the type of dealer: InSD stands for Initials, Spot Dealer.

6. One of the authors, Urs Bruegger, is a former trader who worked for five years on the trading floor of GB1.

7. The global "presence" of GB1 extends far beyond these bridgeheads. In 1997 the bank had a staff of eleven thousand working in fifty offices in thirty countries on six continents.

8. A significant body of literature deals with aspects of what Goffman calls the interaction order (for overviews of important dimensions, see Stone and Farberman 1981; Fine 1984; Scheff 1990). Our purpose is merely to indicate some of those features that seem central to the creation of global spheres and need to be respecified in regard to this involvement. There is also by now an interesting body of work on human machine interaction (see, for example, Suchman 1987; Turkle 1995) and related ethnomethodological studies of work (for overviews, see Ten Have and Psathas 1995; Button 1993; see also Goodwin 1995), but our focus is on transactions in which the computer becomes transparent and third parties are charged with guaranteeing its (and the software's) functioning.

9. As Goffman (1983, 2) explained in his 1982 presidential address to the American Sociological Association: "My concern over the years has been to promote acceptance of this face-to-face domain as an analytically viable one, a domain which might be titled, for want of any happy name, the *interaction order.*"

10. Deals may be based on speculation (attempting to exploit price differences at different points in time), arbitrage (exploiting the price differences between different markets), and hedging (reducing a risk that someone already faces); in a competitive global environment, all require quick reactions to offers and demands and quick repositionings for further moves.

11. These differ from the important patterns of "vigilance" and "restraint" that Abolafia (1996a) describes in that they are built into traders' everyday practices rather than residing in specific cycles of trading behavior.

12. The Association Cambiste Internationale (1996, 1) compiles and periodically reissues a *Code of Conduct,* which was first published in 1975. It does not deal with legal matters but "aims to set out the manner and spirit in which business should be conducted." The fifty-nine-page booklet includes definitions and abbreviating conventions, addresses behavioral issues such as substance abuse, and makes specific recommendations regarding confidentiality and dealing procedures. The published code is extended and interpreted by an informal code of honor.

13. It should be noted that economists have long emphasized the importance of understanding how knowledge is implicated in the price mechanism and more generally in economic behavior. Particularly relevant here are Hayek's pathbreaking ideas for which he received the Nobel Prize in 1974. For an overview of Hayek's notions, see Streissler (1994). For a further, early example, see Stigler (1961).

14. To give some examples, culture provides the categories and understandings that enable us to engage in economic action (DiMaggio 1994, 24), regulatory frameworks and government policies may induce or discourage market investments (Abolafia 1996a), and exchange depends on the institution of contract and its noncontractual elements, as Durkheim emphasizes (Barber 1995, 399).

15. As David Harvey has argued (1989, 239–59), increasing time-compression is a characteristic of the whole process of modernity and of post-industrialization. A similar argument was advanced earlier by Marshall McLuhan (1964, 358), who proposed that electricity establishes a global network of communication that enables us to apprehend and experience media-transmitted events nearly simultaneously, as in a common central nervous system (see also Waters 1995, 35; Giddens 1990, 17–21). These views anticipate global integration by means of a common (media) culture or consciousness rather than by means of economics, in contrast to other approaches (Waters 1995, 33–35; Wallerstein 1974, 1980). Yet what we are after here is something much less general in scope (most of the world is excluded from traders' screen world) and more microlevel in character: a form of time coordination that penetrates all of the participants' interactions and involves dozens of small mechanisms of binding participants into the same time frame.

16. For an interesting historical example of the use of schedules, see Zerubavel (1981, 65ff.).

References

Abolafia, Mitchel Y. 1981. "Taming the Market: Self-regulation in the Commodity Futures Industry." Ph.D. diss., State University of New York at Stony Brook.
———. 1984. "Structured Anarchy: Formal Organization in the Commodities Futures Market." In *The Social Dynamics of Financial Markets,* edited by Patricia A. Adler and Peter Adler. Greenwich, Conn.: JAI Press.

———. 1996a. *Making Markets: Opportunism and Restraint on Wall Street.* Cambridge, Mass.: Harvard University Press.

———. 1996b. "Hyper-Rational Gaming." *Journal of Contemporary Ethnography* 25(2): 226–50.

———. 1998. "Markets as Cultures: An Ethnographic Approach." In *The Laws of the Markets,* edited by Michel Callon. Oxford: Blackwell.

Albrow, Martin. 1996. *The Global Age.* Oxford: Polity Press.

Association Cambiste Internationale. 1996. *Code of Conduct.* Paris: Kremer-Muller & Cie, Foetz.

Austin, John L. 1962. *How to Do Things with Words.* Oxford: Oxford University Press.

Baker, Wayne E. 1981. "Markets as Networks: A Multimethod Study of Trading Networks in a Securities Market." Ph.D. diss., Northwestern University.

———. 1984. "The Social Structure of a National Securities Market." *American Journal of Sociology* 89(4): 775–811.

———. 1990. "Market Networks and Corporate Behavior." *American Journal of Sociology* 96(3): 589–625.

Baker, Wayne E., Robert R. Faulkner, and Gene A. Fisher. 1998. "Hazards of the Market: The Continuity and Dissolution of Interorganizational Market Relationships." *American Sociological Review* 63(2): 147–77.

Bank for International Settlements. 2002. *Triennial Central Bank Survey of Foreign Exchange and Derivatives Market Activity in March 2001: Final Results. Preliminary Global Data.* Basle: BIS.

Barber, Bernard. 1995. "All Economies Are 'Embedded': The Career of a Concept and Beyond." *Social Research* 62(2): 387–413.

Burt, Ronald. 1983. *Corporate Profits and Cooptation: Networks of Market Constraints and Directorate Ties in the American Economy.* New York: Academic Press.

———. 1992. *Structural Holes: The Social Structure of Competition.* Cambridge, Mass.: Harvard University Press.

Button, Graham, ed. 1993. *Technology in Working Order.* London: Routledge.

Callon, Michel. 1998. "An Essay on Framing and Overflowing: Economic Externalities Revisited by Sociology." In *The Laws of the Markets,* edited by Michel Callon. Oxford: Blackwell.

Carruthers, Bruce, and Sarah Babb. 1996. "The Color of Money and the Nature of Value: Greenbacks and Gold in Postbellum America." *American Journal of Sociology* 101(6): 1556–91.

Clark, Colin, and Trevor Pinch. 1995. *The Hard Sell: The Language and Lessons of Street-wise Marketing.* London: HarperCollins.

Collins, Randall. 1981. "Micro-Translation as a Theory-Building Strategy." In *Advances in Social Theory and Methodology: Toward an Integration of Micro- and Macro-Sociologies,* edited by Karin Knorr Cetina and Aaron Cicourel. London: Routledge & Kegan Paul.

Davis, John. 1992. *Exchange.* Buckingham: Open University Press.

DeLaPradelle, Michèle. 1995. "Market Exchange and the Social Construction of a Public Space." *French Cultural Studies* 6: 359–71.

DiMaggio, Paul. 1994. "Culture and the Economy." In *The Handbook of Economic Sociology,* edited by Neil Smelser and Richard Swedberg. Princeton, N.J.: Princeton University Press.

DiMaggio, Paul J., and Walter W. Powell. 1991. "Introduction." In *The New Institutionalism in Organizational Analysis,* edited by Walter W. Powell and Paul J. DiMaggio. Chicago: University of Chicago Press.

Dobbin, Frank R. 1994. "Cultural Models of Organizations: The Social Construction of Rational Organizing Principles." In *Sociology of Culture: Emerging Theoretical Perspectives,* edited by Diana Crane. Oxford: Basil Blackwell.

Dobbin, Frank R., and John R. Sutton. 1998. "The Strength of a Weak State: The Rights Revolution and the Rise of the Human Resources Management Divisions." *American Journal of Sociology* 104(2): 441–76.

Drew, Paul, and John Heritage. 1992. *Talk at Work: Interaction in Institutional Settings.* Vol. 8. Cambridge: Cambridge University Press.

Drucker, Peter. 1993. *Post-capitalist Society.* New York: HarperBusiness.

Dutton, William H., ed. 1996. *Information and Communication Technologies: Visions and Realities.* Oxford: Oxford University Press.

Etzioni, Amitai. 1993. *The Spirit of Community: Rights, Responsibilities, and the Communitarian Agenda.* New York: Simon & Schuster.

Fine, Gary Alan. 1984. "Negotiated Orders and Organizational Cultures." *Annual Review of Sociology* 10: 239–62.

Fligstein, Neil. 1996. "Markets as Politics: A Political-Cultural Approach to Market Institutions." *American Sociological Review* 61(4): 656–73.

Fligstein, Neil, and Iona Mara-Drita. 1996. "How to Make a Market: Reflections on the Attempt to Create a Single Market in the European Union." *American Journal of Sociology* 102(1): 1–33.

Garfinkel, Harold, Michael Lynch, and Eric Livingston. 1981. "The Work of Discovering Science Constructed with Material from the Optically Discovered Pulsar." *Philosophy of the Social Sciences* 11: 131–58.

Geertz, Clifford. 1978. "The Bazaar Economy: Information and Search in Peasant Marketing." *Supplement to the American Economic Review* 68(2, May): 28–32.

Giddens, Anthony. 1990. *The Consequences of Modernity.* Stanford, Calif.: Stanford University Press.

Goffman, Erving. 1972. "The Neglected Situation." In *Language and Social Context: Selected Readings,* edited by Pier Paolo Giglioli. Harmondsworth: Penguin.

———. 1981. "Response Cries." In *Forms of Talk.* Philadelphia: University of Pennsylvania Press.

———. 1983. "The Interaction Order." *American Sociological Review* 48(1, February): 1–17.

Goodwin, Charles. 1995. "Seeing in Depth." *Social Studies of Science* 25(2): 237–74.

Granovetter, Mark. 1985. "Economic Action and Social Structure: The Problem of Embeddedness." *American Journal of Sociology* 91(3): 481–510.

Harvey, David. 1989. *The Condition of Postmodernity: An Inquiry into the Origins of Cultural Change.* New York: Blackwell.

Heath, Christian, Marina Jirotka, Paul Luff, and Jon Hindmarsh. 1995. "Unpacking Collaboration: The Interactional Organization of Trading in a City Dealing Room." *Journal of Computer Supported Cooperation Work* 3(2): 147–65.

Husserl, Edmund. 1960. *Cartesian Meditations.* The Hague: Nijhoff.

Knorr Cetina, Karin. 1981. "Introduction." In *Advances in Social Theory and Methodology: Toward an Integration of Micro- and Macro-Sociologies,* edited by Karin Knorr Cetina and Aaron Cicourel. London: Routledge & Kegan Paul.

Lash, Scott, and John Urry. 1994. *Economies of Signs and Space.* London: Sage Publications.

McLuhan, Marshall. 1964. *Understanding Media.* London: Routledge.

Mead, George Herbert. 1934. *Mind, Self, and Society.* Chicago: University of Chicago Press.

Natanson, Maurice. 1962. "Introduction." In Alfred Schutz, *Collected Papers,* vol. 1. The Hague: Nijhoff.

Portes, Alejandro. 1995. "Economic Sociology and the Sociology of Immigration: A Conceptual Overview." In *The Economic Sociology of Immigration,* edited by Alejandro Portes. New York: Russell Sage Foundation.

Sandel, Michael J. 1982. *Liberalism and the Limits of Justice.* Cambridge, Mass.: Cambridge University Press.

Sassen, Saskia. 1991. *The Global City.* Princeton, N.J.: Princeton University Press.

Scheff, Thomas J. 1990. *Microsociology.* Chicago: University of Chicago Press.

Schegloff, Emanuel A. 1987. "Between Macro and Micro: Contexts and Other Connections." In *The Micro-Macro Link,* edited by Jeffrey C. Alexander, Bernhard Giesen, Richard Munch, and Neil J. Smelser. Berkeley and Los Angeles: University of California Press.

Schutz, Alfred. 1964. *Collected Papers II: Studies in Social Theory,* edited and introduced by Arvid Broodersen. The Hague: Nijhoff.

———. 1967. *The Phenomenology of the Social World.* Evanston, Ill.: Northwestern University Press.

Schutz, Alfred, and Thomas Luckmann. 1973. *The Structures of the Life-World.* Evanston, Ill.: Northwestern University Press.

Simmel, Georg. 1981. "On Visual Interaction." In *Social Psychology Through Symbolic Interaction,* edited by Gregory P. Stone and Harvey A. Farberman. New York: John Wiley.

Smelser, Neil, and Richard Swedberg, eds. 1994. *Handbook of Economic Sociology.* Princeton, N.J.: Princeton University Press.

Smith, Charles W. 1981. *The Mind of the Market.* London: Croom Helm.

———. 1990. *Auctions: The Social Construction of Value.* Berkeley and Los Angeles: University of California Press.

———. 1993. "Auctions: From Walras to the Real World." In *Explorations in Economic Sociology,* edited by Richard Swedberg. New York: Russell Sage Foundation.

Soros, George. 1994. *The Alchemy of Finance.* New York: John Wiley.

Stigler, George J. 1961. "The Economics of Information." *Journal of Political Economy* 69(3): 213–25.

Stone, Gregory P., and Harvey A. Farberman. 1981. *Social Psychology Through Symbolic Interaction.* New York: John Wiley.

Strange, Susan. 1988. *States and Markets.* London: Pinter.

Streissler, Erich W. 1994. "Hayek on Information and Socialism." In *The Economics of F. A. Hayek,* vol. 2, edited by Marina Colonna, Harald Hagemann, and Omar Hamouda. Aldershot: Elgar.

Suchman, Lucy A. 1987. *Plans and Situated Actions: The Problem of Human-Machine Communication.* Cambridge: Cambridge University Press.

Swedberg, Richard. 1994. "Markets as Social Structures." In *The Handbook of Economic Sociology,* edited by Neil Smelser and Richard Swedberg. Princeton, N.J.: Princeton University Press.

———. 1997. "New Economic Sociology: What Has Been Accomplished, What Is Ahead?" *Acta Sociologica* 40(2): 161–82.

Swedberg, Richard, and Mark Granovetter. 1992. "Introduction." In *The Sociology of Economic Life,* edited by Mark Granovetter and Richard Swedberg. Boulder, Colo.: Westview Press.

Ten Have, Paul, and George Psathas, eds. 1995. *Situated Order.* Washington: International Institute for Ethnomethodology and Conversation Analysis and University Press of America.

Turkle, Sherry. 1995. *Life on the Screen.* New York: Simon & Schuster.

Uzzi, Brian. 1997. "Social Structure and Competition in Interfirm Networks: The Paradox of Embeddedness." *Administrative Science Quarterly* 42(1): 35–67.

Wallerstein, Immanuel. 1974. *The Modern World System.* New York: Academic Press.

———. 1980. *The Capitalist World-Economy: Essays.* Cambridge: Cambridge University Press.

Walzer, Michael. 1990. "The Communitarian Critique of Liberalism." *Political Theory* 18(1): 6–23.

Waters, Malcolm. 1995. *Globalization.* London: Routledge.

White, Harrison. 1981a. "Production Markets as Induced Role Structures." In *Sociological Methodology,* edited by Samuel Leinhardt. San Francisco: Jossey-Bass.

———. 1981b. "Where Do Markets Come From?" *American Journal of Sociology* 87(3, November): 517–47.

———. 1993. "Markets as Production Networks." In *Explorations in Economic Sociology,* edited by Richard Swedberg. New York: Russell Sage Foundation.

Wiley, Norbert. 1994. *The Semiotic Self.* Chicago: University of Chicago Press.

Williamson, Oliver. 1981. "The Economics of Organization: The Transaction Cost Approach." *American Journal of Sociology* 87(3, November): 548–77.

Zaner, Richard. 1964. *The Problem of Embodiment: Some Contributions to a Phenomenology of the Body.* The Hague: Nijhoff.

Zelizer, Viviana. 1988. "Beyond the Polemics on the Markets: Establishing a Theoretical and Empirical Agenda." *Sociological Forum* 3(4): 614–34.

———. 1994. *The Social Meaning of Money.* New York: Basic Books.

———. 1998. "The Purchase of Intimacy." Unpublished paper. Princeton University, Department of Sociology, Princeton, N.J.

Zerubavel, Eviatar. 1981. *Hidden Rhythms: Schedules and Calendars in Social Life.* Berkeley and Los Angeles: University of California Press.

———. 1982. "The Standardization of Time: A Sociohistorical Perspective." *American Journal of Sociology* 88(1): 1–23.

Part III

HOW NETWORKS
SHAPE MARKETS

8

OBLIGATION, RISK, AND OPPORTUNITY IN THE RENAISSANCE ECONOMY: BEYOND SOCIAL EMBEDDEDNESS TO NETWORK CO-CONSTITUTION

Paul D. McLean and John F. Padgett

THE NEW Economic Sociology (Granovetter 1990) has performed salutary work in uncovering the social ligaments underlying interactions and decisionmaking in contemporary markets. In so doing, it has shattered the one-sided image of *homo oeconomicus* and the economistic fallacy that the economic sphere has a life of its own and imperatives that determinately shape all action, including, for example, the choice of business partner or trading alter (Polanyi 1944/1957; Granovetter 1985; cf. Williamson 1994). In key instances, it has elegantly documented the interweaving of economic and social logics in economic practice and in participants' talk about that practice (see, for example, Uzzi 1996).

At the same time, in its zeal to demonstrate the embeddedness of economic life in "underlying" social relations, it has sometimes overemphasized one direction of flow between the economic and social spheres of action, or economic and social networks, at the expense of the other. The economistic assumption that the economy is substantively detached from the social has been replaced by a more purely analytical separation of the two, but the fact that economic life *is* itself inherently a social sphere of life—that it is a key component of the social fabric—has not always been sufficiently kept in mind (Krippner 2001). By placing various social networks, or spheres of activity, or fields, on an equal footing, we could more explicitly address their porous interpenetration, or *co-constitution,* rather than the simple determination of one by the other. In this chapter, we explore the co-constitution of economic and other social networks in early-fifteenth-century Florence, a society at the center of medieval European commerce, the birthplace of a new humanistic culture, and a historical case for which a truly unparalleled volume of social network information has survived.

In particular we find strikingly similar patterns and strategies of elite action in Florentine economic networks, on the one hand, and in marital and political networks, on the other, suggesting similar generative processes at work in both.

Although this idea of co-constitution is implicit in a good deal of the economic sociological literature, various exemplary studies and foundational statements unwittingly provide a rhetorical justification for bracketing the impact of the economic on the social and focusing mainly on the impact of the social on the economic.[1] Here we might consider Harrison White's pathbreaking article "Where Do Markets Come From?" (1981), as well as the title of his recent book *Markets from Networks* (2002), both of which—if only rhetorically—suggest particular attention to the derivation of economic networks from other sources. Mark Granovetter's (1974) and Wayne Baker's (1984) seminal studies of the labor market and a securities market, respectively, stress the social and spatial integuments of economic networks. Ezra Zuckerman (1999) has persuasively argued that even a phenomenon as sacrosanct to economists as price formation can be explained to a significant extent on the basis of social processes. The excellent literature on the variety of contemporary capitalisms (for example, Hamilton and Biggart 1988; Guillén 1994, 2001; Schneper and Guillén, this volume) emphasizes the intractable limits on the structural and behavioral convergence of various capitalist economies and the limitations on the diffusion of economic practices posed by national cultural and institutional differences—perhaps reinforcing a sense of the boundedness of economic logic by social factors.[2] And we have seminal studies of the way in which essential instruments of economic life, such as money, are imbued with social meanings that limit their fungibility (Zelizer 1994). But economic sociologists must continue to break free of the "I told you so" mold of showing that economic phenomena can be explained by means of independent "social" variables; instead, they need to document that the economy is an important sphere of social opportunity and socially directed action itself.[3] Further, the co-constitution of economic and other social networks is grounded—certainly in our case, arguably in others (see, for example, Scott, this volume)—in the participation of actors or organizations with multiple roles and multiple identities simultaneously in all of these networks. These actors have the capacity for switching between identities and between logics or rhetorics of presenting themselves and constructing relations with each other.

Beyond "Traditional" Versus "Modern"

When we turn to the analysis of historical markets, we are doubly presented with this lopsided view of the social embeddedness of economic life, for it has remained more or less taken for granted that the embeddedness of the market in past times was much more substantial and far-reaching than it is today.[4] Economic sociologists have increasingly looked for residues of the past in contemporary economic life (for example, Róna-Tas 1994; Stark 1996; Davis, this volume); less have we bothered to investigate seemingly "modern" elements of economic life in the past or the particular implications for economic development of the mixing and melding of modern and traditional elements in past markets. Undoubtedly the best of the new institutionalism-oriented economic sociology has engaged seriously with the past, in particular the historical construction of conceptions of corporate control, industrial policy, property rights, trade associations, and the like (see, for example, Fligstein 1990; Dobbin 1994; Roy 1997; Gao, this volume). But a presentist bias has remained steadfastly in place in social networks–oriented economic sociology. The result is a body of historically informed analysis of economic action and institutional environments, but little historically informed analysis within economic sociology of economic *interactions,* of variations in the structure of economic networks over time, or of the link between past actors' economic strategies and their social obligations—or more simply, between historical instances of economic and social exchange.[5]

Discussion among historians and comparative historical sociologists of the emergence of the early modern European state provides something of a model for a rethinking of markets in past times. No longer does the narrative of the unidirectional, quasi-teleological emergence of the rationalized, bureaucratized, and disciplined state stand up to scrutiny. Instead, scholars acknowledge the variety of regime types (Ertman 1997) and the contingency of the victory of the sovereign state (Spruyt 1994).[6] More specifically, for the Italian city-states, historians recognize: the intersection of putatively "modernizing" *and* "traditionalizing" tendencies in the same institutions; the blurring of public and private (Chittolini 1996) next to bona fide "politico-juridical transformation" of the state and increasing recognition of the state as an autonomous actor (Fubini 1994); respect for constitutional tradition juxtaposed with an increasingly self-conscious and self-interested Machiavellianism among political leaders (Rubinstein 1966; Kent 2000); the simultaneous practice of "forward-looking" and "backward-looking" forms of landholding in adjacent locales (Emigh 1998); the retrenchment of personalistic, clientage-based politics on the issue of taxes next to, in response to, and in fact completely interwoven with fiscal institutional innovation (Conti 1984; Molho 1996; McLean 2002); and a smattering of locally negotiated, tradition-based contracts with subject cities in the midst of the consolidation of the regional state (Cohn 1999; Connell and Zorzi 2000). Contemporary and historical markets and states become harder to characterize in simple terms and harder to distinguish from one another in their basic structural principles. Without further laboring the critique of modernization theory,[7] we encourage economic sociologists to identify the different value of different types of network ties in economic life and to investigate economic networks as sites for the creation, modification, and ultimately historical transformation of the social fabric in toto.

Obligation, Risk, and Opportunity

To develop a more nuanced picture of early European commerce and industry is to take seriously both of the "goals" of economic practice articulated in the famous epigraph that graced the first page of many Renaissance Florentine businessmen's account books: "To the Glory of God and profit."[8] Florentine merchant-bankers and manufacturers avidly pursued profit and assiduously shunned loss; at the same time, they carefully pursued honor and assiduously avoided shame (Weissman 1982).[9] Economy and honor clearly went together: as Lionardo, a character in Leon Battista Alberti's *Libri della famiglia* (1969, 144) tells us, "among occupations, there are quite a few, both honorable and highly esteemed, by means of which wealth in no small measure may be gained," by which he meant precisely the occupations we examine in this chapter (187, 196). And the practitioners of these occupations forged industries of tremendous economic importance. The Florentines who pursued merchant-banking dominated European commerce for most of the thirteenth, fourteenth, and fifteenth centuries. Florentine wool manufacturers were the chief suppliers of high-quality woolen goods to the entire continent, especially in the fourteenth century, while Florentine silk manufacturing likewise achieved a position of continentwide importance in the fifteenth century.[10]

Classic economic historical research has examined how and when the Italians pioneered vital devices of commercial activity such as double-entry bookkeeping, bills of exchange, limited liability partnerships, and holding companies (see, for example, Sapori 1926, 1932, 1970; de Roover 1944, 1966; Melis 1962, 1991; Lopez 1976; Lane 1977; Goldthwaite, Settesoldi, and Spallanzani 1995). Yet notwithstanding compelling evidence for viewing late medieval Italy as the birthplace of modern capitalism, historians have also noted that in terms of motivation and organization the Florentine economy lacked certain features integral to contemporary capitalism as economists define it. For example, despite its decentralization into a multitude of privately owned and operated small companies, hardly any mention is made in contemporary documents of competition as a key element of the market (Goldthwaite 1987, McLean and Padgett 1997, n. 45). Florentines esteemed "ink-stained hands" (Alberti 1969, 14) and the precise bookkeeping they implied, but clearly valued them equally as a signal of diligence, sobriety, and rectitude.

Whereas partnerships operated more continuously in business than did the short-term joint ventures (commenda) of the medieval period, they still operated for short fixed periods, usually two or three years, at which point the books were closed and balanced and shares of profit or loss distributed to the partners and any outside investors. Sometimes the same partnerships re-created themselves, but often new combinations of partners were formed. Although individuals typically worked in the same industry for their entire career, it was not uncommon for them to disappear from active partnership periodically. Moreover, the participatory nature of the Florentine state required all citizens, regardless of their commercial activities, to serve periodically in administrative offices outside the city or in legislative offices within the city (the occupants of which were sequestered in the Signorìa for the duration of their term). These civic duties could not help but affect citizens' ability to participate in or oversee their commercial activities fully. Yet political participation was, if anything, a more vital component of a life well led than was commercial enterprise. In short, the population of actors in the market was subject to continual change.

Thus, we are still left with the task of understanding the interweaving of technical and institutional innovations with the broader cultural and political context of Florence and drawing out the sociological implications of the intersection of the profit motive with the honor motive so neatly articulated by Ronald Weissman (1982). How did Florentines construct and innovatively adapt markets to pursue economic gain while simultaneously pursuing and fulfilling social obligations? How did they use shared dimensions of identity to create trust between traders and between lenders and borrowers? Conversely, how did they use joint economic activity to create or reinforce other shared dimensions of identity? In other words, how did they activate different "logics" of association (Davis, this volume), redolent with different moral guidelines, to pursue both social and economic goals? To what extent was the particular structuring of economic activity isomorphic with or constitutive of structural patterns in other fields of Florentine social life? This chapter adumbrates that market structure and the strategies that constructed it at two levels simultaneously—the choosing of partners in business and the choosing of recipients of credit—and then links this picture to snapshots of Florentine society from other angles. Florentine merchants built biographies, or careers, out of and through a number of linked spheres of life: economic activity, political participation, the vitality of neighborhoods, and kinship-based "belongingness."

We develop this framework concerning economic behavior in Renaissance Florence by elaborating on the interwoven themes of obligation, risk, and opportunity, each of which can be construed both economically and socially. *Obligation* was manifested in choices of career (as families typically participated in the same industry transgenerationally). It was also palpably felt and acted upon in the choice of partners in business and the choice of trading alters, as if partnering and trade were "embedded" (in the narrow sense outlined earlier) in more durable social networks and group memberships. Yet the feeling of obligation resonated both economically and socially: for example, the silk merchant Goro Dati wrote that

> as a result of the adversity which overtook us in Barcelona, and of the suspicions concerning Simone's ventures and the calumnies that were spread about, we were very short of credit. So we were forced to withdraw from business and collect whatever we could pay our creditors, borrowing from friends and using

all our ingenuity, suffering losses, high interest and expense in order to avoid bankruptcy and shame. And although my partner was in favor of going bankrupt so as to avoid some losses and expenditure, I was resolved to face ruin rather than loss of honor. (Brucker 1967, 130)[11]

Consequently, it is fair to say that social obligations had economic consequences, and that economic obligations had social consequences, with both sets of consequences entering into every decision. This is because many Florentines were both businessmen and citizens, both profit-seekers and social status–seekers, with cross-fertilization of these spheres of life accomplished through the actors who linked them.

Risk was present certainly in the daring Mediterranean commercial ventures ably celebrated by the Florentines themselves and commemorated by earlier generations of historians. Yet Quattrocento Florentines experienced new kinds of risks as well. In the early 1300s, the single most salient threat to large, stand-alone, family-run banks came from defaulting borrowers such as the kings of England and Naples; by the early Quattrocento, it appears to have come in the form of runs on the bank and problems of cash flow in a *network* of banks that did not come into being until the later fourteenth century.[12] The economic well-being of Florentine businessmen was threatened by the demands put on them by others to whom they were connected and, specifically in the market, by the extent of their indebtedness relative to their capital and the vulnerability of the entire interconnected system to the failure of its component parts. Simply put, their networks exposed them to costs as well as benefits. Yet the words of Giovanni di Pagolo Morelli suggest their pragmatic, multi-pronged, multiple-network approach to the problem of exposure to risk:

Be courteous: make an effort to acquire one friend or more in your neighborhood, and do whatever good you can for him, and don't trouble yourself about putting yourself in his care. If you are rich, be content to buy friends with your money, if you can't obtain them otherwise; try to marry into families of good citizens, well-loved and powerful; and if there is in your neighborhood someone to help you and to put yourself close to, draw near to this person. (Branca 1986, 190; our translation)[13]

Money, marriage, and vicinanza (emotional ties to neighbors) all served as devices for reducing risk, each being exploited opportunistically according to context or situation. Switching between strategies or arenas of identity represented a key skill in the management of honor and profitability.

Opportunity is in the first place the "profit" component of the picture: far-flung economic networks provided businesses with manifold opportunities for making money. And as the case of the famous merchant of Prato, Francesco Datini, suggests, involvement in these economic networks could become the basis for achieving social acceptance, despite the strength of Florentine status consciousness (Mazzei 1880; Trexler 1980). More precisely, though, Florentines, and in particular Florentine bankers, found ways to capitalize on the *variety* of kinds of social ties linking them to each other and to their respective clients, and they adopted relatively new techniques (such as double-entry bookkeeping and current accounts) for recording these ties in order to pursue new investments and sources of profit. Florentines' social identities were multiple, and opportunities for achieving new revenues, particularly in the emerging silk industry, appear to have been forged through subtle management of these diverse identities.

In what follows we describe in abbreviated narrative form the findings of our empirical study of how Florentine economic networks and social networks impinged on each other.[14] To begin that story, we turn to a discussion of the available data.

Documents for a Study of Florentine Market Structure

The details of the collection of the data used to support the description of the Florentine market offered in this chapter are provided elsewhere (see McLean and Padgett 1997), although we have gathered additional data since then augmenting our coverage of the market. For present purposes, a shorter account can be offered. The partnership and transactional data are drawn from the Florentine *Catasto* of 1427, a remarkable document in the history of public fiscal administration (see Herlihy and Klapisch-Zuber 1985). All Florentine households, as well as those in the surrounding contado, were required to submit a statement in a standardized format to city officials of their total assets in land, holdings in the public debt, investments in and revenues from commercial enterprise, and interpersonal loans so that officials could assess more reliably how to distribute the tax burden in the city. As part of this massive data collection project, officials required the operators of companies to submit a copy of the balance sheets from their companies, offering summary information on the outstanding flows of business between all companies in the market, Florentine and foreign, as of a particular point in time: July 12, 1427. These bilanci survive in the portate version of household tax records in the Archivio di Stato in Florence. We focused chiefly on gathering transactional (credit-debt) information on all companies in the largest and most prestigious industries in the economy, namely, banking (including international merchant-banking, import-export companies, and domestic banking engaged in both commercial credit and personal lending operations), silk manufacture, wool manufacture, cloth retailing, and cloth dyeing. We coded the presence (absence) of ties and their value in florins for all dyadic pairs of companies within and between these industries. The estimated percentage of all credits and all value of credits coded by us are reported in table 8.1. Overall, we estimate that our dataset contains about one-third of all transactions engaged in by all the companies in our selected industries; these transactions account for 60 to 65 percent of the florin value of all the credits and debts amassed by these companies.[15]

Based on our collection of the "credits" data through the reading of the bilanci, we were able furthermore to develop a census of companies in these industries and to characterize companies in terms of their industry, geographic location (Florence chiefly, but also a variety of other Italian cities such as Pisa, Venice, Rome, and Ancona and a variety of other European mercantile centers such as London, Bruges, Barcelona, Avignon, and Montpelier), size of their capital investment (corpo), and number of ties and aggregate value of the ties they maintained. We found conclusive evidence for the existence of forty-five international merchant-banks, twenty Pisa-based import-export-oriented banks,[16] fifty-three domestic banks, thirty-five cloth retail establishments (ritagliatori), forty-six silk manufacturers, 123 wool manufacturers (forty-one of them in the high-quality San Martino district), and eighteen cloth dyers.[17] These numbers concur almost precisely with estimates provided in historical monographs on the wool and silk industries (Hoshino 1980; Edler de Roover 1966; see also Tognetti 2002, 25); no precise estimates besides ours exist for the other industries.

Naturally we also identified the partners active in each company. It was rare in the early 1400s for companies to have more than three partners (by which is typically meant individuals with a stake in the start-up capital of the company), and consequently it is quite possible to characterize companies in terms of the attributes of their partners. More specifically, for each partner[18] we coded the following information:

- The name of his family (that is, his patrilineage)
- His social status, based on the earliest date at which any member of his family was selected for the Florentine priorate, the commune's chief governing body (here discrete status classifications are based on discrete waves of new entry into the priorate; for details, see Padgett 2001)
- The actual two-month periods during which the partner served on the priorate
- The year the partner first sat on the Sei della Mercanzia, an administrative body of merchants charged with resolving disputes between companies or between companies and private individuals
- The partner's year of birth, used for determining age cohorts
- The partner's household wealth in 1427
- The partner's parish, neighborhood (gonfalone), and quarter of residence in 1427
- The name of the partner's wife's family, if available
- The factional affiliation of the partner himself and/or his family when conflict between Medici supporters and Albizzi regime loyalists broke out in the early 1430s[19]

TABLE 8.1 *Estimated Size and Percentage Coverage of the Market in Our Sample of Export-Oriented Industries in Florence, 1427*

	Seen Bilanci[a]				Unseen Bilanci[a]			Overall			
	Debts Coded	Number of Companies	Trans-actions Coded	Value Coded	Number of Companies	Trans-actions Coded (Estimate)	Value Coded (Estimate)	Bilanci Seen	Trans-actions Coded (Estimate)	Value Coded (Estimate)	Estimated Total Credits (Florins)
International merchant-banks	1,364	16	25.4%	44.3%	29	19.4%	70.2%	35.6%	23.8%	45.4%	1,418,387
Florence and Pisa merchant-banks	1,172	16	31.0	58.0	4	4.3	9.4	80.0	28.7	56.2	535,761
Domestic banks	4,194	39	46.9	71.2	14	25.0	66.8	73.6	44.7	70.7	2,150,706
All merchant-banks	6,730	71	39.1	60.1	47	19.7	64.0	60.2	37.3	60.4	4,104,854
Cloth retail	2,705	26	22.3	50.4	9	12.0	23.1	74.3	21.1	47.5	592,033
Silk production	1,765	37	33.4	81.2	9	20.0	[?]	80.4	33.4	81.2	281,424
Wool production, San Martino	1,726	31	48.5	79.4	10	8.9	18.8	75.6	47.6	78.8	359,732

(Table continues on p. 202.)

TABLE 8.1   Continued

	Seen Bilanci[a]			Unseen Bilanci[a]			Overall			
	Debts Coded	Number of Companies	Transactions Coded	Value Coded	Number of Companies	Transactions Coded (Estimate)	Value Coded (Estimate)	Bilanci Seen	Transactions Coded (Estimate)	Value Coded (Estimate)	Estimated Total Credits (Florins)
Via Maggio	434	17	35.7	84.1	10	14.2	35.9	63.0	31.1	75.5	39,058
San Pancrazio	200	6	44.0	59.7	2	—	—	75.0	44.0	59.7	23,291
San Pier Scheraggio	108	4	32.9	98.1	5	17.6	31.9	44.1	25.4	66.2	8,127
All Garbo	—	27	37.2	77.3	17	15.6	34.4	61.4	32.3	70.0	70,476
Unknown	795	21	42.3	64.3	18	29.7	98.3	53.8	39.8	67.2	173,080
Total wool	3,263	79	44.3	75.8	45	23.2	68.2	63.7	41.4	75.0	603,288
Cloth Dyers	619	10	27.4	47.5	8	32.9	51.6	55.6	28.7	50.0	67,364
Totals	—	223	34.9	64.2	118	20.3	44.3	65.4	33.4	62.3	—

Source: Authors' compilation.

a. The percentage of transactions coded for "seen bilanci" companies equals the sum of the number of coded credits/debts for all "seen bilanci" companies in a given industry, divided by the sum of the total number of credits/debts of those companies in that industry. The same formula was used to calculate the percentage of florin value for "seen bilanci" companies within each industry. Totals were also coded, whenever they were available from campione summary statements of company records, for a subset of "unseen bilanci" companies in each industry. The percentage of numbers of credits and of florin values of credits coded for this subset of "unseen bilanci" was used, within each specific industry, to estimate totals for the remaining companies for which totals information was otherwise lacking. Then this formula was used for each complete industry, summing coded numbers and values for all companies, as well as estimated total numbers and values, to estimate the overall percentage of coverage and size of each industry.

Armed with these attributes of the partners, and with the attributes of companies both as units of commercial enterprise and as assemblages of partners, we have been able to examine both patterns in partnership formation and patterns in the offering of credits and their empirical relationship to each other.

The Social Bases of Partnership: Family, Neighborhood, and Social Status

To examine partnership formation, we took a census of all persons active in each of our industries and coded all possible dyadic pairs (within each industry) for whether or not they engaged in a business partnership with each other. To repeat, the idea was to probe for connections between kinship networks and social, geographic, and political affiliations (and the social identities they confer), on the one hand, and patterns of partnership formation, on the other. In another paper (Padgett and McLean 2002), we explicitly assess the weight that each of these networks and affiliations carried relative to each other in structuring partnership. For present purposes, we simply present in tabular form an indication of their several relationships, with partner choice broken down by industry (table 8.2).

Across all industries, the greatest percentage of actually existing partnership dyads were formed within status groups. But given that the target population of available partners of similar social status is much larger than the

TABLE 8.2   *Early-Fifteenth-Century Florentine Partnerships Congruent with Other Social Relations*

	Flowing Through Nuclear Family	Flowing Through Extended or Nuclear Family	Flowing Through Gonfalone	Flowing Within Status Groups
Banking sector	22.3% (=66/296)	31.1% (=92/296)	16.9% (=50/296)	76.4% (=226/296)
Wool sector (including ritagliatori)	21.4 (=68/318)	31.4 (=100/318)	18.5 (=58/318)	54.1 (=172/318)
Silk industry	14.3 (=14/98)	28.6 (=28/98)	20.4 (=20/98)	57.1 (=56/98)
Total[a]	20.2 (=148/732)	30.0 (=220/732)	18.0 (=130/732)	62.0 (=454/732)

Source: Authors' compilation.
a. Total includes cloth dyeing companies and a few miscellaneous companies in addition to the other categories enumerated.

target population of family members, the most striking criterion framing choice of business partner for Florentines was kinship, and in particular nuclear family ties: over 30 percent of partner dyads were within-family dyads, and fully one out of five partnership ties actually existing was between brothers or between fathers and sons. Although pairings between brothers-in-law or fathers- and sons-in-law were far less common, when such ties were present between individuals in the same industry, they typically did eventuate in the formation of a partnership, especially in banking, such as in the case of Cosimo de' Medici, who had married into the Bardi family in 1413, or the banking partnership of Francesco di Filippo Frescobaldi and his brother-in-law, Iacopo di Vannozzo Bardi. A similar case is that of Bartolomeo di Verano Peruzzi, who had married the sister of his partner in a Pisa bank, Giovanni di Domenico Giugni, in 1402.[20] Partnership was also forged on the back of more extended kinds of kinship relations: approximately one out of ten existing partnerships had extended kinship (that is, shared patrilineage beyond and exclusive of the nuclear level) behind it. Extended kinship was used especially by silk manufacturers (compare columns 1 and 2 in table 8.2), which was an emerging but as yet lower-prestige industry with relatively fewer patrician participants but more substantial capital requirements than other manufacturing industries. These facts may well have prompted would-be silk merchants to combine resources across same-kin households to a greater extent than was true for other market participants.

With family we see almost entirely the structuring effect of other social networks and groupings on economic choices. But this limited perspective is considerably challenged when we address the relevance to partnership formation of neighborhood and social status, which are also of substantial importance, as indicated in tables 8.2 and 8.3.

On the surface we can see that being from the same neighborhood was an important determinant in selecting partners, although this criterion was stronger in nonbanking industries and, as we shall see, among non-high-status bankers.[21] For most market participants, neighborhood (vicinanza) offered a local field for matching partners to each other, no doubt because vicinanza carried not only a geographic spatial connotation but also a connotation of psychological proximity and achieved trust (Klapisch-Zuber 1985). Accordingly, not only was neighborhood a field in which to search; it was also a "logic" of affiliation and a rhetoric of trustworthiness to invoke. Consequently, at the most aggregate level partnering appears to have followed a logic of concentric circles: first pick from one's own family, then from among close neighbors, and then from further afield only if need be.[22] Matching of partners by status group appears quite pronounced, but again, we must remember that status groups are much larger than the other groupings examined here. Moreover, for the most "traditionalist" of industries—wool production—within-status-group partnering is not particularly preponderant; men of modest status often teamed up with partners from groups

TABLE 8.3   *Patterns in Same-Status Partnering by Different Status Groups, by Industry: Differences in Reliance on Family and Neighborhood in Early-Fifteenth-Century Florence*

	Dyads from Each Status Group	Same-Status Partners from Same Family	Same-Status Partners from Same Gonfalone
Banking sector (76.4 percent partnering within status group)			
Magnates and popolani	84.1%	31.6%	15.8%
New men	6.2	71.4	85.7
Unadmitted to priorate	9.7	81.8	27.3
Wool sector (54.1 percent partnering within status group)			
Magnates and popolani	69.8	60.0	28.3
New men	24.4	66.7	28.6
Unadmitted to priorate	5.8	n/a[a]	40.0
Silk industry (57.1 percent partnering within status group)			
Magnates and popolani	39.3	81.8	36.4
New men	46.4	38.5	38.5
Unadmitted to priorate	14.3	n/a[a]	0.0

Source: Authors' compilation.

a. The absence of family names for most partners unadmitted to priorate makes it difficult to determine whether their partners were kin or not.

of higher social status, suggesting the kind of master-apprentice model of partnership that had been more dominant throughout the economy across all industries in the mid-1300s.

However, as we cut a little more deeply into the numbers, we can see more clearly the importance of status and the way it intersected, or crosscut, neighborhood.[23] Table 8.3 focuses on the same-status partner dyads but examines patterns of within-family and within-neighborhood partnering for the different status groups.[24] The differences between status groups, especially within banking, are quite pronounced. High-status bankers clearly chose high-status partners from *outside* their own families to a greater extent than any other group did. And they chose high-status partners from *outside* their own neighborhoods to an even greater extent. Thus, rather than bank partnering choices being embedded in neighborhood identities in a straightforward way, they apparently were reflectively constructed to crosscut those identities where possible. And this other identity that stitched together high-status banking partnerships was shared social status. The most pronouncedly elite actors in the most pronouncedly elite industry reached out to each other across locales, thus defying modal partnering strategies in the economy as a whole. By contrast, new men in the banking industry were typically frozen out of these elite partnerships and overwhelmingly constrained to seek partners from within their own neighborhood.

Thus, we can imagine the network of partnership ties spatially this way: largely composed of locally forged ties, ostensibly on the basis of strong-tie social connections, but with a *financial* elite of (also) *socially* elite popolani and magnate bankers spanning neighborhood locales, to form companies that sat at the core of the economy, with greater geographical reach and greater capacity for capital accumulation. Two logics of partnership formation co-existed, and sometimes both were operational in the same company: one "traditionalist" and local (to put it crudely), the other more "modern," expansive, and cosmopolitan.[25]

This hybrid design parallels the structuring principles of the Florentine marriage market in the late fourteenth and fifteenth centuries: the ongoing importance of neighborhood for most actors, combined with strategically forged, cross-neighborhood marriages by elite actors, particularly those most involved in factional politics (Cohn 1980; Padgett and Ansell 1993; Padgett 1994). In other words, economic partnering strategies were yet another facet of the institutional transition from a guild corporatist regime to a reggimento that was more consensualist, based on civic humanism, but also elitist (Najemy 1982). The search for marriage allies and the search for banking partners were similar, even as substantially different search criteria were applied by different status groups in these "markets." Which networks mattered was a matter of strategic choice directed by, we believe, the escalating political tensions that originated in the Ciompi revolt of 1378–82, the value of one's status, and the increasing legitimacy afforded members of the Florentine elite to distinguish themselves from the ordinary rank-and-file citizenry. Neither search for "allies" was straightforwardly grounded in "underlying" social networks.

The Social Bases of Credit: Family, Neighborhood, and Social Status in a Different Light

Next we turn to a discussion of the structuring of the giving and receiving of commercial credit. Here again family, and in particular nuclear family, had a profound impact on choice of trading alter. This was especially true when companies transacted multiple credits simultaneously with each other, a pattern that occurred to a disproportionate extent in the banking industry. Nonetheless, that effect was not the dominant one: the most powerful predictor of whether two companies did business with each other is simply the number of ties we might expect them to have had based on their overall involvement in the market—that is, the expected number of ties between companies if creditors and debtors distributed their ties uniformly within that market. This is an important reminder of the limitations of reading historical cases of markets as if their embeddedness in "underlying" social networks were all-encompassing.[26] As a matter of fact, companies spread most of their ties around, while concentrating a certain proportion of business on a select few alters, in a manner similar to the hybrid strategy pursued by Brian Uzzi's garment manufacturing firms (1996) or Baker's automobile manufacturers (1990).

Another point of similarity between Florentine markets and contemporary ones comes from the importance of interlocks. Consortia of banks located in different cities, with separate account ledgers, often with different managing partners or different lead partners named in each city, and sometimes attached to wool or silk production companies, engaged in heavy trading and cash transfers among themselves. The "holding company" (de Roover 1966, 6) with relatively autonomous branches was an organizational innovation fairly new to the time (although the much larger banks of the early 1300s also maintained numerous branches throughout Europe) and was most famously associated with the Medici and their system of interconnected banks in Florence, Rome, and Venice, as well as their wool shop in Florence. Yet the Medici were by no means the only practitioners of this form: the Giugni, Nelli, and Barbadori families, as well as Cosimo de' Medici's cousin Averardo di Francesco de' Medici, Bartolomeo di Verano Peruzzi, Toso di Albizzo da Fortuna, Lutozzo di Iacopo Nasi, and Andrea de' Pazzi, sat astride a number of interconnected business ventures whose operations were mutually supportive.[27]

Lest we again jump to conclusions about the "embeddedness" of economic networks, however, it is important to note that the structuring effect of family differed at various times in Florentine history. If anything, the shift *away* from the huge family-based partnerships that characterized banking in the early fourteenth century (see Padgett 2001) is what made possible the exchange of credit among separate companies operated by *separate* branches of the patrilineage evident in the early fifteenth century. The replacement of the consolidated family business with a network of companies maintaining current accounts with each other did not eliminate the importance of family as a social institution affecting the economy, but that structuring effect happened in a different way. Furthermore, the effect of shared patrilineage on the giving of credits in certain industries was the inverse of its effect on partnership. Family was important for the formation of silk manufacturing partnerships, but to such an extent that unpartnered family members were hardly left in the field to do company-to-company business with each other. This hints at the different styles or forms of organization characterizing these different industries—a topic to which we return later in the chapter.

When we get beyond family, we return to the thornier but more interesting influences of social status and neighborhood. Once again, we explicitly assess the relative importance of all of these factors for the exchange of credit elsewhere (Padgett and McLean 2002), but for simple expository purposes, table 8.4 reports on the extent to which each of them independently appears linked to concrete exchanges, broken down by sector. Table 8.4 also reports on the tendency for a credit between two companies in any given market to be reciprocated with a credit flowing in the opposite direction.

The most striking finding here concerns banks. Whereas citywide social status identity was invoked to construct elite banking partnerships, neighborhood identity was used to a dramatic extent to construct the credit ties of these ostensibly most cosmopolitan actors to alter companies. This strategy was practiced even by a substantial subset of actors not even living presently in their home neighborhoods (namely, Florentine bankers abroad and merchant-banking companies in Pisa). On the one hand, "social status" is far too broad a category to capture how incestuous the giving and receiving of credit really was at the banking core of the economy, what with its emerging networks of familially tied companies. On the other hand, it is far too narrow to account for the volume of status boundary-crossing exchange in numerous markets,

TABLE 8.4 *Commercial Credits Flowing Through Social Relations in Early-Fifteenth-Century Florence*

	Flowing Through Family (Extended or Nuclear)[a]	Flowing Through Gonfalone[a]	Flowing Within Status Groups[a]	Flowing Reciprocally
Banking sector	24.8% (=236/953)	41.8% (=398/953)	59.0% (=562/953)	44.8% (=427/953)
Banking and wool	8.1 (=76/941)	22.5 (=212/941)	52.9 (=498/941)	14.6 (=137/941)
Banking and silk	4.5 (=19/424)	20.3 (=86/424)	43.6 (=185/424)	21.2 (=90/424)
Wool sector (including ritagliatori)	3.0 (=35/1162)	15.4 (=179/1162)	47.5 (=552/1162)	9.9 (=115/1162)
Silk industry	2.0 (=3/153)	13.1 (=20/153)	30.0 (=46/153)	5.2 (=8/153)
Total[b]	8.2 (=390/4735)	22.0 (=1042/4735)	48.4 (=2292/4735)	19.7 (=933/4735)

Source: Authors' compilation.
a. Shared patrilineage, gonfalone of residence, and social status are computed dichotomously as presence/absence of *at least* one partner dyad of this type.
b. Total includes cloth dyeing companies and a few miscellaneous companies, in addition to the other categories enumerated.

including within the banking industry itself. Elite bankers partnered with each other—the market for partners was stratified—but they did not fail to extend credit to lower-status bankers resident in their home neighborhoods. The use of neighborhood identity was not as strong when bankers extended credit to (or accepted credits from) wool and silk merchants, yet it was more important than when companies in those industries did business among themselves.

At a gross level, examination of the chains of production in this economy (that is, leaving aside the banking system and its interconnections) also reveals status-crossing exchange, despite the homophily that characterized partnership formation. The fairly youthful and new man–populated silk industry successfully sought outlets for its production with some of the most entrenched merchant-banker popolani. Meanwhile, the master-apprentice-style wool companies, even those owned by high-status popolani, sold much of their product on consignment to Florentine ritagliatori, a majority of whom were new men or individuals not yet admitted to the priorate—that is, men beneath the typical wool merchant in social station. In other words, on the basis of a crude classification of the status-group character of each major "occupational group," the step from production to distribution flowed across status lines to a considerable extent.

As we noted earlier, banks invested significantly in "neighborhood" as a frame or an identity facilitating credit relations, both among themselves (over and above the strong effect of family ties) and in their dealings with wool and silk manufacturers. We elaborate further on that finding here. Banks were unquestionably the engine of the Florentine economy, in terms of capital resources, number of credits, and the importance of the functions they served as suppliers of cash, raw materials, and distribution networks for cloth producers. Purely from the standpoint of economic imperatives, bankers needed to develop stable, institutionalized relationships with each other; for example, banks depended on constantly fluctuating foreign exchange rates and the regular reportage of such rates to each other for writing the bills of exchange that were one of their main sources of profit (de Roover 1966). Although we do not know precisely when it happened, the character of banking changed in the course of the 1300s, some time after the bankruptcy of the major family-based companies in the 1320s, 1330s, and 1340s. Banks moved away from serving primarily (or at least most saliently) as the creditors of nobles and toward serving as depositories for the riches of nobles, clerics, and affluent Florentines.[28] They settled more fully into the role of broker looking for profit-making opportunities at the interstices of a great variety of economic operations in Florence and abroad. As brokers in the market, they acted as agents for other kinds of actors and interacted with each other, not only on their own behalf but also on behalf of their nonbank correspondents. Consequently, the banking system at the core of the economy required a system of current accounts between companies acting on each other's behalf to keep the economy working smoothly.

But the population of banks, by virtue of partnering choices, was cleaved along status lines. Had status-consciousness continued to dominate, there would have remained debilitating holes in the banking network. The solution was to use the time-honored identity of neighborhood to reach out across status boundaries and forge trust. Unwillingness to form partnerships with new men could not and did not carry over into a willingness to forgo the economic opportunities that could accrue from such ties. Therefore, we argue, the system of credit anchored by the banking industry resembled a patron-client structure operating as an "addendum" to the activities at the core of the market (Eisenstadt and Roniger 1984, ch. 5). Banking elites reached down across status boundaries to neighborhood locals they knew, not so much to constitute the majority of their business but to extend their networks and fill gaps in them and to overcome the rigidities of a system rich in ascriptive status distinctions. Taking this line of argument a step further, the combination of cross-neighborhood banking partnerships with the dominant logic of within-neighborhood commercial credit enabled elite bankers, by virtue of their partnerships, to obtain access to the credit relationships available in multiple neighborhoods, thus multiplying their economic opportunities. Whether this was a self-conscious economic strategy we cannot say, but the four largest banks, of any type, and seven of the top twenty in terms of volume of credits were in fact partnerships forged across neighborhood (and even quarter) boundaries.

The logic of neighborhood as a socially sanctioned identity was adapted and applied by bankers in an incrementally learned way to forge ties with other industries as well. Here the desiderata of maximizing profit and seizing opportunities for growth were consonant with and pursued through channels that had already been cognitively legitimized. For one thing, "sponsorship" by banks must have dramatically stimulated the growth of the Florentine silk industry, which we know was only just beginning to grow in the early 1400s and had not yet really taken off (Tognetti 2002, 26ff.), partly supplanting the increasingly moribund wool industry that had been the bread-and-butter of Florentine prosperity over the previous century or more. Merchant-bankers saw and capitalized on an opportunity to make money off a new set of producers largely endowed with less social status by both bringing them the raw materials they needed and providing outlets to foreign markets, along the way pulling silk merchants into their accounting practices and into their schemata of organizing economic relations. That is to say, banks began to infiltrate and recharacterize the silk industry with their own logic of search and patterning of relations. In banks' support of the silk industry we find a situation in which the very character of the market was clientelistic: elite actors reached across status barriers to forge ties—especially strong, reciprocal ones (as in table 8.4, column 4)—with clients on the basis of shared neighborhood identity. Clientage did not crosscut the central organizing principle of the system as a whole and make it function more smoothly; rather, it was the constitutive principle of the market. What we know about past and future participation in the priorate by the individuals running these companies confirms this depiction of the market: since worthiness for the priorate was both formally and informally assessed by notables in one's own neighborhood who conducted the scrutinies (the examination and assessment of citizens' eligibility or worthiness for holding high office), economic ties forged through neighborhood but across statuses ought to have resulted in positive judgments of new men and their fitness for office. The market acted as a kind of testing ground for later inclusion in the reggimento—an idea made more persuasive considering the relative youth of many merchants. The simple corollary of this is that a considerable number of cross-status economic ties would involve, by definition, people previously not chosen to be among the elite of the city. Given the fact that a number of silk merchants operating in the 1420s later became staunch supporters of the Medici regime, the clientage depiction of this market becomes even more compelling.[29]

While the "traditional" logic of neighborhood was being adaptively harnessed to the emergence of a new industry in the case of silk, and in turn the logic of search for alters there was reinforcing or "co-constituting" the emergent political field, the situation in wool was somewhat the opposite. Neighborhood was still significant for forging ties between the banking industry and wool companies, especially for reciprocally offered credits. Yet the relationship between banks and wool in the aggregate was evaporating: higher-quality wool producers were now sending goods to ritagliatori to a significant extent rather than to domestic or international banks, and indeed ties between lower-quality woolen cloth producers and big banks were significantly absent. The wool industry was retreating in prominence and retreating from the European market, even though the quality of Florentine production remained high and may even have been improving (Hoshino 1980). Sergio Tognetti (2002) attributes this retreat to the fact that the labor costs of wool production were significantly higher than those for silk, at a time when the population had dwindled (following the Black Plague in the midfourteenth century) and the price of labor had risen substantially. Thus, it is possible to cite a purely economic reason for the substitution of silk for wool, even though state policy no doubt also played a considerable role in the shift. Assuming Tognetti is right, in the case of wool, social embeddedness tugged at but did not overpower profit-making concerns. Neighborhood loyalties were the last bastion of social obligation between the banking industry and a wool industry on the decline rather than the cutting edge of a new partnership—a constraining tie rather than an opportunity.

That elite bankers tried to manage their social networks to a considerable extent is evident in the words of Giannozzo Alberti in the *Libri della famiglia*. The character Giannozzo corresponds to a merchant-banker in our data, a seventy-year-old partner in the concern of Giannozzo e Antonio di Tommaso Alberti &

Co of Venice who was co-head of the richest Alberti household, which was the twentieth-richest household in all of Florence in 1427. He comments:

> Do you know what a friend of mine does? In other ways his character is most upright and disciplined, but perhaps on matters of finance he is a little close. He has a technique for dealing with irresponsible people who come with their importunate demands under color of friendship, kinship and old acquaintance. The greetings of such a fellow he returns with an infinite number of greetings. If he smiles, my friend returns a warmer smile. If he praises him, my friend praises him still more than he has been praised. . . . To all his words and his whining, my friend lends a willing ear, but when he comes to the story of his needs, my friend immediately invents some of his own to tell, and as the man comes to the point of actually asking him, in conclusion, for a loan or at least to stand surety for one—suddenly he is deaf. He misunderstands and gives a reply to something else, and quickly changes the subject. (Alberti 1969, 239)

In short, notes Giannozzo, "we know well how to simulate goodwill or how to avoid friendship in order to suit our situation" (263). In effect bankers were playing this artful game (McLean 1998) of managing their networks of amici and vicini (friends and neighbors) in the pursuit of profit without loss of honor.

The Independent Importance of Market Structure

We move now out of the nitty-gritty details of market structure—details that indeed confirm the relevance of social networks and of various social dimensions of identity to the construction of a market, but more specifically demonstrate that economic decisions are selectively embedded in social networks and that economic and social fields are co-constitutive—to a final view of the logic of production as a whole in this export-oriented economy. There is no question but that the economy had a structure of its own and that ties between companies were driven by an "industry logic" as well as by social or political-cultural logics. That is, companies played distinctive and mutually supportive roles in the production process. We have alluded to some of these roles already, but we focus on them more explicitly here.

Over and above the putative influence of social network ties, certain markets manifested a higher-than-expected number of transactions. Figure 8.1 maps these flows graphically.

The solid lines in figure 8.1 depict market interfaces with more ties than would be expected if companies had distributed their credit completely evenly throughout the market, *and* taking into account the various social connections that were part of the scaffolding of this economy. The first thing to note is the volume of business among various types of banks. International merchant-banks contracted ties among themselves, as did domestic banks, to a remarkable extent. Pisa-based import-export banks were likewise tied to

FIGURE 8.1   *The Flow of Business in Early-Fifteenth-Century Florence, Over and Above Shared Social Ties*

———▶ 1) Higher than expected number of ties: the dominant steps in the chain of production and/or financial flows

---▶ 2) Frequently reciprocally given credits: markets with current accounts and/or credit flowing in both directions

········▶ 3) Significantly more-than-expected nonzero dyads: asymmetrically organized markets—on wool side, a consignment system; on younger silk side, a fluid market with imprecise roles

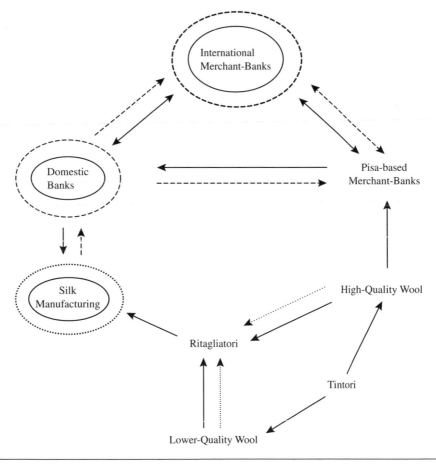

Source: Authors' compilation.

banks abroad and to domestic banks, although they were not so tied to each other. Consequently, the network of banks was a network within the network of the market as a whole; this graphically indicates what we claimed earlier, namely, that banks were the engine of the economy, facilitating the flow of credit and servicing Florence's manufacturing industries at both the raw materials and distribution ends. Furthermore, note the dashed lines connecting these various types of banks to each other and the dashed lines encircling domestic and international banks, indicating that these banks dealt relationally with each other. By this, we mean that a credit flowing in one direction between banks is typically paired with a credit flowing in the opposite direction, an indication of the use of a dual accounting system whereby the corresponding banks did abundant business on each other's behalf (the per noi and per loro accounts discussed by de Roover [1944], as well as the conti correnti [current accounts] for which we find considerable evidence in our companies' balance sheets).

Next, reading up from the bottom of figure 8.1, we can see that Florentine woolen cloth flowed disproportionately into the hands of cloth retailers, largely for domestic consumption. Only some of the cloth produced by high-end manufacturers went to Pisa-based banks for export, and the volume of flow in that direction was not as substantial with respect to baseline expectations as the flow to the local retailers. This, combined with the significant flow of credits from cloth dyers to cloth manufacturers, indicates that the wool industry functioned as a consignment system in which specific roles in production were highly specialized, with credits (goods) flowing chiefly in one direction.

Finally, we can see how the silk industry differed from wool, the traditional staple of the Florentine economy, in two fundamental ways. First, contrary to the consignment system of specialized production traveling along commodity chains, the relatively youthful silk industry was organized as a "cloud" of producers doing business with each other, fluidly moving between supplier, manufacturer, and distributor roles. As "generalists" to a greater extent than the highly specialized and routinized wool manufacturing companies, silk companies were able to give or receive credits (of various sorts) with other silk companies as opportunities arose. Thus, this industry was roughly similar in certain respects to collections of actors like Silicon Alley or groups of Internet start-ups (see, for example, Girard and Stark 2001): companies gave credit or took it in response to a dynamic situation; there were lots of new people; they did not adopt apprenticeship-type relationships; status was a less imposing barrier to exchange than in other markets; and everybody functioned like an independent contractor. Furthermore, they may have been slower to adopt the highest standards of accounting practices (Edler de Roover 1966, 236).[30]

Second, and equally important, silk was tied differently to the banking core of the economy. Here we can see graphically the emergent organization of the silk-based component of the Florentine economy, spurred on by domestic bank investment, an organization that was to become solidified as domestic bankers from the late 1430s on moved more forcefully into positions of ownership and added silk companies to their portfolios (Tognetti 2002).

Credit was vital to Florentine companies to an extent that we may find difficult to comprehend. The volume of debt they carried relative to their capital—the extent to which they were leveraged—was substantially higher than is the case for contemporary firms; in other words, they were exposing themselves to a great deal more risk in the market than we today consider advisable. These figures are reported in table 8.5. This was particularly true of banks, both banks overseas and those with a Florentine tavola (branch): notwithstanding the greater capital invested in these companies by the partners (as the top half of the table indicates), the debt-capital ratio of these companies was markedly higher than for manufacturing or strictly retailing

TABLE 8.5   *Average Capital of Early-Fifteenth-Century Florentine Companies in Key Industries and Degree of Indebtedness with Respect to Invested Capital*

	N	Corpo Only	Corpo Plus Sopraccorpo[a] + Profits	All Previous Plus Inventory	All Previous Plus Personal Wealth
Average capital (corpo) in florins					
Merchant banks	23	5,080	5,751	6,973	8,910
Domestic banks	24	6,375	9,941	10,119	12,574
Cloth retail	21	4,305	5,348	7,102	7,141
Silk	25	3,568	3,928	4,851	5,227
Wool, San Martino (high-quality)	30	3,239	3,654	4,373	4,658
Wool, other (lower-quality)	24	2,030	2,233	2,517	2,681
Average leverage (total debt/capital)					
Merchant banks	12	5.42	4.98	3.62	2.77
Domestic banks	14	4.93	3.29	3.20	2.36
Cloth retail	14	2.20	1.66	1.15	1.14
Silk	19	0.94	0.86	0.66	0.60
Wool, San Martino	23	1.17	1.04	0.84	0.79
Wool, other	16	0.54	0.48	0.41	0.37

Source: Authors' compilation.
a. Sopraccorpo designates lump-sum payments to companies, by partners or others, distinct from start-up capital, yet expressly designated as additions to the capital base of the company.

companies, and it was so regardless of how expansively we define the capital the partners could have available to them in the event of a run on the bank. The extent to which companies were dependent on each other for dependable repayment of credits offered indicates the degree to which the trustworthiness of one's alters must have been integral to all decisions to offer credit. This made the social embeddedness of economic action essential, though such embeddedness could not simply be acted upon with no reflection about the consequences.

One of the primary functions of banks in this economy was to carry debt for manufacturing companies. Banks accepted credits from manufacturing firms and each other (not to mention individual depositors, for whom we have considerable information not yet analyzed) in the form of both merchandise (for example, finished cloth offered on consignment) and cash deposits. Finished cloth was sold abroad for a profit; cash was used to pursue promising investment opportunities. This function of banks—essentially as brokers in a complexly structured economy—differed substantially from their most salient function in the heyday of Florentine banks a century earlier in the early 1300s. Then, even though commerce was already vital to the great banking houses, and even though usury laws posed substantial barriers to the collection of interest, lending was the key to profit. It appears—although documentation of the sort we have for 1427 is lacking—that little in the way of a banking "system" had yet emerged. By 1427 bankers had made two clear discoveries: the risk of default by monarchs and great lords was very high, thus threatening solvency; and debt could just as viably be the path to profit as could credit. The two discoveries are together touched on by the old banker Giannozzo Alberti in a conversation with Adovardo Alberti in book 3 of the *Libri della famiglia:*

> ADOVARDO: But what about lending money, Giannozzo? What if some noble lord asks you for a loan, as happens every day?
>
> GIANNOZZO: I would sooner give him twenty as a gift than a hundred on loan. I would gladly avoid him altogether so as to have to do neither. (Alberti 1969, 236)

Ultimately Adovardo responds: "Then I shall be prudent and, in accordance with your advice, shall avoid all dealings with great lords. *Should I find myself nonetheless engaged in some commerce with them, I shall always ask for cash.* If, in spite of all, a demand is made of me, I shall give a minimum" (238; our emphasis).

Accepting deposits, such as those accepted by the Medici bank in Rome from leading clerics, and then sending them where they were needed or could be most profitably invested was preferable to collecting interest. The trick was to see and capitalize on opportunities for profit arising from the very same network structure that simultaneously created the new risks of constipated cash flow and burdensome requests for repayment.

Conclusion: A Nuanced Understanding of Embeddedness

Economic sociologists cannot simply state that social relations undergird economic relations, or that the economy is embedded in social life. We must move on to concrete specification of the kinds of social relations that matter, to which kinds of economic relations, and thence to a specification of types of network co-constitution. The central broad implications of our research include the following:

- Different types of social ties matter for different types of economic relations.
- Different types of social relations (and the identities they represent) intersect, softening or reinforcing each other in different ways in different situations, to effect economic ties.
- In certain instances, we should think of economic ties (as did Adam Smith) as the basis for emergent social bonds rather than as only the result of underlying social ties.
- Social ties can be understood to provide both opportunities and constraints for economic action.
- Social ties reflect actor identities, which act as frames (Goffman 1974) for organizing conduct in the world and adapting old experiences to new situations.
- The same economic actors are capable of simultaneously entertaining multiple logics of affiliation, and hence of adopting multiple justifications for coproduction, creating and/or supporting different but coexisting markets (or industrial sectors) with fundamentally different principles of organization.
- The process of adaptation through old frames can go hand in hand with the use of new, seemingly modernizing technologies, and the flourishing of technological innovations can be delayed until new patterns of social relations make them apt solutions to emerging problems.

Taking all of these arguments into account, we can say both that individual markets have their own characteristics and that historical markets and contemporary ones differ less in their fundamental operating principles than we have hitherto expected. Finally, concerning the Renaissance Florentine economy in particular, we have argued, among other things, that highly status-conscious Florentines spoke multivocally in the market. They highlighted social status to create city-spanning companies and networks of companies that constituted the engine driving the whole economy but downplayed status to gather the business that fueled that engine.

Notes

1. The bracketing of the impact of the economic on the social is arguably a result of the desire of economic sociologists to distinguish themselves from the transaction-cost economics perspective (Williamson 1994) and the resource dependency view (Pfeffer and Salancik 1978), both of which emphasize an economistic rationale for network formation. These views have had considerable influence within sociology itself.

2. This is not always the case. For example, arguably the extensive literature on corporate interlocks has tried to investigate both the consequences of preexisting ties for interlock structures and patterns of economic behavior and (conversely) the consequences of interlock network position for "non-economic" practices such as corporate philanthropy (see Galaskiewicz and Burt 1991; Powell and Smith-Doerr 1994).

3. We need look no further than Adam Smith (1776/1976, I:519) himself to recall that commerce "ought naturally to be . . . a bond of union and friendship." The implication is that social solidarity may arise from economic exchange rather than being exchange's precondition, as, for example, Durkheim (1893/1984) took it to be.

4. Allan Silver (1990) notes that the Scottish Enlightenment philosophers regarded the liberation of economic exchange from the constraints of friendship as morally desirable, expanding the possibilities of market growth, on the one hand, and reducing the admixture of instrumentality in friendship, on the other.

5. Bruce Carruthers (1996) is an outstanding exception to this generalization. He also offers a refreshing reminder of the value of a historical perspective for the analysis of contemporary economic issues (Carruthers 2001). We may also consider Pierre Bourdieu's (1986; 1990; 1998, 75–92; 2000) work on the convertibility of multiple types of capital and his analysis of the dynamics of gift exchange as programmatic for thinking about the interpenetration of the economic and the social more thoroughly, despite his periodic assertions concerning the "autonomization" of specific "fields," which, he suggests, occurs progressively in history.

6. Somewhat similarly, some economic historians (for example, Goldstone 2000; Pomeranz 2000) are cogently driving home the argument that the dominance of the West and the victory of its form of capitalism was hardly inevitable. More generally, the timing of the beginning of modernity is a subject of immense debate (see, for example, Goldstone 1998).

7. As a matter of fact, despite having become a veritable straw man for critiques of the uniqueness of modern Western capitalism, Weber's (1905/2002, 26) distinction between the form and the spirit of capitalism and his reminder that "rather than being in 'lawful' dependency, the capitalist form of an economy and the spirit

in which it is operated in fact exist generally in a less determinant relationship" is a rough yet illuminating cue for the study of the Renaissance Italian economy.

8. The opening invocation from the ledger of the Covoni company of the mid-fourteenth century offers a more elaborate contextualization of late medieval economic activity: "In the name of God and the Virgin His Mother Madonna Saint Mary and of all the saints of Paradise and of all the court of heaven, that they give us grace to do well and to speak well and to profit, in both our souls and [our] bodies" (Sapori 1970; our translation).

9. As to the profit motive, contemporary memoirs indicate, for example, disdain for profit-making on holy days (Dati) and support for the idea that tested friendship, not impersonal market mechanisms, formed the proper basis for success (Morelli).

10. It is not completely unwarranted to see in these industries and their organization the historical ancestry of the industrial-district, high-end goods production of contemporary northern Italy (see, for example, Lazerson 1988; Piore and Sabel 1984). Robert Putnam (1993) makes a similar (though to our minds less persuasive) claim for the continuity between late-medieval communal democracy and twentieth-century civic institutions in northern Italy.

11. In the original, the last sentence here highlights even more clearly the parallel calculation of profit and honor: "io diliberai più tosto volere rimanere *disfatto dell'avere che dell'onore*" (Branca 1986, 552, our emphasis)—literally, "dispossessed of riches rather than of honor." We may refer again to Adam Smith (1776/1976, I:363), here on the subject of bankruptcy, in support of Dati's view of the interpenetration of economic and social/moral concerns: "Bankruptcy is perhaps the greatest and most humiliating calamity which can befal [*sic*] an innocent man."

12. Anthony Molho (1971, 153) attributes the failure of a number of banks in the mid-1420s specifically to the inability of the Dieci di balìa to repay the short-term loans forced on the banks to pay mercenaries in the service of the commune, a situation not unlike what happened in the first half of the fourteenth century. In general, however, cash was in short supply while taxes went up, no doubt leading many depositors to withdraw funds placed in banks or demand prompt payment for goods shipped on consignment, thus threatening the survivability of the system as a whole.

13. Morelli regarded exposure to risk as practically an existential condition of life in Florence and offers advice to his progeny in the form of meditations on the various obstacles faced by "orphans" trying to make their way in the world, a condition he endured himself. Florentine merchants do appear to have used companies with whom they traded to get detailed information on price movements, market demand, and product quality to reduce uncertainty, but it is not clear that the threat of malfeasance in particular was especially high—at least, it was not as significant as it appears to have been in Genoese and Venetian overseas trade. Letters exchanged between merchants were extremely useful in monitoring trade and transport activities (Lane 1977). Another character in Alberti's (1969, 266) *Della famiglia,* Adovardo, claims that in all matters of the world one must be "farseeing, alert, and careful in the face of fraud, traps, and betrayals," but it

seems to us the gravest danger faced in the market was not so much being duped by others but rather being shunned by them during periods of vulnerability.

14. Our other joint work (Padgett and McLean 2002) provides far more extensive discussion of this relationship, as well as more discussion of the dynamics of the Florentine economy (changes of organizational form, changes in the prominence of different industries) and Florentine political organization leading up to 1427 and then beyond. We also offer there detailed statistical demonstrations supporting the narrative provided in this chapter.

15. These percentages may appear low, but the totals provided or estimated for all companies include ties to companies outside our selected export-oriented industries and ties to individuals rather than companies (a number especially large for cloth retailers and, to some extent, domestic banks). We have systematically collected data of these latter types as well but do not discuss them in this chapter. Thus, the "totals" by which we are dividing are substantially inflated with respect to the number and value of the specific type of transactions that concern us here.

16. Florence captured Pisa in 1406, finding it an especially attractive addition to the emerging Florentine territorial state because of the access it afforded Florentine merchants to the Mediterranean. Hence, we expect to see Florentine merchant-banking concerns active in Pisa especially oriented to the import of raw materials for Florentine cloth manufacturers and the export of Florentine cloth to overseas markets.

17. All of these companies were owned and operated by Florentines. Thus, we are not claiming, for example, that forty-five international merchant-banks in total operated in 1427 throughout Europe, but that we are able to document forty-five such banks operated by Florentines.

18. All individuals in our data are men. Women were important contributors to the Florentine economy as a whole, and specifically as weavers in the silk industry, but they did not serve as the owners or managers of large export-oriented companies.

19. Data on priorate participation were taken from the *Priorista descritto a Tratte riscontro con quello delle riformagioni e con alter scritture publiche,* held in the Newberry Library, Chicago. This manuscript is an eighteenth-century copy of the official list of elected Priors, the *Priorista Mariani,* the original source of which is located in the Archivio di Stato di Firenze (ASF) in the collection entitled *Manoscritti,* 248–52. Data concerning membership on the Sei della Mercanzia come from similar archival lists (*Fondo della Mercanzia,* ASF). Data on partner age were calculated from the birth date information available in the Florentine archives' *I libri d'età,* although age information is also available for many persons in the campioni of the catasto. Data on wealth and residence are comprehensively available in the 1427 catasto. Data on marriages come from the *Carte dell'Ancisa* in the Florentine archives, as well as from various published nineteenth-century sources. Data on factional affiliation was taken from Kent

(1978), who collected it from primary documentary sources such as the confession offered by Ser Niccolo Tinucci and contemporary patronage letters.

20. Business partnerships did not similarly eventuate in future marital ties, even though many participants in the market went on to marry women from economically active families.

21. The city contained sixteen gonfaloni, so to find upwards of one-sixth of all partnerships forged within neighborhoods, and upwards of one-fifth of all credits offered within neighborhoods, as reported in table 8.4, is quite noteworthy.

22. Thus, Giannozzo degli Alberti (1969, 200) comments in the *Libri della famiglia:* "Don't believe that a kinsman would ever cheat you if you treated him like a kinsman. What relative of yours would not rather deal with you than with a stranger? A stranger, indeed, only joins you to gain what he can for himself." Giovanni Morelli adds to this notion of concentric circles of relations, at least with respect to the aim of marriage: "First [look] in the neighborhood (gonfalone), next in the quarter. And although concerning this matter much were already written down earlier on [in this ricordanza], I still want you to remember it: make sure your relative is a merchant, that he be rich, long-established in Florence, Guelf, publicly respected, beloved by all, amicable and good in every action" (Branca 1986, 195–96; our translation).

23. It should be emphasized that when discussing status, we are talking about the *social* status (and hence a social *identity*) of the partners of companies, not the market status of the companies themselves. This use is distinct from that of Podolny (for example, Podolny 1993). For many cases, even when status is quite detached from product quality, it is perfectly appropriate to think of it as an ordinal variable (status ranking). For us, although Florentine statuses can be arrayed in an ordinal fashion, they also refer very much to categorical differences between groups. Hence, it sometimes seems reasonable to use the term "classes" in reference to these groups (as in Padgett and Ansell 1993), not because their members share a common relation to the means of production but because of a certain degree of antagonism between these groups and because certain distinct styles and other cultural connotations adhere to them severally.

24. By "high-status" bankers we refer to those who were members of the popolani families who traced their first participation in communal politics to the origins of the republic in the late thirteenth century or who were members of magnate families—either families reputed to have martial sensibilities and genealogies stretching back well before 1282 or families who at one time or another had achieved a degree of power and influence that threatened the regime and had been sanctioned accordingly. By "new men" we refer in this chapter to members of all families admitted to the priorate between 1343 (roughly the time of the Black Plague and coincident with a surge in new entrants to the priorate) and 1427. By "unadmitted" we refer to members of families not admitted to the priorate by 1427.

25. Among the banks joining partners of high status from different neighborhoods we may identify the most famous bank, that of Cosimo and Lorenzo de' Medici

(in partnership with Ilarione Bardi). But we may also find the banks of Averardo de' Medici &Co (in partnership with Andrea Bardi), Rede di Vieri Guadagni & Co (in partnership with Andreolo Sacchetti), Antonio da Rabatta &Co (in partnership with Bernardo Canigiani), Neri Capponi &Co (in partnership with Niccolo and Bernardo Giugni), Berto and Ridolfo Peruzzi &Co (in partnership with Carlo Benizzi), and Niccolo da Uzzano &Co (in partnership with Michele del Bene). We often assume that the Medici bank was unique, but in this particular respect it was typical.

26. Of course, it should also be a reminder not to read market structure anachronistically through our own conceptual lens. Although the Florentine export-oriented economy was relatively deconcentrated, a trait often taken to be integral to "pure" markets (for a more extensive discussion, see McLean and Padgett 1997), as we noted earlier this structure was not apparently generated through the mechanism of competition. Rather, we sense that the widespread dispersion of ties may have been facilitated by the institutional infrastructure of the guilds and the corporate sensibility of production they continued to foster. More important, it was maintained by the urge to reduce risk through portfolio diversification and by merchants' desire to build their careers and support themselves socially by expanding the number of their contacts in all domains of social life.

27. Of these, da Fortuna is noteworthy for having an interest in companies in four different industries: banking, cloth retailing, wool manufacture, and miscellaneous goods peddling (le merce). The richest Giugni household—including the brothers Bernardo, Giovanni, and Niccolo di Domenico Giugni—had members involved in more than half a dozen separate companies spanning multiple types of banking enterprises, retailing, and wool manufacturing. Somewhat similarly, five Benizzi brothers lived in one household, but three of them were partners in otherwise completely non-overlapping banking companies. Here we have a case of what might well be called "interlocks" at one remove from direct participation in multiple companies by single individuals.

28. The most famous example here is the Medici bank in Rome, which had no corpo of its own but accepted a number of very substantial deposits from various cardinals and papal officials (de Roover 1966, 208).

29. A warning is in order here. Although we identify structural similarities between the pattern of market exchanges, on the one hand, and the emergent dominant logic of political organization, on the other, we cannot assert that specific clients (in the economic sense) became political clients of particular members of the social and economic cum political elite to a statistically significant extent. The isomorphism here is "logical" or "institutional," not relational at the dyadic level.

30. The key difference between banking and silk was that although silk companies were "generalist" in character, and thus credits of different sorts *could* flow in both directions between pairs of silk companies at the same time, in fact they did *not*. A simple reason for this could be the lack of social ties forging the silk industry. In this respect at least, the silk industry functioned rather differently from contemporary industrial districts (Powell and Smith-Doerr 1994).

References

Alberti, Leon Battista. 1969. *The Family in Renaissance Florence.* Translated by Renée Neu Watkins. Columbia: University of South Carolina Press.

Baker, Wayne E. 1984. "The Social Structure of a National Securities Market." *American Journal of Sociology* 89(4): 775–811.

———. 1990. "Market Networks and Corporate Behavior." *American Journal of Sociology* 96(3): 589–625.

Bourdieu, Pierre. 1986. "The Forms of Capital." In *Handbook of Theory and Research for the Sociology of Education,* edited by John G. Richardson. New York: Greenwood Press.

———. 1990. *The Logic of Practice.* Translated by Richard Nice. Stanford, Calif.: Stanford University Press.

———. 1998. *Practical Reasons.* Cambridge: Polity Press.

———. 2000. *Les Structures sociales de l'économie.* Paris: Éditions du Seuil.

Branca, Vittore, ed. 1986. *Mercanti scrittori: Ricordi nella Firenze tra Medioevo e Rinascimento* (Merchant Writers: Memoirs in Florence from the Middle Ages to the Renaissance) [*Paolo da Certaldo, Giovanni Morelli, Bonaccorso Pitti e Domenico Lenzi, Donato Velluti, Goro Dati, Francesco Datini, Lapo Niccolini, e Bernardo Machiavelli*]. Milan: Rusconi.

Brucker, Gene, ed. 1967. *Two Memoirs of Renaissance Florence: The Diaries of Buonaccorso Pitti and Gregorio Dati.* New York: Harper Torchbooks.

Carruthers, Bruce G. 1996. *City of Capital: Politics and Markets in the English Financial Revolution.* Princeton, N.J.: Princeton University Press.

———. 2001. "Current Prospects for Economic Sociology, or Back to the Future, Part II." *Accounts: A Newsletter of Economic Sociology* 2(1, Fall): 3–4.

Chittolini, Giorgio. 1996. "The 'Private,' the 'Public,' the State." In *The Origins of the State in Italy, 1300 to 1600,* edited by Julius Kirshner. Chicago: University of Chicago Press.

Cohn, Samuel Kline. 1980. *The Laboring Classes in Renaissance Florence.* New York: Academic Press.

———. 1999. *Creating the Florentine State: Peasants and Rebellion, 1348 to 1434.* Cambridge: Cambridge University Press.

Connell, William J., and Andrea Zorzi. 2000. *Florentine Tuscany: Structures and Practices of Power.* New York: Cambridge University Press.

Conti, Elio. 1984. *L'Imposta diretta a Firenze nel Quattrocento, 1427–1494* (Direct Taxation in Florence in the 1400s, 1427–1494). Rome: Istituto storico italiano per il medio evo, Palazzo Borromini.

De Roover, Raymond. 1944. "Early Accounting Problems of Foreign Exchange." *Accounting Review* 19: 381–407.

———. 1966. *The Rise and Decline of the Medici Bank.* New York: W.W. Norton.

Dobbin, Frank. 1994. *Forging Industrial Policy: The United States, Britain, and France in the Railway Age.* New York: Cambridge University Press.

Durkheim, Émile. 1893/1984. *The Division of Labor in Society.* Translated by W. D. Halls. New York: Free Press.

Edler de Roover, Florence. 1966. "Andrea Banchi, Florentine Silk Manufacturer and Merchant in the Fifteenth Century." *Studies in Medieval and Renaissance History* 3: 223–85.

Eisenstadt, Shmuel N., and Luis Roniger. 1984. *Patrons, Clients, and Friends.* Cambridge: Cambridge University Press.

Emigh, Rebecca Jean. 1998. "The Mystery of the Missing Middle-Tenants: The 'Negative' Case of Fixed-Term Leasing and Agricultural Investment in Fifteenth-Century Tuscany." *Theory and Society* 27(3): 351–75.

Ertman, Thomas. 1997. *Birth of the Leviathan: Building States and Regimes in Medieval and Early Modern Europe.* New York: Cambridge University Press.

Fligstein, Neil. 1990. *The Transformation of Corporate Control.* Cambridge, Mass.: Harvard University Press.

Fubini, Riccardo. 1994. *Italia Quattrocentesca: Politica e diplomazia nell'età di Lorenzo il Magnifico* (Italy in the 1400s: Politics and Diplomacy in the Age of Lorenzo the Magnificent). Milan: Franco Angeli.

Galaskiewicz, Joseph, and Ronald S. Burt. 1991. "Interorganization Contagion in Corporate Philanthropy." *Administrative Science Quarterly* 36(1): 88–105.

Girard, Monique, and David Stark. 2001. "Distributing Intelligence and Organizing Diversity in New Media Projects." Paper presented to the conference Beyond the Firm: Spatial and Social Dynamics of Project Organization. University of Bonn, Bonn, Germany (April 27–28).

Goffman, Erving. 1974. *Frame Analysis: An Essay on the Organization of Experience.* New York: Harper & Row.

Goldstone, Jack A. 1998. "The Problem of the 'Early Modern' World." *Journal of the Economic and Social History of the Orient* 41(3): 249–84.

———. 2000. "The Rise of the West—Or Not? A Revision to Socioeconomic History." *Sociological Theory* 18(2): 175–94.

Goldthwaite, Richard A. 1987. "The Medici Bank and the World of Florentine Capitalism." *Past and Present* 114(February): 3–31.

Goldthwaite, Richard A., Enzo Settesoldi, and Marco Spallanzani. 1995. *Due libri mastri degli Alberti: Una grande compagnia di Calimala, 1348–1358* (Two Ledgers of the Alberti: A Great Company of the Calimala Guild, 1348–1358). Florence: Cassa di Risparmio di Firenze.

Granovetter, Mark. 1974. *Getting a Job: A Study of Contracts and Careers.* Chicago: University of Chicago Press.

———. 1985. "Economic Action and Social Structure: The Problem of Embeddedness." *American Journal of Sociology* 91(3): 481–510.

———. 1990. "The Old and the New Economic Sociology." In *Beyond the Marketplace,* edited by Roger Friedland and A. F. Robertson. New York: Aldine de Gruyter.

Guillén, Mauro F. 1994. *Models of Management: Work, Authority, and Organization in a Comparative Perspective.* Chicago: University of Chicago Press.

———. 2001. *The Limits of Convergence: Globalization and Organizational Change in Argentina, South Korea, and Spain.* Princeton, N.J.: Princeton University Press.

Hamilton, Gary G., and Nicole Woolsey Biggart. 1988. "Market, Culture, and Authority: A Comparative Analysis of Management and Organization in the Far East." *American Journal of Sociology* 94(supp.): S52–94.

Herlihy, David, and Christiane Klapisch-Zuber. 1985. *Tuscans and Their Families: A Study of the Florentine Catasto of 1427.* New Haven, Conn.: Yale University Press.

Hoshino, Hidetoshi. 1980. *L'Arte della lana in Firenze nel basso medioevo* (The Wool Industry in Florence in the Late Middle Ages). Florence: Leo S. Olschki Editore.

Kent, Dale. 1978. *The Rise of the Medici: Faction in Florence, 1426 to 1434.* Oxford: Oxford University Press.

———. 2000. *Cosimo de' Medici and the Florentine Renaissance: The Patron's Oeuvre.* New Haven, Conn.: Yale University Press.

Klapisch-Zuber, Christiane. 1985. *Women, Family, and Ritual in Renaissance Italy.* Chicago: University of Chicago Press.

Krippner, Greta R. 2001. "The Elusive Market: Embeddedness and the Paradigm of Economic Sociology." *Theory and Society* 30(6): 775–810.

Lane, Frederic C. 1977. "Double Entry Bookkeeping and Resident Merchants." *Journal of European Economic History* 6: 177–91.

Lazerson, Mark H. 1988. "Organizational Growth of Small Firms: An Outcome of Markets and Hierarchies?" *American Sociological Review* 53: 330–42.

Lopez, Robert S. 1976. *The Commercial Revolution of the Middle Ages, 950 to 1350.* Cambridge: Cambridge University Press.

Mazzei, Lapo. 1880. *Lettere di un notaro a un mercatante del secolo XIV, con altre lettere e documenti,* a cura di Cesare Guasti (The Letters of a Notary to a Merchant in the Fourteenth Century, with Other Letters and Documents, edited by Cesare Guasti). 2 vols. Florence: M. Cellini.

McLean, Paul D. 1998. "A Frame Analysis of Favor-Seeking in the Renaissance: Agency, Networks, and Political Culture." *American Journal of Sociology* 104(1): 51–91.

———. 2002. "Fiscal Innovation and Traditional Motivation in the Renaissance State: The Case of Early Quattrocento Florence." Unpublished paper. Rutgers University, New Brunswick, N.J.

McLean, Paul D., and John F. Padgett. 1997. "Was Florence a Perfectly Competitive Market? Transactional Evidence from the Renaissance." *Theory and Society* 26(2,3): 209–44.

Melis, Federigo. 1962. *Aspetti della vita economica medievale: Studi nell'Archivio Datini di Prato* (Aspects of Medieval Economic Life: Studies Using the Datini Archive in Prato). Siena: Leo S. Olschki Editore.

———. 1991. *L'Azienda nel medioevo* (The Firm in the Middle Ages). Edited by Marco Spallanzani. Florence: Le Monnier.

Molho, Anthony. 1971. *Florentine Public Finances in the Early Renaissance, 1400 to 1433.* Cambridge, Mass.: Harvard University Press.

———. 1996. "The State and Public Finance: A Hypothesis Based on the History of Late Medieval Florence." In *The Origins of the State in Italy, 1300 to 1600,* edited by Julius Kirshner. Chicago: University of Chicago Press.

Najemy, John M. 1982. *Corporatism and Consensus in Florentine Electoral Politics, 1280 to 1400.* Chapel Hill: University of North Carolina Press.

Padgett, John F. 1994. "Marriage and Elite Structure in Renaissance Florence, 1282 to 1500." Paper presented to the meeting of the Social Science History Association. Chicago (November 17–20, 1994).

———. 2001. "Organizational Genesis, Identity, and Control: The Transformation of Banking in Renaissance Florence." In *Networks and Markets,* edited by James E. Rauch and Alessandra Casella. New York: Russell Sage Foundation.

Padgett, John F., and Christopher K. Ansell. 1993. "Robust Action and the Rise of the Medici, 1400 to 1434." *American Journal of Sociology* 98(6): 1259–1319.

Padgett, John F., and Paul D. McLean. 2002. "Economic and Social Exchange in Renaissance Florence." Working paper 02-07-032. Santa Fe, N.M.: Santa Fe Institute.

Pfeffer, Jeffrey, and Gerald R. Salancik. 1978. *The External Control of Organizations: A Resource Dependence Perspective.* New York: Harper & Row.

Piore, Michael, and Charles Sabel. 1984. *The Second Industrial Divide.* New York: Basic Books.

Podolny, Joel M. 1993. "A Status-Based Model of Market Competition." *American Journal of Sociology* 98(4): 829–72.

Polanyi, Karl. 1944/1957. *The Great Transformation.* Boston: Beacon Press.

Pomeranz, Kenneth. 2000. *The Great Divergence: China, Europe, and the Making of the Modern World Economy.* Princeton, N.J.: Princeton University Press.

Powell, Walter W., and Laurel Smith-Doerr. 1994. "Networks and Economic Life." In *The Handbook of Economic Sociology,* edited by Neil J. Smelser and Richard Swedberg. Princeton, N.J., and New York: Princeton University Press and Russell Sage Foundation.

Putnam, Robert D. 1993. *Making Democracy Work: Civic Traditions in Modern Italy.* Princeton, N.J.: Princeton University Press.

Róna-Tas, Ákos. 1994. "The First Shall Be Last? Entrepreneurship and Communist Cadres in the Transition from Socialism." *American Journal of Sociology* 100(1): 40–69.

Roy, William G. 1997. *Socializing Capital: The Rise of the Large Industrial Corporation in America.* Princeton, N.J.: Princeton University Press.

Rubinstein, Nicolai. 1966. *The Government of Florence Under the Medici, 1434 to 1494.* Oxford: Oxford University Press.

Sapori, Armando. 1926. *La Crisi delle compagnie mercantili del Bardi e dei Peruzzi* (The Crisis of the Bardi and Peruzzi Merchant-Banks). Florence: Leo S. Olschki Editore.

———. 1932. *Una compagnia di Calimala ai primi del Trecento* (A Company of the Calimala Guild in the Early 1300s). Florence: Leo S. Olschki Editore.

———. 1970. *Libro Giallo della compagnia dei Covoni* (The Yellow Ledger of the Covoni Company). Milan: Istituto Editoriale Cisalpino.

Silver, Allan. 1990. "Friendship in Commercial Society: Eighteenth-Century Social Theory and Modern Sociology." *American Journal of Sociology* 95(6): 1474–1504.

Smith, Adam. 1776/1976. *An Inquiry into the Nature and Causes of the Wealth of Nations.* Edited by Edwin Cannan. Chicago: University of Chicago Press.

Spruyt, Hendrik. 1994. *The Sovereign State and Its Competitors: An Analysis of Systems Change.* Princeton, N.J.: Princeton University Press.

Stark, David. 1996. "Recombinant Property in East European Capitalism." *American Journal of Sociology* 101(4): 993–1027.

Tognetti, Sergio. 2002. *Un'industria di lusso al servizio del grande commercio: Il mercato dei drappi serici e della seta nella Firenze del Quattrocento* (A Luxury Industry in the Service of International Commerce: The Silken Cloth and Raw Silk Market in Florence in the 1400s). Florence: Leo S. Olschki Editore.

Trexler, Richard C. 1980. *Public Life in Renaissance Florence.* Ithaca, N.Y.: Cornell University Press.

Uzzi, Brian. 1996. "The Sources and Consequences of Embeddedness for the Economic Performance of Organizations: The Network Effect." *American Sociological Review* 61(4): 674–98.

Weber, Max. 1905/2002. *The Protestant Ethic and the Spirit of Capitalism.* 3rd ed. Translated by Stephen Kalberg. Los Angeles: Roxbury Publishing.

Weissman, Ronald F. E. 1982. *Ritual Brotherhood in Renaissance Florence.* New York: Academic Press.

White, Harrison C. 1981. "Where Do Markets Come From?" *American Journal of Sociology* 87(3): 517–47.

———. 2002. *Markets from Networks: Socioeconomic Models of Production.* Princeton, N.J.: Princeton University Press.

Williamson, Oliver E. 1994. "Transaction-Cost Economics and Organization Theory." In *The Handbook of Economic Sociology,* edited by Neil J. Smelser and Richard Swedberg. Princeton, N.J., and New York: Princeton University Press and Russell Sage Foundation.

Zelizer, Viviana A. 1994. *The Social Meaning of Money: Pin Money, Paychecks, Poor Relief, and Other Currencies.* New York: Basic Books.

Zuckerman, Ezra. 1999. "The Categorical Imperative: Securities Analysts and the Illegitimacy Discount." *American Journal of Sociology* 104(5): 1398–1438.

9

THE EFFECTS OF DOMAIN OVERLAP AND NON-OVERLAP ON ORGANIZATIONAL PERFORMANCE, GROWTH, AND SURVIVAL

Heather A. Haveman and Lisa A. Keister

O VER THE past twenty years research in organizational theory has increasingly acknowledged that organizations are not independent entities that rely exclusively on their own strategic advantages and competencies. Rather, researchers have come to realize, firms are dependent, like other social actors, on others in their environments, most often other organizations. Studies in four well-established research traditions—organizational ecology, the new institutionalism, social-network analysis, and resource dependence—have demonstrated the value of analyzing both the determinants and outcomes of interfirm interdependence. This research has shown that interorganizational relations can be either competitive or mutualistic. *Competitive* relations arise between organizations that draw on the same scarce resources. Each organization in a competitive system reduces the vitality of others in the system. *Mutualistic* relations arise between organizations that depend on each other for maintenance and survival. Mutualistic relations generally arise between organizations that draw on dissimilar sets of resources, but they sometimes also emerge where the firms draw on the same sets of resources. In either case, each organization in a mutualistic system improves the vitality of some or all of the organizations in the system.

One of the most fruitful efforts to understand the sources of competition and mutualism among organizations has been launched by organizational ecologists. Ecological studies of competition and mutualism build on the general proposition that organizational domains—the claims organizations stake out for themselves in terms of the clients they serve, the goods and services they produce, and the production, administrative, and distribution technologies they employ (Levine and White 1961; Thompson 1967)—

determine both organizations' resource requirements and demand for their products, and thus determine opportunities for interactions (Hawley 1950, 31–36; 1968, 10–44).[1] Similarities and differences among the domains of organizations within a population shape competitive and mutualistic interactions, respectively.

Miller McPherson and his colleagues (McPherson 1983; McPherson and Ranger-Moore 1991; McPherson, Popielarz, and Drobnic 1992; McPherson and Rotolo 1996) have examined voluntary associations and defined organizational niches on the basis of association members' characteristics—specifically, education, age, occupation, and sex. William Barnett and Glenn Carroll (1987) have defined the domains of telephone companies on the basis of technology (common-battery versus magneto) and legal form (mutual versus commercial company). Joel Baum and Jitendra Singh (1994a, 1994b) have defined the niches inhabited by day care centers according to the age ranges of the children served. Regardless of how organizational domains or niches are defined empirically, organizations whose domains overlap compete over common pools of scarce resources and limited client demand. The greater the overlap between two organizations' domains—and therefore the greater the overlap between the resources used and the clientele targeted by those organizations—the stronger the competition between those organizations. In contrast, organizations inhabiting completely different domains do not compete at all because they do not depend on the same resources or clientele; such organizations may benefit each other through mutualistic interactions that derive from either symbiosis or commensalism.

In this chapter, we build on Hawley (1950, 1968) and extend McPherson (1983) and Barnett and Carroll (1987) to propose that competition between organizations emerges from overlaps between organizations' domains and therefore overlaps between resources used and clientele targeted. In contrast, mutualism between organizations generally stems from *non-overlaps* between organizational domains: organizations inhabiting completely different domains often benefit each other through symbiotic interactions. Further, mutualism between organizations occasionally stems from shared interests rooted in partial domain overlaps: organizations inhabiting similar (not identical) domains often benefit each other through commensalistic interactions. We develop and test a model that involves both competition arising from domain overlap and mutualism arising from a combination of domain overlap and non-overlap.

We extend previous research on domain overlap in four ways. First, we develop a more elaborate theory of noncompetitive interactions. Second, we develop refined measures of domain overlap and non-overlap by weighting an organization's activities by the magnitude of its participation in each sector of its domain—each group of clients served and type of goods or services produced. Third, we investigate whether the effects of domain overlap and non-overlap are size-localized—that is, stronger among firms of similar size (compare Hannan and Ranger-Moore 1990; Hannan, Ranger-Moore, and Banaszak-Holl 1990; Baum and Mezias 1992). Fourth, we follow McPherson and his colleagues (McPherson and Ranger-Moore 1991; McPherson and Rotolo 1996) and extend the range outcomes studied using the domain-overlap model from the long-term consequences of competitive interaction (organizational founding and failure) to more immediate outcomes (growth and economic performance).

This chapter's focus on the impact of competition and mutualism among organizations with varying domains and therefore varying (sub)forms necessarily—given the limitations on our data and the publisher's expectations concerning reasonable chapter length—begs three questions that are answered in other chapters of this volume. First, we beg the question of how competitive and mutualistic interactions stemming from domain overlap and non-overlap affect both interorganizational relations and the nature and location of organizational domains. The chapter by Richard Scott, which deftly summarizes an important co-authored book (Scott et al. 2000), describes the consequences of interactions among health care organizations for several types of interorganizational relations and for domains claimed by various health care populations. The growth of multihospital systems from the mid-1960s to late 1970s forged strong links between hospitals. Hospital domains shrank to a core set of services under an emerging logic of managerial control in the 1980s and 1990s; consequently, new kinds of health care organizations sprang up to serve several delimited peripheral areas. We see, therefore, that commensalistic mutualism among hospitals within a system was augmented by new symbiotic mutualistic relations between them, on the one hand, and supporting players, such as physician groups and end-stage renal disease centers, on the other. Second, we evade the question of whether and to what extent the organizations we study actively cooperate to limit the competitive effects of domain overlap. Bai Gao's chapter on the rise of trade associations and cartels in prewar Japan picks up where the lack of data forces us to leave off. He shows that state policies concerning property rights catalyzed the rise of an "associational order" in which cartels and trade associations could dominate and dictate limits to competition and mutualism. Gao's chapter highlights the third question that is not addressed in our study, namely, the role of the state in determining the forms and economic consequences of interorganizational relations. The chapter by Charles Perrow, which offers a skillful digest of his recent book (Perrow 2002), is similarly concerned with this issue. In contrast to Gao's study of the Japanese government's promotion of associationalism, Perrow demonstrates how the American state's concern for minimizing government had the unanticipated consequence of benefiting huge firms most. The issue of power, which we touch on only lightly, looms large in Gao's chapter, and even larger in Perrow's.

Forms of Competition and Mutualism

Relations between organizations, like relations between organisms and individuals, can be defined along two dimensions, one ranging from commensalism to symbiosis and the other ranging from pure competition through predation and parasitism to full mutualism (Hawley 1950, 36–41; 1968, 30–38; Aldrich 1999, 301–10).[2] Commensalism ("eating from the same table") involves relations between similar organizations; symbiosis involves relations between dissimilar organizations. In relations characterized by pure competition, both parties lose; in relations characterized by predation and parasitism, actors experience different outcomes, and individual actors may lose but aggregates of actors (populations) may gain. In mutualistic relations, similar benefits accrue to both actors. Figure 9.1 summarizes the variety of relations between organizations that result from considering the interplay between these two dimensions.

Pure competition describes head-to-head turf battles between pairs of organizations (Lucent and Northern Telecom in electronic networks, for example, or Coke and Pepsi in soft drinks). It also describes widespread and indirect scrambling for scarce resources among large coteries of firms (dozens of PC manufacturers worldwide jousting for market share or myriad small retail outlets in a city vying to sell food and sundries). In contrast, *commensalistic mutualism* often takes the form of industry associations (such as the National Association of Manufacturers and the American Banking Association) lobbying for expanded resources or more favorable legal regimes or collections of similar firms indirectly benefiting their members through mere existence and size (for example, the benefits from the taken-for-grantedness that accompanies increases in the number of organizations in an emerging industry such as biotechnology or cellular telephone service).

Asymmetric symbiotic relations, which are partly competitive and partly mutualistic, involve either *predation* (for example, relations between large corporations with deep pockets and law firms that specialize in class-action suits, or relations between highly diversified firms and leveraged-buyout specialists that seek to dismantle conglomerates) or *parasitism* (for example, relations between large corporations and management consultants pushing the latest "best practice," or relations between advertisers and Internet website creators). In such relations, one population typically loses while the other gains, although both can lose. In contrast, *symbiotic mutualism* includes relations in which both populations gain: direct relations between suppliers and their customer organizations (between business schools and consulting firms, for example, or between semiconductor integrated circuit manufacturers and the producers of many consumer and industrial goods), as well as community-building efforts between organizations that are functionally dissimilar (such as members of a chamber of commerce promoting municipal development interests). Symbiotic mutualism can

FIGURE 9.1   *Forms of Relations Between Organizations*

	Commensalism (Relations Between Similar Organizations)	**Symbiosis** (Relations Between Dissimilar Organizations)
One or both parties lose	**Pure Competition** • *Head-to-head battles* between pairs of organizations or among small groups of organizations (direct competition) • *General resource squeezing* by groups of organizations whose resource demands are large relative to the environmental carrying capacity (diffuse competition)	**Asymmmetric Symbiotic Relations** • *Predation:* one organization or one group of organizations feeding off another (direct or diffuse relationship)—the prey provides sustenance to the eater • *Parasitism:* one organization benefiting from another (direct relationship)—the host provides resources (may be nonlethal to the host), shelter, or distribution for the parasite; the parasite provides some service for the host
Both parties win	**Commensalistic Mutualism** • *Coalition formation or sociopolitical legitimation* derived from joint activity by groups of similar organizations (direct mutualism) • *Cognitive legitimation* derived from sheer numbers of organizations (diffuse mutualism)	**Symbiotic Mutualism** • *Customer and supplier relations* (direct mutualism) • *Coalition formation or sociopolitical legitimation* derived from joint activity by differentiated communities of organizations (direct mutualism) • *Visibility and legitimacy* accorded differentiated communities of organizations (direct mutualism)

Source: Authors' compilation.

involve tangible or material links, such as the physical infrastructure that connects the distribution networks of local producers seeking to reach wider markets (for example, local telephone companies interconnecting to offer longer-distance service) or to smooth out local imbalances in supply and demand (for example, networks of regional electric-power producers cooperating to balance supply and demand across Canada and the United States). Finally, a diffuse form of symbiotic mutualism occurs when visibility and legitimacy are accorded to clusters of differentiated firms (such as stores located in antique, art, or other specialized shopping districts in cities, or high-technology firms located in industrial parks or particular regions of the country).[3]

In the sections that follow, we explain how overlaps and non-overlaps in organizational domains create a system of competitive and mutualistic relations between organizations.

Domain Overlap and Competition

Scholars have long proposed that competitive interactions are strongest among organizations that rely on similar sets of scarce resources: the more similar the resource requirements, the greater the potential for competition (Hannan and Freeman 1977, 1989). Resource requirements, in turn, are a function of organizational domain, of activity in various product and client markets (see, for example, Meyer 1975; Haveman 1992), or of technological fields (see, for example, Podolny, Stuart, and Hannan 1996; Wade 1996). Holding constant the overall availability of resources and the level of customer demand, the competitive pressure felt by any organization is a function of how many, and to what extent, other organizations depend on the same resources.

Network analyses of organizations resonate with ecological thought. Perhaps the most famous is Harrison White's (1981, 2002) argument that markets (which can be interpreted, rather loosely, as equivalent to ecological niches) are socially constructed: firms observe what rivals do and react by avoiding competition through differentiation. Our analysis cannot be said to fall precisely within this line of work, but it is related. We do not investigate the social construction of markets—for example, organizations' moves into and out of product or client markets as a response to domain overlap. But we do study other important consequences of domain overlap. We also do not study the direct interorganizational ties that are common in network studies using White's ideas. But we do study role-equivalent (rather than structurally equivalent) ties among organizations whose domains overlap. Joint involvement in product or client markets creates a network of *indirect* ties between organizations. Domain overlap links organizations to each other through relations with clients in various niches; organizations with overlapping domains are involved in similar types of exchange relations, but not necessarily with the exact same partners (Winship and Mandel 1983; Winship 1988).

Several streams of research have extended the basic density-dependence model of organizational ecology (Hannan and Freeman 1987, 1988; Hannan and Carroll 1992) to investigate the relationship between the extent of domain overlap and competition. The three reviewed here focus on similarities between organizations based on size, geographic location, and strategic group membership.

Size Michael Hannan and John Freeman (1977, 945–46) have proposed that although organizations of different sizes may produce similar goods and services, they depend on different mixes of material, financial, informational, and human resources. This logic implies that organizations compete most intensively with other organizations of similar size and that the level of competition declines with the distance between firms on a size gradient. Studies of several organizational populations—Manhattan banks and life insurance companies (Hannan, Ranger-Moore, and Banaszak-Holl 1990), Manhattan hotels (Baum and Mezias 1992), U.S. health maintenance organizations (Wholey, Christianson, and Sanchez 1992), U.S. credit unions (Amburgey, Dacin, and Kelly 1994), New York life insurance companies (Ranger-Moore, Breckenridge, and Jones 1995), and Japanese banks (Han 1998)—support the size-localized competition hypothesis.

Geography   Researchers in organizational ecology have modified the density-dependence model to consider density in geographically bounded subpopulations: William Barnett and Glenn Carroll (1987) have studied local and nonlocal subpopulation density in telephone companies, and Anand Swaminathan and Gabriele Wiedenmayer (1991) and Glenn Carroll and James Wade (1991) have investigated density-dependence among breweries at the regional, state, and city levels. Two related studies show that density-dependent competition operates more locally than does density-dependent legitimation. Michael Hannan and his colleagues (1995) have contrasted the effects of within-nation density (which captures legitimation) and between-nation density (which captures competition) on foundings of automobile manufacturers in Continental Europe, while Lyda Bigelow and her colleagues (1997) have contrasted the impacts of national density (which captures legitimation) and regional density (which captures competition) on foundings of U.S. automobile manufacturers. Other scholars have studied the effects of geographic proximity—overlapping geographic domains—on firms' competitive interactions (Baum and Mezias 1992; Baum and Haveman 1997; Haveman and Nonnemaker 2000). Taken together, these studies show that competitive pressures within organizational populations are often segmented geographically.

Strategic Groups   Research on strategic groups assumes that meaningful subgroups of organizations can be identified in terms of organizational strategies (McGee and Thomas 1986) and that the strength of the competitive pressures impinging on any organization depends on the location of its rivals in competitive space. Warren Boeker (1991) and Glenn Carroll and Anand Swaminathan (1992) have shown that members of two relatively new strategic groups in the U.S. brewing industry—brewpubs and microbreweries—respond to very different competitive pressures than do traditional mass producers. Similarly, William Barnett (1993) has found that competition is localized within strategic groups in the U.S. telephone industry. And Carroll and Swaminathan (2000) have demonstrated that in the U.S. brewing industry, strategic group membership (organizational form identity) is reinforced by cultural forces; because the cultural identities that accompany strategic group membership are emergent phenomena, they are difficult to manipulate, and so strategic group membership has persistent effects on competitive inter-actions (see Carroll and Hannan 2000, 67–74).

In sum, as overlap between organizational domains increases, so does competition. This relationship holds whether organizations' domains are defined in terms of size (as a proxy for structure and strategy and therefore resources), geographic location (as a proxy for spatially localized customer demand and resources), or strategic group membership (as a proxy for tech-nology, client group, product market, and/or cultural identity and therefore customer demand and resources).

We are concerned here with the consequences of domain overlap for three important organizational outcomes: economic performance, growth, and failure. Holding constant overall levels of resources and demand, domain overlap causes organizations to compete for the resources (skilled employees, funding, raw materials and components) and the customer demand they need to thrive. When domain overlap is great, organizations must search widely for resources, pay large sums to acquire resources, and often accept low-quality resources. Moreover, they must also work hard to attract and retain cus-tomers—that is, they must advertise and promote products and accept low prices for their products. In sum, when domain overlap is great, organizations' input and operating costs are high and their revenues are low; hence, their eco-nomic performance suffers. Moreover, when domain overlap is great, many rivals battle over scarce resources and limited customer demand; hence, growth (the expansion of organizational resource use and the customer base) is hampered. Growth is also hampered because the poor economic perfor-mance that attends great domain overlap diminishes the stocks of surplus resources that are needed to fuel growth. Finally, because economic perfor-mance suffers when domain overlap is great, organizations are more vulner-able to failure. Therefore, we hypothesize that:

As domain overlap increases, economic performance worsens (hypothesis 1).

As domain overlap increases, organizational growth slows (hypothesis 2).

As domain overlap increases, the chance of organizational failure rises (hypothe-sis 3).

Domain Non-Overlap and Mutualism

Relations between organizations with overlapping domain sectors are compet-itive, and the level of competition increases with the extent of domain overlap. In contrast, relations between organizations with non-overlapping domains can be mutually beneficial. Indeed, research on business groups shows that mem-bership in an interorganizational network improves member firm performance by facilitating cooperation and economizing on control (Lincoln, Gerlach, and

Ahmadjian 1996; Keister 1998, 2000). More generally, organizations operating in non-overlapping niches may help each other through the symbiosis created by their complementary differences or through the commensalism created by the commonality of their interests (Hawley 1950, 36–42). As discussed earlier, symbiotic mutualism can take various forms: interorganizational learning through benchmarking; client referrals in times of temporary undercapacity; and increases in overall customer demand as sales in one domain stimulate sales in another, related domain. Also as discussed earlier, commensalistic mutualism can take various forms: enhanced visibility and therefore enhanced legitimacy with suppliers, customers, and oversight agencies; increased volume and quality of complementary goods and services; increased volume and quality of specialized inputs, including skilled workers; cooperative advertising and promotion campaigns; and coordinated government lobbying efforts. We consider how each of the two types of mutualism develops.

Symbiotic Mutualism　The theory of niche-partitioning in industrial systems (Carroll 1985) suggests two mechanisms by which symbiotic mutualism can develop between organizations whose niches do not overlap. The first mechanism involves flows of benefits from generalists to specialists. As industries that are subject to economies of scale mature, they tend to become more concentrated; that is, industry participants decrease in number and become larger and more generalized. The few large generalists that operate in concentrated industries tend to focus on serving the densely populated center of the industry's demand space and to ignore the sparsely populated periphery. These underserved peripheral sectors are available for exploitation by specialists; hence, specialists can enter concentrated industries and thrive because generalists release to specialists the demand in the periphery and the resources needed to meet this demand. Symbiotic mutualism thus develops because the domains of specialists and generalists become ever more differentiated as industry concentration increases, and so their domains come to overlap less and less.

The second mechanism by which symbiotic mutualism develops between organizations with non-overlapping domains involves flows of benefits from specialists to generalists. Because specialists tend to be small, their costs tend to be higher than those of large generalists. Therefore, to earn the same profits, specialists must charge higher prices than generalists. Specialists can do this because they focus on particular domain sectors (they offer distinctive products, market to small customer groups with distinctive needs, and use specialized production and distribution systems) and because their customers are willing to pay more for goods and services that meet their idiosyncratic needs. Specialists' pricing behavior has consequences for generalist organizations. When specialists charge more for their goods and services, all customers may become a little less price-sensitive. This reduction in customer price-sensitivity allows generalists to raise their prices too.[4]

Commensalistic Mutualism   Research on the evolution of legitimacy in organizational populations (Hannan and Freeman 1989; Aldrich and Fiol 1994; Suchman 1995) suggests several related mechanisms by which such commensalistic mutualism develops. When an organizational form is new and its adherents are few, its goals and operations are not well understood— that is, the organizational form is not legitimated, not taken for granted as an acceptable social, economic, political, or cultural agent. As the density of an organizational form increases, however, it becomes increasingly taken for granted and amasses sociopolitical support (two instances of commensalistic mutualism among members of that form). The fates of all members of that form are improved when density-dependent legitimacy increases.

Another instance of commensalistic mutualism is discussed by Howard Aldrich and Marlene Fiol (1994) and Mark Suchman (1995). Organizations can use several strategies to establish, maintain, or enhance their legitimacy by manipulating actors in their environment—for example, product advertising, image advertising, and selective publication of data concerning technical performance. All of these manipulations are likely to benefit not just the focal organization but also other organizations in the same population by increasing awareness and acceptance of the general categories of goods and services produced by all organizations in the population. To the extent that such manipulations are more frequent when there are more organizations around, then such commensalistic benefits increase with density.

Commensalistic mutualism can also take the form of material, rather than cultural, benefits. As the density of an organizational form increases, organizations that supply goods, services, and trained workers to organizations with this form are more willing to make their production processes more specialized to meet the particular needs of this form. For example, vocational schools are likely to train workers in particular skilled trades when school administrators perceive large-scale demand for such specialized workers in a large or growing industry. More reliable supplies of other, specialized complementary goods and services may also develop as organizational-form density increases and suppliers come to depend more on exchanges with members of this form.

Finally, commensalistic relations between organizations whose domains overlap only a little can take the form of cooperative advertising and promotion campaigns or coordinated government lobbying efforts. Both types of action serve to improve understanding of and demand for the goods and services produced by organizations in the entire population.

Caveat: Limits to Mutualism   Relations among organizations with non-overlapping domains may not be purely mutualistic. Mutualism, especially mutualism deriving from symbiosis, develops only to the extent that the product, client, and technology categories used to define various domain sectors are not substitutes—that is, to the extent that the organizations making and selling various products do not target a common general pool of customers, require similar generic resources, or rely on similar production systems. Organizations in the same population with non-overlapping domains may compete with each other to the extent that the product classes, client groups, or technology fields constituting these domain sectors are similar with respect to some aspect of resource acquisition or customer demand—that is, to the extent that these domain sectors overlap partially.

The difference between purely mutualistic and partly mutualistic and partly competitive cross-niche relations is most easily explained with examples. Consider the day care and financial services industries. Day care centers can be grouped into sectors based on the ages of the children they enroll (Baum and Singh 1994a, 1994b). Day care centers operating in different age markets are pure complements: they provide similar services to mutually exclusive client groups. Day care centers serving, for example, preschool-age children facilitate the operation of day care centers serving children of other ages, such as toddlers or school-age children. Together, organizations in this population offer services over the full range of children's ages. The existence of day care centers catering to children of all ages increases overall demand for child care services. In addition to these indirect, market-expanding effects of organizations in non-overlapping niches, direct spillover benefits occur between organizations in non-overlapping niches: day care centers that enroll younger children may refer clients to day care centers that enroll older children as their charges mature beyond their particular domain. Thus, day care centers in non-overlapping niches (non-overlapping age ranges for children) engage in completely mutualistic interactions.

In contrast, financial services firms are grouped into sectors based on a combination of the clientele they serve (consumer or commercial) and the products they sell (loans and other investments). For example, the U.S. General Accounting Office (1991, 63–66) classifies savings and loans (thrifts) into five main categories: traditional (focusing on home mortgages and mortgage-backed securities), commercial (making business loans and commercial mortgage loans, as well as consumer nonmortgage loans), mortgage banking (servicing other institutions' consumer and commercial mortgage loans), security and equity investment (investing heavily in service-corporation subsidiaries, corporate securities, and mortgage-backed securities), and real estate development (holding real estate for development and resale and investing heavily in construction loans). The services provided by thrifts in different sectors are in some cases partial substitutes for each other; for instance, consumers can borrow money to buy either houses (from "traditional" thrifts) or cars (from "commercial" thrifts). The financial services offered by thrifts in these two sectors vary greatly in risk levels, term lengths, and rates and structures of return to the lending institution; indeed, that is why these are deemed by industry analysts to be distinct domains. But both sectors depend on general demand for consumer credit. Hence, thrifts operating solely in one product or client market (such as traditional thrifts) may compete to some extent with thrifts operating solely in another product or client market (such as commercial thrifts) if both markets serve the same clientele and involve products that are at least partial substitutes—that is, if both markets depend on some general demand, such as the demand for consumer credit. But thrifts that deal with mutually exclusive client groups (consumer versus commercial) and thrifts that sell distinctly different products to a common client group do not compete at all; instead, such thrifts engage in purely mutualistic interactions.

Balancing both possible consequences of domain non-overlap—competitive and mutualistic spillovers from one domain sector to another—we expect that organizations whose domains are in non-overlapping sectors will develop at least partly mutualistic interactions. Following this logic, we predict:

As domain non-overlap increases, economic performance improves (hypothesis 4).

As domain non-overlap increases, organizational growth accelerates (hypothesis 5).

As domain non-overlap increases, the chance of organizational failure falls (hypothesis 6).

Research Design

We test these hypotheses using data on savings and loan associations (thrifts) operating in California between 1977 and 1987. Although the traditional core domain of thrifts is residential mortgage lending, deregulatory initiatives in 1980 and 1982 broadened the allowed scope of investment and lending activities for these firms. Thrifts operate in eight product and client markets that constitute eight distinct domain sectors: residential mortgages, nonresidential mortgages, mortgage-backed securities, consumer nonmortgage loans, commercial loans, direct investments in real estate, corporate and government securities, and service-corporation subsidiaries (for descriptions of these markets, see U.S. GAO 1991, 63–66, and Haveman 1992, 56–58).[5] Because thrifts can invest in such a wide variety of assets, the industry has become quite heterogeneous. Many thrifts remain focused on the traditional residential mortgage business. But others have adopted new strategies: some have become primarily commercial lenders, some offer mortgage-banking services (servicing loans originated at other institutions), others invest heavily in corporate and mortgage-backed securities, while still others have moved into real estate development. The wide array of business strategies and the large number of markets open to thrifts facilitate the investigation of how similarities and differences between these organizations influence competition and mutualism in this industry.

Data

Our data come from thrift regulators. The Federal Home Loan Bank Board in Washington, D.C., has compiled detailed financial reports of all regulated thrifts. These reports provide the balance sheets and income statements from which we draw most of our data. Other data on California thrifts, primarily headquarters location, date of founding, and information on mergers and acquisitions, come from the annual *Directories of Members* published by the Federal Home Loan Bank of San Francisco and from a merger file compiled by federal regulators. The data cover all savings and loans operating between June 1977 and March 1987. The data are semiannual from 1977 to 1983 and quarterly from 1984 on. To facilitate econometric corrections for violations of the assumptions of the classical linear model, we aggregated quarterly data into semiannual data for our analysis of both continuous dependent variables (economic performance and growth); however, to maximize information, we retained quarterly data for our analysis of the discrete dependent variable (failure). We updated all variables at the end of each period. We measured independent and control variables at the beginning of each period and dependent variables at the end of each period.

From the population of California thrifts, we selected thrifts headquartered in the state's three largest metropolitan areas: Los Angeles (163 thrifts), San Diego (26 thrifts), and San Francisco–San Jose (67 thrifts). (The appendix lists the cities included in these metropolitan areas.) Our sample contains 77 percent of the thrifts in the population in this time period (249 out of 322). We treated the three metropolitan areas as separate arenas of competition and pooled information on thrifts headquartered in each of the three areas. We judged the metropolitan area to be an appropriate unit of aggregation for studying competitive and mutualistic interactions because thrifts' primary activities, mediating consumer savings activities and home mortgage lending, tend to be local in nature (Friend 1969; Gart 1989). The fact that the names of these organizations frequently include a city or county supports this contention; First Federal Savings and Loan of Fresno and Century City Savings and Loan Association are typical California thrift names. We also judged that parameter estimates on performance, growth, and failure would be the same for thrifts operating in the three metropolitan areas because thrifts in the three areas tend to be subject to similar economic conditions and are performing similar functions in all three local economies; hence, pooling data on the three areas not only improves statistical power but is appropriate.

Measures of Independent Variables
Overlap Density

We measured domain overlap in four ways. First, we measured *overlap density* as:

$$\text{overlap density}_{it} = \frac{\sum\limits_{j \neq i} \left(\sum\limits_{m} D_{imt} \times D_{jmt} \right)}{\sum\limits_{m} D_{imt}}$$

where D_{imt} equals one if firm i invests in market m at time t and zero otherwise, and D_{jmt} equals one if firm j invests in market m at time t and zero otherwise.[6] This formula counts the number of markets in which firm i meets every other firm j, aggregates this count over all firms j in the population, and scales it by the number of markets in which firm i operates. Thus, overlap density is equivalent to the average number of competitors that firm i meets across the m markets that constitute its domain at time t. The range of this variable is zero to $N_t - 1$, where N_t equals organizational population density at time t. Neither extreme value is likely. When overlap density equals zero, there is no competition between the focal organization and any of the other organizations in the population. When overlap density equals population density minus one, the focal organization competes with all other organizations in the population, in all markets.

Domain-overlap measures are generally asymmetric, in that firm i can have a different competitive impact on firm j than vice versa. For example, thrifts that offer only residential mortgages do not compete with those that offer only consumer nonmortgage financial services, but both of these types of specialist organizations compete with generalist organizations that are active in both markets. Thus, domain overlaps are complete for organizations that specialize in either residential mortgages or consumer nonmortgage loans, but only partial for organizations that serve both consumer financial markets. This means that generalist lenders represent a greater competitive threat to specialist lenders than vice versa.

Since many thrifts are active in some of the eight markets we study on a very small scale, we followed Haveman (1993) and calculated overlap density by setting a threshold of *5 percent of total assets* of the focal firm to mark substantial investment in each market.[7] Hence, D_{imt} is set equal to one if firm i's investment in market m is at least 5 percent of its total assets. We also set a threshold of 1 percent of market share to demarcate the presence of other organizations in the focal market at a level substantial enough to influence the behavior of the focal organization. Hence, D_{jmt} is set equal to one if firm j's share of market m is at least 1 percent. We did not use a threshold based on the relative importance of the market for firm j, such as 5 percent of firm j's total assets, because we did not want to bias our measure against large firms and because we wanted to construct this variable from the focal firm's perspective. We reasoned that all firms with substantial market shares will be seen as significant competitors by any market incumbent.

Overlap Mass

Second, we weighted domain overlap by the magnitude of the overlapping organizations' activities in various markets. This allows us to discriminate between the effects of two different organizations that a focal firm meets in several markets, if the primary activities of one competitor are in the same markets as the focal firm and the primary activities of the other competitor are in different markets than the focal firm. Accordingly, we introduce a new measure of domain overlap, *overlap mass:*

$$\text{overlap mass}_{it} = \frac{\sum_{j \neq i} \left(\sum_m S_{imt} \times S_{jmt} \right)}{\sum_m S_{imt}},$$

where S_{imt} is the constant dollar amount firm i invests in market m at time t and S_{jmt} is the amount firm j invests in market m at time t. (We used the dollar value of investments to calculate overlap mass because that measure fit our research site best. Other scholars might use other measures of market share, such as the dollar value of sales or unit volume of sales.) For each market, we multiplied firm i's investment by firm j's investment and summed across all markets. We aggregated this dollar amount over all firms j in the population, and then scaled this by the total investments of firm i across all of its markets (total size). Thus, this variable measures the average mass of competitors that firm i meets in the m markets that constitute its domain at time t. The range of this variable runs from zero, at which point there is no overlap and therefore no competition between the focal organization and any of the other organizations in the population, to the total investments of all other organizations in the population (population mass), at which point the focal organization overlaps with and therefore competes with all other organizations in the population, in all markets.

Size-Localized Overlap Density and Mass

The foregoing definitions of domain overlap assume that domain overlap has uniform and ubiquitous competitive effects on all organizations in a population. But as noted earlier, previous research suggests that competition is constrained by differences in organizational size (see, for example, Hannan and Freeman 1977; Hannan and Ranger-Moore 1990; Wholey, Christianson, and Sanchez 1992). To examine whether the competitive effects of overlap density and mass are size-localized, we weighted these measures by the closeness of pairs of firms in terms of size, as follows:

$$\text{Size-localized Overlap Density}_{it} = \sum_{j \neq i} \left[\frac{\sum_{m} [(D_{imt} \times D_{jmt}) \div (|S_{it} - S_{jt}| + 1)]}{\sum_{m} D_{imt}} \right]$$

$$\text{Size-localized Overlap Investment}_{it} = \sum_{j \neq i} \left[\frac{\sum_{m} [(I_{imt} \times I_{jmt}) \div (|S_{it} - S_{jt}| + 1)]}{\sum_{m} I_{imt}} \right]$$

where S_{it} is the size of firm i at time t and S_{jt} is the size of firm j at time t, in terms of total assets. These measures weight our original domain-overlap measures by the inverse of the distance between the focal organization and each of the other organizations in the population. We add one to the absolute value of the distance between the focal organization and each of the other organizations to constrain this weight to range between zero (when $|S_{it} - S_{jt}|$ is very large) and one (when $S_{it} = S_{jt}$ and $|S_{it} - S_{jt}| = 0$).

As the value of size-localized domain overlap increases, the extent to which other organizations' resource requirements overlap with those of the focal organization increases *and* the size-based distance between the focal organization and overlapping organizations decreases; together, these factors drive competition between the focal organization and overlapping organizations to higher levels. The maximum for size-localized overlap density is organizational population density (minus one for the focal organization); for size-localized overlap investment, it is the total investments of all other organizations in the population (population mass minus the investments of the focal organization). At the maximum for both variables, the focal organization competes with all other organizations in the population. But these maxima are unlikely to occur because they require all organizations in the population to be identical in size *and* domain.

Non-Overlaps

Domain non-overlap is the complement of domain overlap. Our first measure of domain non-overlap, *non-overlap density,* counts organizations whose resource requirements are not similar to those of the focal organization:

$$\text{non-overlap density}_{it} = N_t - \text{overlap density}_{it} - 1,$$

where N_t is the number of firms operating at time t (population density).

Similarly, our second measure, *non-overlap mass*, is the complement of overlap mass:

$$\text{non-overlap mass}_{it} = \sum_{j \neq i} \sum_m S_{jmt} - \text{overlap mass}_{it},$$

where $\Sigma\Sigma S_{jmt}$ represents the total investment in all markets by all firms except the focal organization (population mass minus the focal organization's investments).

Our third and fourth measures are size-localized equivalents of non-overlap density and mass, defined as follows:

$$\frac{\text{size-localized}}{\text{Non-overlap density}_{it}} = N_t - 1 - \text{size-localized overlap density}_{it},$$

and

$$\frac{\text{size-localized}}{\text{Non-overlap mass}_{it}} = \sum_{j \neq i} \sum_m S_{jmt} - \text{size-localized overlap mass}_{it},$$

where N_t is population density at time t and $\Sigma\Sigma S_{jmt}$ is population mass at time t (minus the focal organization).

Comparing Overlaps and Non-Overlaps

These measures of domain overlap and non-overlap are complex, and it is reasonable to conclude that non-overlap is merely the opposite of overlap. It is not. Instead, each measure of domain non-overlap is the complement of one measure of domain overlap. To illustrate this point, table 9A.1 shows the domains of six hypothetical thrifts, along with calculations of domain-overlap and -non-overlap measures; for the purposes of this exercise, we assume that these six thrifts constitute the entire industry. One of the hypothetical thrifts is very large, with investments in all eight markets, and five thrifts are medium-size to small, with investments in varying subsets of the eight markets. Rows 1 through 8 of table 9A.1 show the dollar value of investments (in millions of dollars) by each thrift in each domain sector. Row 9 shows the total size of each thrift, where total size equals investments in all eight domain categories plus fixed assets and other assets. Rows 10 through 13 show the values for four of the domain-overlap and domain-non-overlap measures, calculated using the formulae given earlier.

One nonobvious result is that the largest thrift (thrift A), which operates in all eight domain sectors, does *not* have the highest value for overlap density. On the contrary, it has the lowest value. Because in this example we are considering thrifts in a single time period, overlap and non-overlap density are complements; therefore thrift A also has the highest value for non-overlap density. This result comes about because only one of the other, smaller thrifts (thrift C) is nearly as diversified as thrift A. Therefore, although thrift A operates in all markets, it meets very few competitors, on average, across those markets. In contrast, the firm that operates in the only market that all other firms operate in (thrift D in the residential mortgage market) has the maximum possible value for overlap density and the minimum possible value for non-overlap density.

Measures of Dependent Variables

The first outcome we study is *economic performance,* measured using net income. To compare firms of different sizes, our models control for total firm assets; hence, our analyses are equivalent to estimating the effects of domain overlap and non-overlap on return on assets, which is recognized by industry analysts as the best scale-independent measure of performance in this industry (see, for example, Cole 1971), because it allows comparisons between joint-stock and mutual companies. Our second outcome is *growth,* the one-period change in firm size. This is measured in terms of total assets. Total assets and net income, like all other dollar amounts, were corrected for inflation using a GDP deflator index.

Our third outcome, *failure,* is measured with an indicator variable set equal to one if the firm under study dissolved or underwent involuntary merger at the end of the period and zero otherwise. Thrifts seldom disband outright. Instead, regulators tend to negotiate with potential investors (usually other, healthier thrifts) to acquire failing firms. Regulators underwrite the costs of these mergers, in effect selling failed thrifts for the assessed value of their investment portfolios, reimbursing depositors and other creditors, and absorbing a loss in the process (Woerheide 1984, 172–77). We distinguish between involuntary mergers (those forced by regulators or by impending insolvency) and voluntary mergers (those entered into freely, without coercion). Some forced mergers are noted by regulators, but most mergers are not recorded as either voluntary or involuntary. For these, we followed Haveman (1992) and used a simple classification rule: any thrift with zero or negative net worth in the period immediately prior to merger was coded as undergoing involuntary merger; any disappearing thrift with positive net worth was coded as undergoing voluntary merger. Failure thus encompasses three types of events: mergers that were explicitly labeled as federally supervised (and therefore involuntary), outright liquidations, and mergers of firms with zero or negative net worth. This classification scheme is a conservative one in that voluntary mergers (which may well be the result of success) are very unlikely to be classified as involuntary (which are undoubtedly the result of failure).

Measures of Control Variables

Our analyses control for both organizational and environmental factors that are likely to influence the success and survival of savings and loan associations. In analyses of economic performance, we controlled for size by including assets invested in each of ten categories: eight product or client markets and the two non-investment categories (fixed and other assets). In analyses of growth, we controlled for prior size (total assets) and overall diversification of investments across the eight product or client markets. In analyses of survival, we controlled for investments in each of the eight product or client markets and the two non-investment categories. We measured overall diversification using an index of diversity (Berry 1974, 62–63; Blau 1977, 9):

$$\text{Diversification}_{it} = \sum_m P_{imt}^2,$$

where P_{imt} is the proportion of its assets that firm i invests in market m at time t. In analyses of all three outcome variables, we also controlled for organizational age, measured in terms of the number of years since founding.

Our environmental control variables capture external factors that influence the intensity of competition independent of domain overlap and non-overlap: the presence of competing financial institutions and demand for thrift services. On the supply side, we counted the number of commercial banks operating in California. On the demand side, we controlled for the effects of housing sales (total house sales in California) and the gap between short- and long-term interest rates (which assesses the difference between thrifts' costs of funds from deposits and thrifts' uses of funds to underwrite mortgages).

Model Specification and Estimation

Economic Performance

We investigated economic performance using models of the following general form:

$$Y_{it_1} = \alpha Y_{it_0} + \beta' X_{it_0} + \varepsilon_{it_1},$$

where Y_{it_1} is the value of the dependent variable (net income) for firm i at the end of a period (at time t_1), Y_{it_0} is its value at the beginning of the period (at time t_0), X_{it_0} is a vector of independent and control variables measured at the beginning of the period, and ε_{it_1} is the error term.

Growth

We estimated logistic growth models of the following form:

$$\log[S_{it_1}] = \gamma \log[S_{it_0}] + \beta' X_{it_0} + \varepsilon_{it_1},$$

where S_{it_1} is the size (assets) of firm i at the end of a period, S_{it_0} is the value of this variable at the beginning of the period, X_{it_0} is a vector of independent and control variables measured at the beginning of the period, and ε_{it_1} is the error term. When the size distribution is skewed to the right, as it is for this organizational population, the error term in this equation is normally distributed (Ijiri and Simon 1977).

In analyses of both economic performance and growth, we pooled multiple observations over time for each organization. It is likely, then, that the assumption of independence required for ordinary least squares (OLS) regression is violated. This violation may result in biased parameter estimates. To correct this bias, we estimated fixed-effects models. We subtracted the value of each variable from its mean across all observations on an organization and suppressed the intercept. This is equivalent to introducing one dummy variable for each firm but is easier to estimate, since it eliminates the addition of a large number of variables to the dataset (Judge et al. 1982, 478–88).

We also corrected for serial correlation of errors, which can result from model misspecification caused by omitted variables. Such model misspecification introduces errors whose effects are felt in the coefficient estimates for the lagged dependent variable and the independent variables. For models that include the lagged dependent variable, as these do, serial correlation confounds the disturbance term with the effect of the lagged dependent variable. When exogenous variables are correlated with the lagged dependent variable, estimates of all parameters are biased and inconsistent (see Ostrom 1978; Judge et al. 1982; Greene 1990). When models contain the lagged dependent variable and error terms are serially correlated, OLS will not yield accurate estimates of the error term and hence will not provide consistent estimates of serial correlation. To deal with this problem, the technique of instrumental variables should be used (Ostrom 1978, 53–55; Greene 1990, 440–45). This involves estimating the lagged dependent variable using variables that are *not* correlated with the error term and substituting this estimate into the earlier model. The most common suggestion is to regress the dependent variable on current and lagged independent variables (see, for example, Ostrom 1978, 55; Greene 1990, 448). The lagged values of the predictions of the independent variable are substituted into the earlier model, which then yields consistent estimates of the errors.

We corrected for first- and second-order serial correlation within each organization's time series using a pseudo-generalized–least squares estimation technique (Ostrom 1978, 53–55; Judge et al. 1982, 442–46; Greene

1990, 440–45). Estimates of the first- and second-order serial correlation parameter (constant across the industry) were derived from the AUTOREG procedure in SAS.[8]

Failure

For our analysis of organizational failure, we employed event-history methods. The dependent variable is the instantaneous rate of failure (involuntary merger or liquidation). We used the Gompertz specification, which is a monotonic function of time:

$$\gamma_{it} = \exp[\beta'X_{it} + \gamma t]$$

where β is a vector of coefficients, X_{it} is a vector of time-varying variables measured at the start of each period, γ is the time-dependent coefficient, and t is the time clock (organizational age). This log-linear specification constrains the failure rate to be non-negative. We used Nancy Brandon Tuma's (1993) maximum-likelihood program RATE to estimate these models. Estimation with RATE allows right-censored observations to be used in estimating parameters, thereby avoiding biases that result from eliminating censored observations or from treating censored observations as though events occur when the observation period ends (Sørensen 1977; Tuma and Hannan 1984).

One problem with our research design must be addressed, namely, left truncation. Left truncation occurs whenever data are unavailable on the initial conditions and past history of the actors under study (Cox and Oakes 1984, 177–78). This study begins in 1977. Firms that operated in the California thrift industry before 1977 and disappeared before that date are not part of the population analyzed; only thrifts that were still alive in 1977 are included in the data. The sample of firms we study is thus unavoidably chosen contingent on their being part of the industry at the start of the observation period. This selection criterion creates bias if it is correlated with the outcome under study (Heckman 1979; Berk 1983; Tuma and Hannan 1984). If the factors that cause a firm to continue to operate until 1977 are related to the factors that cause it to survive after 1977, then there is sample-selection bias. Previous research has shown that organizational age influences organizational survival (see, for example, Freeman, Carroll, and Hannan 1983). Thus, in investigating organizational survival in this sample, we are likely to be confronted with sample-selection bias; however, sample-selection bias is attenuated to the extent that a large proportion—about half—of the firms studied entered our sample after the beginning of our observation period.

To address the issue of sample-selection bias, we controlled for the age of all organizations, including those with left-truncated life histories. Thus, we condition our estimates of survival rates on organizational age. This strategy yields unbiased estimates because it controls for the only aspect of past history that is of interest in semi-Markov models, namely, duration in state (Yamaguchi 1991, 7–8; Guo 1993).[9] This strategy has the further advantage of using all available information, thus maximizing statistical power.

Results

Table 9.1 presents means, standard deviations, and correlations for the variables included in the analysis. Note that the measures of domain overlap and non-overlap are complements, not opposites. As we might expect, the correlation between each pair of measures is always moderately high (ranging from .63 to .86). But for three out of four pairs of variables, the correlation is positive, indicating that firms that have a high level of overlap between their domains and the domains of other thrifts also tend to have a high level of non-overlap. This result occurs for two reasons. First, we pool data on eighteen six-month periods; we do not just compare firms within any single time period. (If we did the latter, each overlap measure would be the complement to one non-overlap measure, and the correlation between each pair of measures would be minus one.) Second, our mass-based measures pool data on firms whose investments in the eight markets vary greatly in magnitude, where investment levels are not perfectly correlated with market density. Third, our size-localized measures pool data on firms of varying sizes, which are therefore calculated within varying size-based windows.

Tables 9.2 through 9.4 present multivariate analyses of the impact of domain overlap on economic performance, firm growth, and failure, respectively. In each table, models 1 and 2 assess the impact of overlap density and overlap mass, while models 3 and 4 investigate their size-localized counterparts. We discuss each outcome in turn.

Table 9.2 shows strong support for our theory: overlap density, overlap mass, and their size-localized counterparts all have negative and statistically significant effects on economic performance, congruent with hypothesis 1. As the domain overlap between any savings and loan association and other associations increases, the focal association's economic performance worsens. This pattern holds whether we simply count the number of investment markets or measure the dollar value of investments in those markets. And the pattern holds whether we measure domain overlaps with all other savings and loan associations or domain overlaps with just similarly sized ones.

Table 9.3, which presents estimates of growth in savings and loans' asset bases, demonstrates that domain overlap slows growth significantly. This finding holds regardless of how domain overlap is measured. In all models, parameter estimates for all four measures of domain overlap—overlap density, overlap mass, and their size-localized counterparts—are negative and statistically significant. These results strongly support hypothesis 2.

TABLE 9.1   *Descriptive Statistics for California Savings and Loan Associations, 1977 to 1986*

	1	2	3	4	5	6	7
Mean	1.65	587.90	0.025	5.41	183.40	48.40	61.77
Standard deviation	31.43	1674.00	0.156	12.99	23.80	11.69	12.92
1. Net income	—	0.208*	−0.018	0.448*	−0.212*	0.006	0.100*
2. Assets	—	—	−0.019	0.772*	−0.399*	0.015	0.040*
3. Firm failure	—	—	—	0.002	0.012	0.026	−0.059*
4. Overlap density	—	—	—	—	−0.626*	−0.014	−0.104*
5. Non-overlap density	—	—	—	—	—	−0.002	0.728*
6. Overlap mass	—	—	—	—	—	—	0.002
7. Non-overlap mass	—	—	—	—	—	—	—
8. Size-localized overlap density	—	—	—	—	—	—	—
9. Size-localized non-overlap density	—	—	—	—	—	—	—
10. Size localized overlap mass	—	—	—	—	—	—	—
11. Size-localized non-overlap mass	—	—	—	—	—	—	—
12. Age	—	—	—	—	—	—	—
13. Bank density	—	—	—	—	—	—	—
14. Diversification	—	—	—	—	—	—	—
15. Housing sales	—	—	—	—	—	—	—
16. Interest-rate gap	—	—	—	—	—	—	—

Source: Authors' compilation.
Note: These statistics were calculated on pooled cross-sectional and time-series data comprising 3,740 observations on 315 savings and loan associations operating in San Francisco, San Diego, or Los Angeles between 1977 and 1986.
* $p < .05$

Finally, table 9.4 shows event-history analyses of the impact of domain overlap on thrift failure rates. As with our analyses of organizational performance and growth, this table shows clearly that domain overlap decreases survival chances (that is, it increases failure rates). All parameter estimates for the theoretical variables—no matter how they are measured—are positive and statistically significant, offering consistently strong support for hypothesis 3.

A final consistency to note in our results is that the effects of the non-overlap variables on economic performance, growth, and survival are always opposite to those of the overlap variables, as anticipated by hypotheses 4, 5, and 6. These results, which hold across all three outcomes and all four measures, support the notion that organizations of the same form in non-overlapping

8	9	10	11	12	13	14	15	16
0.006	188.78	0.002	61.82	29.13	3.48	0.504	4.01	1.65
0.001	18.61	0.008	12.92	29.13	0.921	0.163	1.067	1.89
0.206*	−0.025	0.189*	0.100*	0.099*	−0.036*	0.041*	0.069*	−0.019*
0.970*	0.049*	0.932*	0.040*	0.369*	0.062*	−0.057*	−0.023	0.037*
−0.028	0.001	−0.018	−0.059*	0.007	−0.013	0.043*	−0.089*	−0.015
0.690*	−0.102*	0.690*	−0.104*	0.435*	−0.115*	0.016	0.058*	−0.065
−0.272*	0.839*	−0.339*	0.728*	−0.384*	0.679*	−0.385*	−0.304*	0.171*
0.035*	−0.013	0.067*	0.003	0.208*	−0.212*	0.507*	0.306*	−0.205*
0.150*	0.856*	0.052*	0.090*	−0.185*	0.780*	−0.540*	−0.126*	0.349*
—	0.157*	0.959*	0.149*	0.282*	0.165*	−0.084*	−0.056*	0.084*
—	—	0.072*	0.856*	−0.159*	0.775*	−0.475*	−0.313*	0.161*
—	—	—	0.052*	0.308*	0.060*	0.004	−0.004	0.024
—	—	—	—	−0.184*	0.780*	−0.539*	−0.126*	0.349*
—	—	—	—	—	−0.193*	0.142*	0.121*	−0.095*
—	—	—	—	—	—	−0.666*	−0.651*	0.544*
—	—	—	—	—	—	—	0.404*	−0.417*
—	—	—	—	—	—	—	—	−0.377*
—	—	—	—	—	—	—	—	—

niches help rather than harm each other, either through the symbiosis created by complementary differences or through the commensalism created by commonality of interests (Hawley 1950, 29–38). Further, these results indicate that the mutualistic effects of non-overlap greatly outweigh any competitive effects that may arise because the eight domain sectors are partial substitutes for each other or are similar with respect to resource requirements. Increases in the number of organizations that do *not* overlap with the focal organization's domain always improve that organization's economic performance, accelerate its growth, and lessen its chances of failure.

One important assumption we make in these analyses is that all organizations with overlapping domains create an equal amount of competition for any focal organization, so that each competitor has an equally strong negative effect

TABLE 9.2   *The Effects of Domain Overlap on the Economic Performance of California Savings and Loan Associations, 1977 to 1986: Feasible GLS Estimates*

	Model 1	Model 2	Model 3	Model 4
Net income$_{t-1}$	0.521*** (0.033)	0.555*** (0.033)	0.449*** (0.033)	0.448*** (0.032)
Overlap density	−0.184*** (0.054)	—	—	—
Non-overlap density	0.154* (0.067)	—	—	—
Overlap mass	—	−0.143* (0.070)	—	—
Non-overlap mass	—	0.013 (0.115)	—	—
Size-localized overlap density	—	—	−0.755*** (0.179)	—
Size-localized non-overlap density	—	—	0.123* (0.064)	—
Size-localized overlap mass	—	—	—	−0.046*** (0.008)
Size-localized non-overlap mass	—	—	—	0.105*** (0.031)
Asset portfolio				
Residential mortgages	−0.037*** (0.003)	−0.028*** (0.003)	−0.030*** (0.004)	−0.044*** (0.003)
Nonresidential mortgages	0.046*** (0.008)	0.046*** (0.008)	0.041*** (0.009)	0.033*** (0.008)
Mortgage-backed securities	−0.065*** (0.005)	−0.055*** (0.005)	−0.067*** (0.005)	−0.057*** (0.005)

(Table continues on p. 253.)

on organizational performance and survival, and each non-overlapping organization has an equally strong positive impact. However, some firms may exert different patterns of influence, for reasons we do not capture here. Models of multimarket contact and competition predict that firms that meet in multiple markets (multiple domain sectors) do not compete as strongly against each other as firms that meet in a single market. Instead, firms that operate in multiple markets will refrain from aggressive action against the competitors they meet in multiple markets because they fear retaliation. Ironically, because possible harm from aggressive action is greater among rivals who meet in multiple domain sec-

TABLE 9.2   *Continued*

	Model 1	Model 2	Model 3	Model 4
Consumer non-mortgage loans	0.143*** (0.018)	0.138*** (0.018)	0.144*** (0.019)	0.153*** (0.017)
Commercial non-mortgage loans	−1.151*** (0.181)	−1.203*** (0.179)	−1.197*** (0.179)	−1.267*** (0.176)
Direct investments in real estate	0.422*** (0.025)	0.318*** (0.025)	0.320*** (0.026)	0.327*** (0.025)
Cash and investment securities	0.017** (0.007)	0.019** (0.007)	0.014 (0.008)	0.014* (0.007)
Service corporation investments	0.078*** (0.013)	0.077*** (0.013)	0.085*** (0.013)	0.089*** (0.013)
Fixed assets	1.103*** (0.112)	1.111*** (0.112)	1.103*** (0.113)	1.069*** (0.109)
Other assets	−0.098*** (0.020)	−0.098*** (0.020)	−0.101*** (0.020)	−0.092*** (0.019)
Age	0.832 (1.390)	−0.764 (1.462)	0.887 (1.390)	−0.356 (1.460)
Bank density	0.191 (3.954)	2.611 (4.164)	−0.240 (3.955)	−0.888 (4.060)
Housing sales	3.075*** (0.762)	2.529 (1.453)	3.227*** (0.762)	1.270 (1.460)
Interest-rate gap	0.365 (0.392)	0.596 (0.389)	0.412 (0.392)	0.585 (0.391)
R-squared	0.23	0.22	0.22	0.23

Source: Authors' compilation.
Notes: Standard errors are in parentheses below point estimates. To procure consistent estimates in the presence of autocorrelation, we estimated the lagged dependent variables using instrumental variables and used this estimate in our analyses.
* $p < .05$; ** $p < .01$; *** $p < .001$ (two-tailed t-tests)

tors than among rivals who meet in a single domain sector, actual harm from aggression is weaker. Fear of great reciprocal harm forestalls opponents who meet in multiple domains from using their strongest weapons against each other. In this case, the competitive interaction between two organizations with overlapping domains would decrease with the number of domain sectors in which they meet. Our assumption of equal competitive pressure is consistent with past research on domain overlap, and exploring the possibility of the mutual forbearance caused by multimarket contact is beyond the scope of this chapter. Yet an extension of this model to address the nature and impact of multipoint con-

TABLE 9.3   *The Effects of Domain Overlap on the Growth of California Savings and Loan Associations, 1977 to 1986: Feasible GLS Estimates*

	Model 1	Model 2	Model 3	Model 4
Log (assets)$_{t-1}$	0.481*** (0.024)	0.412*** (0.026)	0.470*** (0.024)	0.477*** (0.024)
Overlap density	−0.003*** (0.001)	—	—	—
Non-overlap density	0.002** (0.001)	—	—	—
Overlap mass	—	−0.007*** (0.001)	—	—
Non-overlap mass	—	0.002** (0.001)	—	—
Size-localized overlap density	—	—	−0.286** (0.103)	—
Size-localized non-overlap density	—	—	0.003** (0.001)	—
Size-localized overlap mass	—	—	—	−0.001* (0.000)
Size-localized non-overlap mass	—	—	—	0.002** (0.001)
Diversification index	−0.091 (0.075)	−0.271*** (0.079)	−0.057 (0.072)	−0.061 (0.072)
Age	0.068*** (0.011)	0.076*** (0.012)	0.076*** (0.011)	0.061*** (0.012)
Bank density	0.055* (0.027)	0.024 (0.028)	0.048* (0.026)	0.043 (0.028)
Housing sales	0.024*** (0.012)	0.021* (0.012)	0.024* (0.012)	0.024* (0.012)
Interest-rate gap	0.007*** (0.002)	0.008*** (0.002)	0.007** (0.002)	0.007** (0.002)
R-squared	0.32	0.31	0.32	0.32

Source: Authors' compilation.
Notes: Standard errors are in parentheses below point estimates. To procure consistent estimates in the presence of autocorrelation, we estimated the lagged dependent variables using instrumental variables and used this estimate in our analyses.
* $p < .05$; ** $p < .01$; *** $p < .001$ (two-tailed t-tests)

TABLE 9.4   *The Effects of Domain Overlap on the Hazard Rate of Firm Failure Among California Savings and Loan Associations, 1977 to 1986: Gompertz Models*

	Model 1	Model 2	Model 3	Model 4
Constant	0.251*** (0.051)	0.267*** (0.062)	0.218*** (0.040)	0.225*** (0.024)
Overlap density	0.039*** (0.011)	—	—	—
Non-overlap density	−0.045*** (0.011)	—	—	—
Overlap mass	—	0.021** (0.010)	—	—
Non-overlap mass	—	−0.030** (0.017)	—	—
Size-localized overlap density	—	—	15.020*** (4.547)	—
Size-localized non-overlap density	—	—	−0.046*** (0.011)	—
Size-localized overlap mass	—	—	—	0.010** (0.005)
Size-localized non-overlap mass	—	—	—	−0.034* (0.017)
Age	0.006 (0.005)	0.003 (0.003)	0.003 (0.004)	0.008 (0.008)
Asset portfolio				
Residential mortgages	0.002** (0.000)	0.001** (0.000)	0.003* (0.001)	0.001* (0.000)
Nonresidential mortgages	0.002* (0.001)	0.002* (0.001)	0.004** (0.002)	0.004*** (0.001)
Mortgage-backed securities	−0.004** (0.002)	−0.004** (0.002)	0.004** (0.002)	−0.004** (0.002)
Consumer non-mortgage loans	−0.010** (0.005)	−0.008** (0.004)	−0.010* (0.006)	−0.010** (0.005)
Commercial non-mortgage loans	−0.038*** (0.007)	−0.026*** (0.005)	−0.050*** (0.009)	−0.029*** (0.008)
Direct investments in real estate	0.008 (0.006)	0.011 (0.007)	0.008 (0.006)	0.010 (0.006)
Cash and investment securities	−0.006*** (0.002)	−0.006*** (0.002)	−0.004** (0.002)	−0.006*** (0.002)

(*Table continues on p. 256.*)

TABLE 9.4   *Continued*

	Model 1	Model 2	Model 3	Model 4
Service corporation investments	0.008** (0.004)	0.008** (0.004)	0.007* (0.004)	0.007* (0.004)
Fixed assets	−0.030 (0.023)	−0.025 (0.022)	−0.047 (0.026)	−0.027 (0.022)
Other assets	−0.008 (0.007)	−0.005 (0.007)	−0.008 (0.007)	−0.007 (0.007)
Bank density	−2.717*** (0.461)	−3.487*** (1.112)	−2.217*** (0.487)	−3.507*** (1.107)
Housing sales	−15.120*** (2.458)	−19.020*** (4.255)	−13.030*** (2.472)	−18.400*** (4.288)
Interest-rate gap	0.118*** (0.061)	0.007 (0.055)	0.117*** (0.060)	0.006 (0.054)
χ^2	75.49	62.54	72.63	62.53
Degrees of freedom	16	16	16	16

Source: Authors' compilation.
Notes: Standard errors are in parentheses below point estimates. These models were estimated on 3,256 observations covering 232 thrifts and 106 failure events.
* $p < .05$; ** $p < .01$; *** $p < .001$ (two-tailed t-tests)

tact would be worthwhile. The extension could design measures of domain overlap and non-overlap that are sensitive to the system of mutual forbearance that develops among multipoint rivals. This would involve weighting the competitive effect of rival j by a declining function of the number of markets in which j and the focal firm i meet.

Conclusion

A fundamental concern of organizational theory is relationships between organizations and their environments, which are largely composed of other organizations. Organizations interact with each other in many ways, but their interactions can usually be classified as either competitive or cooperative (mutualistic). In this chapter, we have examined interactions among organizations in a single industry whose domains overlap. That is, we focused on organizations that sell similar products and target the same pool of clients. Because their products and prospective clients are similar, these organizations have similar resource requirements. We argued that domain overlap increases competition for scarce resources, while non-overlap (the absence of domain overlap) facilitates mutualistic, cooperative outcomes. We explored empirically how the nature of the relations between organizations affects organizational financial performance, growth, and failure. We argued that competitive interactions worsen performance and growth and increase the chance of failure, while cooperative, mutualistic interactions improve performance and growth and reduce the chance of failure.

Our results provide strong evidence that domain overlap and non-overlap have the predicted effects. We found remarkable consistency in results across all three outcomes. Moreover, these results proved robust to the way domain overlap and non-overlap are measured. We counted the number of markets in which a focal organization meets its competitors (overlap density), we weighted this count by the magnitude of organizational investments in those markets (overlap mass), and we constrained domain overlap to weight most heavily firms of similar size to the focal organization (size-localized overlap density and size-localized overlap mass). No matter what measure we used, we found domain overlap to have deleterious effects on organizational performance, growth, and survival, and domain non-overlap to have beneficial effects.

This study demonstrates the importance of examining the differences among an industry's participants. Our findings are fundamental to the literature on diversification, which to this point has focused almost exclusively on within-organization sources of competitive advantages. Here we show how diversification strategies can affect between-organization patterns of competition and cooperation, and thus how an organization's position relative to its rivals can generate competitive advantages and disadvantages. Moreover, the prescriptive implications of this research are clear: managers and entrepreneurs should not seek markets that are devoid of competitors, but rather markets where many incumbents are engaged in activities different from or complementary to those of their own venture. Finally, our results suggest that organizational decision-makers may want to focus their attention on more fine-grained differentiation of their competitors in terms of market presence, the importance of that market presence to those competitors (the degree of investment by competitors), and whether those competitors are similar or different in size to their own firm.

Appendix

Cities Included in the Three California Metropolitan Areas Studied

Los Angeles

Alhambra	Camarillo
Altadena	Colton
Anaheim	Compton
Bellflower	Costa Mesa
Beverly Hills	Covina
Brea	Culver City
Buena Park	Encino

Fillmore
Fontana
Fountain Valley
Fullerton
Gardena
Garden Grove
Glendale
Hawthorne
Hollywood
Huntington Beach
Inglewood
Irvine
Laguna Beach
Long Beach
Los Angeles
Malibu
Manhattan Beach
Marina Del Rey
Mission Viejo
Montebello
Monterey Park
Newport Beach
Northridge
Ontario
Orange
Oxnard

Pacific Palisades
Pasadena
Placentia
Pomona
Redlands
Redondo Beach
Riverside
Rosemead
San Bernadino
San Clemente
San Fernando
San Gabriel
San Marino
Santa Ana
Santa Monica
Santa Paula
Signal Hill
South Pasadena
Torrance
Upland
Van Nuys
West Covina
Westlake Village
Westminster
Whittier
Wilmington

San Diego

Carlsbad
Chula Vista
Encinitas
Escondido
La Jolla

La Mesa
Oceanside
Rancho Santa Fe
San Diego

San Francisco

Alameda
Berkeley

Burlingame
Campbell

Concord		San Francisco
Danville		San Jose
El Cerrito		San Leandro
Hayward		San Mateo
Lafayette		San Rafael
Mill Valley		San Ramon
Oakland		Santa Clara
Pacifica		South San Francisco
Palo Alto		Sunnyvale
Pleasanton		Vallejo
Redwood City		Walnut Creek
San Carlos		

TABLE 9A.1   *Example Calculations for Domain Overlap and Non-Overlap Measures*

Domain Sector (Market)	Thrift A	Thrift B	Thrift C	Thrift D	Thrift E	Thrift F
Residential mortgages	23	4	10	12	4	22
Nonresidential mortgages	8	5	3	0	0	3
Mortgage-backed securities	15	8	1	0	0	0
Consumer nonmortgage loans	9	2	1	0	1.5	0
Commercial loans	4	1	1	0	0	0
Direct investments in real estate	8	0	0	0	0	10
Corporate and government securities	9	0	1	0	0	0
Service corporation subsidiaries	4	0	1	0	0.5	0
Overall firm size (millions of dollars)	80	20	18	12	6	35
Overlap density	2.38	3.00	2.86	5.00	3.33	3.00
Non-overlap density	2.63	2.00	2.14	0.00	1.67	2.00
Overlap mass	21.03	26.01	45.42	67.00	52.96	38.81
Non-overlap mass	69.97	124.99	107.58	92.00	112.04	97.19

Source: Authors' compilation.
Note: Rows 1 through 8 show the dollar value of investments by each thrift in each domain sector. Row 9 shows the total size of each thrift (total investments across all eight domain sectors). Rows 10 through 13 show the values for four measures of domain overlap and non-overlap, which are calculated using the formulas provided in the text.

We thank seminar participants at the University of California at Berkeley, the University of Chicago, the University of Alberta, Cornell University, Carnegie-Mellon University, and the University of Utah for their constructive comments. We also thank Joel Baum for his collaboration on an earlier version of this chapter.

Notes

1. We use the terms "domain" and "niche" interchangeably, and in this chapter we study the actual behavior patterns of organizations. Thus, the organizational domains we study correspond to realized niches, not fundamental niches. For a discussion of fundamental versus realized niches, see Hannan and Freeman (1989, 95–98).

2. A third dimension of interorganizational relations, direct versus diffuse, is of less importance to our analysis. Direct relations involve small numbers (often pairs) of organizations whose fates are intimately linked in conflict or cooperation. In contrast, diffuse relations involve larger numbers of organizations, and the fate of any organization in a system of diffuse relations is only indirectly linked with the fate of any other single organization through congestion or cognitive legitimation (see Hannan and Freeman 1989). Here we note whether the particular relations we are discussing are direct or diffuse, but we do not dwell on these differences.

3. For reasons of conceptual clarity, we do not examine in this study either of the types of asymmetric symbiotic relation, predation and parasitism. Instead, we focus on all three symmetric relations: commensalistic competition, commensalistic mutualism, and symbiotic mutualism.

4. In support of this speculation, there is anecdotal evidence of price increases by generalists (mass producers) in the wake of price increases by specialists (microbrewers) in the U.S. brewing industry (Glenn Carroll, personal communication, 1997).

5. Thrifts also have investments that are not directly related to any product or client market: fixed assets (primarily buildings and equipment) and other assets (a small residual category).

6. When we calculated overlap density, we actually used the following formula, which is algebraically equivalent to the definitional formula:

$$\text{overlap density}_{it} = \sum_m \left(D_{imt} \times \sum_{j \neq i} D_{jmt} \right) \Big/ \sum_m D_{imt}.$$

7. Conversations with accounting researchers who study the thrift industry confirm that the 5 percent threshold is a reasonable one (Christopher Stinson and Frederick Lindahl, personal communications, 1993).

8. Time series varied in length across the firms in our data. Hence, we could not use the TSCS procedure, which estimates autoregressive models on balanced, pooled, time-series data (data in which there are n firms and all n firms have t records). The AUTOREG procedure assumes a single time series. To prevent the program from estimating autoregressive parameters across different firms' time series, we inserted two blank records at the end of each firm's time series. Conversations with SAS technical consultants indicate that padding the data this way yields correct within-firm estimates for the first- and second-order serial correlation parameters. Conversations with SAS technical consultants also reveal that the TSCS procedure does not function if the data contain any missing values, so

we could not use that procedure even if we inserted enough blank records to make all firms' time series the same length. We thank Andrew Henderson for suggesting this technique.

9. Semi-Markov models assume that hazard rates are independent of previous history, but they allow these rates to depend on duration in a state; see Tuma and Hannan (1984, 92–95) or Guo (1993).

References

Aldrich, Howard E. 1999. *Organizations Evolving.* Thousand Oaks, Calif.: Sage Publications.

Aldrich, Howard E., and Marlene Fiol. 1994. "Fools Rush In? The Institutional Context of Industry Creation." *Academy of Management Review* 19(4): 645–70.

Amburgey, Terry L., Tina Dacin, and Dawn Kelly. 1994. "Disruptive Selection and Population Segmentation: Interpopulation Competition as a Segregating Process." In *Evolutionary Dynamics of Organizations,* edited by Joel A. C. Baum and Jitendra V. Singh. New York: Oxford University Press.

Barnett, William P. 1993. "Strategic Deterrence Among Multipoint Competitors." *Industrial and Corporate Change* 2: 249–78.

Barnett, William P., and Glenn R. Carroll. 1987. "Competition and Mutualism Among Early Telephone Companies." *Administrative Science Quarterly* 32: 400–21.

Baum, Joel A. C., and Heather A. Haveman. 1997. "Love Thy Neighbor? Differentiation and Spatial Agglomeration in the Manhattan Hotel Industry." *Administrative Science Quarterly* 41: 304–38.

Baum, Joel A. C., and Stephen J. Mezias. 1992. "Localized Competition and Organizational Failure in the Manhattan Hotel Industry." *Administrative Science Quarterly* 37: 580–604.

Baum, Joel A. C., and Jitendra V. Singh. 1994a. "Organizational Niche Overlap and the Dynamics of Organizational Mortality." *American Journal of Sociology* 100: 346–80.

———. 1994b. "Organizational Niche Overlap and the Dynamics of Organizational Founding." *Organization Science* 5: 483–501.

Berk, Richard A. 1983. "An Introduction to Sample Selection Bias in Sociological Data." *American Sociological Review* 48: 386–98.

Berry, Charles H. 1974. *Corporate Growth and Diversification.* Princeton, N.J.: Princeton University Press.

Bigelow, Lyda S., Glenn R. Carroll, Marc-David Seidel, and Lucia Tsai. 1997. "Legitimation, Geographical Scale, and Organizational Density." *Social Science Research* 26(4): 377–98.

Blau, Peter M. 1977. *Inequality and Heterogeneity.* New York: Free Press.

Boeker, Warren. 1991. "Organizational Strategy: An Ecological Perspective." *Academy of Management Journal* 34(3): 613–35.

Carroll, Glenn R. 1985. "Concentration and Specialization: Dynamics of Niche Width in Populations of Organizations." *American Journal of Sociology* 90(6, May): 1262–83.

Carroll, Glenn R., and Michael T. Hannan. 2000. *The Demography of Corporations and Industries.* Princeton, N.J.: Princeton University Press.

Carroll, Glenn R., and Anand Swaminathan. 1992. "The Organizational Ecology of Strategic Groups in the American Brewing Industry from 1975 to 1990." *Industrial and Corporate Change* 1: 65–97.

———. 2000. "Why the Microbrewery Movement? Organizational Dynamics of Resource Partitioning in the American Brewing Industry After Prohibition." *American Journal of Sociology* 106: 715–62.

Carroll, Glenn R., and James B. Wade. 1991. "Density Dependence in the Evolution of the American Brewing Industry Across Different Levels of Analysis." *Social Science Research* 20: 271–302.

Cole, David W. 1971. "Measuring Savings and Loan Profitability." *Federal Home Loan Bank Journal* (October): 1–7.

Cox, David Roxbee, and D. Oakes. 1984. *Analysis of Survival Data.* London: Chapman and Hall.

Freeman, John, Glenn R. Carroll, and Michael T. Hannan. 1983. "The Liability of Newness: Age Dependence in Organizational Death Rates." *American Sociological Review* 48: 692–710.

Friend, Irwin, ed. 1969. *Study of the Savings and Loan Industry.* Washington, D.C.: Federal Home Loan Bank Board.

Gart, Alan. 1989. *An Analysis of the New Financial Institutions: Changing Technologies, Financial Structures, Distribution Systems, and Deregulation.* New York: Quorum.

Greene, William H. 1990. *Econometric Analysis.* New York: Macmillan.

Guo, Guang. 1993. "Event-History Analysis for Left-Truncated Data." In *Sociological Methodology 1993,* edited by Peter Marsden. Oxford: Basil Blackwell.

Han, Joon. 1998. "The Evolution of the Japanese Banking Industry: An Ecological Analysis, 1783 to 1945." Ph.D. diss., Stanford University.

Hannan, Michael T., and Glenn R. Carroll. 1992. *Dynamics of Organizational Populations: Density, Competition, and Legitimation.* New York: Oxford University Press.

Hannan, Michael T., Glenn R. Carroll, Elizabeth A. Dundon, and John Charles Torres. 1995. "Organizational Evolution in a Multinational Context: Entries of Automobile Manufacturers in Belgium, Britain, France, Germany, and Italy." *American Sociological Review* 60(4): 509–28.

Hannan, Michael T., and John Freeman. 1977. "The Population Ecology of Organizations." *American Journal of Sociology* 83: 929–84.

———. 1987. "The Ecology of Organizational Founding: American Labor Unions, 1836 to 1985." *American Journal of Sociology* 92(4, January): 910–43.

———. 1988. "The Ecology of Organizational Mortality: American Labor Unions, 1836 to 1985." *American Journal of Sociology* 94(1, July): 25–42.

———. 1989. *Organizational Ecology.* Cambridge, Mass.: Harvard University Press.

Hannan, Michael T., and James R. Ranger-Moore. 1990. "The Ecology of Organizational Size Distributions: A Microsimulation Approach." *Journal of Mathematical Sociology* 15: 65–89.

Hannan, Michael T., James R. Ranger-Moore, and Jane C. Banaszak-Holl. 1990. "Competition and the Evolution of Organizational Size Distributions." In *Organi-*

zational Evolution: New Directions, edited by Jitendra V. Singh. Newbury Park, Calif.: Sage Publications.

Haveman, Heather A. 1992. "Between a Rock and a Hard Place: Organizational Change and Performance Under Conditions of Fundamental Environmental Transformation." *Administrative Science Quarterly* 37(1): 48–75.

———. 1993. "Follow the Leader: Mimetic Isomorphism and Entry into New Markets." *Administrative Science Quarterly* 38(4): 593–627.

Haveman, Heather A., and Lynn Nonnemaker. 2000. "Competition in Multiple Geographic Markets: The Impact on Market Entry and Growth." *Administrative Science Quarterly* 45(2): 232–67.

Hawley, Amos H. 1950. *Human Ecology: A Theory of Community Structure.* New York: Ronald Press.

———. 1968. *Human Ecology: A Theoretical Essay.* Chicago: University of Chicago Press.

Heckman, James J. 1979. "Sample Selection Bias as Specification Error." *Econometrica* 47(1, January): 153–61.

Ijiri, Yuji, and Herbert A. Simon. 1977. *Skew Distributions and the Sizes of Business Firms.* New York: North Holland.

Judge, George G., G. Carter Hill, William E. Griffiths, Helmut Lütkepohl, and Tsoung-Chao Lee. 1982. *Introduction to the Theory and Practice of Econometrics.* New York: John Wiley.

Keister, Lisa A. 1998. "Engineering Growth: Business Group Structure and Firm Performance in China's Transition Economy." *American Journal of Sociology* 104(2): 404–40.

———. 2000. *Chinese Business Groups: The Structure and Impact of Interfirm Relations During Economic Development.* New York: Oxford University Press.

Levine, Sol, and Paul E. White. 1961. "Exchange as a Conceptual Framework for the Study of Interorganizational Relationships." *Administrative Science Quarterly* 5(4): 583–601.

Lincoln, James R., Michael L. Gerlach, and Christina L. Ahmadjian. 1996. "Keiretsu Networks and Corporate Performance in Japan." *American Sociological Review* 61(1): 67–88.

McGee, John, and Howard Thomas. 1986. "Strategic Groups: Theory, Research, and Taxonomy." *Strategic Management Journal* 7: 141–60.

McPherson, J. Miller. 1983. "An Ecology of Affiliation." *American Sociological Review* 48(4, August): 519–32.

McPherson, J. Miller, Pamela A. Popielarz, and Sonia Drobnic. 1992. "Social Networks and Organizational Dynamics." *American Sociological Review* 57: 153–70.

McPherson, J. Miller, and James R. Ranger-Moore. 1991. "Evolution on a Dancing Landscape: Organizations and Networks in Dynamic Blau Space." *Social Forces* 70(1, September): 19–42.

McPherson, J. Miller, and Thomas Rotolo. 1996. "Testing a Dynamic Model of Social Composition: Diversity and Change in Voluntary Groups." *American Sociological Review* 61(2): 179–202.

Meyer, Marshall W. 1975. "Organizational Domains." *American Sociological Review* 40(5, October): 599–615.

Ostrom, Charles W. 1978. *Time-Series Analysis: Regression Techniques.* Beverly Hills, Calif.: Sage Publications.

Perrow, Charles. 2002. *Organizing America: Wealth, Power, and the Origins of Corporate Capitalism.* Princeton, N.J.: Princeton University Press.

Podolny, Joel M., Toby E. Stuart, and Michael T. Hannan. 1996. "Networks, Knowledge, and Niches." *American Journal of Sociology* 102(3): 659–89.

Ranger-Moore, James, Robert S. Breckenridge, and Daniel L. Jones. 1995. "Patterns of Growth and Size-Localized Competition in the New York Life Insurance Industry, 1860 to 1985." *Social Forces* 73(3): 1027–49.

Scott, W. Richard, Martin Ruef, Peter J. Mendel, and Carol A. Caronna. 2000. *Institutional Change and Health Care Organizations: From Professional Dominance to Managed Care.* Chicago: University of Chicago Press.

Sørensen, Åage B. 1977. "Estimating Rates from Retrospective Questionnaires." In *Sociological Methodology 1977,* edited by David Heise. San Francisco: Jossey-Bass.

Suchman, Mark C. 1995. "Managing Legitimacy: Strategic and Institutional Approaches." *Academy of Management Review* 20: 571–610.

Swaminathan, Anand, and Gabriele Wiedenmayer. 1991. "Does the Pattern of Density Dependence in Organizational Mortality Rates Vary Across Levels of Analysis? Evidence from the German Brewing Industry." *Social Science Research* 20(1): 45–73.

Thompson, James D. 1967. *Organizations in Action.* New York: Harper & Row.

Tuma, Nancy Brandon. 1993. *Invoking RATE.* Palo Alto, Calif.: DMA Corp.

Tuma, Nancy Brandon, and Michael T. Hannan. 1984. *Social Dynamics: Models and Methods.* Orlando, Fla.: Academic Press.

U.S. General Accounting Office. 1991. *Thrifts and Housing Finance: Implications of a Stricter Qualified Thrift Lender Test.* Washington: U.S. Government Printing Office.

Wade, James. 1996. "A Community-Level Analysis of Sources and Rates of Technological Variation in the Microprocessor Market." *Academy of Management Journal* 36: 1218–44.

White, Harrison C. 1981. "Where Do Markets Come From?" *American Journal of Sociology* 87(3, November): 517–47.

———. 2002. *Markets from Networks: Socioeconomic Models of Production.* Princeton, N.J.: Princeton University Press.

Wholey, Douglas R., Jon B. Christianson, and Susan M. Sanchez. 1992. "Organizational Size and Failure Among Health Maintenance Organizations." *American Sociological Review* 57(6): 829–42.

Winship, Christopher. 1988. "Thoughts About Roles and Relations: An Old Document Revisited." *Social Networks* 10: 209–31.

Winship, Christopher, and Michael Mandel. 1983. "Roles and Positions: A Critique and Extension of the Blockmodeling Approach." *Sociological Methodology,* edited by Samuel Leinhardt. San Francisco: Jossey-Bass.

Woerheide, Walter J. 1984. *The Savings and Loan Industry: Current Problems and Possible Solutions.* Westport, Conn.: Quorum Books.

Yamaguchi, Kazuo. 1991. *Event-History Analysis.* Newbury Park, Calif.: Sage Publications.

Part IV

HOW ECONOMIC IDEAS
SHAPE MARKETS

10

COMPETING LOGICS IN HEALTH CARE: PROFESSIONAL, STATE, AND MANAGERIAL

W. Richard Scott

O BSERVERS of health care delivery systems in the United States have been amazed at the extent and rapidity of change during the past two decades. After watching for many years the numbing spectacle of systems displaying "dynamics without change," in Robert Alford's (1972) cogent phrase, observers following recent developments and attempting to understand their characteristics, causes, and consequences suddenly have much to ponder.

For a very long time—well into the first half of the twentieth century—professionals were in a position to determine what patients required and the terms on which they could expect to receive services. While the patients being served fared well, concerns increased regarding those who were in need but unable to gain access to the system. A broad social movement put pressure on political figures to develop programs to serve those less fortunate, and the state stepped in to ensure greater equity of access. However, ever-rising costs and dwindling support for the expansive welfare state ushered in an era of retrenchment and cost-containment within which managers and market mechanisms have played a prominent role. This is the history we attempt to recount and examine.

The systems involved are complex and varied, the forces at work manifold and intricately interrelated, and the speed of change alarmingly swift. At the present juncture, patients are concerned and confused; physicians, nurses, and other providers are beleaguered and often angry; politicians are uncertain and conflicted; managers and health care administrators are stressed and sometimes vilified; and investors and financial analysts are seeking to learn whether there are profits to be made out of illness. The former world of the independent physician ministering to the medical needs of his (*sic!*) patients under simple fee-for-service arrangements, in sometime cooperation with nonprofit, independent community hospitals, seems a distant dream.

These arrangements that were so stable for so long—from the 1920s into the 1960s—appeared largely impervious to change. One would be hard-pressed to find a comparably stable system among other arenas of social activity during the first half of the twentieth century. It would be equally difficult to identify a large system that has changed so quickly. The rapidity and multidimensional nature of the transformation attest to the truth of Roysden Greenwood and C. R. Hinings's (1996) generalization that highly institutionalized sectors, by definition, resist change, but when change occurs, they can become transformed rapidly. A highly structured field can undergo rapid destructuration.

How did it happen that the least changeable, most highly institutionalized sector of this earlier time began so suddenly to unravel before our eyes? That is the difficult question this chapter attempts to address. The question is sufficiently large and complex that any answer must be incomplete and partial. My analysis is based on conceptual work and empirical investigations carried out by a team of researchers over a five-year period, reported in more detail in our book *Institutional Change and Health Care Organizations: From Professional Dominance to Managed Care* (Scott, Ruef, Mendel, and Caronna 2000). In this work, my colleagues and I endeavor both to shed some light on the changes that occurred during the last half-century in health care delivery systems in one metropolitan area of this country and to develop an analytical framework to help guide other studies of profound institutional change. Although our systematic empirical dataset extends only to 1995, the major trends we document have continued up to the present time.

Conceptualizing and Measuring Institutional Change

Conceptual Framework

Most studies of health care organizations focus on a single organization or on a few organizations of the same type; they are also primarily cross-sectional or they examine short time periods. Such studies can address important questions but are not very useful when we are trying to understand larger forces that operate over extended periods of time and necessarily affect, and work through, many diverse organizations. To broaden the range of organizations studied, we chose to examine the *organizational field:* "those organizations that, in the aggregate, constitute a recognized area of institutional life: key suppliers, resource and product consumers, regulatory agencies, and other organizations that produce similar services or products" (DiMaggio and Powell 1983, 148). (I employ the terms "field" and "sector" interchangeably; see Scott and Meyer 1983.)

I adopt the convention of organizational sociologists and characterize the health care arena as an "organizational field" rather than as a "market"—a term that might be preferred by some of the other contributors to this volume. Under the traditional conception of market—a system of exchange in which the behavior of each actor is optimal, resulting in an efficient equilibrium—it is obvious that a field is not a market. However, pushed along by economic sociologists and institutional economists, the concept of market is gradually being reformulated to resemble more closely that of organizational field. A growing collection of scholars, including sociologists Mark Granovetter (1985) and Neil Fligstein (2001) and economists Douglass North (1990) and Avner Greif (forthcoming), are developing the view that markets are socially, culturally, and politically constructed, that they are greatly dependent on and shaped by the actions of the state, and that whatever equilibrium is established may not reflect the most efficient ordering of actors and economic processes (see Dobbin, this volume).

In spite of this growing convergence, I employ the concept of organizational field here to emphasize (1) the extent to which organizations are the most critical actors; (2) the role of political processes—both broader societal and field-specific—in supporting and constraining systems of production and consumption; (3) the power of cultural-cognitive and normative forces as they shape economic actors and their interests and actions; and (4) the ways in which economic activities are organized into relatively distinctive clusters with fairly demarcated boundaries. The notion of field "connotes the existence of a community of organizations that partakes of a common meaning system and whose participants interact more frequently and fatefully with one another than with actors outside of the field" (Scott 1994, 207–8). Within a field, we find social actors, both individuals and collectives, exchange systems ("organization sets"), diverse types of organizations ("populations"), and governance structures. In examining the health care field, we focus on selected types of providers of health care services but also include as important organizational actors in our study the purchasers of health care services (for example, employers and governmental agencies), fiscal intermediaries (insurance companies, health plans), and oversight structures (professional associations, regulatory agencies).

We also sought to examine changes in the health care field over an extended period of time. Too much of the organizational literature focuses on local variations in organizational form and functioning, ignoring broad, major currents of change as new ways of working or of organizing work replace older practices and forms (see Meyer 1994; Scott and Christensen 1995). A longitudinal focus on the organization field allows us to contemplate (1) diverse kinds of organizations; (2) changes in relations (exchange, competitive, ownership, contractual) among these organizations; (3) changes in the boundaries of individual organizations; (4) changes in the boundaries of organizational forms or populations (organizations of the same type); (5) the emergence of new types of organizations; and (6) changes in the boundaries of the field itself.

We embrace an open systems conception that emphasizes that if we are to understand changes in organizations and organizational forms over time, it is necessary to attend to changes in their environments, both the material resources on which they depend and the institutional frameworks on which they draw (Scott 2003). The *material-resource environment* is "that facet of the environment most directly relevant to viewing the organization as a production system depending on and transforming scarce resources" (Scott et al. 2000, 18). It includes factors affecting supply and demand (for example, numbers of physicians, demographic characteristics of an area's population; insurance coverage of patients), technologies (including both specialized medical equipment and information processing), and the structure of the industry as it affects the flow of resources among competitors and exchange partners.

Of particular interest are the *institutional environments* that influence the structure and behavior of individuals and organizations. Although many analysts conflate organizational and institutional structures, we insist on the advantages to be gained by analytically distinguishing between them. Institutions are defined as regulative, normative, and cultural-cognitive frameworks that, in combination, provide stability and meaning to social life (Scott 2001, 48). Individual organizations can develop their own distinctive norms and beliefs—"corporate cultures"—that, in turn, provide symbolic (normative and cultural-cognitive) frameworks that affect their behavior (see Selznick 1957; Schein 1992). However, we focus primarily on those wider symbolic frameworks operating at the field level—or even the societal level—that provide legal requirements, normative guidelines, cognitive models, and cultural logics affecting the full range of actors (both individual and collective) operating in that societal arena.

To examine changes in institutional environments, we found it useful to distinguish among three components: institutional logics, institutional actors, and governance systems.

- *Institutional logics* are sets of "material practices and symbolic constructions which constitute [a field's] organizing principles and which are available to organizations and individuals to elaborate" (Friedland and Alford 1991, 248). Changes in the prevailing logics, including rules (such as, should alternative practitioners be allowed to treat patients?) and belief systems (such as, should the federal government pay for health care?), represent significant changes in an organizational field.

- *Institutional actors* include both individuals who occupy specified roles and collective actors, such as organizations or associations, as they function to both create and carry (embody) institutional logics. Changes in the number and type of institutional actors—such as an increase in the number of health economists or a decline in the number of community hospitals—reflect significant alterations in the nature of an organizational field. We are also, of course, interested in examining changes in relations between actors.

- *Governance systems* are "those arrangements which support the regularized control—whether by regimes created by mutual agreement, by legitimate hierarchical authority or by non-legitimate coercive means—of the actions of one set of actors by another" (Scott, Mendel, and Pollack 2004). We can learn much about the underlying processes of organizational fields by attending closely to the changing nature of power and authority structures operating above the level of the individual organization.

In our view, a sociologically informative portrait of significant changes in the health care field can be drawn by recording changes over time in institutional logics, actors, and governance structures and their interrelations and as they relate to changes in material-resources. But it is also important to recognize that no organizational field is completely insulated from changes in wider social, economic, and cultural conditions. Some of the sources of change in organizational fields are endogenous to the field, but others are exogenous, arising from outside the field to influence and penetrate it and perhaps alter its boundaries. Such changes could stem, for example, from wider societal shocks (like depressions and wars), changes in broader political alignments and ideologies, or significant reform movements.

Empirical Case

To arrive at a feasible research design, we elected to limit our collection of data on health care to selected populations of organizations located in a single, large metropolitan area—the San Francisco Bay Area—and to focus on the last half of the twentieth century, specifically 1945 to 1995. Five populations (types) of organizations were selected for systematic study: hospitals, integrated health care systems, home health agencies (HHAs), health maintenance organizations (HMOs), and end-stage renal disease centers (ESRDCs). The populations were selected to reflect both more traditional forms (hospitals) and newer forms (HHAs, ESRDCs, and HMOs) as well as more diffuse forms (hospitals and integrated health care systems) and more specialized forms (HHAs and ESRDCs). The Bay Area is a large, rapidly growing metropolitan area—the population increased from 2.2 to 6.1 million between 1945 and 1995. It was selected to serve as a case of a large, expanding metropolitan region, but not in any way as representative of developments in other regions. Indeed, in important respects the Bay Area was an outlier, being in the forefront of change in health care delivery systems and serving as the home for the Kaiser Permanente system, a prototype for the new modes of service provision.

Although we restricted our study of organizational actors to a single metropolitan area, our examination of institutional logics and governance structures took into account developments at broader levels: regional, state, and national. Geographical boundaries may be employed to delimit the range and numbers of actors (individual and collective) affected by a set of forces but should not be used to exclude from study those actors and processes that are producing and conveying the new rules, norms, and cultural models. Scholars attempting to understand the dynamics of organizational fields must attend to both horizontal (exchange and competitive) and vertical (hierarchical) influences and to both local and distant forces. Early studies of interorganizational relations within communities often neglected to take into account the important connections between branch and headquarter units or between local units and regulatory agencies at the state and national levels (Scott and Meyer 1983). Fields encompass both organizational actors and relevant governance structures (Scott 1994).

Charting Change in Health Care Organizations
Changing Distributions of Institutional Actors

We begin by examining changes in institutional actors. Focusing on actors, we believe, provides a good descriptive account of changes in the demography of the field. Both individual and collective actors are of interest, but rather than attending to their individuating features, we emphasize their institutionalized components: the *roles* of individuals and the *forms* of organizations.

Within the Bay Area, individual consumers of health care services during the period of our study were becoming much more numerous, more urbanized, and more educated. Health care providers were also growing in numbers and becoming more specialized. Between 1945 and 1990, the physician-to-population ratio increased from 180 per 100,000 residents to over 300, and whereas in 1945 fewer than 30 percent of physicians were specialized, by 1990 more than 80 percent had qualified for such certification. At the national level, health care administrators became increasingly professionalized throughout the period, and the locus and nature of their training changed as well. In 1949, twelve training programs for health administrators were recognized, but by 1994 there were over sixty such programs. Earlier administrators received their training primarily in schools of public health, whereas later ones increasingly elected business school settings. By 1994 over one-third of the training programs for health administrators were either located within or affiliated with business schools (Scott et al. 2000, 216).

Organizational forms are defined by institutionalized models that specify what types of work are to be done by what types of personnel in what ways. The models also prescribe what kinds of social functions are to be insulated from one another or permitted to interact. During the period of our study traditional forms such as hospitals were confronted by new, competing models of health care delivery. Home health agencies, a reinvention of an earlier form, visiting nurse associations, emphasized home-based services as an alternative to expensive in-patient approaches. End-stage renal disease centers began as a specialized service within hospitals but increasingly were set up as independent units, an instance of a diffuse organizational service becoming "unbundled" and redeployed as a free-standing entity. Both of these forms depended greatly for their development on new, improved technologies as well as on specific public policies. ESRDCs also were buoyed by an unusual disease-specific federal funding program (Rettig and Levinsky 1991).

For their part, hospitals were set upon from all sides and confronted with competition from the new, specialized forms, reduced funding from health plans and federal agencies, and increased costs associated with higher patient acuity and advanced treatment techniques. Survival tactics included increased interdependence and collaboration with exchange partners, cooperation with former competitors, and the negotiation of contractual or ownership ties with the newly emerging delivery systems. These tactics often resulted in the creation of multiunit, integrated health care systems—systems that varied enormously in scope, "size, geographical spread, formal structure, type of ownership, degree of control, importance and permanence of connections, and, generally, in extent of 'systemness' " (Scott et al. 2000; see also Shortell et al. 2000). Hospitals, increasingly, are no longer free-standing, independent organizations but components of larger systems.

Without question, the most innovative and controversial organizational form to emerge during this period was the health maintenance organization. Adapting and extending an earlier prepaid direct services model that had long been condemned by the American Medical Association (AMA) as subordinating medical decisionmaking to economic criteria, HMOs were embraced by Washington politicians and policymakers in the early 1970s as a solution to reining in escalating health care expenditures (Starr 1982). HMOs represent a *hybrid* organization that blends two or more elements from (formerly) distinct forms of organizations (Haveman and Rao 2004). In this novel form, medical care delivery is combined with the insurance-financial function such that the economic effects of clinical decisions directly affect providers. Physicians practicing in HMOs are, to a variable degree, placed "at risk" financially for the medical decisions they make. The creation of the HMO provides a strong instance of the way in which new organizational forms embody new institutional logics, supporting and constraining individual actors to adopt new decision criteria and modes of practice.

Increases or decreases in the number of organizations embodying a given form provide one of the simplest and most powerful indicators of change occurring in an organizational field. Ecologists have argued that the prevalence of an organizational form is a valid indicator of that form's cultural-cognitive legitimacy—its "taken-for-grantedness" as the appropriate arrangement for carrying out a set of activities (Carroll and Hannan 1989). We extend this argument to suggest that comparing the *relative* density of organizational populations operating in the same field at the same time provides a good indicator of how these forms are faring in the competitive struggle for patients, dollars, and legitimacy. How were the five organizational forms doing relative to one another in the San Francisco Bay Area between 1945 and 1995?

Figure 10.1 reports changes in density for four of the five populations of interest. Eighty-two hospitals existed in the Bay Area in 1945, and eighty-two were still operating in 1992. (Of course, these were not necessarily the same hospitals.) As the Bay Area population tripled during this period, hospitals increased in numbers to a peak of one hundred fifteen in 1965 before beginning their slow but continuing decline. Indeed, those still surviving were shrinking: their capacity utilization dropped from about 75 percent to under 65 percent during this period. By contrast, the number of HMOs increased from only one provider in 1945 (one of the two original branches of Kaiser

FIGURE 10.1   *Bay Area Organizational Health Care Populations, 1945 to 1992*

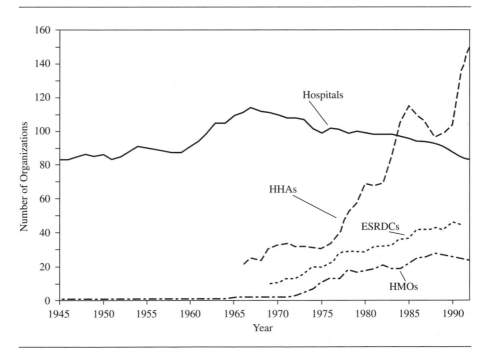

Source: Scott et al. (2000, 89). © The University of Chicago Press, 2000. Reprinted with permission.

Permanente) to twenty-three in 1995; HHAs increased over sevenfold, from twenty-one in 1966 to one hundred forty in 1995; and ESRDCs increased more than fourfold, from ten units in 1969 to forty-five in 1993. Data for the final population—integrated health care systems with Bay Area members— are not included in the figure but can be quickly summarized. The number of integrated health care systems more than doubled, from seven in 1945 to seventeen in 1995. The proportion of hospitals that were system members increased from under 15 percent in 1945 to almost 70 percent in 1995. The most important conclusion from this demography of organizational forms is that in the Bay Area, community hospitals—the diffuse, traditional form—have been losing out to the newer, more specialized provider forms (Scott et al. 2000, ch. 3).

Our data also reveal a shift in ownership arrangements among health care forms. Two distinctions are important: public versus private ownership and, if the latter, nonprofit versus for-profit status. Public ownership of health care facilities shows a marked decline. Government-owned hospitals declined from 40 percent in 1945 to 25 percent in 1992. There are virtually no publicly owned forms among the newer, specialized organizations. Hospitals continued to retain their nonprofit status, but among the specialized organizations (HMOs, ESRDCs, HHAs) the ratio of for-profits exceeded that of nonprofits in every case (Scott et al. 2000, ch. 4). Considering trends among all populations, Bay Area health care organizations during the period of study became increasingly privatized and for-profit, but hospitals, the most traditional population, remained predominantly nonprofit even as they moved toward privatization. Such trends are broadly consistent with those occurring in the country as a whole (see Gray and Schlesinger 2002).

Finally, if we examine the extensiveness of relations among provider organizations, we observe growing interdependence among all of them. Today's hospitals are much more likely than earlier versions to be affiliated with integrated health care systems. For example, in the Bay Area only about 10 percent of the hospitals in 1945 were affiliated with health care systems, whereas by 1995, 70 percent of the hospitals had become members of a system. Similarly, both horizontal and vertical integration among the various types of organizations had increased. All three specialized organizational types—HMOs, HHAs, and ESRDCs—were more likely to be affiliated with "chains" of similar forms. Vertical integration—between hospitals, HHAs, HMOs, and ESRDCs—also substantially increased after 1980, in the form of either contractual or ownership ties. More recent trends favor contracts over ownership (Scott et al. 2000, ch. 8).

In sum, in our longitudinal case study of changes in the health care delivery systems of the San Francisco Bay Area, we observed an organizational field within which significant populations of organizations were moving rapidly toward higher levels of specialization, concentration, private ownership, for-profit orientation, and interdependence.

Certainly, organizations and their leaders can by their actions influence the speed and direction of change. Prominent players in the Bay Area included Dr. Russell Lee, the founder of one of the earliest and most successful multi-specialty medical groups, and Henry J. Kaiser and Dr. Sidney Garfield, who together founded Kaiser Permanente, a prototype HMO-integrated health care system. On the other hand, most organizations reflect rather than instigate change. New models are more likely to emerge outside of organizations—this is particularly true of the kinds of organizations we are considering—as a consequence of changes in material resources (including new technologies), institutional logics (including political ideologies and professional practices), or governance systems (including public, associational, and corporate). To move from the "how" to the "why" of societal change, we need to examine changes in resources, beliefs, and power.

Explaining Change in Health Care Systems
Material Resources

Significant changes have occurred on both the demand and supply sides of health care. Demand for medical services rose as the number of individuals covered by insurance plans—public, commercial, and employer-sponsored—increased. Over time purchasers became increasingly concentrated, because of both the growing role of public programs and changes on the private side, including the growth of purchasing coalitions among employers (Berghold 1990) and greater consolidation of health plans (Robinson 1995, 1999). Major developments on the supply side included the increased specialization of individual providers, especially physicians, and the increasing ratio of physicians to the population, as described earlier. In addition, alternative providers, such as chiropractors and acupuncturists, increased in numbers and legitimacy.

Concentration among buyers in purchasing power (through medical insurance, employer associations, or public programs), together with increased competition (because of greater numbers) and fragmentation in interests (due to specialization) among physicians, reduced the economic bargaining power of physicians. Membership in specialty associations grew while membership in the general medical society, the American Medical Association, waned. These trends, in combination, worked to weaken the market position of physicians, as well as their political power, in the latter decades of the twentieth century.

Developments in health care systems were also greatly influenced by the expanding medical science base and associated pharmaceutical and techno-logical advances. Medical care services became more efficacious and expensive. The new technologies were both more powerful and more portable, encouraging the decentralization and specialization of service settings. Developments in information technologies made possible the current, complex contractual arrangements among physicians, health care organizations, and funding units, including public agencies and medical plans. A single medical plan can contract with and exercise fiscal oversight over diverse, geographically dispersed physicians and medical groups in a region.

Increased demand coupled with improved technologies and greater numbers of specialized providers have produced ever-increasing health care expenditures. Throughout the second half of the twentieth century, national health care expenditures rose continuously, from 4 percent of gross domestic product (GDP) in 1940 to almost 14 percent in 1995. Since the early 1970s, annual increases in health care prices have regularly exceeded the consumer price index (CPI). Not surprisingly, much health policy since 1970 has been aimed at reining in health care costs.

Material resources and their availability, distribution, and concentration have clear effects on organizational fields. However, these economic effects are always mediated through a set of changing social mechanisms and cultural lenses. The "demand" for a doctor's services is never a direct function of physician supply, insurance coverage, and disease patterns. The institutional landscape intervenes to guide preferences and choices and to construct and constrain available solutions.

Institutional Logics and Governance Systems

Having described some of the important changes that have occurred in the numbers and types of individual and collective actors and in material resources, we turn now to examine the remaining institutional components: logics and governance systems.

Institutional logics are the belief systems and basic assumptions that motivate and guide the behavior of field participants. Changes in belief systems—cognitive and normative structures—constitute fundamental changes in institutional environments (Alexander and D'Aunno 1990). To be active and in play, logics require carriers: individuals and organizations that affirm, embody, transmit, and act in accordance with the principles. Different logics tend to be associated with different types of actors. If the numbers and power of particular types of actors increase, the logics they carry increase in prevalence and influence and are more likely to be instantiated in reconstructed governance systems. Our empirical observations suggest that in the U.S. health care system three primary sets of logics—associated with three different governance regimes—were dominant at different times during the last half-century.

Era of professional dominance, 1920s to 1964. From the early part of the twentieth century until the mid-1960s, physicians enjoyed an unprecedented degree of "cultural authority" in the realm of medical services (Freidson 1970; Starr 1982). This era of professional dominance was characterized by the preponderance of independent practice and by physicians' ability to insist that their professional autonomy be recognized in the structuring of hospital staffs and financing arrangements. The overriding logic during this period was a focus on *quality of care*—at the clinical, not the epidemiological level—as defined by the physician. This value was employed to justify the physician's resistance to managerial and financial controls and to fuel the "medical arms race." The primary governance structures employed were professional systems, both formal and informal, operating at national, state, and local levels. The American Medical Association served as the unified and unchallenged voice of organized medicine (Garceau 1941). Public agencies played a secondary and circumscribed role. At the national level, they functioned primarily to subsidize the development of infrastructure (for example, federal funding for medical research and for hospital construction following World War II). At the state level, they served to reinforce professional controls (such as licensure systems). In this manner and at this time, the American approach to health care governance resembled the associational order adopted by Japan, as described by Bai Gao (this volume).

These institutional arrangements were firmly in place for a half-century and seemed unalterable. But signs of tension and weakness began to become evident around mid-century. From the 1950s forward, health care expenditures began their fluctuating but steady increase as physicians were unconstrained by financial or organizational controls in their pursuit of quality care—an objective also associated with enhanced professional income. And after 1960 the unity of physicians began to erode. The growth in medical specialization resulted not just in heightened expertise (and expense) but also in increased fragmentation of physicians' interests. Membership in specialty associations soared, but membership in the AMA began its decline—from a high of nearly 80 percent of practicing physicians in the 1950s to a low of 40 percent in 1990 (Scott et al. 2000, ch. 6). Thus, endogenous forces—unconstrained resource consumption fueled by the single-minded pursuit of medical logics and growing fragmentation in the political interests of physicians—opened the gates to change.

Era of federal involvement, 1965 to 1982. The year 1965 was without doubt the high-water mark of the Great Society programs spearheaded by President Lyndon Johnson and a Democratic congress. A societywide movement aimed at combating sources of inequality based on income or ethnicity was introduced into health care and translated as a need to improve access to services for underserved populations. In 1965 Congress passed the Medicare and Medicaid acts, providing publicly funded health care to the elderly and the indigent. For the first time the U.S. government was in the business of paying for direct health care services to large numbers of citizens: virtually overnight, the federal government became the purchaser of almost half of all medical services. The medical profession was still sufficiently strong and unified to ensure that the payment mechanisms accommodated concerns for physician autonomy (Starr 1982), but not strong enough to block legislation denounced by AMA leaders as leading to "socialized medicine." *Equity of access*—a political rather than a medical value—had joined quality of care as a guiding institutional logic.

Suddenly new types of actors—that is, actors who were new to the field (politicians, federal policymakers, and administrative officials)—were engaged in and occupied positions of power in the health care sector. They created new public governance structures at all levels. Funds had to be dispensed and accounted for, and because the new source of funds stimulated increased expenditures, new types of regulative and rate-setting agencies were soon created. The total number of federal health-related regulatory agencies overseeing Bay Area health care organizations grew from under ten in 1950 to over ninety by 1975 (Scott et al. 2000, 198). Physicians were obliged to share governance functions with bureaucrats, a situation that led to increased fragmentation in governance systems and inconsistent demands on provider systems. John Meyer and I (Meyer and Scott 1983) argue that organizations subject to conflicting demands from institutional agents of their environments are likely to suffer reduced legitimacy. Health care organizations found themselves in an increasingly conflicted environment, with physicians, managers, and patients all less certain of their rights and roles.

Era of managerial control and market mechanisms, 1983 to the present. As with the wider societal forces fueling the Great Society movement of the 1960s, the market-managerial era was primarily the product of broad (even international) changes in political ideologies of appropriate governmental structures. Earlier models of "public utility regulation," which had not succeeded in containing inflationary pressures in health care, became discredited as tools too easily captured by organized providers. During the Reagan period, these approaches began to be dismantled in health care and other sectors as a general wave of deregulation swept away many of the privileges previously enjoyed by the physicians' guild (Robinson 1999). Faith was instead placed in market-based controls as health providers were encouraged to compete on the basis of price and service. The new logic of public management applied to health care stressed the central importance of *efficiency* in medical care delivery.

Also originating outside the health care sector, a secondary logic that stressed the value of consumer choice and responsibilities began to appear in health care discourse (see Herzlinger 1997). An unanticipated consequence of this movement was to legitimate the application of conventional market mechanisms in a sector formerly declared exempt from such "commercial" considerations. Policy designers introduced incentives to encourage first consumers (with the use of deductibles and copayments) and then providers (using risk-sharing approaches) to reduce both the demand for and the supply of medical care services (Melhado 1988). Of course, the creation of a new health care delivery form, the HMO, was one of the principal mechanisms designed to alter physician incentives. Promulgated as the solution of choice by the Nixon administration in the early 1970s, this form did not begin its period of rapid growth until the early 1980s, when service requirements were relaxed and for-profit plans included.

More generally, a wide range of new organizational forms—including multispecialty groups, independent practice associations (IPAs), preferred provider organizations (PPOs), and physician-hospital organizations (PHOs)—were devised that, to a varying but increasing extent, subjected physicians to a wide variety of incentive systems and managerial controls (Robinson 1999). These forms have rapidly diffused (Scott et al. 2000, 86–88). Even traditional forms, such as community hospitals, are being incorporated within and sub-ordinated to these wider organizational governance systems. Managers, long marginalized in the health care sector, have moved to center stage (Leicht and Fennell 2001). Attentive to changes in the locus of authority, physicians increasingly seek managerial training, and a growing subset have been certi-fied as "physician executives" (Montgomery 1990).

In addition, corporate America determined that there was money to be made in delivering medical services. For-profit firms and health plans were rapidly introduced, and in 1975 the first company specializing in health ser-vices had found its way on to the list of the one thousand largest American cor-porations. By 1995 nearly thirty such companies were in business (Scott et al. 2000, 231).

The rhetoric of deregulation and market mechanisms implies that public controls over the delivery of health care are being dismantled. Such is not the case. Except for a slight decline in the mid-1970s, public governance systems have continued to grow in numbers. Federal health-related regulatory bodies with authority over Bay Area health care providers increased from approxi-mately ninety in 1975 to over one hundred thirty in 1995 (Scott et al. 2000, ch. 6). Thus, public controls continue to be exercised; only the mode of con-trol has changed.

In sum, in this third (and current) era, professional autonomy is more cir-cumscribed, while public, market, and managerial controls have been greatly expanded. After decades of being treated as an exception to the corporate models adopted by virtually all other industrial (including service) sectors, the health care field now increasingly resembles mainstream sectors in its orga-nizational forms and institutional logics.

The dynamics of change we have observed involve both endogenous and exogenous forces. Professionals were dominant for many decades, but over time they proved to be unable to organize in ways that could curb insupport-able cost increases or even to retain their own internal solidarity and political unity. Their declining political strength rendered them incapable of resisting two political tidal waves (both originating from outside health care), the first coming from the left, the second from the right. First, liberal reformers, under the banner of reducing inequality, broadened access to health care but were then forced to erect complex regulatory systems to deal with the resulting financial crisis of escalating costs. In the second wave, conservative reformers, wrapped in the bunting of free markets, attempted to increase efficiency by restructuring incentives and relying on more conventional organizational (managerial) controls.

Each of the three logics—physician-defined quality, public concern with equity of access, and managerial emphasis on efficiency and increased profits—was supported by (or gave rise to) a different governance structure (the professional association, the public bureaucracy, the private corporation) and carried by different types of actors, both individual and collective. A simple summary of this history would be to claim, using categories proposed by Wolfgang Streeck and Philippe Schmitter (1985), that the governance of the health care sector progressed from an association- to a state- to a market-centered framework. Although this statement captures the sequence of governance systems, it conceals the complexity of current arrangements. Professionals and their associations have not been replaced but continue to exert important power, particularly in research, educational, and clinical contexts. The state has by no means withdrawn from the scene but exerts its influence through a variety of mechanisms, earlier fiscal and regulatory controls having now been augmented by managerial and market tools. Exhibiting a process referred to as "bricolage" (Douglas 1986), sector actors, both individual and collective, have constructed new combinations of governance structures out of preexisting forms. Earlier regimes provide "a repertoire of already existing institutional principles (e.g., models, analogies, conventions, concepts) that actors use to create new solutions in ways that lead to evolutionary change" (Campbell 1997, 22).

Destructuration of Organizational Fields

Our study may be placed in a broader theoretical context if it is viewed as an instance of structuration-destructuration processes. Anthony Giddens's (1979, 1984) discussion of structuration emphasizes the ways in which social structures must continually be produced and reproduced by actors who construct schemata, enforce and alter rules, and deploy resources (see also Sewell 1992). These social structures are both the product of past actions and the context for current behavior. Institutions represent social structures that are strongly entrenched, giving "solidity" to social structures across time and space (Giddens 1984, 24), but even such structures are subject to change.

Paul DiMaggio (1988, 1991) insists that power and interests underlie all institutional arrangements. However, because most early institutional analysts concentrated on the diffusion of successful organizing models and on the processes leading to increasing isomorphism among organizational participants, the role of power and interests has been overlooked. As DiMaggio observes:

> The neglect by researchers of structuration processes provides a one-sided vision of institutional change that emphasizes taken-for-granted, nondirected, nonconflictual evolution at the expense of intentional (if boundedly rational), directive, and conflict-laden processes that define fields and set them upon trajectories that eventually appear as "natural" developments to participants and observers alike. (DiMaggio 1991, 268)

As an antidote, DiMaggio suggests that researchers focus on the early stages of the construction of an organizational field—a time when struggle and contention are likely to be more visible. Winners and losers can be identified as some groups overcome others in the struggle to write the rules and control the resources. DiMaggio's (1991) study of the art museum field in the United States and Yves Dezalay and Bryant Garth's (1996) study of the transnational field of commercial arbitration represent strong empirical case studies of the contending forces at work in the period when these fields were being constructed. But the role of power and interests can also be observed during periods when highly institutionalized fields confront crisis. Fields can undergo processes of destructuration as well as structuration. Our case describes an episode of the former during which entrenched interests were challenged, reconstituted, and forced to share power with new types of actors.

My colleagues and I view the changes occurring in the U.S. health care system during the second half of the twentieth century as an instance of the destructuration of, and beginning attempts to restructure, an organization field. DiMaggio and Powell (1983, 65) note that fields vary over time in their degree and type of structuration—their structural order and cultural coherence. They propose four markers of increased structuration: extent of interaction, sharply defined interorganizational structures, increase in information available, and development of mutual awareness. We build on and extend these criteria, identifying eight dimensions along which the structuration of fields can vary (Scott et al. 2000, 258–60).

1. Funding centralization: The extent to which financial resources employed by field actors are concentrated
2. Unity of governance: The extent to which governance structures are congruent in jurisdiction and consistent in the rules enforced
3. Public versus private mode of governance: The extent to which one mode of governance exercises uncontested power and authority over the field

4. Structural isomorphism: The extent to which organizational actors conform to a single or limited number of archetypes or structural models

5. Coherence of organizational (population) boundaries: The extent to which organizational forms in the sector exhibit clear, well-demarcated boundaries

6. Consensus on institutional logics: The extent to which central actors embrace and adhere to the same general beliefs and recipes for action

7. Organizational linkages: The extent to which there is a relatively high number of formal linkages among organizational actors

8. Clarity of field boundaries: The extent to which field actors are insulated from intrusions by "external" actors and logics

Using empirical evidence from our description of changes in the health care sector, we can broadly characterize the state of the field on each indicator during the three eras identified. Our conclusions are summarized in table 10.1. The general trend across the three eras is one of increased destructuration. Governance structures have become less unified. Structural isomorphism has been reduced so that a greater diversity of organizational forms now operate in the field. The coherence of organizational boundaries has been greatly reduced, and many blended and hybrid forms have been created. Consensus on institutional logics has been reduced: patients are confused by the multitude of plans; providers are less secure in their practice arrangements; and there is disagreement as to how health care should be funded. Field boundaries have become more permeable. The health care sector is no longer seen as a distinctive and protected arena and is more subject to external influences and alien logics and actors. Destructuration of the field has proceeded in all these ways during the past fifty years.

On the other hand, such processes are complex and do not all move in the same direction or at the same pace. Centralization of funding—an important

TABLE 10.1   *Field Dimensions and Institutional Eras*

	Professional Dominance	Federal Involvement	Market Orientation
Funding centralization	Low	High	Med
Unity of governance	High	Med	Low
Public/private mode of governance	Low	Med	Med
Structural isomorphism	High	Med	Low
Coherence of organizational boundaries	High	Med	Low
Consensus on logics	High	Med	Low
Organizational linkages	Low	Med	High
Clarity of field boundaries	High	Med	Low

Source: Scott et al. (2000, 362). © The University of Chicago Press, 2000. Reprinted with permission.

stimulant to increased structuration (see DiMaggio 1983)—increased between the first and second eras but did not lead to increased coherence in programmatic authority. Linkages among organizational actors have also increased, so that the field is now more densely connected. It appeared for a time that new corporate systems and hospital "chains" would increase order and provide more comprehensive and integrated care arrangements, but this did not come about. There is increased interdependence but reduced predictability and coherence.

With respect to shifting power and conflicting interests, the story is largely one of physicians being forced to share power with, first, federal agencies and their administrators, and then with corporate managers. The early rules that favored professional providers have been revised to incorporate first the interests of political actors and subsequently the interests of corporate managers and investors. Physicians and other professional providers exercise less control over resources, more of which are claimed by corporations. But on the other hand, some entrepreneurial physicians have moved quickly to exploit new resources made available by governmental programs. Sadly, general consumer and public health interests have not been advanced by the developing arrangements. However, the health care field remains a work in progress.

The first portion of this chapter draws heavily on an earlier paper prepared for Mick and Wyttenbach (2003). Helpful comments on this version were received from Carol A. Caronna.

References

Alexander, Jeffrey A., and Thomas A. D'Aunno. 1990. "Transformation of Institutional Environments: Perspectives on the Corporatization of U.S. Health Care." In *Innovations in Health Care Delivery: Insights for Organization Theory,* edited by Stephen S. Mick. San Francisco: Jossey-Bass.

Alford, Robert R. 1972. "The Political Economy of Health Care: Dynamics Without Change." *Politics and Society* 2: 127–64.

Berghold, Linda. 1990. *Purchasing Power in Health: Business, the State, and Health Care Politics.* New Brunswick, N.J.: Rutgers University Press.

Campbell, John L. 1997. "Mechanisms of Evolutionary Change in Economic Governance: Interaction, Interpretation. and Bricolage." In *Evolutionary Economics and Path Dependence,* edited by Lars Magnusson and Jan Ottosson. Cheltenham, Eng.: Edward Elgar.

Carroll, Glenn R., and Michael T. Hannan. 1989. "Density Dependence in the Evolution of Populations of Newspaper Organizations." *American Sociological Review* 54(4): 524–48.

Dezalay, Yves, and Bryant G. Garth. 1996. *Dealing in Virtue: International Commercial Arbitration and the Construction of a Transnational Legal Order.* Chicago: University of Chicago Press.

DiMaggio, Paul J. 1983. "State Expansion and Organizational Fields." In *Organizational Theory and Public Policy,* edited by Richard H. Hall and Robert E. Quinn. Beverly Hills: Sage.

———. 1988. "Interest and Agency in Institutional Theory." In *Institutional Patterns and Organizations: Culture and Environment,* edited by Lynne G. Zucker. Cambridge, Mass.: Ballinger.

———. 1991. "Constructing an Organizational Field as Professional Project: U.S. Art Museums, 1920 to 1940." In *The New Institutionalism in Organizational Analysis,* edited by Walter W. Powell and Paul J. DiMaggio. Chicago: University of Chicago Press.

DiMaggio, Paul J., and Walter W. Powell. 1983. "The Iron Cage Revisited: Institutional Isomorphism and Collective Rationality in Organizational Fields." *American Sociological Review* 48(2): 147–60.

Douglas, Mary. 1986. *How Institutions Think.* Syracuse, N.Y.: Syracuse University Press.

Fligstein, Neil. 2001. *The Architecture of Markets: An Economic Sociology of Twenty-first-Century Capitalist Societies.* Princeton, N.J.: Princeton University Press.

Freidson, Eliot. 1970. *Profession of Medicine: A Study in the Sociology of Applied Knowledge.* New York: Dodd, Mead.

Friedland, Roger, and Robert R. Alford. 1991. "Bringing Society Back In: Symbols, Practices, and Institutional Contradictions." In *The New Institutionalism in Organizational Analysis,* edited by Walter W. Powell and Paul J. DiMaggio. Chicago: University of Chicago Press.

Garceau, Oliver. 1941. *The Political Life of the American Medical Association.* Cambridge, Mass.: Harvard University Press.

Giddens, Anthony. 1979. *Central Problems in Social Theory: Action Structure and Contradiction in Social Analysis.* Berkeley: University of California Press.

———. 1984. *The Constitution of Society.* Berkeley: University of California Press.

Granovetter, Mark. 1985. "Economic Action and Social Structure: The Problem of Embeddedness." *American Journal of Sociology* 91(3): 481–510.

Gray, Bradford D., and Mark Schlesinger. 2002. "Health." In *The State of Nonprofit America,* edited by Lester M. Salamon. Washington, D.C.: Brookings Institution Press.

Greenwood, Roysden, and C. R. Hinings. 1996. "Understanding Radical Organizational Change: Bringing Together the Old and New Institutionalism." *Academy of Management Review* 21(4): 1022–54.

Greif, Avner. Forthcoming. *Comparative and Historical Institutional Analysis.* New York: Cambridge University Press.

Haveman, Heather, and Haygreeva Rao. 2004. "Hybrid Forms and Institution/Organization Coevolution in the Early California Thrift Industry." In *How Institutions Change,* edited by Walter W. Powell and Daniel L. Jones. Chicago: University of Chicago Press.

Herzlinger, Regina E. 1997. *Market-Driven Health Care: Who Wins, Who Loses in the Transformation of America's Largest Service Industry?* Reading, Mass.: Addison-Wesley.

Leicht, Kevin T., and Mary L. Fennell. 2001. *Professional Work: A Sociological Approach.* Malden, Mass.: Blackwell.

Melhado, Evan M. 1988. "Competition Versus Regulation in American Health Policy." In *Money, Power, and Health Care,* edited by Evan M. Melhado, Walter Feinberg, and Harold M. Swartz. Ann Arbor, Mich.: Health Administration Press.

Meyer, John W. 1994. "Rationalized Environments." In *Institutional Environments and Organizations: Structural Complexity and Individualism,* edited by W. Richard Scott and John W. Meyer. Thousand Oaks, Calif.: Sage Publications.

Meyer, John W., and W. Richard Scott. 1983. "Centralization and Legitimacy Problems of Local Governments." In *Organizational Environments: Ritual and Rationality,* edited by John W. Meyer and W. Richard Scott. Beverly Hills, Calif.: Sage Publications.

Mick, Stephen S., Mindy E. Wyttenbach, eds. 2003. *Advances in Health Care Organization Theory.* San Francisco: Jossey-Bass.

Montgomery, Kathleen. 1990. "A Prospective Look at the Specialty of Medical Management." *Work and Occupations* 17(2): 178–97.

North, Douglass C. 1990. *Institutions, Institutional Change, and Economic Performance.* Cambridge: Cambridge University Press.

Rettig, Richard, and Norman Levinsky, eds. 1991. *Kidney Failure and the Federal Government.* Washington, D.C.: National Academy Press.

Robinson, James C. 1995. "Health Care Purchasing and Market Changes in California." *Health Affairs* 14(4): 117–30.

———. 1999. *The Corporate Practice of Medicine: Competition and Innovation in Health Care.* Berkeley: University of California Press.

Schein, Edgar H. 1992. *Organizational Culture and Leadership.* 2nd ed. San Francisco: Jossey-Bass.

Scott, W. Richard. 1994. "Conceptualizing Organizational Fields: Linking Organizations and Societal Systems." In *Systemrationalitat und Partialinteresse,* edited by Hans-Ulrich Derlien, Uta Gerhardt, and Fritz W. Scharpf. Baden-Baden, Germ.: Nomos Verlagsgesellschaft.

———. 2001. *Institutions and Organizations.* 2nd ed. Thousand Oaks, Calif.: Sage Publications.

———. 2003. *Organizations: Rational, Natural, and Open Systems.* 5th ed. Upper Saddle River, N.J.: Prentice-Hall.

Scott, W. Richard, and Søren Christensen. 1995. "Crafting a Wider Lens." In *The Institutional Construction of Organizations: International and Longitudinal Studies,* edited by W. Richard Scott and Søren Christensen. Thousand Oaks, Calif.: Sage Publications.

Scott, W. Richard, Peter J. Mendel, and Seth Pollack. 2004. "Environments and Fields: Studying the Evolution of a Field of Medical Care Organizations." In *How Institutions Change,* edited by Walter W. Powell and Daniel L. Jones. Chicago: University of Chicago Press.

Scott, W. Richard, and John W. Meyer. 1983. "The Organization of Societal Sectors." In *Organizational Environments: Ritual and Rationality,* edited by John W. Meyer and W. Richard Scott. Beverly Hills, Calif.: Sage Publications.

Scott, W. Richard, Martin Ruef, Peter J. Mendel, and Carol A. Caronna. 2000. *Institutional Change and Healthcare Organizations: From Professional Dominance to Managed Care.* Chicago: The University of Chicago Press.

Selznick, Philip. 1957. *Leadership in Administration: A Sociological Interpretation.* New York: Harper & Row.

Sewell, William. 1992. "A Theory of Structure: Duality, Agency, and Transformation." *American Journal of Sociology* 98(1): 1–29.

Shortell, Stephen M., Robin R. Gillies, David A. Anderson, Karen Morgan Erickson, and John B. Mitchell. 2000. *Remaking Health Care in America: The Evolution of Organized Delivery Systems.* San Francisco: Jossey-Bass.

Starr, Paul M. 1982. *The Social Transformation of American Medicine.* New York: Basic Books.

Streeck, Wolfgang, and Philippe C. Schmitter. 1985. "Community, Market, State—and Associations? The Prospective Contribution of Interest Governance to Social Order." In *Private Interest Government: Beyond Market and State,* edited by Wolfgang Streeck and Philippe C. Schmitter. Beverly Hills, Calif.: Sage Publications.

11

TALKING ABOUT PROPERTY IN THE NEW CHINESE DOMESTIC PROPERTY REGIME

Deborah S. Davis

IN JANUARY 1998 the most popular legal advice journal in Shanghai published the following exchange between a reader and the editor of the journal's biweekly advice column:

COMRADE EDITOR,

The home where I now live with my mother originally was a publicly owned dwelling belonging to my father's employer and rented by my father. After the implementation of the housing reforms, I put out the cash to buy the home. In October 1996 my father died. My older brother not only did not come to console my mother, but even declared that he had inheritance rights to the home and was prepared to go to court to sue me. Please tell me, given that I purchased the home for which my father was previously the lessee when my father was still alive, does my older brother have any inheritance rights?

SIGNED: *Wu Min*

READER WU MIN:

In order to answer the question raised in your letter, we think it is necessary first to clarify what is an estate. According to Article 3 of the National Law of Inheritance, an estate is defined as all personal legal property handed down when a citizen dies, including the citizen's income, citizen's home, savings, and items of daily use, a citizen's tools, livestock, and household furnishings, a citizen's copyrights and patent rights, and other legal property. If the home where you now live with your mother or any part of this home belonged to your father as his personal legal property when he was alive, then when he passed away, that part of his property becomes his estate, and as his estate, your elder brother has inheritance rights. But if the situation was otherwise, that is, if as you state in your letter, the home was a publicly owned dwelling belonging to your father's work unit, and after the housing reform you purchased it, . . . then this home does not qualify as your father's personal legal property, does not qualify as his estate, and your older brother has no inheritance rights.

Minzu yu Fazhi 1(1998): 46

I first read this exchange between Wu Min and the editors of *Minzu yu Fazhi* in the fall of 1998 while conducting a study of the social consequences of privatizing Shanghai housing stock. Integral to the project were comparisons between statutory definitions of property rights and popular expectations toward ownership under the new conditions of market socialism. Review of the statutes documented a stepwise commodification of the rights of use, the rights of control, and the rights to alienate and transfer ownership, but they could not capture changes in popular attitudes. Even household surveys that documented which occupational groups were most likely to become owners did not adequately reveal how Shanghai residents understood their new rights as property owners (Davis 2002, 2003). Yet, as previous work on the reallocation of property rights in India, Latin America, and Eastern Europe has shown, new property regimes imposed from above are revised and resisted by the larger population in order to protect and assert their own immediate interests (Agarwal 1994; Deere and León 2001; Hann 1998; Stark 1996).

Moreover, as Christopher Hann (2002) and Katherine Verdery (1999) have demonstrated in their analyses of property disputes in postsocialist Europe, changes in property rights are most fundamentally about creating new relationships around property rather than the drafting of formal statutes. Therefore, the point of departure for understanding the institutionalization of a postsocialist property regime is investigation of how individuals—or groups of individuals—differentiate among different people's relationships to things. Or as Verdery (1999, 76) concludes in her study of postsocialist Romania: "Property is . . . about the boundaries between self and non-self, . . . and the self can also be collective." Only when we can identify enduring logics of entitlement within the moral argument and behavior of social actors can we understand the institutions of the postsocialist property regime.

The focus on the social construction of economic institutions extends, of course, beyond the particularities of the market transitions of postsocialist economies in Europe or China and exemplifies a core precept of economic sociology that, as Frank Dobbin (this volume) concludes, seeks "to develop explanations that root economic behavior in society" and privileges "human-made conceptions of how to be rational" over universal economic laws or "economic ideals that transcend society." The authors of several of the early chapters of this volume (for example, Charles Perrow and Bai Gao) illustrate how cognitive and normative frameworks at the national level create political institutions that over time produce enduring national distinctions. William Schneper and Mauro Guillén, in their study of hostile takeovers, also illustrate what Dobbin sees as the power of cultural tool kits when they demonstrate the key role of the "cognitive acceptance of stock trading" and "normative legitimacy for private property." My work on contemporary China thus works within the larger epistemological world of economic sociology but enters the discussion at the grassroots rather than national level by listening to individuals talk about competing claims to newly privatized, transferable real estate assets. Like Christopher Hann and Katherine Verdery, I am listening to the language of protagonists in property disputes in order to identify logics of entitlement that define social positions. And like many other authors in this volume, I use close study of one particular taken-for-granted socioeconomic phenomenon to demonstrate how a core economic institution—in this case, the institution of private property—is socially defined and institutionalized. Specifically through analysis of the transcripts from sixteen focus groups that discussed Wu Min's letter to the editor of *Minzu yu Fazhi,* this essay explicates how Shanghai men and women simultaneously drew on both the moral values of pre-Communist family justice and their past experiences with state socialism to understand competing claims to newly commodified private property. In this way, the essay demonstrates the importance of approaching the comparative study of property regimes in terms of bundles of meanings embedded in the institutions of family and kinship, the party-state, and the market.

The Rise and Fall of Collective Ownership

For the Communist victors in the Chinese Civil War, the superiority of collective ownership decisively shaped all public policy after the establishment of the People's Republic of China in October 1949. For urban households, one immediate outcome was precipitous disinvestment in privately owned dwellings and rapid institutionalization of housing as a decommodified welfare benefit.[1] Then, between 1992 and 1998, the central leadership abandoned this position and enthusiastically endorsed the advantages of private homeownership (Davis 2003; Li 1999; Tong and Hays 1996; Wang and Murie 1999; Zhou and Logan 1996). The impact of this repudiation was dramatic. At the end of the Mao era, less than 15 percent of the urban population had lived in privately owned dwelling; by 1999 not only was most real estate commodified, but most residents had become homeowners, according to *Zhongguo Fangdichan Bao* (Chinese Real Estate News) on May 19, 2000 (see also Li 2000).[2]

Because of the party's unwavering preference for collective ownership between 1950 and 1980, two generations of city-dwellers had lived within a decommodified residential property regime in which no one could buy new residential property and the majority lived in apartments allocated by their employers as a welfare benefit (Bian et al. 1997; Chen and Gao 1993; Davis 1993; Lee 1995; Lee 1988). Under these conditions, the concept of the home as family property, which had been central in pre-Communist years, atrophied to the point of extinction.

At marriage, urban couples queued with the housing office of their employers or the municipal real estate bureau. There was no possibility of taking a loan or using family savings to purchase a new dwelling. Moreover, because public investment for new housing estates dried up in the 1960s, crowding increased to the point that three-generation living was more common during the 1970s than it had been twenty years earlier (Wang and Murie 1999; Whyte 1993).

However, even when parents sheltered married children and created multigeneration households, urban apartments could function neither as family property nor as a parental estate. During the collective era enterprise housing could not be sold, rented out, or inherited by the tenants. Rather, within the decommodified property regime the criteria for making a just claim to an urban home were politicized and bureaucratic.

In need of a new apartment, employees approached the housing officer citing unbearable crowding or an intolerable commute. In turn, the officials in the housing office decided which "supplicants" were most worthy (Davis 1993). Within an overarching logic of need, housing was assigned on the basis of job rank and seniority. However, if an individual applicant was politically tainted because he or she was the child or grandchild of a pre-1949 capitalist or had close relatives who had fled to Taiwan, that person's request would be deemed less worthy than that of the individual whose family tree included no such political pariahs. High-ranking military officers and party officials lived in separate compounds, but even they were assigned rental units by rank and seniority.

When the employee registered as the head of the household died, the surviving spouse was permitted to remain, but the right to rent could not routinely be passed on to the next generation. And in no case could children who were not coresident inherit the right to rent the home, use the dwelling as collateral for a loan, or sell use-rights to create a legacy. Thus, when the housing reforms of the 1990s recommodified urban housing stock and made the family home into fully capitalized, alienable property (Davis 2003; Gu 2001; Wang and Murie 1999), the new policies necessitated new logics of entitlement.

To identify the criteria for just property claims as defined by the party-state and its agents, we can turn to court cases and media coverage (Davis 1999). However, neither the statutes and casebooks nor the news media can capture the understandings of ordinary citizens. In particular, such sources are silent as to how individuals or groups of citizens understand and negotiate competing claims. Yet from prior work on "claim-making" in capitalist versus socialist settings and urban versus rural ones (Burawoy and Verdery 1999; Singer 2000; Thireau and Wang 2001), we know that the criteria that ordinary citizens invoke to decide just possession—or dispossession—create the practices of new property regimes and define subsequent property relations. For this essay, I turned away from casebooks and media to focus groups created specifically to capture the popular discourse emerging in postsocialist Shanghai.

The Data and Research Design

Disputes over the inheritance of a parental estate by two or more heirs provide an ideal setting to capture the vocabulary, syntax, and logic of claims to property. By asking a variety of men and women to discuss their views of how best to divide a parental estate, we have a natural laboratory to record potentially competing logics of entitlement. For several reasons, however, it is not easy to gather data systematically in this "natural laboratory." First, most individuals deal with the division of a parental estate only once or twice in their lifetime, and only a small number of heirs ever dispute the division. Thus, in a random sample of even a large population there will be few respondents who could draw from personal experience since the onset of housing reform. Second, inheritance disputes are painful experiences that are not easy to discuss with strangers, even in the abstract. And finally, there are widely circulating "correct answers" for how best to divide a parental estate. For example, in urban China most respondents know that legally men and women should have equal property rights and that parents should care for all their children equally well. Yet those justifying their claim to a parental estate may find that "incorrect answers" are actually the most decisive, or they may invoke multiple criteria simultaneously.

To overcome these barriers to data collection and also take advantage of the natural laboratory of inheritance disputes, I ran a series of focus groups in which I asked each group to respond to Wu Min's letter. A pretest was done in the summer of 1999 when I asked two groups of women and two groups of men divided by age to discuss the letter.[3] However, because the men and women who held blue-collar or service jobs systematically deferred to the college-educated professionals, I subsequently assembled groups that were homogenous on gender, occupational class, and age. The first groups met in July 2000, the second ones in May 2002. In each of these two sessions, the group met for ninety minutes, seated around a table in a medium-size meeting room. Each session was led by a professional associate. The leader explained that the research goal was to understand the impact of the recent housing reforms, but the leader asked no specific question and offered no hypothesis. None of the participants had known each other prior to the sessions, and none were chosen because they had experienced an inheritance dispute. In each session the leader read Wu Min's letter and then asked the participants how they would answer him. Over the course of the ninety-minute session the leader encouraged every participant to speak. In both sessions respondents discussed more than one dispute and were asked for their reactions.[4] All sessions were recorded and then transcribed in Chinese.[5]

The Language and Logic of Property Claims

When the magazine editor answered Wu Min, he focused first on the definition of personal legal property as defined by the 1985 inheritance law and then concluded that the decisive issue was whether or not the father had ever owned the home prior to his death as personal legal property. Because the father had not owned the property as his personal legal property, the editor wrote, the older brother had no claim. Thus, in his answer the editor disregarded considerations about Wu Min's current coresidency with his mother, his past joint household with his father, and his claim that his older brother had been unfilial. In short, in contrast to some legal scholars (Foster 1998, 1999) who have praised the Chinese justice system for linking behavior and bequests in the Chinese case law, the *Minzu yu Fazhi* editor invoked a straightforward market logic that disregarded the letter writer's coresident status and the older brother's unfilial behavior: the younger son had used his own money to buy the apartment from his father's employer, and thus the younger son had all rights of ownership.

The men and women in the focus groups perceived Wu Min's situation as far more complicated than it had appeared to the magazine editor, and they spent a great deal of time evaluating the information on the family's past and current domestic relationships. Only one fifty-year-old female manager took the inheritance law as her first point of departure, and only four other professionals and one young male truck driver made the inheritance law central to their discussion. Also of note was that even after these individuals had framed their argument in terms of the law, no one else in their group responded with further discussion of the law.[6] Instead, the participants overwhelmingly evaluated the competing claims of Wu Min and his brother by invoking principles of entitlement rooted in the norms of family justice or in the regulatory practices of state socialism. Moreover, they were able to invoke both the logic of family justice and the logic of the regulatory state even as they accepted the rights of individual ownership and market exchange. Let us now examine in detail the vocabulary and logic of their multidimensional arguments about just property claims in postsocialist Shanghai.

Family Justice

In each group several participants emphasized the need to preserve family harmony and to consider the past and current behavior of all family members. Thus, someone in each group qualified his or her views in terms of the need to be fair in dealing with family obligations and the actual needs of each family member. In group 1—the only group in which all four participants quickly agreed that the older brother had no inheritance rights[7]—there also was consensus that more than a simple legal decision was involved. For example, participant 1, who was the first to cite the decisive role of new legal procedures, qualified his position by suggesting the possibility that contrary to Wu Min's statement, the older brother may have been more filial to the father than the younger, and that if this were true, then the older brother should get at least a share. Participant 3, a thirty-four-year-old male computer programmer, then amplified this point by emphasizing the need for siblings to treat one another equitably in order to avoid the trauma of lifelong enmity.

In group 2, two women supported the older brother, one supported the younger brother, and one could not make up her mind. Nevertheless, all four of these young professional women grounded their decision in some aspect of family relationships. Most notably, they stressed that a history of coresidency and the relative housing needs of the two siblings could trump the letter of the law. Participant 6, a thirty-year-old female researcher who actually supported the older brother on the assumption that the younger brother had purchased the home at a steep discount, also made clear that the older brother's claim was not absolute. She summarized her view this way:

> I think that the elder brother should still have a part of the inheritance. How-ever, I think that he should consider that the younger brother had been support-ing his parents for so many years. He did not fulfill his duty to support his parents, and in fact his younger brother had been shouldering this duty. In that case, the elder brother might consider that although he had the right, consider-ing the circumstances, he should give up the right of inheritance.

This concern with coresidence and the years of support that the women in group 2 articulated also emerged during all twelve subsequent groups and was given even greater elaboration. In the following remarks, participant 24, a twenty-four-year-old female factory worker, participant 27, a fifty-one-year-old male electrician, and participant 40, a thirty-four-year-old female factory worker, explain the importance of mitigating circumstance regardless of which sibling's claim they favored:

> PARTICIPANT 24: I think the older son should have the right to inherit because the par-ents' or the father's housing could be inherited by every member of the family. Each child had a share. Even though this younger brother bought the place, I think the other children still had the right to co-inherit, right? However, it is necessary to investigate the behavior of the other children, right? Because this letter did not mention the duty of the children, they should investigate to see if they fulfilled their filial responsibility to sup-port the parents. There should be an investigation, and they should decide according to the particular circumstances.

> PARTICIPANT 27 (*when asked if he had a solution*): I would say, what on earth was the elder brother thinking? The mother is living with the younger brother, right? Now, he bought this place, and from now it became the house of their family. If the elder brother wants to support the mother and also pay some money, then they can divide the place equally in the future. But right now the elder brother has another home, and the younger has only this one he shares with their mother. Currently the younger son is living with the mother and caring for her. If the elder brother wants to take care of her, wants some prop-erty rights, and also offers some money, then he can have half or a third. They can easily negotiate.

> PARTICIPANT 40: The mother's arrangements should be followed. The apartment should be given to whomever the mother chooses. It also depends on how the older son fulfilled

his duties to his elders. If he did not fulfill his duties, then his demand for half the apartment should not be considered at all. But if he was adequately filial, then he should get some reward.

The other central criterion that the women in group 2 introduced and that subsequently surfaced in every group was the question of necessity.[8] Thus, when one participant asked others to consider the housing situation, most agreed that if the older brother had inadequate housing, then the younger brother needed to find a way to help him even if legally the younger brother had full property rights. Participant 13, a fifty-one-year-old female statistician, summarized this typical understanding of the primacy of necessity:

Everyone hopes all things could conform to reason and law, but in fact what is legal is not necessarily reasonable. For instance, in this case it is not very reasonable from the perspective of moral principle, but it is legal from the perspective of law. The younger brother bought the place, and it became his legal property. According to the law, the elder brother did not have the right to inherit it. But if the older brother was in financial difficulties, and if his own home was crowded, from the perspective of moral principle the younger brother should somehow aid him financially. This would be reasonable, but the law would not protect it.

But when participants raised the possibility that the older brother was already well housed and therefore had no pressing need for new accommodation, the argument became even more multidimensional. In the comments of participant 8, a twenty-eight-year-old manager at an insurance company, and participant 60, a twenty-nine-year-old truck driver, we see how familiarity and experience with the regulatory state contextualized the invocation of the logic of family justice.

PARTICIPANT 8: Different people will have different ways to deal with this issue, right? For example, if this elder brother was well-to-do and had his own home, then he probably won't want this place. Because, after all, he was already living elsewhere, and he did not take good care of his parents, while the younger brother did take care of them. Also, when the younger brother bought this place, he must have made the purchase relying on his father, because normally when you buy discounted housing, the one with the longest employment history gets the biggest discount. So ordinarily, the younger brother's employment history would not have been used. There should have been an agreement between the younger brother and the parents. But whether the older brother was informed is not clear. Just now [participant] 6 mentioned this issue of discounts. This house was not a fully commercial sale—it was rather after-sale public housing, and there must have been a big discount. The elder brother must enjoy part of that discount. Of course, in practice the older brother could consider that the younger brother supported the parents more, and the older brother could not ask for the money. However, his right is still there.

PARTICIPANT 60: This was the situation of my own family. My father has a flat. It originally belonged to my father's aunt, who had never married. My dad was her nephew. Auntie had four nephews and nieces in Shanghai. At that time, only my auntie had her official household registration at that publicly owned apartment, so if after she died, in terms of household registration, no one else was involved and the apartment would then be taken by the state. So then my mother spoke with Auntie about whether we could register someone else (in addition to Auntie) as a household member. My auntie agreed, and afterward my mother discussed it with the other uncles. They said none of them had the possibility to move a registration, and none had the energy to work on this. So my mother then moved my household registration into my auntie's house. In 1993, when the sale of publicly owned flats to sitting tenants began, my uncles noted that because this apartment was my auntie's, they also had inheritance rights. Afterward my whole family moved into the place, and we took care of Auntie. Two years later she died. Afterward we went to seek the advice of a lawyer, and he said that my uncles absolutely did not have inheritance rights because at that time (when we moved my household registration) publicly owned flats could not be inherited; rather, it was a question of the names on the official household registry. Whoever had their name in the household registry, then they were the heirs.

Regulatory State Socialist Logic and Housing Assets

During the first set of focus groups in 2000, at least one participant in each group spontaneously distinguished between the situation of Wu Min and situations where the home had either been an old private home that had always been in a family's possession prior to the reforms or was newly built commercial property. When the property at issue was an old private home, participants agreed that both sons would have equal claims regardless of their current residency, on the grounds that all family members were entitled to a share when, as participant 7 put it, the home had been handed down from "the ancestors." By contrast, when the property was a newly built commercial flat, participants thought that only the current owner had a claim. However, as discussion progressed some participants focused on the source of the money used to pay for the commercial property, arguing that if parents had paid for a child's commercial property, then other siblings might indeed have a claim. Thus, in discussion of all types of housing, the logic of family justice remained a key moral anchor.

Most complicated were disputes, like that between Wu Min and his brother, in which the property had originally been a publicly owned rental home. In these cases, participants entwined the logic of the regulatory state with that of family justice. For example, in the earlier remarks of participant 8, we hear how decisive were the special discounts that the state had given to sitting tenants when public housing was privatized. And participant 60 shows us how strictly families understood their rights to residential property and ownership within the administrative regulations of the household registration bureaucracy.

On the basis of these distinctions rooted either in individual household registration or more generally within the socialist property regime, we identify a second major axis of entitlement: a "regulatory state socialist logic" that was invoked even by those who consistently stressed the centrality of new legal procedures. For example, we hear this clearly in the answer of participant 3, a thirty-four-year-old programmer at a private Web company, as he explains how the past experience of housing as a welfare benefit of the regulatory state affected even the undisputed claim of an only son.

> Before I rented my old place, my dad had rented the place. But when my employer was going to assign me a new rental place, they calculated my allocation including the space my dad had rented and assigned me the bigger flat that I later bought in my name. But my father ultimately had half of the use rights . . . at least half. So in my heart it is impossible to make him move out. Even if I had to move, I would not make him move out. Right? After all, without my father's place in the beginning, I wouldn't have had this place.

Contingent Entitlements

Participants in the July 2000 focus groups spontaneously differentiated the situation of Wu Min, whose family home had originally been a publicly owned flat, from situations in which families lived in a home they had owned continuously since 1949 or in a home purchased outright since 1990. In short, people navigated with a moral gyroscope that triangulated between three systems of residency and ownership. However, because not every person in the 2000 focus groups relied on these distinctions, and not every group spent equal time embedding its arguments in these property distinctions, I could not be sure that the logics of entitlement really pivoted around housing type. Thus, in May 2002 I organized a second round of focus groups in which participants considered Wu Min's original dispute with his brother, disputes over a parental home that had always been privately owned, and a third dispute in which the home was a newly built commercial property.[9] The conditions of the father's death, current coresidence, and lack of concern for the mother were identical in each case, but in the second two cases there was no history of the home having originally been a rental in the father's name.

Overall, the pattern of response in the two sets of focus groups was identical. In 2002, as in 2000, only one-third of the participants agreed with the editor that the previously publicly owned rental unit now indisputably belonged to the younger brother.[10] Rather, as illustrated in the quotes from participants 40 and 60, participants weighted the relative needs of the two brothers, the amount of care each had given to the parents, past patterns of coresidency, the specifics of household registration, and the source of the money and the meaning of state discounts.

But as in 2000, the logic of entitlement varied systematically with the type of housing stock. When the home had always been owned by the family, only 9 percent (three out of thirty-two) of the participants would deny the older brother's claim. By contrast, when the home was a formerly public apartment, 27 percent (ten out of thirty-one) held this view, and when the home was a new commercial flat, 72 percent (twenty-three out of thirty-two) were confident that the older brother's ownership claims were groundless. Among the participants in May 2002, we also can identify a distinctive vocabulary, emphasis, and order of argument according to the type of property in dispute. Let me now summarize the pattern for the three types of homes.

The Always Privately Owned Home and the Logic of the Family Estate

In the case of the always privately owned home, participants more quickly focused on the situation of the mother than in any of the other cases. I quote from an exchange between a forty-seven-year-old clerk and a fifty-five-year-old textile worker:

> PARTICIPANT 32: If mother is still alive, the older brother then should not raise this thing about inheriting a home. If mother is not alive, then, just as these several comrades said, everyone gets equal shares.

> PARTICIPANT 33: Just now everyone spoke really well. What I have heard is also my view. I have no other view. If mom is alive, then mom is the first heir and the older brother cannot raise this thing about dividing the property. The house was the dad's, so to demand a division now is simply outrageous. If mom is not alive, then he and the younger brother both have inheritance rights.

These remarks were made in the first three minutes of a discussion among four middle-aged women with blue-collar service jobs, but there was a similar focus on the rights of the mother in the other groups. In the group of middle-aged professional women, participant 36, who was the second to speak in her group, immediately emphasized the mother's legal right to half the father's property. In the group of younger women with blue-collar service jobs, participant 41, a thirty-four-year-old clerk, stressed the importance of the sons' care of their mother. In her view, if the older brother cared for the mother less than the young son, he still had an inheritance claim to the family home, but his share should be proportional to the care he gave. However, at the end of the discussion among these young women in blue-collar and service jobs, participant 43, a twenty-eight-year-old cashier at a supermarket, moved away from viewing the mother as a passive object of concern and emphasized her right to dispose of the house as she wished: "If mother wanted to give a share to the older son, then she could give it." These issues of the mother's rights as the father's heir, the importance of filial behavior toward the mother, and the mother's power to decide also appeared among young female professionals and all the male groups when the property under dispute was one that had always been privately owned.

In assessing claims to the always privately owned home, many participants in May 2002 raised the question of a will, an argument that was not raised very often in July 2000. Across the eight groups in 2002, the argument was the same. If the father had written a will and cut out the older son, then, participants agreed, the older had no claim. But if there was no will, then the older son had a claim to the family property, as did all family members. However, the size of the older son's claim and the time at which he could take his share would be decided by all members' current needs and past behavior. Participant 39, a forty-nine-year-old administrator, explained her views:

> Well, if we look at it from the perspective of the property law, then I agree with [participants] 36 and 37 [that both brothers have the right to inheritance unless the father left a will cutting out the older son]. But here there is a question about how to divide the property. I think in regard to assessing the care of the parents, as was just pointed out by [participant] 38 [participant 38 had linked the older brother's share to the degree of care], care for a parent can be provided in many forms. If one doesn't live with the parent, one can still fulfill one's duty to care in other ways. Here the younger brother lived with the mother, so physically he was there to give care. I also am thinking the mother is still alive, so actually they have not arrived at the time to divide the property. If the older brother now insists on dividing the property, then I think he is expropriating his mother's inheritance right, and morally he shouldn't make this claim.

The Previously Publicly Owned Rental Unit and the Logic of the Regulatory State

When participants discussed the case of the formerly publicly owned home, their first question frequently centered on the names on the deed and the names on the household registration, both at the time of the dispute and when the property was first purchased. Thus, in contrast to the arguments about the always privately owned house—in which the technical-legal issue was whether or not the father had explicitly disinherited an interstate heir—here the question related to the bureaucratic procedures of the household registration system created by the Communist party-state. According to this line of reasoning, ownership claims pivoted around the technicalities of the Communist household registration system regardless of which names were on the deed. Participant 49, a forty-six-year-old man working in a Chinese medicine factory, drew on his own experience to demonstrate this logic:

PARTICIPANT 49: The key is that previously this was a rented place, and now [they] want to buy the property rights, so you take the household registration book and you go and register. Those people not officially registered simply have no connection.

GROUP LEADER: You mean that those who are not included in the household registry have no property interests?

PARTICIPANT 49: Right, absolutely none.

GROUP LEADER: If other brothers who are not officially registered as residents come to discuss the situation at the time the house goes on sale and they decide that the younger brother will put up the money, then the older ones have no inheritance right, right? But if at that time the older brothers considered that the younger brother was in financial difficulty and so he put up the money, then what?

PARTICIPANT 49: It still belongs to the younger brother. Just like when I bought my old place. I went to the real estate office to handle all the procedures for the contract; they verified the names on the household registration book and closed the deal. Those others whose names were not in the registration book then had no relationship to this real estate property.

But while the language of the state registration system framed the discussion of Wu Min's case in both July 2000 and May 2002, few participants saw the administrative procedure of the household registration system as definitive, as did participant 49. Rather more representative was the perspective that participant 60 attributed to his mother in making claims to the childless aunt's home, or the perspective of participant 47, whose remarks will conclude this section. In these more typical arguments, participants weighed competing property claims within a moral framework that entwined the logic of family justice with the logics of the state and the market.

I know a case. This was public housing. The father passed away, and the elder son was discussing with the younger son about buying the house. At that time, the younger son clearly indicated that he would not participate. He had already bought a one-hundred-square-meter place with three bedrooms and two living rooms elsewhere, and his family even hired a maid. He was very well-to-do. At that time, the elder son and his wife were both laid off and had no money. Their relatives in Hong Kong were sympathetic with the elder son and offered some money to help the elder son buy the place. Now this house is worth 300,000 yuan, and the younger son then requested that he would also have a chance to inherit part of the place. His reason was that the parents were not fair to the children. The elder son said to the younger son, "You were in such good situations that you could buy a one-hundred-square-meter house while I was laid off? Why should you come back and take a share?" The younger son said, "If you don't agree, I'll go to court and sue you." The elder son said, "Let's see each other in the court." After some time, the younger son came back and told the elder son, "Forget it. We siblings should not become enemies. If you give me 50,000 yuan, I'll let it pass, and I can feel justified." The elder son did not agree. After some more time, the younger son said 8,000 yuan would do, and the elder son agreed, but told his younger brother: "If you want that 8,000 yuan, you'll have to wait till my child starts to work."

I've heard that this issue is still not resolved. The younger son even transferred his household registration back to his mother's place, but the housing certificate used the elder son's name. The younger son said, "Anyway, you shall need my signature if you want to sell this place." The elder son said, "I'm living here till my death and will never sell it." All the other family members, including the mother, supported the elder son.

The Newly Built Commercial Home and the Logic of the Law and the Market

When the dispute involved newly built commercial housing and the letter identified the younger brother as the property owner, not a single participant said that the older brother had an undisputed claim to the apartment, and 72 percent definitively rejected his demand for any share of the flat after the father's death. Moreover, in comparing the content and sequence of the discussion of the new commercial flat with those for the other two kinds of property, respondents in all groups spoke more consistently in what I call a logic of the law and the market. However, the logic of family justice still established priorities and emphasis.

Thus, for example, the question that raised doubts and created sustained discussion was not about the presence or absence of a will, the names on the household registry, or the quality of filial care. Rather, the issue that animated the debate over the commercial real estate dispute was the source of financing. Many thought that if the parents had made a major contribution to the purchase by the younger brother, and if the older brother had received nothing from the parents to buy a home of his own, then the younger brother had the legal rights to the house but was obliged to give his older brother a monetary gift. On the other hand, if the older brother already was well housed, then the younger brother did not need to give him anything, and the older brother's demand was totally unreasonable. I conclude by quoting from an exchange between two young professional women to illustrate how even when the situation of commercial housing is first presented within the framework of market transactions and legal definitions, ownership claims continued to be understood in terms of the morality of intergenerational family ties.

PARTICIPANT 45: I think the older brother has no right to this flat. Commercial housing belongs to whoever purchased it. However, if the younger son was really nice and felt that the relationship with his brother was strong and that the brothers depended on each other for their survival, or if the older brother was in financial difficulty, then the younger brother could give the older one some compensation. But that is really for him to decide.

PARTICIPANT 44: I agree with [participant] 45. The younger brother's name was the name on the certificate of ownership, so it was the younger son's property. As for the source of the money, it has no influence. Even if you had evidence that the money came from the mother's bank account, as [participant] 46 mentioned before, or even if his parents openly gave the money, the parents must have known that the younger brother's name was on the certificate of ownership. So that proves that it was their intention to give it to the younger one as a gift.

Logics of Entitlement in a Postsocialist Domestic Property Regime

When the Chinese leadership relegitimated private ownership and enthusiastically created the new hybrid of market socialism, they opened the way for private real estate development and created the conditions for a new logic of entitlement defined by rules of individual property and private ownership.

Not only was it now good to get rich, but entrepreneurs became exemplars of modernity, and private real estate investment a primary engine of economic growth. Local governments and state-owned banks, which had systematically treated housing as a nonproductive welfare good, now imposed mandatory provident funds and urged urban residents to take advantage of twenty-year home mortgages. Emblematic of the new commercial discourse of market socialism were advertisements in Shanghai's largest publicly owned newspaper that urged readers to "buy a home, become a boss!" (Fraser 2000, 35).

When scholars first evaluated the trajectory for privatizing ownership claims in China, they focused on the privatization of industrial assets and land (Putterman 1995; Oi and Walder 1999). The argument was framed in the language of economists and legal scholars. One extremely useful distinction first introduced by the nineteenth-century lawyer Sir Henry Maine and more recently popularized by the economist Harold Demsetz (1967) was to disaggregate property ownership into three distinct bundles of rights: the right of use or control, the right to derive income or return, and the right to transfer or alienate. In this chapter and elsewhere (Davis 2003), I build on these well-established distinctions because they usefully disaggregate the omnibus concept of market transition into more analytic processes that facilitate comparisons across nations and historical eras. However, as others have documented—most notably, the anthropologist Christopher Hann (1998, 2002)—the semantic distinctions between rights of use, return, and alienation fail to incorporate the moral reasoning and conceptual distinctions of ordinary people as they develop a logic of just ownership in postsocialist societies.

Thus, as we learned from the discussion of the focus-group participants, despite the rapid creation of a new urban property regime, Shanghai residents rely on a moral calculus that incorporates the experience of earlier eras of state socialism and pre-Communist familism even as they accept the legitimacy of market-based individual property rights. However, they also see the contradictions between new property laws and the need for justice when the house itself has a history as collectively owned property or when the desire for family harmony and justice justifies multiple claims. For these Shanghai residents, therefore, the bundles of newly marketized property claims could best be allocated by relying on a bundle of meanings that triangulate between the moral logics of the party-state, the property markets, and family justice.

In her pathbreaking study of the social meaning of money, Viviana Zelizer (1994) addresses the misconceptions in previous one-dimensional assumptions about market money that presumed that increased monetization transforms society and drives out nonpecuniary values. Through a study of household budgeting, gift-giving, and U.S. welfare reforms between 1870 and 1930, Zelizer employs the concept of earmarking to demonstrate how the seemingly "qualitatively neutral" (12) currency of market exchange is used by consumers to "preserve moral categories" (24). Even as monetization and rationalization offer increased opportunity to depersonalize economic transactions, she points out, earmarking of money becomes ever more elaborated. Moreover, Zelizer argues, social categories and norms are as likely to direct economic practices as vice versa, and they are particularly salient at moments of conflict or difficulty.

In contemporary urban China, we observe another example of the centrality of social norms and the utility of earmarking during a period of increased monetization and marketization. Prior to 1990, the majority of urban residents lived in collectively owned flats that were distributed as a workplace benefit and for which they paid minimal rents. Homeownership was a residual of the pre-Communist era, and a fully elaborated socialist property system defined legal rights and duties. Within a decade the entire situation was turned on its head. Private ownership has now become the norm, the legal system consistently stands on the side of individual property rights, and the party-state is pressing for ever greater monetization of goods and services. Yet, at moments of conflict, such as that confronted by Wu Min, people reject the market-based, legal logic of the magazine editor and ground their decisions by earmarking the properties according to the rules under which families first established residency. When the property at issue had been a private home of the family before 1949, they disregard the legal argument about what constitutes an estate and instead emphasize a moral logic of family justice rooted in millennia of Confucian familism. When the property at issue had originally been a collectively owned rental, they invoke both the logic of family justice and their experience with the socialist regulatory state. Even when the property is a newly built commercial property that has had no existence prior to market reforms, people continue to give weight to the norms of sibling equity, family unity, and filial piety. Comparative analysis of property rights gains precision and rigor when we unbundle the rights into component claims. Grounding these claims in past experiences and the moral arguments of those who claim those rights reveals the societal matrix and practices in which a new property regime becomes institutionalized.

The author wishes to thank Professor Hanlong Lu and his colleagues at the Shanghai Academy of Social Sciences, who supervised the focus groups and transcriptions; without their outstanding professional support, the analysis in this chapter would have been impossible. A Cheng-Lee faculty research grant from Yale University provided the necessary financial support.

Notes

1. In China's biggest cities, between 10 and 20 percent of housing remained privately owned after 1950. But most of these privately owned homes were simple, usually dirt-floored cottages without modern plumbing. By contrast, all new modern residential dwellings built after 1951 were collectively owned property provided as a welfare benefit. By the 1970s the percentage of owners had stabilized at about 15 percent. Rents averaged less than 5 percent of household incomes, and for the wealthiest families with the largest flats, rents were trivial (Gu 2001; Whyte and Parish 1984, 82).

2. Because of the influx of migrants from rural areas who rarely purchased a home, the percentage of privately owned dwelling units exceeds the percentage of households who had an ownership claim, but whether we estimate ownership levels for total population or for total households, the slight majority are owners. In any case, most housing units have been privatized and are either rented out by the owner or owner-occupied.

3. Half of the group were under age thirty-five, and half were between forty-five and fifty-five.

4. In 2000 the second letter described a dispute among three siblings over a mother's bequest. In 2002, in addition to Wu Min's original letter, participants were read two other letters in which the family situation was identical but the house in dispute either had always been privately owned or was a commercial property built since 1980.

5. All quotes from the original letters and from the focus groups were translated for this essay by the author or by Ms. Jin Gao. Word counts and word searches were done only with the Chinese transcripts.

6. What was also striking was that even after the facilitator read aloud the editor's reply to initiate a second round of discussion, not even those who had cited the law earlier cited it again.

7. The key point for these young male professionals was that the older brother had his name was on the deed—a fact that was not presented in the information they were given to discuss but that they projected onto the case.

8. Although I did make numerical tallies of how many times certain phrases or words were used in each group or by each individual, I do not rely primarily on frequencies to compare the relative importance of an argument across groups or between individuals. In each group the facilitator allowed the group to develop its own dynamic, and as a result, the groups varied in the amount of time they focused on any one topic. Thus, what I have done in the text is to note whether an issue was raised in a group and then to look at the range of criteria that were invoked.

9. In addition to using the original letter from *Minzu yu Fazhi,* we also presented the two additional disputes as letters to the editor. In the second dispute, the letter read:

COMRADE EDITOR,

I lived in a home with my mother that was originally my father's privately owned home. After my father died in November 2000, my older brother not only did not come to console my mother but even declared that he had inheritance rights and was prepared to go to court to sue me. Please tell me: does my older brother still have inheritance rights to this place?

In the third dispute, the letter read:

COMRADE EDITOR,

I live with my mother in a commercial flat, and I am the owner. After my father died in November 2000, my older brother not only did not come to console my mother but even declared that he had inheritance rights and was prepared to go to court to sue me. Please tell me: does my older brother still have inheritance rights to this place?

10. In 2000, ten of the thirty-one participants said the older brother had no rights; in 2002, nine of thirty-three said the brother had no rights.

References

Agarwal, Bina. 1994. *A Field of One's Own.* Cambridge: Cambridge University Press.
Bian Yanjie, John Logan, Hanlong Lu, Yunkang Pan, and Ying Guan. 1997. "Work Units and Housing Reform in Two Chinese Cities." In *Danwei: The Changing Chinese Workplace in Historical and Comparative Perspective,* edited by Xiaobo Lu and Elizabeth Perry. Boulder, Colo.: Westview Press.
Burawoy, Michael, and Katherine Verdery, eds. 1999. "Introduction." In *Uncertain Transition: Ethnographies of Change in the Postsocialist World.* Lanham, Md.: Rowman & Littlefield.

Chen Xiangming and Xiaoyuan Gao. 1993. "China's Urban Housing Development in the Shift from Redistribution to Decentralization." *Social Problems* 40(2, May): 266–83.

Davis, Deborah. 1993. "Urban Households: Supplicants to the State." In *Chinese Families in the Post-Mao Era,* edited by Deborah Davis and Stevan Harrell. Berkeley: University of California Press.

———. 1999. "The 1985 Law of Succession at the End of the 1990s." In *China Review 1999,* edited by Chong Chor Lau and Geng Xiao. Hong Kong: Chinese University of Hong Kong Press.

———. 2002. "When a House Becomes His Home." In *Popular China,* edited by Perry Link, Richard P. Madsen, and Paul Pickowicz. London: Rowman & Littlefield.

———. 2003. "From Welfare Benefit to Capitalized Asset." In *Housing and Social Change,* edited by Ray Forrest and James Lee. London: Rowman & Littlefield.

Deere, Carmen Diana, and Magdalena León. 2001. *Empowering Women: Land and Property Rights in Latin America.* Pittsburgh: University of Pittsburgh Press.

Demsetz, Harold. 1967. "Toward a Theory of Property Rights." In *Ownership, Control, and the Firm.* Oxford: Blackwell.

Foster, Frances H. 1998. "Towards a Behavior-Based Model of Inheritance?" *University of California at Davis Law Review* 32(1): 77–126.

———. 1999. "Linking Support and Inheritance." *Wisconsin Law Review* 6: 1199–1257.

Fraser, David. 2000. "Inventing Oasis." In *The Consumer Revolution in Urban China,* edited by Deborah Davis. Berkeley: University of California Press.

Gu, Edward. 2001. "Dismantling the Chinese Mini-welfare State." *Communist and Post-Communist Studies* 34: 91–111.

Hann, Christopher M. 1998. *Property Relations: Renewing the Anthropological Tradition.* Cambridge: Cambridge University Press.

———. 2002. *Postsocialism.* London: Routledge.

Lee Peter Nan-shong. 1995. "Housing Privatization with Chinese Characteristics." In *Social Change and Social Policy in Contemporary China,* edited by Linda Wong and Stewart MacPherson. Aldershot, Eng.: Avebury.

Lee Yok Shiu. 1988. "The Urban Housing Problem in China." *China Quarterly* 115(September): 387–407.

Li Ling Hin. 1999. *Urban Land Reform in China.* London: Macmillan.

Li Xuefan. 2000. "Chengshi Zhumin Zhufang." *Beijing Fangdichan* (March 15): 18–22.

Oi, Jean, and Andrew Walder, eds. 1999. *Property Rights and Economic Reform in China.* Stanford, Calif.: Stanford University Press.

Putterman, Louis. 1995. "The Role of Ownership and Property Rights in China's Economic Transition." *China Quarterly* 144(December): 1047–64.

Singer, Joseph William. 2000. *Entitlement: The Paradoxes of Property.* New Haven, Conn.: Yale University Press.

Stark, David. 1996. "Recombinant Property in East European Capitalism." *American Journal of Sociology* 101(4): 993–1027.

Thireau, Isabelle, and Wang Hansheng. 2001. *Disputes au village chinois.* Paris: Éditions de la maison des sciences de l'homme.

Tong Zhongyi, and R. Allen Hays. 1996. "The Transformation of the Urban Housing System in China." *Urban Affairs Review* 31(5): 625–58.

Verdery, Katherine. 1999. "Fuzzy Property." In *Uncertain Transition: Ethnographies of Change in the Postsocialist World,* edited by Michael Burawoy and Katherine Verdery. Lanham, Md.: Rowman & Littlefield.

Wang Ya Ping, and Alan Murie. 1999. *Housing Policy and Practice in China.* New York: Macmillan.

Whyte, Martin K. 1993. "Wedding Behavior and Family Strategies in Chengdu." In *Chinese Families in the Post-Mao Era,* edited by Deborah Davis and Stevan Harrell. Berkeley: University of California Press.

Whyte, Martin K., and William L. Parish. 1984. *Urban Life in Contemporary China.* Chicago: University of Chicago Press.

Zelizer, Viviana. 1994. *The Social Meaning of Money.* Princeton, N.J.: Princeton University Press.

Zhou Min, and John Logan. 1996. "Market Transition and the Commodification of Housing in Urban China." *International Journal of Urban and Regional Research* 20(3): 400–21.

12

SACRED MARKETS AND SECULAR RITUAL IN THE ORGAN TRANSPLANT INDUSTRY

Kieran Healy

S INCE THE 1970s, organ transplantation has been transformed from an experimental therapy of last resort into a common medical procedure. A network of organ procurement organizations (OPOs) has grown up to collect and distribute organs in the United States. Along with the government and the medical profession, these organizations have worked in various ways to increase the supply. Demand for human organs has increased sharply since the mid-1980s, and the number of people currently waiting for a transplant exceeds the number of available organs by a factor of more than ten. Because of the increasing structural pressure on the procurement system, the need to convince people to become organ donors is very great, and the search for alternative ways to meet demand has led to proposals to provide some kind of financial incentive to donors or their families. Over a period of about thirty years we have moved from a period of public ambivalence or even suspicion about transplantation to the real prospect of market exchange in organs.

Sociological approaches to the emergence and spread of markets focus on the empirical questions of how markets are institutionalized and legitimated, how they are adapted to particular circumstances, and how (or whether) they are resisted. Other chapters in this volume show that distinctive cultures of exchange may develop in explicitly profit-driven contexts. Karin Knorr Cetina and Urs Bruegger demonstrate the emergence of norms of trading from the ground up in electronic currency markets. William Schneper and Mauro Guillén show that hostile takeovers are not simply a matter of market opportunity or corporate law but depend also on the institutionalization of stock trading and the prevalence of cultural individualism. Currency trading and corporate raiding are innovations within an already well entrenched set of economic institutions. But markets may also develop for goods already governed by some other principle of exchange. This is the problem of commodification.

Discussions of commodification are most often grounded in the philosophical problem of establishing what is and is not commodifiable in general (Radin 1996; Walzer 1983; Anderson 1993). This chapter, by contrast, focuses on the cultural and organizational work involved in procuring and legitimately exchanging a potentially controversial good in practice. Debates about commodification tend to gloss over this process, but it is central to understanding how a new, potentially threatening practice becomes morally acceptable—and indeed virtuous—over time. I argue that transplant advocates developed a specific cultural account of donation to resolve these problems. An *account* is a coherent body of reasons and evaluations that can be used to explain and legitimate some practice or activity (Wuthnow 1996; Scott and Lyman 1968). This account can be seen to emerge in the promotional materials and professional handbooks of OPOs, in books and memoirs about organ donation, and in the media coverage of donation issues. It amounts to a script, a set of "feeling rules" for the experience of organ donation, in Arlie Hochschild's (1985) sense. I argue that this account is prescriptive rather than descriptive: it presents the ideal experience, what one ought to feel in these circumstances, rather than what many people actually experience. Evidence for this comes from a number of facts: advocates of organ donation tried more than one approach before settling on the current rules; themes found in earlier sources are not found in later ones; the popular account focuses on atypical cases; and documentary and interview evidence shows a much wider spectrum of feeling about organ donation than the official account suggests. This process has, in turn, made it possible to consider seriously and explicitly for-profit forms of exchange in human organs that were originally beyond the pale.

My argument is in three parts. First, I outline the theoretical approach. I show how Viviana Zelizer's (1992) work on the life insurance industry provides the theoretical resources to approach this issue sociologically. Second, I discuss the efforts of donor families and transplant professionals to make organ donation a worthwhile and appropriate act. I trace the development of their account of donation and show how it has tended to rely on a particular set of arguments and stories. Third, I examine the growing importance of monetary incentives in organ procurement. I show how practical systems of payment for organs recognize the expressive role of money and argue that commodification is not a simple yes-or-no choice.

Organ Donation and Commodification

Why focus on the transplant industry? Unlike more exotic human goods (for a survey, see Andrews and Nelkin 2001), organs are widely exchanged in the United States through a well-regulated and carefully monitored system that can deliver them from donor to patient with great speed. Their exchange is much better institutionalized than more cutting-edge technologies, and so people have had an opportunity to develop practical responses to organ donation and cultural accounts of it. This is important, since what is of interest here is how organ donation is presented and understood by those involved.

At the same time, it is only since 1980 that organ transplants have been possible on a wide scale (thanks to a new generation of immunosuppressive drugs), so the practice is still new compared to a few other human goods (such as blood) that have been around longer. Although the organ supply has grown in the past ten years, it has not kept pace with demand. The shortfall is severe, and it produces many tragic, unusual, or otherwise vivid cases—a sick child waits for a new heart, a famous sports player gets a new liver, the family of a brain-dead accident victim refuses consent to donate, and so on. One response to the shortfall is to introduce a financial incentive for organs—to create a production market for them. But commercial traffic in organs seems disturbing, even obscene, to many. An altruistic system seems the only justifiable solution. The result has been a classic commodification debate.

How should we think about this issue? With a few notable exceptions (Simmons, Marine, and Simmons 1977; Fox and Swazey 1974, 1992), sociologists have not paid much attention to organ transplants. But we do know a good deal about how people think and talk about their own altruism (Wuthnow 1991, 1995), how they use money to express social ties (Zelizer 1992), and how they manage money in personal relationships (Nelson 1998). Research in this area suggests that the problem of commodification is not about the encroachment of the market on some untouched region of society. Rather, it is about the ways in which people account for their own actions and the place of money in their lives.

Take life insurance. As documented by Zelizer (1979, 1992), life insurance was a controversial product in its early days and is a good example of moral debate about commodification. Though promoted by legislatures, life insurance companies were unsuccessful in the first half of the nineteenth century. Americans did not want to buy any. This changed between 1840 and 1860, at which time insurance companies grew rapidly. By the late nineteenth century, life insurance was commonplace, and the earlier controversy about it had abated.

Life insurance threatened to assess a person's life in financial terms. Compared to other goods up for commodification, it seems quite harmless. We would say that, unlike slavery, for example, it doesn't *really* put a cash value on you as a person. But many nineteenth-century commentators felt it was just that: life insurance was "merchandising in human life" and "turning a very solemn thing into a mere commercial transaction" (quoted in Zelizer 1992, 291). Americans did not want to buy life insurance because they did not want to put a price on their heads.

There is also a close relationship between life insurance and death. A policy yields its reward when the owner dies, so buying life insurance meant tempting fate. Life insurers were aware of "the mysterious connection between insuring life and losing life," as customers confessed their fear that taking out a policy would hasten their death (Zelizer 1992, 292). Such views are typical of the many traditional, magical strategies used to ward off death and illness (for example, not mentioning death by name, or not speaking the name of an illness for fear of contracting it). Social processes or professions related to death are usually subject to magic rituals of this kind. With life insurance, the involvement of money required further ritual effort. The result was interesting. Death was not profaned by money. Rather, money could be transmuted into an offering of sorts, and life insurance made possible a proper, respectable—even lavish—funeral. Thus,

> the dual relationship between money and death—actual as well as symbolic—is essential to the understanding of the development of life insurance. Sacrilegious because it equated cash with life, life insurance became on the other hand a legitimate vehicle for the symbolic use of money at the time of death. (Zelizer 1992, 294)

In short, Zelizer argues, insurers had to reconcile the demands of business for profit with the sacred aspects of the good in question. One did not simply triumph over the other. Rather, contradictions were overcome through "the transformation of monetary evaluations of death into a ritual . . . life insurance assumed the role of a secular ritual that emphasized remembrance through money" (Zelizer 1992, 294).

The correspondence between life insurance and organ transplantation is not perfect, of course, and the comparison should not be drawn too strongly. The goods differ in their tangibility, in the structure of payment, and in the relation between providers and beneficiaries. The life insurance industry created a tradable commodity in a controversial area, but the market for insurance did not threaten an already existing system of gift exchange. Further differences could easily be enumerated. Yet the comparison remains worthwhile, because exchange in transplant organs crosses boundaries similar to those that Zelizer identifies for life insurance, and the framework she uses to approach the insurance case can fruitfully be applied to transplantation.

Organ procurement is done with care, but it could hardly be more invasive. It is difficult to make this procedure acceptable to people. In circumstances where there is a great shortage of organs—and the market seems like a possible solution to this problem—these difficulties are exacerbated. In the next section, I trace the production and propagation of a cultural account of organ procurement that morally justifies this procedure and tries to motivate people to participate in it.

Building an Account of Organ Donation

Organ donation is a novel medical procedure that, in most cases, demands a remarkable sacrifice from someone who has just lost a close relative, usually through a violent accident. It is not obvious that people should consent to donation under these circumstances. Ruth Richardson (1996, 68) has argued that the closest historical analogue to organ harvesting is the dissection of the dead for anatomical study: "Both depend upon an accessible supply of dead bodies. Each damages the dead body for the sake of what is generally seen as a greater good. Both processes break cultural taboos." Many religious doctrines pose potential stumbling blocks for donation. Some societies—Japan is the most prominent example—have opposed organ donation and transplants (Lock 1996). Even when generally accepted, organ procurement can spark moral controversy, as Linda Hogle's (1999) study of organ procurement in Germany shows.

I argue that we can trace how organ donation has been rationalized by OPOs and made meaningful by donor families. Zelizer describes three ways in which secular rituals developed around life insurance, in each case through the efforts of insurance providers and religious activists. First, it became a way for the bereaved to come to terms with the death of a loved one. Second, it became a moral act with religious significance. Third, it became a way to guarantee one's memory after death, and thus a kind of immortality. Her categories can be applied to the present case. We find a similar cultural account and body of secular ritual emerging in the contemporary world of transplant organs.

To make my argument, I rely on three sources of data. First, I examined promotional material, official reports, policy statements, and other discussion papers originating with OPOs or their coordinating agency, the United Network for Organ Sharing (UNOS). Second, I collected a comprehensive sample of book-length journalistic accounts and personal memoirs of organ donation published between 1980 and 1999. These books began to appear with increasing frequency in the 1980s. The official sources reflect the interests of the OPOs in increasing the organ supply and represent their best efforts at convincing potential donors that giving organs is worthwhile.[1] Like the advocates of life insurance, they lay out arguments in favor of a practice that trespasses on questions of life and death in a disturbing way. The stories told in the popular books add narrative detail and emotional depth to these policy arguments. I argue that they act as a cultural resource, a way of familiarizing the public with the rules and ideals of this new practice. They publicize the experiences of those who have been affected, providing rich, personalized narratives about donation. (These books can be found in the references.) Third, I sampled the *New York Times* (through the Lexis-Nexis database) for all stories appearing between January 1, 1980, and December 31, 1999, that had the words "organ," "donor," or "transplant" in the headline or lead paragraph. The initial search yielded 1,012 news items for the whole period. After checking each story, 14 were eliminated as irrelevant, leaving 998 items. Figure 12.1 shows the trend in coverage over the

FIGURE 12.1   New York Times *News Items on Organ Transplantation or Donation, 1980 to 1999*

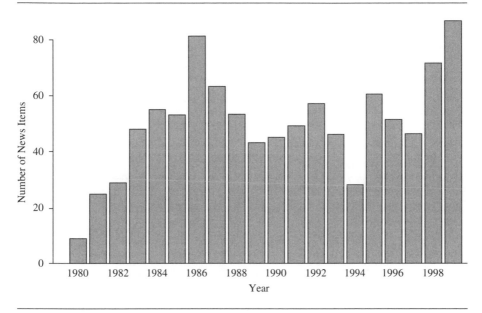

Source: Author's compilation.

twenty-year period sampled. The median number of stories per year is 50, with a minimum of 9 (in 1980) and a maximum of 86 (in 1999).

A Way to Cope with Bereavement

Between 1830 and 1870, life insurance companies justified their product as a way of coming to terms with death. Far more than a financial safety blanket, life insurance was a consolation "next to that of religion itself" (quoted in Zelizer 1992, 294). In the first issue of the *American Life Assurance Magazine* (1860), Morris Franklin asserted that life insurance could "alleviate the pangs of the bereaved, cheer the heart of the widow and dry the orphan's tears."

The florid prose style is no longer in fashion, but UNOS makes the same argument about becoming an organ donor:

> At the time of your death, your family will be asked about organ donation. Sharing your decision with your family will spare them the added burden of having to guess your wishes at a difficult time. . . . Carrying out your wish to save other lives can provide your family with great comfort in their time of grief. (United Network for Organ Sharing 1999)

313

In most cases, a donor becomes available for organ procurement through violent or accidental death.[2] The victims are often young, and their deaths are unexpected and meaningless. OPOs stress how the organ donation can help a family make sense of such a tragedy and give some meaning to it. A number of journalistic and firsthand accounts from the donor family side have been published (see Gutkind 1990; Pekkanen 1986; Schomaker 1995; Green 1997). In addition to books like these, volunteer donor organizations encourage donor families to tell their stories, most of which are now commonly available online. For example, the Transweb Memorial website (http://www.transweb.org/) has memorials for about sixty donors.

These testimonies movingly articulate the grief of the families involved and relate their responses to the procurement request. They generally confirm the claims of the OPOs about the benefits of donation. Donating organs can invest an otherwise senseless death with some meaning. Alice Sanders (1999) is a typical example. She tells how she consented to have her husband's organs donated: "A day of sorrow for us turned into a very bright day for several families, as we were able to donate kidneys and the liver. My thought several times that day was how excited those recipients must have been when their pagers went off, knowing that they were getting a 'second chance.' "

In *The Nicholas Effect* (1997), Reg Green describes the killing of his seven-year-old son Nicholas during a botched carjacking while the family was on holiday in Italy. They consented to donate their child's organs to the Italian procurement system. Seven Italians received Nicholas's organs. The story understandably provoked a tremendous response in Italy (resulting, among other things, in a jump in the donation rate there), and in the book Green describes his feelings about what came of his son's death.

This case brings out some subtle aspects of the gift relationship. Green's case provoked so much sympathy in Italy because a terrible thing happened to him while he was a visitor there. If you agreed when you read that the Italian response was "understandable," then you shared an assumption about a host's obligations to guests. It seems fair to say that the Italian reaction would not have been as strong if the victim had been a local resident. This may seem odd, because we normally care more for those closer to us. But group identity can produce feelings of responsibility, and even shame, in this way. These feelings were amplified when Reg Green acted generously toward the group.

As Marcel Mauss long ago recognized, gift-giving creates a bond of solidarity as the giver shares what he has, but also a relationship of superiority as he creates a debt that must be repaid (Godelier 1999, 12). Italy was doubly in debt to Green. The strong popular reaction can be seen as an expression of the feeling that the wrong done to him as a guest, combined with his selfless reaction to it, created a debt that was almost impossible to discharge. The country was shamed by a stranger's unwarranted generosity.

The feelings expressed in the online memorials are much more varied than those in the published books. Not all articulate the benefits of donation as well as Alice Sanders, or manage to find meaning in the way the Green family did. Often they consist of only a short note or poem expressing grief, nothing more. Sometimes writers express resentment at the anonymity of the donation procedure; in the Transweb memorial for the donor Carl Zimmerman, his sister implores: "Oh, recipients, where are you, you who live because our beloved donor has died? Can you not acknowledge your appreciation to your anonymous donor's beloved family? After all, the organ didn't come from a donor, it came from my beloved brother."

We have no comparable literature describing the experiences of those who refuse consent to donate. We do know that a substantial percentage of donation requests are refused—perhaps as many as 50 percent (Gortmaker 1998)—indicating that the OPOs need to work hard to make donation a standard choice.

The Transweb memorials are public, but they are much less refined than the books on the subject. Though the books recount great suffering on the part of the families involved, they are positive and life-affirming. They lay out a template for those who might be put in the same situation, leading these readers through to the moment of closure and acceptance. The books' aim is to describe the stages of feelings toward organ donation that a potential donor family typically goes through, even though it is clear that not every donor family completes this sequence with a decision to consent to donate. The narrative structure of the books aimed at adults follows the argument of the OPOs that donation helps families cope with death. Like the insurance companies, they stress the alleviation of the "pangs of the bereaved."

This template for the secular ritual of organ donation is quite well established. The stock of cultural resources available to assist its broad acceptance is large (books, television documentaries, newspaper articles, and so on). As an indication of how entrenched this view now is, it is significant that books aimed at children have begun to appear. *Precious Gifts: Barklay and Eve Explain Organ and Tissue Donation* (Carney 1999) and *Lizzy Gets a New Liver* (Ribal 1997) both lay out the process of organ and tissue donation for young children. *Precious Gifts* is aimed at four- to eight-year-olds. The publisher's description notes that the book will help "children and adults understand the process of organ and tissue donation. The determination of brain death and its meaning is clearly portrayed. The process of family decision-making is poignantly illustrated. A list of words and definitions is provided to enhance understanding."

The place of children in this cultural account is interesting in another way too. As organ donation became more common, media attention focused disproportionately on transplant cases involving infants and children. As can be seen from figure 12.2, *New York Times* coverage of child transplants rose and fell during the 1980s. Coverage peaked in 1984 (at more than 38 percent of

FIGURE 12.2   New York Times *News Items About Infants and*
Children as a Percentage of All News Items About
Organ Donation or Transplantation, 1980 to 1999

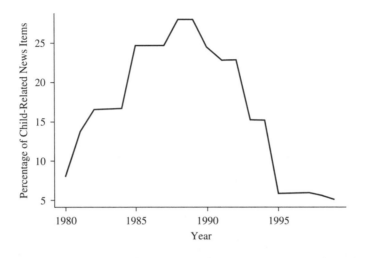

Source: Author's compilation.
Note: Percentages are based on a smoothed (running median) plot of the number of such stories.

total coverage) with the story of Baby Fae, the "baby with the baboon heart." It remained high throughout the 1980s. Most of these stories were about children getting transplanted and (often) dying shortly afterward. By 1995 coverage of children had fallen to about 7 percent of total coverage, and it would stay there. The era of transplant "poster children" in the 1980s may have done much to acquaint people with organ donation.

We might be inclined to think it quite natural that organ donation should become a part of the mourning process for a family member lost in an accident. This would be a mistake. Indeed, in the early 1980s it was not clear to those involved whether a request for organs would make things better or worse for the grieving family. Writing in 1985, Arthur Caplan (1987, 264) noted that "often the [nursing] staff may be concerned about the impact of the donation request on the acutely grieving family and may preclude the family's opportunity to donate [by not asking]." Integrating organ donation into grieving required a good deal of cultural work. A combination of survey research conducted by the OPOs, widely circulated firsthand testimony from donor families, and required request laws that deprive nurses of any discretion in the matter have essentially eliminated the idea (at least among transplant professionals) that a sympathetic request for organs could cause harm.[3]

A Moral Act for Family or Community

Religious leaders play an important role in making practices like organ donation acceptable. Church authorities in many religious traditions support organ donation. Their main concern has been to ensure that the donation is altruistic and that the donor is dead before the organs are removed. The accurate determination of death is important for theological reasons. In Catholic teaching, the soul must have left the body before organ harvesting can occur. Any tendency to redefine the moment of death is suspicious, as this might make it easier for doctors to give up on patients in order to harvest their organs.[4] I cannot discuss the issue of defining brain death here (for a detailed discussion, see Zaner 1988), but as long as there is no money involved and the donor has died, most Christian church authorities are not against organ donation.

By contrast, Orthodox Judaism has had more trouble assimilating organ donation to existing law and practice. There is more opposition to organ donation among Jewish religious authorities, who are also more divided on the issue. Rabbis who favor it have had to make strong efforts to integrate organ donation into existing theology and ritual. Those in favor say that "the preservation of human life supersedes all *halachic*[5] prohibitions, except for the three cardinal sins: idolatry, adultery and murder. Thus, procurement of cadaver organs for life-saving purposes need not pose a major problem, since the various prohibitions cited would be overridden by the supreme requirement to save a life" (Twersky, Gold, and Jacob 1991, 190). A difficulty is that influential halachic opinion identifies the absence of a pulse as a necessary condition for determining death. This is almost never the case with organ donation, where the potential donor is brain-dead but otherwise functioning. In their educational and promotional material, UNOS and the OPOs circulate material from Jewish authorities favoring donation (see *The Jewish Voice* 1996).

Even though most religions accept or encourage voluntary donation, these endorsements go against the grain of many other religious views on questions about human goods and human life that arise in other areas, such as genetic engineering or fetal research.[6] Support for organ donation in the Catholic Church is weakened by concerns over the definition of brain death, which leads some conservative church members to oppose organ donation. Considering the Catholic Church's ambivalence on the issue as well as the difficulties within Judaism, we should not be surprised by the widespread belief that religious officials oppose donation. A 1990 survey found that 61.5 percent of respondents believed that some major Western religions do not support it (Horton and Horton 1990). In response, UNOS and various individual OPOs collect and publicize official religious policies on organ donation and offer guidebooks to ministers on their role in the process (United Network for Organ Sharing 1998).

For most churches, the problem of organ transplants solved itself once they solved the problem of brain death. These churches focused on overcoming the problem of organ donation's proximity to death. The other boundary problem—where human goods change hands for money—remained in the background, since there seemed to be little prospect of the legal sale of organs in any form. This may change, as I discuss later.

A Way to Ensure One's Memory

The third feature of the cultural account of organ donation is the idea that donation is a way to live on (and do good) after death. Donor families, OPOs, and the media all express this sentiment. The Donor Memorial Quilts Project, like the AIDS quilt, remembers the sacrifice of organ donors. A more direct expression of this idea is that the donor spiritually as well as physically lives on in the recipient. Helen Batten and Jeffrey Prottas's (1987) follow-up study of organ donor families found that 68 percent of them agreed that the deceased relative could live on in someone else through donation. This sentiment is very common in the journalistic literature.[7] OPOs also draw on it in their efforts to recruit people to sign organ donor cards.

For example, a New Jersey OPO, the Sharing Network, organizes public information sessions during which donor families and transplant recipients talk about their experiences. At a 1999 session held at Princeton University, one participant, Jack Locicero, spoke about his daughter Amy, who was one of six people killed by Colin Ferguson in 1993 on a crowded Long Island Railroad commuter train. In his talk, he described the decision that he and his wife had made to donate Amy's organs and how they had since become "like family" to some of the recipients (Locicero 1999). Members of these families described their feeling that Amy lives on through the transplantation of her organs. Kinlike ties have developed between the Lociceros and these families, especially the recipient of Amy's heart, a woman named Arlene. They visit one another, and Arlene sends flowers to Amy's mother on Mother's Day. When they first met, Arlene embraced Amy's mother and said, "The heart that beats in me once beat in your womb."

I highlight this case because, although such stories are common in the media, they are rare in practice. In the Lociceros' case, they ended up meeting the recipients of their daughter's organs because of the publicity that the shooting received. *People* magazine picked up the story and traced the patients who had received the organs. Donor families are normally given the age, gender, and general location of each recipient, but not their names. Nevertheless, much of the donor literature (though not the written OPO material) focuses on these unusual cases where families meet. The idea of the continuing life of the donor in the body of the transplant recipient is especially forceful in these cases. John Pekkanen (1986, 213) quotes one family member as saying: "I don't really see why we should have rules against these meetings. . . . I sure think it would help heal a lot of anger and hurt."

The available evidence suggests that donor families are unhappy with the information they receive about the recipients of their gift. In a valuable but unpublished pilot study, Maria Banevicius (1992, 35) interviewed donor families about their experiences with donation. She found that all the families would have liked to receive some follow-up information about the recipient. One suggested a letter "maybe once a year. . . . I don't need to know every breath they take but you would like to know that they're okay or they're not okay." Another respondent said: "Wouldn't it be nice to be able to drop somebody a note, saying congratulations I'm glad everything went well for you. It was my relative who's [sic] part you received and I'm so glad to know you're no longer on dialysis, or that you can get up and go to work or go play tennis again. But there isn't that kind of an exchange, and why?" (36).

Most donor families will not meet "their" organ recipients, and the feeling that their loved one lives on must be more abstract. Again, narrative accounts act as a road map for the emotions. They show how donors and donor families can have a meaningful sense of the continuing survival of the donor and how an emotional tie can thus develop between the families. This ideal, however, must be promoted, since it is not the only possible response. Evidence for the alternatives is available from both donors and recipients. Victoria Poole's *Thursday's Child* (1980, 257) describes her son Sam's illness and eventual heart transplant. After his transplant, Sam reacted to his new heart: "My new heart likes me; I can feel it. Boy, am I glad I don't ever have to know where it came from or whose it was. I don't ever want to know. It's my heart now, and nobody is going to take it away from me." This attitude is not found in the more recent literature.

On the donor family side, Banevicius found that although the families wanted more information, they were not always happy when they got it. In particular, four of her ten respondents were surprised and somewhat upset to find that "their" transplant recipient was not whom they imagined. One said:

> There was a 42-year-old man that had gotten the heart and in a way it was, which I now realize is silly, but it was almost a disappointment that it wasn't a 19-year-old girl. It could be because it would have been like my daughter was living again because, it would have been someone the same age she was. (Banevicius 1992, 38)

And another:

> I found it a little bit disconcerting that an 18-year-old heart went into such an— I don't want to say such an old person but it would be my hope that it would be someone younger, that would have 40 or 50 years left of their life. I don't want to say it was a waste, but I think that it would be more valuable maybe in somebody in their 20s. (Banevicius 1992, 38)

These reactions, on both sides, again point toward the active construction of a particular way of understanding the transplant process and the possibility that the official version will diverge from the complex feelings of donor families and recipients. The dominant meaning attributed to the organ donation, as found in the Lociceros' experience and most of the book-length accounts, is perhaps the better, more satisfying one, but it is not inherent to the experience of donation.

The Expressive Role of Money

The National Organ Transplantation Act of 1984 prohibits organ sales. It was enacted partly in response to several reports about people trying to sell kidneys and corneas through the newspapers. The efforts of Dr. H. Barry Jacobs provided a further spur. He planned to buy organs from around the world and sell them at a profit to those who needed them (Kimbrell 1997, 30). Public opposition to such schemes has remained high, despite the organ shortage, and politically the idea has long been thought untouchable.

Organ procurement is a delicate affair that must be handled with great sensitivity if it is to work at all. Those in favor of a purely altruistic system would say that this need for sensitivity and respect is one of the strongest arguments for keeping money and the market as far away from potential donors and their families as possible. They argue that a gift is the only form of exchange appropriate to such a situation. To offer cash for organs would be obscene. Their opponents retort that the real obscenity is a chronic shortage that could be solved by the market. Proposals for market solutions to the organ shortage have been gaining ground recently in the bioethics literature. In the introduction to their recent anthology on the subject, Arthur Caplan and Daniel Coelho (1998, 11) note a shift toward arguments in favor of commodification: "Proposals for outright organ sales are suggested by authors who only years earlier had summarily dismissed any commodification of organs."

This change in attitude seems to be driven in part by the increasing gap between the number of available transplant organs and the number of people who need one. Both in theory and in practice, bioethicists and the transplant community have begun to look for a way to increase the organ supply using some financial incentive. Perhaps because the "feeling rules" for altruistic organ donation are firmly in place—people know what it is, what everyone's motives are, and how they ought to react—using money to reduce the shortage now seems more plausible. The key to understanding the role of money in this area, I argue, lies in its expressive rather than its instrumental qualities. Rewards are set up so that they are commensurate with the organ being exchanged (Espeland and Stevens 1998); the payment reimburses the donor in an appropriate way.

Payment Schemes in Theory

The normative question of whether organs should be bought and sold tends to overwhelm the empirical one. From a sociological perspective, we should be interested in the practical solutions that emerge. Following recent work in economic sociology, I argue that we should expect money to play an expressive role in the exchange of organs. Zelizer's (1994) work on money is about the myriad efforts that people make to arrange and earmark different transfers with tokens of payment so that they express the social relationship between the parties. These efforts become especially creative in cases where a transaction involves something thought to be beyond the reach of utilitarian calculation.

If we look at proposals for organ sales, we find that this expressive aspect becomes more prominent the more practical the proposal is thought to be. Early versions called for a cash bounty to be paid to the donor family on receipt of the organs. This idea is no longer discussed. Instead, those in favor of commodifying organs are careful to qualify what they mean. For instance, Roger Blair and David Kaserman (1991, 421), strong advocates of a market for organs, emphasize:

> Because the issue of organ markets is so emotionally charged and often misunderstood, let us be clear about what is not being proposed. We do not propose barkers hawking human organs on street corners. We do not envision transplant patients, or their agents, dickering for a heart or liver with families of the recently deceased. We do not advocate an auction in which desperate recipients bid against each other for life-sustaining organs.

Instead, their solution is to offer potential suppliers "some fixed payment (either in cash or in the form of a tax credit) in exchange for entering into a binding contract that authorizes the removal of one or more of their organs at death" (421).

Why should they bother with this qualification? Such efforts to distinguish appropriate from inappropriate sales suggest that even market advocates are aware of the need to mark or transform the place of money in this context. The focus on appropriate *tokens* of payment is important. Certain exchanges are ruled out, especially cash payment at the point of sale. Instead, less visible payments are proposed, usually involving money given at a different time, well in advance of any organ procurement. Even these payments may be further restricted to, for instance, a health insurance premium reduction (Hansmann 1989). The futures market created is for an *option* on the organ, should it ever become available. Under such a system, most people's organs would not come up for donation, because they would not die in the appropriate circumstances. In contrast to early schemes that proposed paying the family several thousand dollars (estimated prices varied widely), the amount of money on offer is small. In addition, the form of the payment is commensurate with the item being purchased. The seller receives a small annual reduction in health insurance costs, not a check, a holiday in the Bahamas, or a gift voucher to spend at Wal-Mart. The uncomfortable image of paying cold cash for a warm kidney is kept well away.

Payment Schemes in Practice

These carefully marked and delimited exchanges are just beginning to appear in practice. In March 1999, state health officials in Pennsylvania announced that they would soon begin offering a $300 stipend to help donor families cover funeral expenses. This is the first time that a definite cash amount has been introduced by an OPO in connection with donor families. Families will not receive this money in cash. In fact, it will not be paid to them at all, but to funeral homes. A spokesperson for the Gift of Life Program (the Delaware Valley's OPO) said at the time: "This is absolutely not buying and selling organs. . . . This is about having a voluntary death benefit for a family who gave a gift" (*New York Times* 1999). But of course, the OPO introduced the scheme to boost donation rates. ("The intent is to test it and see if it makes a difference to families," said the same spokesperson.) This is exactly how we would expect money to be introduced in such a case: it might be expected to act as an incentive, but it cannot be presented as one.

Programs such as these could make those who have already struggled to accept organ donation uncomfortable about it again. If the Pennsylvania scheme is widely implemented, we can expect to hear the same arguments that Zelizer documents for life insurance. It is an open question whether religious bodies will reconcile themselves to compensation for organs. From the life insurance case, we can expect there to be two sticking points. First, as I have been arguing, the form of the payment will be crucial. Indirect, noncash transfers (as in the Pennsylvania scheme) will probably be acceptable.

Second, the beneficiary of the transfer also poses a difficulty. Most proposals for futures markets in organs try to eliminate the role of the donor family by making a contract with the donor. But in practice it is donor families who make the decision to donate and are in fact the real donors. Even if the doctors know that the patient had a preference for organ donation (perhaps the patient carried an organ donor card, for example), in practice hospital staff will always defer to the family's wishes. If they refuse consent, the organs will not be harvested. This is so even when there is an organ donor card witnessed as a legal document. The central role of donor families is a big stumbling block to the implementation of schemes of the kind proposed by Hansmann (1989) and Blair and Kaserman (1991).

How commodified will exchange in organs become? At present, organs are given as gifts, and for-profit exchange in them is illegal. However, the media evidence shows that discussion of cash incentives for organs has con-

FIGURE 12.3   New York Times *News Items Mentioning Financial Incentives for Organ Donation as a Percentage of All News Items About Organ Donation, 1980 to 1999*

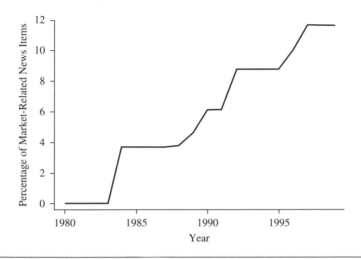

Source: Author's compilation.
Note: Percentages are based on a smoothed (running median) plot of the number of such mentions in headlines or lead paragraphs.

sistently increased since the late 1980s. Figure 12.3 shows a smoothed plot of the number of *New York Times* news items mentioning financial incentives for organ donation over a twenty-year period, as a percentage of all stories about organ donation. The jump in coverage around 1983 and 1984 was caused by early reports about people trying to sell their kidneys and the subsequent passage of the National Organ Transplantation Act of 1984 (which banned the sale of organs). After the act passed, news items about organ sales or financial incentives remained at about 5 percent of all organ donation stories for several years. Beginning in 1990, coverage began to climb again. Later items tend to be policy-oriented discussions of financial incentives as a potential solution to the organ shortage rather than news stories about organ sales.[8]

It is interesting to ask whether the rise in "market talk" about donation is related to the fall in the relative number of stories about infants and children and transplantation. One interpretation is that children are an index of the sacred. Since the late 1980s, transplants have become more and more routine (from a medical point of view). At the same time, demand pressure on the system has increased severely. Associating organ transplants with children might have made them more palatable initially, but such associations might be a liability in the context of a severe shortage and the possibility of a market for organs.

Commodification and Account-Giving

Donor families are not paid cash for their decision to donate, but both the trend of public discussion documented in figure 12.3 and policy experiments like the Pennsylvania program suggest that money is being introduced to the act of donation in subtle ways. Does this mean that organ procurement will ultimately be market-driven?

Some economists take this view. Their argument is that the reasons and excuses offered are just window dressing for the simple expansion of the market into a new arena. The life insurance case shows that people often resist the market on moral grounds only to later accept it as expedient and sensible. Likewise for organ transplants, these economists argue. What would be the problem with an organ market? If it makes you feel better to call the sellers "donors" (as with human eggs), then go ahead. But the suppliers will still get the market rate, whether you call them donors or not.

In contrast, work in economic sociology, along with the efforts of some legal theorists (Radin 1996; Sunstein 1997), points in a different direction. Charles Tilly (1999, 341) comments that, from Zelizer's perspective, "what appear to be narrowly rational economic transactions actually result from pursuit of meaningful social relations. Hence fears that monetization and commodification are desiccating social life have their causality backwards." In this volume, Deborah Davis examines the different "logics of entitlement" that Chinese focus-group members used to resolve hypothetical conflicts over property ownership. Market logic was simply one of several different rationales that were available. "Participants," she says, "weighed competing property claims within a moral framework that entwined the logic of family justice with the logics of the state and the market." Davis's respondents resolved their conflicts over family homes by appealing to the property rules "under which families first established residency." This clarified the basic relations between the parties, and the right logic to apply became clear. In these sorts of cases, the application of a particular logic of action or the choice of a particular token of exchange is fundamentally tied to an underlying social relationship.

Is there evidence to help choose between these alternatives? Some cases do seem better suited to one side than the other. Egg "donors" who are paid thousands of dollars for their services support the window-dressing view. On the other hand, the organ case raises the question of why there is so much window dressing in the first place. Why should people go to such enormous efforts to distinguish forms of payment and ritualize exchanges as they do if the exchange does not express something besides a simple preference?

Even in the restricted area of human goods, there is a good deal of variation that does not conform to any simple pattern. Cash for organs is out of the question at present, but direct payment to women for their eggs is routine. Is the distinction therefore between renewable and nonrenewable body parts? This is a common explanation, but it is wrong. Except in special circumstances, whole blood cannot be bought from blood donors. In fact, a large U.S. cash-for-blood market was dismantled in the 1970s—a clear counterexample to the idea that market exchange must spread to everything in this area sooner or later.[9] This example should give pause to both sides. On the one hand, markets do not inevitably win out. There is no slippery slope toward commodification. But on the other hand, there is no insuperable obstacle that prevents for-profit markets in human goods from being set up. Just such a market existed for blood until 1974, and still exists for plasma. The correspondence of types of goods to kinds of exchange systems is variable, not an immutable fact about human nature. A sociology of commodification ought to be able to account for this variability.

Further, the legitimate *expression* of a market interpretation might vary by social position or by the frequency of the transaction. Most donor families are in that position only once. Medical professionals who are repeatedly involved in organ exchange may have a "backstage" view that sounds more cynical. Backstage cynicism is not uncommon in medicine. For instance, when a person dies in the United Kingdom, a doctor must fill in a form registering the cause of death. There is no charge to the next of kin for this. However, if the body is to be cremated, the doctor charges for the relevant form and also gets another doctor to fill in a similar form, for a total charge of about £60. This is known in the trade as "ash cash." Even here, however, the market talk may represent rhetorical gallows humor more than a real financial incentive (for a discussion of the relationship between market rhetoric and commodification proper, see Radin 1996, 79–101).

Within genuinely cash-oriented markets, some interesting conventions still exist. Egg suppliers normally receive an unspecified gift in addition to the money. The following newspaper advertisement (from the *Columbia Daily Spectator*) is typical: "Although our gratitude cannot be measured in dollars, if we were in your shoes, the least we would expect is: $6,500 plus expenses (and a gift)."[10] Even sperm donors, who are at the very bottom of the status and income hierarchies in the world of human goods, are still donors rather than vendors. It seems that, even if money is involved in these exchanges, people do not want to account for them in market terms. Donors repeatedly insist that they are not motivated by the money. If experiments like the Pennsylvania scheme have the effect of increasing the donation rate, then the trend of in-kind reimbursement is likely to accelerate. But the official account of donation will probably not be told in market language.

Disguised payments, benefits, and gifts to donor families are likely to play an increasingly important role in the organ supply. Is this commodification? It does not conform to the altruistic vision of organ exchange. But it is not the nightmare world of cash for kidneys that many opponents of commodification have in mind. Nor does it much resemble the system of binding contracts with future donors proposed by the more thoughtful advocates of the market. From what we know about the motives of donor families, the organizational effort required to procure organs, and the fragility of consent, there is every reason to believe that these complicated arrangements are a necessary part of motivating the consent to donate, not just window dressing that could be dispensed with if only we were honest with ourselves.

Conclusion

Contemporary debate about medical technology and the market is drawn to novelty, to the brave new worlds opened up by genetic engineering or cloning or xenotransplantation (Cooper and Lanza 2000). The focus is normative, asking what ought to be done with particular goods (to commodify or not to commodify). These are important problems, but I have taken a different tack here. I argued that economic and cultural sociology contribute important insights about how people manage these problems. This approach, developed from historical cases of commodification, makes good empirical predictions about the organ industry. I argued that the chief lesson of these studies is that the empirical reality of organ exchange is likely to be more differentiated and carefully managed than standard debates about commodification might lead us to believe.

Though outside the range of the usual comparison cases, the analogy I began with between the life insurance and organ transplant industries is rich. Life insurance and organ transplants threaten sacred beliefs about death and the body. They bring the threat of utilitarian calculation and the negative influence of money. One possible reaction is to ban such corrupting practices for good. But more often, the practical benefits are large, or the promoting organizations are powerful. The new practice can be reinterpreted so that it is incorporated into existing ritual and reconciled to existing understandings. The cultural account of organ donation can be seen in these terms. Transplant advocates did not force their ideas on an unwilling public. Neither did the account of donation appear by magic to solve the problem of procurement. Rather, there are many ways in which donation might be understood. The cultural work of transplant advocates produced the public version we ended up with. They found ways to incorporate donation into death rituals; they made signing a donor card a morally worthwhile action; and they associated the donation with a kind of social immortality. The result is that public opposition to organ procurement is now almost unknown in the United States, even though people do not like to sign donor cards, families often refuse consent to donate, and the available evidence suggests a much wider range of responses to procurement than one gleans from the official account.

As the organ shortage has worsened, OPOs have begun to explore new ways to give people an incentive to donate. Proposals for commercializing the system by contracting with potential donors misunderstand both how the procurement process works and how people understand it. Paradoxically, opposition to commercialization is buttressed by the same arguments for the "gift of life" that helped legitimate donation and transplantation from the 1970s onward. In response, transplant advocates in favor of some kind of incentive system are beginning to develop payment systems that reimburse without corrupting. A new phase of account-making seems to be under way.

The standard commodification literature tends to miss this organizational and cultural work. Instead, it focuses on abstract questions of commodification or on difficult (and often quite unusual) cases (Zaner 1988; Lamb 1990; Churchill and Pinkus 1990; Childress 1989). Some bioethicists are concerned with the practical application of moral theory (Caplan 1994). But the field as a whole has little to say about the ways in which individuals and organizations have found ways to give meaning to transplantation. Similarly, although some scholars have developed sophisticated conceptual accounts of commodification (Radin 1996; Sunstein 1997; Anderson 1993), they have less to say about the organizational effort and cultural work that go into making these exchanges socially acceptable.

I have argued that, as in similar areas that deal with death or the exchange of human goods, the transplant community has tried to account for itself as a moral actor in a comprehensible and convincing way. In the process it has developed a body of secular ritual to help manage a fragile transaction. This account is under increasing pressure as the gap between supply and demand for organs widens.

The key to understanding what exchange in human goods will look like in the future does not lie in novel technologies or moral recipes. Rather, what is important is the resemblance of such exchange to other markets—for insurance, blood, children, or sex—that are subject to similar cultural work and face comparable organizational problems. The strategies used to make exchanges socially acceptable in these cases will also shape the institutionalization of organ donation.

Thanks to Viviana Zelizer, Paul DiMaggio, Ed Amenta, Lynn Spillman, J. P. O'Carroll, and two anonymous reviewers for helpful comments on earlier versions of this chapter.

Notes

1. I do not mean to suggest that there is no debate among transplant professionals about the best procurement strategies. There are three alternative proposals: (1) increasing the donor pool by pursuing "non-heart-beating" donors more aggressively; (2) eliminating refusals by curtailing the rights of donors or (especially) their families to veto harvesting; and (3) introducing a monetary reward. Type 1 proposals are gaining support in the profession but threaten to undermine

years of effort to educate the public about brain death. Type 2 proposals tend not to have much support. I deal with type 3 proposals in this chapter. I also show that, at different times, there has been some uncertainty among OPOs about which altruistic strategies would work best. At present in the United States there is essentially no organized lobby that opposes organ transplants.

2. For example, motor vehicle accidents caused the death of 26 percent of cadaveric donors in 1997. Homicide or suicide victims accounted for a further 15 percent.

3. But see Norris (1990) for an argument about why required request laws have not succeeded as expected. For survey evidence that donor families are more likely to say that donation helped them deal with their loss, see Batten and Prottas (1987). In addition to these efforts, the position of the organ recovery coordinator became increasingly professionalized as OPOs accumulated specialist knowledge about how to intervene; see Strange and Taylor (1991), Sammons (1988), Williams, Grady, and Sadiford-Guttenbeil (1991), and United Network for Organ Sharing (1995, n.d.).

4. To guard against this, there is a long-standing professional separation between the doctors who declare a patient dead, on the one hand, and the transplant teams who harvest the organs.

5. The halacha is the accumulated body of law and ethics in Orthodox Judaism.

6. There is an overlap here. Although both fetal tissue and organs may be harvested for medical use, most churches do not see the two practices as morally equivalent, because the fetuses involved will normally have been aborted or grown in a test tube.

7. This idea can never be entirely symbolic, since the recipient does carry a physical piece of the donor alive inside them. There are also much stronger versions of it: in her memoir *A Change of Heart* (1997), Claire Sylvia claims that after her heart-lung transplant she developed personality traits—including new tastes for food and clothes—that she later discovered were characteristic of the eighteen-year-old man her new organs came from.

8. Over the period of the sample, horror stories about organs-for-cash did persist but became almost exclusively concerned with foreign reports of organ sales, particularly from India, South America, and Southeast Asia. These stories are excluded from the data in figure 12.3.

9. The mistaken idea that market versus nonmarket exchange neatly lines up with renewable versus nonrenewable body parts probably persists because many people wrongly believe that there is for-profit blood collection in the United States. In fact, almost all of the whole blood collected is freely donated. There is a market for plasma, which complicates the issue. But this only reinforces the point: there is no convenient biological divide that maps onto the social organization of exchange. See Healy (1999) for further discussion.

10. "We have had some fabulous gifts. . . . We have had donors sent on cruises, we have had a year of tuition paid. The donor doesn't know what the gift is going to be. She just knows that there will be a gift, so that way she's still giving her eggs without undue compensation or any form of bribery," said Teri Royal of the Options Egg Donor Agency (quoted in Mead 1999, 62).

References

Anderson, Elizabeth. 1993. *Value in Ethics and Economics.* Cambridge, Mass.: Harvard University Press.

Andrews, Lori, and Dorothy Nelkin. 2001. *Body Bazaar: The Market for Human Tissue in the Biotechnology Age.* New York: Crown.

Banevicius, Maria. 1992. "An Investigation of Cadaver Organ Donor Families Three Years After Donation: A Pilot Study." Master's thesis, Yale University School of Nursing.

Batten, Helen Levine, and Jeffrey Prottas. 1987. "Kind Strangers: The Families of Organ Donors." *Health Affairs* 6: 35–47.

Blair, Roger, and David Kaserman. 1991. "The Economics and Ethics of Alternative Cadaveric Organ Procurement Policies." *Yale Journal of Regulation* 8: 403–52.

Caplan, Arthur. 1987. "Sounding Board: Ethical and Policy Issues in the Procurement of Cadaver Organs for Transplantation." In *Human Organ Transplantation: Societal, Medical-Legal, Regulatory, and Reimbursement Issues,* edited by Dale H. Cowan, Jo Ann Kantorowitz, Jay Moskowitz, and Peter H. Rheinstein. Ann Arbor, Mich.: Health Administration Press.

———. 1994. *If I Were a Rich Man, Could I Buy a Pancreas?* Bloomington: Indiana University Press.

Caplan, Arthur, and Daniel Coelho, eds. 1998. *The Ethics of Organ Transplants.* Amherst, N.Y.: Prometheus Books.

Carney, Karen. 1999. *Precious Gifts: Katie Coolican's Story: Barklay and Eve Explain Organ and Tissue Donation.* Edmond, Okla.: Dragonfly Publishing.

Childress, James F. 1989. "Ethical Criteria for Procuring and Distributing Organs for Transplantation." *Journal of Health Politics, Policy, and Law* 14: 87–113.

Churchill, Larry R., and Rosa Lynn Pinkus. 1990. "The Use of Anencephalic Organs: Historical and Ethical Dimensions." *Milbank Quarterly* 68(2): 147–69.

Cooper, David K., and Robert P. Lanza. 2000. *Xeno: The Promise of Transplanting Animal Organs into Humans.* New York: Oxford University Press.

Espeland, Wendy Nelson, and Mitchell L. Stevens. 1998. "Commensuration as a Social Process." *Annual Review of Sociology* 24: 313–43.

Fox, Renée, and Judith Swazey. 1974. *The Courage to Fail: A Social View of Organ Transplantation and Dialysis.* Chicago: University of Chicago Press.

———. 1992. *Spare Parts: Organ Replacement in American Society.* New York: Oxford University Press.

Godelier, Maurice. 1999. *The Enigma of the Gift.* Chicago: University of Chicago Press.

Gortmaker, Steven L. 1998. "Improving the Request Process to Increase Family Consent for Organ Donation." *Journal of Transplant Coordination* 8: 210–17.

Green, Reg. 1997. *The Nicholas Effect: A Boy's Gift to the World.* Cambridge, Mass.: O'Reilly.

Gutkind, Lee. 1990. *Many Sleepless Nights: The World of Organ Transplantation.* Pittsburgh: University of Pittsburgh Press.

Hansmann, Henry. 1989. "The Economics and Ethics of Markets for Human Organs." *Journal of Health Politics, Policy, and Law* 14: 57–85.

Healy, Kieran. 1999. "The Emergence of HIV in the U.S. Blood Supply: Organizations, Obligations, and the Management of Uncertainty." *Theory and Society* 28(4): 529–58.

Hochschild, Arlie Russell. 1985. *The Managed Heart: Commercialization of Human Feeling.* Berkeley: University of California Press.

Hogle, Linda. 1999. *Recovering the Nation's Body: Cultural Memory, Medicine, and the Politics of Redemption.* New Brunswick, N.J.: Rutgers University Press.

Horton, Raymond L., and Patricia J. Horton. 1990. "Knowledge Regarding Organ Donation: Identifying and Overcoming Barriers to Organ Donation." *Social Science and Medicine* 31: 791–800.

The Jewish Voice. 1996. "Organ Transplant: Soon It May Be a Routine Part of the Jewish Death Ritual" (December).

Kimbrell, Andrew. 1997. *The Human Body Shop: The Cloning, Engineering, and Marketing of Life.* 2nd ed. Washington, D.C.: Regnery.

Lamb, David. 1990. *Organ Transplants and Ethics.* New York: Routledge.

Locicero, Jack. 1999. Talk delivered at Princeton University (April 20).

Lock, Margaret. 1996. "Deadly Disputes: Ideologies and Brain Death in Japan." In *Organ Transplantation: Meanings and Realities,* edited by Stuart J. Younger, Renée Fox, and Laurence J. O'Connell. Madison: University of Wisconsin Press.

Mead, Rebecca. 1999. "Eggs for Sale." *The New Yorker,* August 9, 56–65.

Nelson, Julie. 1998. "One Sphere or Two?" *American Behavioral Scientist* 41: 1467–71.

New York Times. 1999. "Pennsylvania Set to Break Taboo on Money for Organs" (May 6).

Norris, M. K. Gaedeke. 1990. "Required Request: Why It Has Not Significantly Improved the Donor Shortage." *Heart and Lung* 19: 685–86.

Pekkanen, John. 1986. *Donor: How One Girl's Death Gave Life to Others.* Boston: Little, Brown.

Poole, Victoria. 1980. *Thursday's Child.* Boston: Little, Brown.

Radin, Margaret. 1996. *Contested Commodities.* Cambridge, Mass.: Harvard University Press.

Ribal, Lizzy. 1997. *Lizzy Gets a New Liver.* Louisville, Ky.: Bridge Resources.

Richardson, Ruth. 1996. "Fearful Symmetry: Corpses for Anatomy, Organs for Transplant?" In *Organ Transplantation: Meanings and Realities,* edited by Stuart J. Younger, Renée C. Fox, and Laurence J. O'Connell. Madison: University of Wisconsin Press.

Sammons, Bonnie Harris. 1988. "Organ Recovery Coordinators Can Help Family Work Through the Grieving Process." *AORN Journal* 48: 181–82.

Sanders, Alice. 1999. "Discussions and Decisions Save Lives." http://www.transweb.org/reference/articles/donation/alice_sanders.html.

Schomaker, Mary Zimmeth. 1995. *Lifeline: How One Night Changed Five Lives.* New York: New Horizon Press.

Scott, Marvin B., and Stanford M. Lyman. 1968. "Accounts." *American Sociological Review* 33(1, February): 46–62.

Simmons, Roberta, Susan Klein Marine, and Richard Simmons. 1977. *Gift of Life: The Social and Psychological Impact of Organ Transplantation.* New York: John Wiley.

Starzl, Thomas. 1992. *The Puzzle People: Memoirs of a Transplant Surgeon.* Pittsburgh: University of Pittsburgh Press.

Strange, Julie Mull, and David Taylor. 1991. "Organ and Tissue Donation." In *Transplantation Nursing: Acute and Long-term Management,* edited by Marie T. Nolan and Sharon M. Augustine. Norwalk, Conn.: Appleton & Lange.

Sunstein, Cass. 1997. *Free Markets and Social Justice.* New York: Oxford University Press.

Sylvia, Claire. 1997. *A Change of Heart: A Memoir.* Boston: Little, Brown.

Tilly, Charles. 1999. "Power: Top Down and Bottom Up." *Journal of Political Philosophy* 7(3): 330–52.

Twersky, Abraham, Michael Gold, and Walter Jacob. 1991. "Jewish Perspectives." In *New Harvest: Transplanting the Body and Reaping the Benefits,* edited by C. Don Keyes and Walter E. Wiest. Clifton, N.J.: Humana Press.

United Network for Organ Sharing. 1995. *UNOS Organ Procurement Coordinator's Handbook.* Richmond, Va.: UNOS.

———. 1998. *Organ and Tissue Donation: A Reference Guide for Clergy.* 3rd ed. Richmond, Va.: UNOS.

———. 1999. "Share Your Life. Share Your Decision." Informational brochure. Richmond, Va.: UNOS.

———. N.d. *Donation and Transplantation: Nursing Curriculum.* Richmond, Va.: UNOS.

Walzer, Michael. 1983. *Spheres of Justice.* New York: Basic Books.

Williams, Barbara A. Helene, Kathleen L. Grady, and Doris M. Sadiford-Guttenbeil. 1991. *Organ Transplantation: A Manual for Nurses.* New York: Springer Verlag.

Wuthnow, Robert. 1991. *Acts of Compassion: Caring for Others and Helping Ourselves.* Princeton, N.J.: Princeton University Press.

———. 1995. *Learning to Care: Elementary Kindness in an Age of Indifference.* New York: Oxford University Press.

———. 1996. *Poor Richard's Principle: Recovering the American Dream Through the Moral Dimension of Work, Business, and Money.* Princeton, N.J.: Princeton University Press.

Zaner, Richard M., ed. 1988. *Death: Beyond Whole-Brain Criteria.* Boston: Kluwer Academic Publishers.

Zelizer, Viviana. 1979. *Morals and Markets: The Development of Life Insurance in the United States.* New York: Columbia University Press.

———. 1992. "Human Values and the Market: The Case of Life Insurance and Death in Nineteenth-Century America." In *The Sociology of Economic Life,* edited by Mark Granovetter and Richard Swedberg. Boulder, Colo.: Westview Press.

———. 1994. *The Social Meaning of Money.* New York: Basic Books.

Index

Boldface numbers refer to figures and tables.